Study Guide and Workbook to Accompany

Statistics for Business and Economics 12E

Mohammad Ahmadi, PhD

CENGAGE
Learning

Australia • Brazil • Japan • Korea • Mexico • Singapore • Spain • United Kingdom • United States

**Study Guide and Workbook to Accompany:
Statistics for Business and Economics 12E
Mohammad Ahmadi, PhD**

Executive Editors:
 Maureen Staudt
 Michael Stranz

Senior Project Development Manager:
 Linda deStefano

Marketing Specialist:
 Courtney Sheldon

Senior Production/Manufacturing Manager:
 Donna M. Brown

Production Editorial Manager:
 Kim Fry

Sr. Rights Acquisition Account Manager:
 Todd Osborne

For product information and technology assistance, contact us at
Cengage Learning Customer & Sales Support, 1-800-354-9706

For permission to use material from this text or product,
submit all requests online at **cengage.com/permissions**
Further permissions questions can be emailed to
permissionrequest@cengage.com

Compilation © 2014 Cengage Learning
ISBN-13: 978-1-305-01884-6

ISBN-10: 1-305-01884-2

Cengage Learning
5191 Natorp Boulevard
Mason, Ohio 45040
USA

Cengage Learning is a leading provider of customized learning solutions with office locations around the globe, including Singapore, the United Kingdom, Australia, Mexico, Brazil, and Japan. Locate your local office at:
international.cengage.com/region.
Cengage Learning products are represented in Canada by Nelson Education, Ltd.
For your lifelong learning solutions, visit **custom.cengage.com.**
Visit our corporate website at **cengage.com.**

Printed in the United States of America

Study Guide/Workbook to Accompany

Anderson, Sweeney and Williams'

STATISTICS FOR BUSINESS

AND ECONOMICS

TWELFTH EDITION

By:

Mohammad Ahmadi

The University of Tennessee at Chattanooga

CONTENTS

Preface

TO THE READER

This study guide is designed to reinforce and elaborate on the main concepts and ideas of the text by Anderson, Sweeney and Williams. The purpose of this guide is to help the reader more easily understand the material covered in the text. The chapters in the study guide parallel the chapters of the text, and the same notations are used in both. In this twelfth edition, each chapter contains four distinct parts: (1) chapter outline and review, (2) chapter formulas, (3) exercises, and (4) self-testing questions. In part one (chapter outline and review), the material covered in the text is outlined and briefly reviewed. Some of the explanations are phrased differently than the text; but of course, the meaning is the same. In the second part of each chapter (chapter formulas), the formulas that have been introduced in the text are organized in a concise form for easy reference. The same numbering system is used in both so that cross-reference can be easily achieved. Part three (exercises) consists of an extensive exercise section. In this part, two types of exercises are presented. First, for each topic, which is covered in the text, an exercise is given; and then, a step-by-step procedure for the solution of the exercise is presented. The purpose of this section is to show the reader how she/he should approach the problems in order to solve them. For easy reference, all the solved problems are distinctly labeled by

Solved Problem

and denoted by an asterisk (*). These exercises are followed by a series of additional exercises, which the reader must solve. The answers to these latter exercises are provided in the back of each chapter. In part four, I have designed a series of self-testing questions where the reader can test her/his understanding of the concepts covered in each chapter. Following the self-testing questions, an answer key is provided so the reader can evaluate her/his test results. To use this study guide, the reader should review the chapter outline of the study guide, review the problems that are solved completely in order to understand the solution procedure, and then, work as many problems as possible and check the answers for correctness with those provided at the end of each chapter. Finally, the reader should check her/his understanding of the materials covered in the chapter by answering the self-testing questions and checking the answers with the key. I trust the workbook will enhance the reader's understanding of the basic statistical concepts.

I would like to express my great appreciation to my wife Nancy, who typed and edited this manuscript and to my son Michael for preparing the graphs for the manuscript. My special gratitude goes to Ms. Lauren Michelle Lyon for proofreading and meticulously checking the accuracy of the entire manuscript. My thanks also go to Ms. Kayla Delong and David Moore for editing the manuscript and also checking the solutions' accuracy. Also, I would like to thank all my students who encouraged me to write this twelfth edition and the individuals who sent me their valuable comments and suggestions.

If you have any comments, suggestions, or corrections, please send them to me via e-mail at *mohammad-ahmadi@utc.edu* .

Mohammad Ahmadi
Chattanooga, Tennessee

CHAPTER ONE

DATA AND STATISTICS

CHAPTER OUTLINE AND REVIEW

Data are the raw materials of statistics. For obtaining data on variables, four scales of measurement (*nominal, ordinal, interval,* and *ratio*) are used. Furthermore, data can be *categorical* (qualitative) or *quantitative*. Categorical data are labels used to identify attributes of elements and use either *nominal* or *ordinal* scales of measurement; whereas quantitative data indicate the value of a variable, i.e., how much or how many and use either the *interval* or *ratio* scale of measurement. This is an introduction to the concept of statistics, and you will be given a few examples of how statistics can be applied. Statistics can be used to make inferences about characteristics of a population from sample information. Since computer software (such as Microsoft Excel) plays a major role in statistical analysis, you are encouraged to become familiar with and use statistical software that is available to you. The key terms in this chapter are as follows.

Categorical Data is data that provides labels or names for a characteristic of an element and uses either the *nominal* or *ordinal* scale of measurement. Categorical data may be numeric or nonnumeric.

Categorical Variable is a variable with categorical data.

Census is a survey to collect data on the entire population.

Cross-sectional Data is data gathered at the same time or approximately the same time.

Data is factual information that is collected, analyzed, presented, and interpreted. Data may be either *numeric* or *nonnumeric*.

Data Mining is using a combination of procedures from statistics, mathematics, and computer science, for developing useful decision-making information from large data bases.

Data Set is all of the data collected in a particular study.

Data Warehousing is the process of capturing, storing, and maintaining the data.

Descriptive Statistics is the study of the methods of organization, summarization, and presentation of statistical data.

Elements are the entities on which data are collected.

Interval Scale is a scale of measurement that has the properties of an ordinal scale, and the interval between observations is expressed in terms of a fixed unit of measurement. Interval data are always numeric. Example: **temperature**.

Nominal Scale is a scale of measurement that simply uses a label for the purpose of identifying an element. Example: Labels of **male** and **female**.

Observation is the set of measurements or data obtained for a particular element.

Ordinal Scale is a scale of measurement that is used for rank ordering of observations. Example: Classification of **freshman**, **sophomore**, **junior**, **senior**.

Population is the aggregate of all elements of interest in a particular study.

Quantitative Data is data that indicate the quantity of a variable in terms of how much or how many and use either the **interval** or **ratio** scale of measurement. Quantitative data may be discrete or continuous. Discrete data measure "how many," such as the number of people; whereas, continuous data measure "how much," such as the weight of an item. Quantitative data are always numerical.

Quantitative Variable is a variable with quantitative data.

Ratio Scale is a scale of measurement that has the properties of an interval scale, and the ratio of observations is meaningful. In a ratio scale, a zero value is inherently defined. Ratio data are always numeric. Example: **sales, profits**.

Sample is a portion of the population selected to represent the whole population.

Statistical Inference refers to making inferences about the characteristics of the population based on the information taken from the sample.

Statistics is a body of principles that deals with collection, analysis, interpretation and presentation of numerical facts or data.

Time Series Data *is d*ata collected at several successive periods of time.

Variable is a characteristic of interest for the elements.

EXERCISES

*1. The following data set provides information about five college professors.

Name	Specialty	Sex	Age	Rank
Ahmadi	Management	M	49	Full Professor
Keilany	Economics	M	58	Full Professor
Freeman	Entrepreneurship	F	29	Associate Professor
Lyon	Biology	F	30	Assistant Professor
Gehron	Accounting	F	35	Assistant Professor

(a) How many elements are in this data set?

Answer: Elements are entities on which data are collected. In this case, each college professor represents an element. Therefore, in this data set there are five elements.

(b) How many variables are in this data set?

Answer: Variable refers to a characteristic of interest for an element. In this case, four characteristics are being observed. Thus, there are four variables *(specialty, sex, age, and rank)* in this data set.

(c) How many observations are in the above data set?

Answer: The set of data gathered for an element is an observation. For instance, professor Ahmadi (the first element) has the following observation: *Management, M, 49, and Full Professor.* Since there are five college professors in this data set, we say that there are five observations.

(d) Which variables are categorical and which are quantitative variables?

Answer: *Specialty, Sex,* and *Rank* are simply labels, therefore, these three variables are categorical variables. The variable *Age* is a numerical measure and it is a quantitative variable.

(e) Which measurement scale is used for each variable?

Answer: *Specialty* and *Sex* are simply represented by labels such as "Economics" and "M" (for male). Therefore, for these two variables, the measurement is nominal. The variable *Age* is a numerical measure and does have an inherent zero. Therefore, ratio measurement is used for *Age.* Finally, the variable *Rank* classifies professors into various existing ranks ranging from instructor to full professor. Thus, *Rank* is measured using the ordinal scale.

2.   In many universities, students evaluate their professors by means of answering a questionnaire. Assume a questionnaire is distributed to a class of 45 students. Students are asked to answer the following questions:

1. Sex
2. Race (Black, White, Other)
3. Age
4. Number of hours completed
5. Grade point average
6. My instructor is a very effective teacher

1	2	3	4	5
strongly agree	moderately agree	neutral	moderately disagree	strongly disagree

(a)   How many elements are in the above data set?

(b)   How many variables are in this data set?

(c)   How many observations are in this data set?

(d)   Which variables are categorical variables and which are quantitative variables?

(e)   What measurement scale is used for each variable?

3. The following national weather report gives the temperatures and weather conditions on the previous day in cities across the nation.

City	Hi	Lo	Condition
Albany, N.Y.	88	60	cloudy
Chicago	92	64	clear
Dallas-Ft. Worth	89	72	cloudy
Denver	75	54	clear
Hartford	88	61	cloudy
Honolulu	86	70	clear
Kansas City	93	74	clear
Los Angeles	80	62	cloudy
Nashville	94	72	rain
New York City	90	69	rain
Philadelphia	90	67	rain

(a)   How many elements are in this data set?

(b)   How many variables are in this data set?

(c)   How many observations are in the above data set?

(d)   Which variables are categorical variables and which are quantitative variables?

(e)   What measurement scale is used for temperature and weather condition?

*4.   A recent issue of a national magazine reported that in a national public opinion survey conducted among 1200 registered voters, 36 percent favored Candidate A, 34 percent favored Candidate B, and 23 percent were in favor of Candidate C for president.

(a)   What constitutes the population?

Answer: The population is the aggregate of all elements of interest in a study. In the above example, the population will be all the registered voters.

(b)   What is the sample?

Answer: The sample is a portion of the population that represents the population. Hence, the 1200 people who were surveyed represent the sample.

(c)   Based on the sample, what percentage of the population would you think favors none of the candidates?

Answer: Based on this sample, our best estimate is that 36 percent favored Candidate A, 34 percent favored Candidate B, and 23 percent were in favor of Candidate C, or a total of 93 percent indicated a favorite candidate, which means 7 percent did not indicate any preference. Thus, our best estimate is that 7 percent of all registered voters favor none of the three candidates.

(d)   Based on the sample, what percentage of the population would you think favors Candidate C?

Answer: We assume that the sample represents the population. Based on this sample, our best estimate is that 23 percent of all registered voters are in favor of Candidate C. In statistics, this type of estimation is called a "point estimate." That is, determining a measure from a sample and inferring that the best estimate for the population's measure is that of the sample. We shall study the concept of estimation at length in Chapter 8.

Solved Problem

*5. The following table shows the age distribution of a sample of 180 students at a local college.

AGE DISTRIBUTION OF
180 STUDENTS AT A LOCAL COLLEGE

Age of Students	Number of Students
15 - 19	36
20 - 24	44
25 - 29	60
30 - 34	38
35 - 39	2
Total	180

(a) Of the students in the sample, what percentage is younger than 20 years of age?

Answer: There are 36 students whose ages are less than 20. Therefore, the percentage of the students whose ages are less than 20 is calculated as

(36/180) x 100% = 20%

(b) What percentage is at least 30 years of age?

Answer: There are 40 students who are at least 30 (38 in the "30 - 34" category and 2 in the "35 - 39" category). Therefore, the percentage of the students who are 30 or older is calculated as

(40/180) x 100% = 22.22%

(c) Based on this sample, what percentage of the students at the college do you estimate to be younger than 25 years of age?

Answer: There are 80 students who are younger than 25 (36 in the first category and 44 in the second category). Therefore, the percentage of the students (in the sample) who are younger than 25 is

(80/180) x 100% = 44.44%

Since we assume the sample represents the population, our best estimate (based on the sample) is that 44.44% of all the students in the college are younger than 25.

6.   Ahmadi, Inc., a manufacturer of solar panels, is a small firm with 80 employees. The table below shows the hourly wage distribution of the employees:

Hourly Wages (in dollars)	Number of Employees
12 - 15	3
16 - 19	12
20 - 23	18
24 - 27	20
28 - 31	15
32 - 35	10
36 - 39	2
Total	80

(a)   How many employees receive hourly wages of at least $28?

(b)   What percentage of the employees have hourly wages of at least $28?

(c)   What percentage of the employees have hourly wages of $23 or less?

(d)   How many variables are presented in the above data set?

(e)   This data set represents the results of how many observations?

(f)   Which variables are categorical variables and which are quantitative variables?

(g)   What measurement scales are used for the given variables?

7.   The highway patrol is interested in determining the average speed of automobiles traveling on I-75 between Chattanooga and Atlanta. To accomplish this task, the speed of every tenth car passing a particular point on I-75 is recorded.

(a)   What is the population for this study?

(b)   What constitutes the sample?

(c)   Is speed a categorical or quantitative variable?

(d)   What type of measurement scale is used?

8.   In order to assure the quality of wine, the quality control departments of wineries determine the acidity, the correctness of taste, and the aroma. This task is accomplished by opening the seal, determining the quality of the wine, and then discarding the bottle. Do you think the quality control departments use a sampling concept?

9.   The following data show the age distribution of a sample of employees of Research Inc.

Age	Number of Employees
20 - 24	2
25 - 29	48
30 - 34	60
35 - 39	80
40 - 44	10

(a)   What percentage of employees are at least 35 years of age?

(b)   Is the figure (percentage) that you computed in part (a) an example of statistical inference? If no, what kind of statistics does it represent?

(c)   Based on this sample, the president of the company said that "45% of our employees are 35 or older." The president's statement represents what kind of statistics?

(d)   What percentage of the employees are 29 years or younger?

SELF-TESTING QUESTIONS

In the following multiple choice questions, circle the correct answer. An answer key is provided following the questions.

1.   The sample size
a)   can be larger than the population size
b)   is always smaller than the population size
c)   can be larger or smaller than the population
d)   is always equal to the size of the population

2.   A population is
a)   the same as a sample
b)   the selection of a random sample
c)   the collection of all items of interest in a particular study
d)   always the same size as the sample

3.   A portion of the population selected to represent the population is called
a)   descriptive statistics
b)   inferential statistics
c)   a statistic
d)   a sample

4.   The study of the methods of organization, summarization, and presentation of statistical data is referred to as
a)   inferential statistics
b)   descriptive statistics
c)   sampling
d)   inferential sampling

5.   The process of making inferences about the characteristics of the population based on the sample information is termed
a)   descriptive statistics
b)   random sample
c)   inferential statistics
d)   sampling

6. In a random sample of 200 items, 5 items were defective. An estimate of the percentage of defective items in the population is
a) 5.0%
b) 2.5%
c) 200%
d) 10.0%

7. The entities on which data are collected are
a) variables
b) data sets
c) elements
d) sample points

8. The numerical facts are called
a) categorical measures
b) a population
c) a sample
d) statistics

9. Labels or names used to identify attributes of elements are
a) quantitative data
b) categorical data
c) simple data
d) ratio data

10. The labeling of parts as "defective" or "non-defective" is an example of
a) quantitative data
b) categorical data
c) simple data
d) ratio data

11. A characteristic of interest for the elements is
a) a variable
b) an element
c) a data set
d) a sample point

12. In a questionnaire, respondents are asked to indicate whether their home is located in the city or the suburbs. The location is an example of
a) quantitative data
b) categorical data
c) simple data
d) ratio data

13. Arithmetic operations are appropriate for
a) categorical data
b) quantitative data
c) both quantitative and categorical data
d) neither quantitative nor categorical data

14. Weight is an example of a variable with
a) categorical data
b) quantitative data
c) both quantitative and categorical data
d) neither quantitative nor categorical data

15. On a street, the houses are numbered from 300 to 450. The house numbers are examples of
a) categorical data
b) quantitative data
c) both quantitative and categorical data
d) neither quantitative nor categorical data

16. The scale of measurement that allows for the rank ordering of data items is
a) nominal measurement
b) ratio measurement
c) interval measurement
d) ordinal measurement

17. The scale of measurement that is simply a label for the purpose of identifying the attribute of an element is
a) nominal measurement
b) ratio measurement
c) ordinal measurement
d) interval measurement

18. The labeling of parts as "defective" or "non-defective" is an example of
a) ordinal data
b) ratio data
c) interval data
d) nominal data

19. Methods for developing useful decision-making information from large data bases is known as
a) data manipulation
b) data monitoring
c) data base conversion
d) data mining

20. The process of capturing, storing, and maintaining data is known as
a) data manipulation
b) data monitoring
c) data warehousing
d) category analysis

21. The subject of **data mining** deals with
a) methods for developing useful decision-making information from large data bases
b) keeping data secure so that unauthorized individuals cannot access the data
c) computational procedure for data analysis
d) computing the average for data

ANSWERS TO THE SELF-TESTING QUESTIONS

1. b
2. c
3. d
4. b
5. c
6. b
7. c
8. d
9. b
10. b
11. a
12. b
13. b
14. b
15. a
16. d
17. a
18. d
19. d
20. c
21. a

ANSWERS TO CHAPTER ONE EXERCISES

2. (a) 45
   (b) 6
   (c) 45
   (d) Sex, Race, and Teacher effectiveness are categorical
        Age, Number of hours, and Grade point average are quantitative
   (e) Sex: nominal
        Race: nominal
        Age: ratio
        Number of hours: ratio
        Grade point average: ratio
        Teacher effectiveness: ordinal

3. (a) 11
   (b) 3
   (c) 11
   (d) Temperature is quantitative
        Weather Condition is categorical
   (e) Temperature (Hi and Lo): interval
        Weather Condition: nominal

6. (a) 27
   (b) 33.75%
   (c) 41.25%
   (d) 2
   (e) 80
   (f) both variables are quantitative
   (g) ratio (for both variables)

7. (a) All the automobiles on I-75
   (b) All the tenth cars
   (c) quantitative
   (d) ratio

8. Yes, testing is destructive.

9. (a) 45%
   (b) No, it is descriptive statistics.
   (c) statistical inference
   (d) 25%

CHAPTER TWO

DESCRIPTIVE STATISTICS:
TABULAR AND GRAPHICAL PRESENTATIONS

CHAPTER OUTLINE AND REVIEW

In Chapter 1, you were introduced to the concept of statistics; and in exercise *5 of that chapter, you were given a frequency distribution of the ages of 180 students at a local college, but you were not told how this frequency distribution was formulated. Chapter 2 covers how such frequency distributions can be formulated, and this chapter introduces several tabular and graphical procedures for summarizing data. Furthermore, we will discuss how crosstabulations and scatter diagrams can be used to summarize data for two variables simultaneously. The terms for this chapter include the following.

Bar Chart is a graphical method of presenting categorical data that has been summarized in a frequency distribution, a relative frequency distribution, or a percent frequency distribution.

Categorical Data are data that are measured by either nominal or ordinal scales of measurement. Each value serves as a name or label for identifying an item.

Class is a grouping of data elements in order to develop a frequency distribution.

Class Width is the length of the class interval. Each class has two limits. The lowest value is referred to as the lower class limit, and the highest value is the upper class limit. The difference between the upper and the lower class limits represents the class width.

Class Midpoint is the point in each class that is halfway between the lower and the upper class limits.

Crosstabulation is a tabular presentation of data for two variables. Rows and columns show the classes of categories for the two variables.

Cumulative Frequency Distribution is a tabular presentation of a set of quantitative data which shows for each class the total number of data elements with values less than the upper class limit.

Cumulative Relative Frequency Distribution is a tabular presentation of a set of quantitative data which shows for each class the fraction of the total frequency with values less than the upper class limit.

Cumulative Percent Frequency Distribution is a tabular presentation of a set of quantitative data which shows for each class the fraction of the total frequency with values less than the upper class limit.

Dot Plot is a graphical presentation of data, where the horizontal axis shows the range of data values and each observation is plotted as a dot above the axis.

Exploratory Data Analysis is the use of simple arithmetic and easy-to-draw pictures to look at data more effectively.

Frequency Distribution is a tabular presentation of data, which shows the frequency of the appearance of data elements in several non-overlapping classes. The purpose of the frequency distribution is to organize masses of data elements into smaller and more manageable groups. The frequency distribution can present both categorical and quantitative data.

Histogram is a graphical method of presenting a frequency distribution, a relative frequency distribution, or a percent frequency distribution.

Ogive is a graphical method of presenting a cumulative frequency distribution, a cumulative relative frequency distribution, or a cumulative percent frequency distribution.

Percent Frequency Distribution is a tabular presentation of a set of data which shows the percentage of the total number of items in each class. The percent frequency of a class is simply the relative frequency multiplied by 100.

Pie Chart is a graphical device for presenting categorical data by subdividing a circle into sectors that corresponds to the relative frequency distribution or percent frequency distribution of each class.

Quantitative Data are data that are measured by interval or ratio scales of measurement. Quantitative data are numerical values on which mathematical operations can be performed.

Relative Frequency Distribution is a tabular presentation of a set of data which shows the frequency of each class as a fraction of the total frequency. The relative frequency distribution can present both categorical and quantitative data.

Scatter Diagram is a graphical method of presenting the relationship between two quantitative variables. One variable is shown on the horizontal and the other on the vertical axis.

Simpson's Paradox refers to conclusions drawn from two or more separate crosstabulations that can be reversed when data are aggregated into a single crosstabulation.

Skewness is a measure that shows how a distribution compares to a symmetrical distribution. A histogram with a longer tail to the right is said to be skewed to the right; and if it has a longer tail to the left, it is said to be skewed to the left.

Stem-and-Leaf Display is an exploratory data analysis technique that simultaneously ranks orders quantitative data and provides insight into the shape of the underlying distribution.

Trendline is a line that provides an approximation of the relationship between two variables.

Since ***Microsoft Excel*** is a widely used tool for data analysis, I ***strongly*** recommend that you spend some time and learn this software extremely well. If you will be using your own computer, be sure to load "***Data Analysis***" on your computer. To load "Data Analysis," find the Excel's "***Add-ins***" and then select "***Analysis Tool Pack***." Depending on which version of Excel you will be using, the "Add-ins" is located in different places. Go to "help" and search for "Add-ins." Once the "Analysis Tool Pack" is loaded, you will have "***Data Analysis***" available to you that can be used for most of your statistical computations and analyses. If you will be using the university's computer lab, all of the computers should have "Data Analysis" available to you.

Another very useful item in Excel is "f_x" that you can find on the formula bar (Shown below).

You can find numerous statistical procedures under "f_x". Browse through them and become very familiar with the available statistical procedures.

CHAPTER FORMULAS

$$\text{Relative Frequency of a Class} = \frac{\text{Frequency of the Class}}{n} \qquad (2.1)$$

where n = total number of observations

$$\text{Approximate Class Width} = \frac{\text{Largest Data Value} - \text{Smallest Data Value}}{\text{Number of Classes}}$$

$$(2.2)$$

EXERCISES

*1. A student has completed 20 courses in the School of Business Administration. Her grades in the 20 courses are shown below.

A	B	A	B	C
C	C	B	B	B
B	A	B	B	B
C	B	C	B	A

(a) Develop a *frequency distribution* for her grades.

Answer: To develop a *frequency distribution*, we simply count her grades in each category. Thus, the frequency distribution of her grades can be presented as

Grade	Frequency
A	4
B	11
C	5
Total	20

(b) Develop a bar chart for the *frequency distribution*.

Answer: A bar chart is a graphical device for presenting the information of a frequency, relative frequency, or percent frequency distribution for categorical data. Bars of equal width are drawn to represent various classes (in this case, grades). For a *frequency distribution*, the height of each bar represents the frequencies of various classes. Figure 2.1 shows the bar chart for the above data.

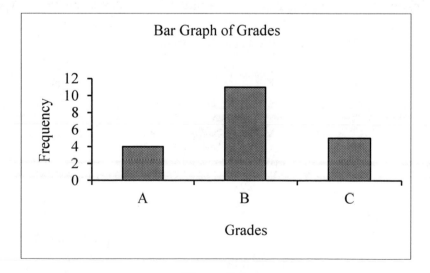

Figure 2.1

(c)   Develop a *relative frequency* distribution for her grades.

Answer: The *relative frequency* distribution is a distribution that shows the fraction or proportion of data items that fall into each category. The relative frequencies of each category are computed by dividing the frequency of each class by the number of observations (equation 2.1). Thus, the relative frequency distribution can be shown as follows.

Grade	Relative Frequency
A	4/20 = 0.20
B	11/20 = 0.55
C	5/20 = 0.25

(d)   Develop a *percent frequency* distribution for her grades.

Answer: A *percent frequency* distribution is a tabular summary of a set of data showing the percent frequency for each class. The percent frequency of a class is simply the relative frequency multiplied by 100. Thus, we can multiply the relative frequencies that we found in part (b) to arrive at the percent frequency distribution. Hence, the percent frequency distribution can be shown as follows.

Grade	Percent Frequency
A	20
B	55
C	25

(e)   Construct a pie chart for the *percent frequency* distribution.

Answer: A pie chart is a pictorial device for presenting a relative frequency and percent frequency distribution of categorical data. The relative frequency distribution is used to subdivide a circle into sections, where each section's size corresponds to the relative frequency of each class. Figure 2.2 shows the pie chart for the student's grades.

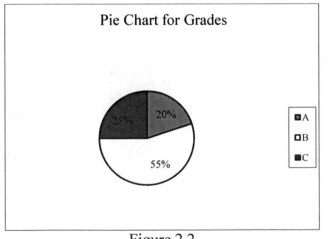

Figure 2.2

2.   There are 800 students in the School of Business Administration at UTC. There are four majors in the school: Accounting, Finance, Management and Marketing. The following shows the number of students in each major:

Major	Number of Students
Accounting	240
Finance	160
Management	320
Marketing	80

(a)   Develop a relative and a percent frequency distribution.

(b)   Construct a bar chart.

(c)   Construct a pie chart.

3.   Thirty students in the School of Business were asked what their majors were. The following represents their responses (M = Management;
A = Accounting; E = Economics; O = Others).

```
A   M   M   A   M   M   E   M   O   A
E   E   M   A   O   E   E   A   M   A
M   A   O   A   M   E   E   M   A   M
```

(a)   Construct a frequency distribution.

(b)   Construct a relative frequency and a percent frequency distribution.

4.   Five hundred recent graduates indicated their majors as follows.

Major	Frequency
Accounting	60
Finance	100
Economics	40
Management	120
Marketing	80
Engineering	60
Computer Science	40
Total	500

(a)   Construct a relative frequency distribution.

(b)   Construct a percent frequency distribution.

Solved Problem

*5. In a recent campaign, many airlines reduced their summer fares in order to gain a larger share of the market. The following data represent the prices of round-trip tickets from New York to Boston for a sample of nine airlines.

120	140	140
160	160	160
160	180	180

Construct a dot plot for the above data.

Answer: The dot plot is one of the simplest graphical presentations of data. The horizontal axis shows the range of data values, and each observation is plotted as a dot above the axis. Figure 2.3 shows the dot plot for the above data. The four dots shown at the value of 160 indicate that four airlines were charging $160 for the round-trip ticket from New York to Boston.

DOT PLOT FOR TICKET PRICES

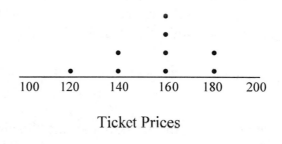

Ticket Prices

Figure 2.3

6. A sample of the ages of 10 employees of a company is shown below.

| 20 | 30 | 40 | 30 | 50 |
| 30 | 20 | 30 | 20 | 40 |

Construct a dot plot for the above data.

*7. The following data elements represent the amount of time (rounded to the nearest second) that 30 randomly selected customers spent in line before being served at a branch of First County Bank.

183	121	140	198	199
90	62	135	60	175
320	110	185	85	172
235	250	242	193	75
263	295	146	160	210
165	179	359	220	170

(a) Develop a frequency distribution for the above data.

Answer: The first step for developing a frequency distribution is to decide how many classes are needed. There are no set rules for determining the number of classes; but generally, using anywhere from five to twenty classes is recommended, depending on the number of observations. Fewer classes are used when there are fewer observations, and more classes are used when there are numerous observations. In our case, there are only 30 observations. With such a limited number of observations, let us use 5 classes. The second step is to determine the width of each class. By using equation 2.2 which states

$$\text{Approximate Class Width} = \frac{\text{Largest Data Value} - \text{Smallest Data Value}}{\text{Number of Classes}}$$

we can determine the class width. In the above data set, the highest value is 359, and the lowest value is 60. Therefore,

$$\text{Approximate Class Width} = \frac{359 - 60}{5} = 59.8$$

We can adjust the above class width (59.8) and use a more convenient value of 60 for the development of the frequency distribution. Note that I decided to use five classes. If you had used 6 or 7 or any other reasonable number of classes, you would not have been wrong and would have had a frequency distribution with a different class width than the one shown above.

Now that we have decided on the number of classes and have determined the class width, we are ready to prepare a frequency distribution by simply counting the number of data items belonging to each class. For example, let us count the number of observations belonging to the 60 - 119 class. Six values of 60, 62, 75, 85, 90, and 110 belong to the class of 60 - 119. Thus, the frequency of this class is 6. Since we want to develop classes of equal width, the last class width is from 300 to 359.

THE FREQUENCY DISTRIBUTION OF WAITING TIMES
AT FIRST COUNTY BANK

Waiting Times (Seconds)	Frequency
60 - 119	6
120 - 179	10
180 - 239	8
240 - 299	4
300 - 359	2
Total	30

(b) What are the lower and the upper class limits for the first class of the above frequency distribution?

Answer: The lower class limit shows the smallest value that is included in a class. Therefore, the lower limit of the first class is 60. The upper class limit identifies the largest value included in a class. Thus, the upper limit of the first class is 119. (**Note:** The difference between the lower limits of adjacent classes provides the class width. Consider the lower class limits of the first two classes, which are 60 and 120. We note that the class width is 120 - 60 = 60.)

(c) Develop a relative frequency distribution and a percent frequency distribution for the above.

Answer: The relative frequency for each class is determined by the use of equation 2.1.

$$\text{Relative Frequency of a Class} = \frac{\text{Frequency of the Class}}{n}$$

where n is the total number of observations. The percent frequency distribution is simply the relative frequencies multiplied by 100. Hence, the relative frequency distribution and the percent frequency distribution are developed as shown on the next page.

RELATIVE FREQUENCY AND PERCENT FREQUENCY DISTRIBUTIONS OF WAITING TIMES AT FIRST COUNTY BANK

Waiting Times (Seconds)	Frequency	Relative Frequency	Percent Frequency
60 - 119	6	6/30 = 0.2000	20.00
120 - 179	10	10/30 = 0.3333	33.33
180 - 239	8	8/30 = 0.2667	26.67
240 - 299	4	4/30 = 0.1333	13.33
300 - 359	2	2/30 = 0.0667	6.67
Total	30	1.0000	100.00

(d)   Develop a cumulative frequency distribution.

Answer: The cumulative frequency distribution shows the number of data elements with values less than or equal to the upper limit of each class. For instance, the number of people who waited less than or equal to 179 seconds is 16 (6 + 10), and the number of people who waited less than or equal to 239 seconds is 24 (6 + 10 + 8). Therefore, the frequency and the cumulative frequency distributions for the above data will be as follows.

FREQUENCY AND CUMULATIVE FREQUENCY DISTRIBUTIONS FOR THE WAITING TIMES AT FIRST COUNTY BANK

Waiting Times (Seconds)	Frequency	Cumulative Frequency
60 - 119	6	6
120 - 179	10	16
180 - 239	8	24
240 - 299	4	28
300 - 359	2	30
Total	30	

The total of the frequency column should equal the final number in the cumulative frequency column.

(e)   How many people waited less than or equal to 239 seconds?

Answer: The answer to this question is given in the table of the cumulative frequency. You can see that 24 people waited less than or equal to 239 seconds.

(f)   Develop a cumulative relative frequency distribution and a cumulative percent frequency distribution.

Answer: The cumulative relative frequency distribution can be developed from the relative frequency distribution. It is a table that shows the fraction of data elements with values less than or equal to the upper limit of each class. Using the table of relative frequency, we can develop the cumulative relative and the cumulative percent frequency distributions as follows:

RELATIVE FREQUENCY AND CUMULATIVE RELATIVE FREQUENCY AND CUMULATIVE PERCENT FREQUENCY DISTRIBUTIONS OF WAITING TIMES AT FIRST COUNTY BANK

Waiting Times (Seconds)	Relative Frequency	Cumulative Relative Frequency	Cumulative Percent Frequency
60 - 119	0.2000	0.2000	20.00
120 - 179	0.3333	0.5333	53.33
180 - 239	0.2667	0.8000	80.00
240 - 299	0.1333	0.9333	93.33
300 - 359	0.0667	1.0000	100.00

NOTE: To develop the cumulative relative frequency distribution, we could have used the cumulative frequency distribution and divided all the cumulative frequencies by the total number of observations, which is in this case 30.

(g)   Construct a histogram for the waiting times in the above example.

Answer: One of the most common graphical presentations of data sets is a histogram. We can construct a histogram by measuring the class intervals on the horizontal axis and the frequencies on the vertical axis. Then we can plot bars with the widths equal to the class intervals and the height equivalent to the frequency of the class that they represent. In Figure 2.4, the histogram of the waiting times is presented. As you note, the width of each bar is equal to the width of the various classes (60 seconds), and the height represents the frequency of the various classes. Note that the first class ends at 119; the next class begins at 120, and one unit exists between these two classes (and all other classes). To eliminate these spaces, each bar is extended from its lower class limit to the lower class limit of the next bar.

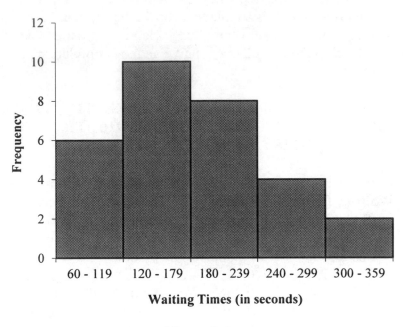

Histogram of the Waiting Times at First County Bank

Figure 2.4

(h)   Construct an ogive for the above example.

Answer: An ogive is a graphical representation of the cumulative frequency, cumulative relative frequency, or cumulative percent frequency distribution. It is constructed by measuring the class intervals on the horizontal axis and the cumulative frequencies (or cumulative relative frequencies or cumulative percent frequencies) on the vertical axis. Then points are plotted ***half a point*** above the class limits (i.e., 119.5, 179.5, 239.5, etc.) at a height equal to the cumulative frequency (or cumulative relative frequency or cumulative percent frequency). One additional point is plotted at 59.5 on the horizontal axis and 0 on the vertical axis. This point shows that there are no data values below the 60 - 119 class. Finally, these points are connected by straight lines. The result is an ogive that is shown in Figure 2.5.

**OGIVE FOR THE CUMULATIVE FREQUENCY DISTRIBUTION
OF THE WAITING TIMES AT FIRST COUNTY BANK**
Waiting Times (in seconds)

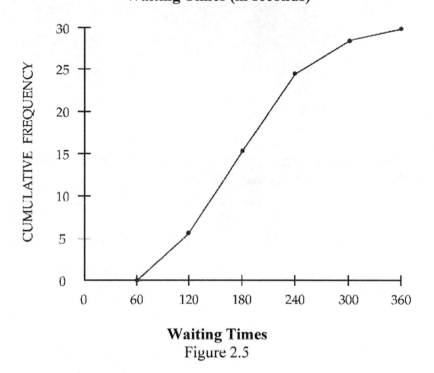

Waiting Times
Figure 2.5

8. The grades of 20 students on their first statistics test are shown below.

71	52	66	76	78
71	68	55	77	91
72	75	78	62	93
82	85	87	98	65

(a) Develop a frequency distribution for the grades. (Let your first class be 50 - 59.)

(b)   Develop a percent frequency distribution.

9.   The sales record of a real estate company for the month of May shows the following house prices in thousands of dollars (rounded to the nearest $1,000).

105	55	45	85	75
30	60	75	79	95

(a)   Develop a frequency distribution and a percent frequency distribution for the house prices. (Use 5 classes and have your first class be 20 - 39.)

(b)   Develop a cumulative frequency and a cumulative percent frequency distribution for the above data.

(c)   What percentage of the houses sold at a price below $80,000?

10. The frequency distribution below shows the yearly income distribution of a sample of 160 Hamilton County, Tennessee residents.

Yearly Income (in thousands of dollars)	Frequency
50 - 54	10
55 - 59	25
60 - 64	30
65 - 69	40
70 - 74	35
75 - 79	20
Total	160

(a) What percentage of the individuals in the sample had incomes of less than $65,000?

(b) How many individuals had incomes of at least $70,000?

11. The ages of 16 employees are shown below.

22	40	34	36
35	27	30	32
39	46	32	48
45	36	41	41

(a) Develop a frequency distribution. Let your first class be 20 - 25.

(b) Develop a cumulative frequency distribution.

12.   The frequency distribution below was constructed from data collected from a group of 250 students.

Height in Inches	Frequency
58 - 63	30
64 - 69	50
70 - 75	20
76 - 81	60
82 - 87	40
88 - 93	30
94 - 99	20
Total	250

(a)   Construct a percent frequency distribution.

(b)   Construct a cumulative frequency distribution.

(c)   Construct a cumulative percent frequency distribution.

Solved Problem

*13. The test scores of 14 individuals on their first statistics examination are shown below.

95	87	52	43	77	84	78
75	63	92	81	83	91	88

a)   Construct a stem-and-leaf display for these data.

Answer: To construct a stem-and-leaf display, the first digit of each data item is arranged in an ascending order and written to the left of a vertical line. Then, the second digit of each data item is written to the right of the vertical line next to its corresponding first digit as follows.

Stem	Leaf				
4	3				
5	2				
6	3				
7	7	8	5		
8	7	4	1	3	8
9	5	2	1		

Now, the second digits are rank ordered horizontally, thus leading to the following stem-and-leaf display.

Stem	Leaf				
4	3				
5	2				
6	3				
7	5	7	8		
8	1	3	4	7	8
9	1	2	5		

b)   What does the above stem-and-leaf show?

Answer: Each line in the above display is called a stem, and each piece of information on a stem is a leaf. For instance, let us consider the fourth line:

Stem	Leaf		
7	7	7	8

The stem indicates that there are 3 scores in the seventies. These values are

75   77   78

Similarly, we can look at line five (where the first digit is 8) and see

Stem	Leaf				
8	1	3	4	7	8

This stem indicates that there are 5 scores in the eighties, and they are

   81   83   84   87   88

At a glance, one can see the overall distribution for the grades. There is one score in the forties (43), one score in the fifties (52), one score in the sixties (63), three scores in the seventies (75, 77, 78), five scores in the eighties (81, 83, 84, 87, 88), and three scores in the nineties (91, 92, 95).

14.   Construct a stem-and-leaf display for the following data.

22	44	36	45	49	57	38	47	51	12
18	48	32	19	43	31	26	40	37	52

Solved Problem

*15. The following is a crosstabulation of starting salaries (in thousands of dollars) of a sample of business school graduates by their gender.

Starting Salary

Gender	Less than $20k	$20k up to $25k	$25k and more	Totals
Female	12	84	24	120
Male	20	48	12	80
Totals	32	132	36	200

(a)   What general comments can be made about the distribution of starting salaries and the gender of the individuals in the sample?

Answer: Using the frequency distribution at the bottom margin of the above table it is noted that majority of the individuals in the sample (132) have starting salaries in the range of $20,000 up to $25,000, followed by 36 individuals whose salaries are at least $25,000, and only 32 individuals had starting salaries of under $20,000. Now considering the right-hand margin it is noted that the majority of the individuals in the sample (120) are female, while 80 are male.

(b)   Compute row percentages and comment on the relationship between starting salaries and gender.

Answer: To compute the row percentages we divide the values of each cell by the row total and express the results as percentages. Let us consider the row representing females. The row percentages (across) are computed as

$(12/120)(100)=10\%$; $(84/120)(100)=70\%$; $(24/120)(100)=20\%$

Continuing in the same manner and computing the row percentages for the other row we determine the following row percentages table:

Starting Salary

Gender	Less than $20k	$20k up to $25k	$25k and more	Totals
Female	10%	70%	20%	100%
Male	25%	60%	15%	100%

From the above percentages it can be noted that the largest percentage of both genders' starting salaries are in the $20,000 to $25,000 range. However, 70% of females and only 60% of the males have starting salaries in this range. Also it can be noted that 10% of females' starting salaries are under $20,000, whereas, 25% of the males' starting salaries fall in this category.

(c)   Compute column percentages and comment on the relationship between gender and starting salaries.

Column percentages are computed by dividing the values in each cell by column total and expressing the results as percentages. For instance for the category of "Less than 20" the column percentages are computed as (12/32)(100)=37.5 and (20/32)(100)=62.5 (rounded). Continuing in the same manner the column percentages will be as follows.

Starting Salary

Gender	Less than $20k	$20k up to $25k	$25k and more
Female	37.5%	63.6%	66.7%
Male	62.5%	36.4%	33.3%
Total	100%	100%	100%

Considering the "Less than $20k" category it is noted that the majority (62.5%) are male. In the next category of "$20k up to $25k" the majority (63.6%) are female. Finally in the last category of "$25k and more" the majority (66.7%) are female.

16.   A survey of 400 college seniors resulted in the following crosstabulation regarding their undergraduate major and whether or not they plan to go to graduate school.

Undergraduate Major

Graduate School	Business	Engineering	Others	Totals
Yes	35	42	63	140
No	91	104	65	260
Totals	126	146	128	400

(a)   Are majority of seniors in the survey planning to attend graduate school?

(b)   Which discipline constitutes the majority of the individuals in the survey?

(c)   Compute row percentages and comment on the relationship between the students' undergraduate major and their intention of attending graduate school.

(d)   Compute the column percentages and comment on the relationship between the students' intention of going to graduate school and their undergraduate major.

*17. The numbers (as well as column percentages) of students who passed or failed Professors Ross and Ahmadi's courses last semester are given below.

	Ross	Ahmadi	Totals
Passed	258 (85.1%)	172 (87.3%)	430
Failed	45 (14.9%)	25 (12.7%)	70
Totals	303 (100%)	197 (100%)	500

(a)   Which professor has the larger percentage of failing grades?

Answer: As you can see from the above table, the percentage of Professor Ross's students who failed the course is 14.9%, which is larger than Professor Ahmadi's failures, which is 12.7%.

(b)   Shown below are crosstabulations of the two professors' pass or fail grades, broken down by graduate and undergraduate courses.

	Ross			**Ahmadi**		
	Graduate	Undergraduate	Totals	Graduate	Undergraduate	Totals
Passed	32 (91.4%)	226 (84.3%)	258	150 (88.2%)	22 (81.5%)	172
Failed	3 (8.6%)	42 (15.7%)	45	20 (11.8%)	5 (18.5%)	25
Totals	35 (100%)	268 (100%)	303	170 (100%)	27 (100%)	197

Which professor shows a higher percentage of failures?

Answer: The above crosstabulations show that in both graduate and undergraduate classes, the percentage of failures are smaller for Professor Ross. The failure rates are 8.6 percent and 15.7 percent for Professor Ross; while the failures are 11.8 percent and 18.5 percent for Professor Ahmadi. In Part a, it appeared that Professor Ross had a higher failure rate. The above inconsistency is known as ***Simpson's paradox***.

Solved Problem

*18. The average grades of 8 students in statistics and the number of absences they had during the semester are shown below.

Student	Number of Absences (x)	Average Grade (y)
1	1	94
2	2	78
3	2	70
4	1	88
5	3	68
6	4	40
7	8	30
8	3	60

Develop a scatter diagram for the relationship between the number of absences (x) and their average grade (y).

Answer: A scatter diagram is a graphical method of presenting the relationship between two variables. The scatter diagram is shown in Figure 2.6. The number of absences (x) is shown in the horizontal axis and the average grade (y) on the vertical axis. The first student has one absence (x=1) and an average grade of 94 (y=94). Therefore, a point with coordinates of x=1 and y=94 is plotted on the scatter diagram. In a similar manner all other points for all 8 students are plotted.

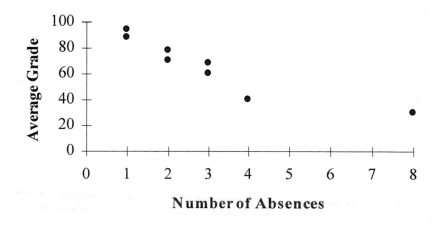

Figure 2.6

The scatter diagram shows that there is a negative relationship between the number of absences and the average grade. That is, the higher the number of absences, the lower the average grade appears to be.

19.   You are given the following ten observations on two variables, x and y.

x	y
1	8
5	15
6	20
4	12
2	10
8	20
9	26
1	5
6	18
8	26

(a)   Develop a scatter diagram for the relationship between x and y.

(b)   What relationship, if any, appears to exist between x and y?

SELF-TESTING QUESTIONS

In the following multiple choice questions, circle the correct answer. An answer key is provided following the questions.

1.   A tabular summary of a set of data, which shows the frequency of the appearance of data elements in several non-overlapping classes is termed
a)   the class width
b)   a frequency polygon
c)   a frequency distribution
d)   a histogram

2.   A tabular summary of a set of data showing classes of the data and the fraction of the items belonging to each class is called
a)   the class width
b)   a relative frequency distribution
c)   a cumulative relative frequency distribution
d)   an ogive

3.   A histogram is
a)   a graphical presentation of a frequency or relative frequency distribution
b)   a graphical method of presenting a cumulative frequency or a cumulative relative frequency distribution
c)   the history of data elements
d)   the same as a pie chart

4.   The length of the interval forming a class is called
a)   the class midpoint
b)   the lower class limit
c)   the upper class limit
d)   the class width

5.   A graphical method of presenting categorical data by frequency distribution is termed
a)   a frequency polygon
b)   an ogive
c)   a bar chart
d)   a categorical chart

Exhibit 2-1
Michael's Rent-A-Car, a national car rental company, has kept a record of the number of cars they have rented for a period of 80 days. Their rental records are shown below:

Number of Cars Rented	Number of Days
0 - 19	5
20 - 39	15
40 - 59	30
60 - 79	20
80 - 99	10
Total	80

6.   Refer to Exhibit 2-1. The class width of the above distribution is
a)   0 to 100
b)   20
c)   80
d)   5

7.   Refer to Exhibit 2-1. The lower limit of the first class is
a)   5
b)   80
c)   0
d)   20

8.   Refer to Exhibit 2-1. If one develops a cumulative frequency distribution for the above data, the last class will have a frequency of
a)   10
b)   100
c)   0 to 100
d)   80

9.   Refer to Exhibit 2-1. The percentage of days in which the company rented at least 40 cars is
a)   37.5%
b)   62.5%
c)   90.0%
d)   75.0%

10.   Refer to Exhibit 2-1. The number of days in which the company rented less than 60 cars is
a)   20
b)   30
c)   50
d)   60

11.   The sum of frequencies for all classes will always equal
a)   1
b)   the number of elements in a data set
c)   the number of classes
d)   a value between 0 to 1

12.   The relative frequency of a class is computed by
a)   dividing the midpoint of the class by the sample size
b)   dividing the frequency of the class by the midpoint
c)   dividing the sample size by the frequency of the class
d)   dividing the frequency of the class by the sample size

13.   If several frequency distributions are constructed from the same data set, the distribution with the narrowest class width will have
a)   the fewest classes
b)   the most classes
c)   the same number of classes as the other distributions since all are constructed from the same data
d)   at least 10 classes

14.   The sum of the relative frequencies for all classes will always equal
a)   the sample size
b)   the number of classes
c)   1
d)   any value larger than 1

15.   In a cumulative relative frequency distribution, the last class will have a cumulative relative frequency equal to
a)   1
b)   0
c)   the total number of elements in the data set
d)   any positive value

16.   In a cumulative percent frequency distribution, the last class will have a cumulative percent frequency equal to
a)   1
b)   0
c)   the total number of elements in the data set
d)   100

17.   A tabular method that can be used to summarize the data on two variables simultaneously is called
a)   simultaneous equations
b)   an ogive
c)   a histogram
d)   crosstabulation

ANSWERS TO THE SELF-TESTING QUESTIONS

1. c
2. b
3. a
4. d
5. c
6. b
7. c
8. d
9. d
10. c
11. b
12. d
13. b
14. c
15. a
16. d
17. d

ANSWERS TO CHAPTER TWO EXERCISES

2. (a)

Major	Relative Frequency	Percent Frequency
Accounting	0.3	30
Finance	0.2	20
Management	0.4	40
Marketing	0.1	10

(b)

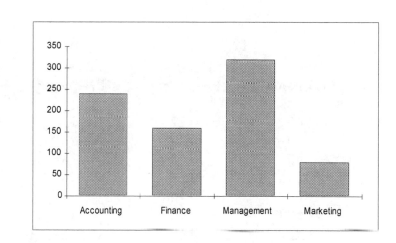

(c)

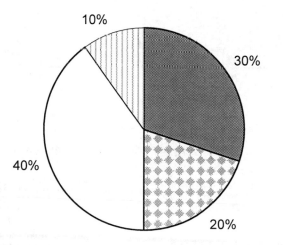

3. (a) and (b)

Major	Frequency	Relative Frequency	Percent Frequency
M	11	0.37	37
A	9	0.30	30
E	7	0.23	23
O	3	0.10	10

4.

		(a)	(b)
Major	Frequency	Relative Frequency	Percent Frequency
Accounting	60	0.12	12
Finance	100	0.20	20
Economics	40	0.08	8
Management	120	0.24	24
Marketing	80	0.16	16
Engineering	60	0.12	12
Computer Science	40	0.08	8
Totals	500	1.00	100

6.

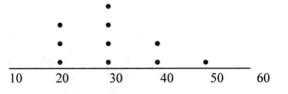

8.

	(a)	(b)
Class	Frequency	Percent Frequency
50 - 59	2	10
60 - 69	4	20
70 - 79	8	40
80 - 89	3	15
90 - 99	3	15
	20	100

9.

Sales Price (In Thousands of Dollars)	(a) Freq.	(a) Percent Freq.	(b) Cum. Freq.	(b) Cum. Percent Freq.
20 - 39	1	10	1	10
40 - 59	2	20	3	30
60 - 79	4	40	7	70
80 - 99	2	20	9	90
100 - 119	1	10	10	100

(c)   70%

10.   (a)   40.625%
     (b)   55

11.

Class	(a) Frequency	(b) Cumulative Frequency
20 - 25	1	1
26 - 31	2	3
32 - 37	6	9
38 - 43	4	13
44 - 49	3	16

12.

Height (In Inches)	Frequency	(a) Percent Frequency	(b) Cumulative Frequency	(c) Cumulative Percent Frequency
58 - 63	30	12	30	12
64 - 69	50	20	80	32
70 - 75	20	8	100	40
76 - 81	60	24	160	64
82 - 87	40	16	200	80
88 - 93	30	12	230	92
94 - 99	20	8	250	100
		100		

14.

Stem	Leaf					
1	2	8	9			
2	2	6				
3	1	2	6	7	8	
4	0	3	4	5	7	8	9
5	1	2	7			

16. (a) No, majority (260) will not attend graduate school
    (b) Majority (146) are engineering major
    (c)

Undergraduate Major

Graduate School	Business	Engineering	Others	Total
Yes	25%	30%	45%	100%
No	35%	40%	25%	100%

Majority who plan to go to graduate school are from "Other" majors. Majority of those who will not go to graduate school are engineering majors.

(d)

Undergraduate Major

Graduate School	Business	Engineering	Others
Yes	27.8%	28.8%	49.2%
No	72.2%	71.2%	50.8%
Total	100%	100%	100%

Approximately the same percentages of Business and engineering majors plan to attend graduate school (27.8% and 28.8% respectively). Of the "Other" majors approximately half (49.2%) plan to go to graduate school.

19. (a)

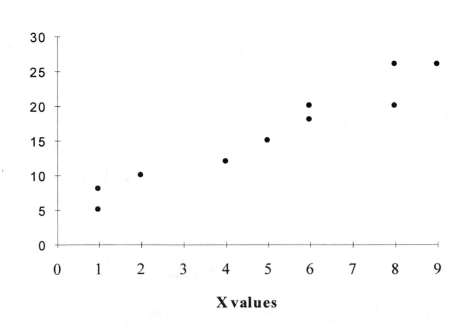

(b) A positive relationship between x and y appears to exist.

CHAPTER THREE

DESCRIPTIVE STATISTICS: NUMERICAL MEASURES

CHAPTER OUTLINE AND REVIEW

In this chapter, we will discuss various numerical measures of location and variability (dispersion), both for ungrouped and grouped data. Furthermore, we will study measures of association between two variables. You will be introduced to the following measures and key concepts.

Measures of Location

Mean is the average value of a data set.

Median is the value in the middle of a data set after the data set has been arranged in ascending (or descending) order. Therefore, the median is the value that divides the data set into two equal groups.

Mode is the most frequently occurring or the most common data value in a data set.

Percentile divides the data set into one hundredths whereas the median divides the data set into two equal groups. Therefore, *when the data set is arranged in ascending order*, the pth percentile is a value such that *at least p percent of the items in the data set have values less than or equal to the value of the pth percentile*. The median is the 50th percentile.

Quartiles divide the data set into four parts; the first quartile (Q_1), second quartile (Q_2), and third quartile (Q_3) are respectively the 25th, 50th, and 75th percentiles.

Weighted Mean is the average value of a data set where each data value is given a weight that reflects its importance.

Measures of Variability (Dispersion)

Coefficient of Variation is a measure that is used for comparing two or more data sets and determining which data set is more dispersed (relative to the average size of data values). The value of the coefficient of variation is the ratio of the standard deviation to the mean multiplied by 100.

Interquartile Range is a measure of variability whose value is equal to the difference between the third and first quartiles ($IQR = Q_3 - Q_1$). It represents the middle 50% of the data when the data set is arranged in ascending or descending order.

Range is the difference between the largest and the smallest values in a data set.

Skewness is a measure of shape of a data distribution. For a symmetrical distribution, skewness is zero. If skewness is positive, the distribution is skewed to the right; and if it is negative, it is skewed to the left.

Standard Deviation is a measure of the absolute variability or dispersion of the data elements around the mean. Its value is equal to the square root of the variance. It is easier to interpret than the variance since it is in the same units as the data.

Variance is a measure of variability or dispersion of the data elements around their mean. Its value is equal to the average of the squared deviation of data elements from their mean (for the population).

Other Key Concepts

Box Plot is a visual presentation of a five-number summary.

Chebyshev's Theorem is a theorem which allows us to determine the percentage of data elements that fall within a specified number of standard deviations from the mean. More specifically, Chebyshev's Theorem states that at least $[1- (1/z^2)]$ of the data elements fall within plus or minus z standard deviations (for z >1) of the mean.

Correlation Coefficient is a numerical measure of linear association between two variables. The coefficient of correlation ranges between -1 to +1. Values close to -1 indicate a strong negative linear relationship and values close to +1 indicate a strong positive correlation.

Covariance is a numerical measure of linear association between two variables. Positive values indicate a positive relationship and negative values show a negative relationship.

Empirical Rule is a rule applied to *bell-shaped* distributions that states approximately what percentage of the items are within 1, 2, and 3 standard deviations of the mean. For data having a bell-shaped distribution, approximately

- 68% of the data values will be within plus or minus 1 standard deviation from the mean.

- 95% of the data values will be within plus or minus 2 standard deviations from the mean.

- Almost all the data values will be within 3 standard deviations from the mean.

Five-Number Summary is an exploratory data analysis technique that uses the following five measures to summarize the data set: smallest value, first quartile, median, third quartile, and largest value.

Grouped Data is when the individual data items (observations) are summarized by a frequency distribution. It must be noted that when the data is grouped and is reported by means of a frequency distribution, the exact values of the individual observations are no longer known.

Outlier is an unusually small or large data value.

Point Estimator is the sample statistic, such as $\overline{X}$, S^2, and S, which are used to estimate population parameters μ, σ^2, and σ.

Population Parameter is a descriptive measure of a population, such as the population mean μ (mu), population variance σ^2 (sigma) and the population standard deviation σ.

Sample Statistic is a descriptive measure of a sample, such as the sample mean $\overline{X}$, sample variance S^2, and the sample standard deviation S.

Z-Score is the number of standard deviations a data value is from the mean. It is referred to as either a *standardized value* or the *Z - Score*.

CHAPTER FORMULAS

$$\boxed{\textbf{Ungrouped Data}}$$

SAMPLE	*POPULATION*

Mean

$$\overline{X} = \frac{\sum X_i}{n} \qquad (3.1)$$

$$\mu = \frac{\sum X_i}{N} \qquad (3.2)$$

where n = sample size

where N = size of population

Interquartile Range

$$IQR = Q_3 - Q_1 \qquad (3.3)$$

(Same as for sample)

where Q_3 = third quartile (i.e., 75th percentile)

Q_1 = first quartile (i.e., 25th percentile)

Variance

$$S^2 = \frac{\sum\left(X_i - \overline{X}\right)^2}{n-1} \qquad (3.5)$$

$$\sigma^2 = \frac{\sum\left(X_i - \mu\right)^2}{N} \qquad (3.4)$$

or

or

$$S^2 = \frac{\sum X_i^2 - n\overline{X}^2}{n-1}$$

$$\sigma^2 = \frac{\sum X_i^2 - N\mu^2}{N}$$

Standard Deviation

$$S = \sqrt{S^2} \qquad (3.6)$$

$$\sigma = \sqrt{\sigma^2} \qquad (3.7)$$

Coefficient of Variation (C.V.)

$$C.V. = \left(\frac{S}{\overline{X}}\right)(100)\%$$

$$C.V. = \left(\frac{\sigma}{\mu}\right)(100)\% \qquad (3.8)$$

z-Score

$$z_i = \frac{X_i - \overline{X}}{S}$$

$$z_i = \frac{X_i - \mu}{\sigma} \qquad (3.9)$$

where z_i = number of standard deviations X_i is from the mean

CHAPTER FORMULAS
(Continued)

SAMPLE	*POPULATION*

Covariance

$$S_{xy} = \frac{\sum(X_i - \overline{X})(Y_i - \overline{Y})}{n-1} \quad (3.10)$$

$$\sigma_{xy} = \frac{\sum(X_i - \mu_X)(Y_i - \mu_Y)}{N} \quad (3.11)$$

Pearson Product Moment Correlation Coefficient

$$r_{XY} = \frac{S_{XY}}{S_X S_Y} \quad (3.12)$$

$$\rho_{XY} = \frac{\sigma_{XY}}{\sigma_X \sigma_Y} \quad (3.13)$$

where

r_{XY} = Sample correlation coefficient

S_{XY} = Sample covariance

S_X = Sample standard deviation of X

S_Y = Sample standard deviation of Y

where

ρ_{XY} = Population correlation coefficient

σ_{XY} = Population covariance

σ_X = Population standard deviation of X

σ_Y = Population standard deviation of Y

Weighted Mean

$$\overline{X} = \frac{\sum w_i X_i}{\sum w_i} \quad (3.15)$$

$$\mu = \frac{\sum w_i X_i}{\sum w_i}$$

where X_i = data value I and w_i = weight for data value I

Grouped Data

Mean

$$\overline{X} = \frac{\sum f_i M_i}{n} \quad (3.16)$$

$$\mu = \frac{\sum f_i M_i}{N} \quad (3.18)$$

where f_i = frequency of class i and M_i = midpoint of class i

Variance

$$S^2 = \frac{\sum f_i (M_i - \overline{X})^2}{n-1} \quad (3.17)$$

$$\sigma^2 = \frac{\sum f_i (M_i - \mu)^2}{N} \quad (3.19)$$

The variance can also be calculated as follows.

$$S^2 = \frac{\sum f_i M_i^2 - n\overline{X}^2}{n-1}$$

$$\sigma^2 = \frac{\sum f_i M_i^2 - N\mu^2}{N}$$

EXERCISES

> **Solved Problem**

*1.   A sample of 9 gasoline stations in London, England had the following prices (in U.S. dollars) for a liter of gasoline:

Gas Station #	Price Per Liter (X_i)
1	$ 1.94
2	1.89
3	2.24
4	2.10
5	2.17
6	1.89
7	2.20
8	1.68
9	1.89

$$\Sigma X_i = \$18.00$$

a)   What is the mean price per liter among the 9 stations?

Answer: The mean refers to the average price, and the average is determined by adding the prices of all nine stations and dividing the sum by 9 (the number of gas stations).

$$\overline{X} = \frac{\Sigma X_i}{n}$$

The $\Sigma X_i = \$18.00$, as shown above on the bottom of column two. Therefore, the mean will be

$$\overline{X} = \frac{\Sigma X_i}{n} = \frac{18.00}{9} = \$2.00$$

Had the above data represented a population, the calculations would have been the same only we would have used the following notations.

$$\mu = \frac{\Sigma X_i}{N}$$

(b)   If gas station number one's price was $5.00 per liter, could a different mean be computed so that it would be a better indication of the central location of data?

Answer: When there are unusually large or unusually small data values in a data set (outliers), we can trim the data by dropping the extreme values and then computing the *trimmed mean*. In this example, we would drop the gas station with the unusually high price of $5.00 per liter and compute the *trimmed mean* for the remaining eight gas stations. Thus the trimmed mean would be the average price for the last eight gas stations, which is $2.01 (rounded).

(c) What is the mode for the above data?

Answer: The mode is the most frequently occurring item in a data set. In the above example, the mode is $1.89, which represents the most common price. Three gas stations had a price of $1.89 per liter.

(d) What is the median of the above data?

Answer: The median is the middle value of a data set, after the data has been arranged in ascending order. Hence, to determine the median, the data is first arranged in ascending order as follows.

$$X_i$$
$1.68
1.89
1.89
1.89
1.94 ← Median
2.10
2.17
2.20
2.24

The data element that is located in the middle of the data set is the median. As shown above, the median for this example is $1.94. It must be noted that in the above example the number of data points was odd, that is, there were an odd number (9) of gas stations. If the data set had an even number of items, then the median would have been the average of the middle two items. Assume we had a sample of 10 gas stations with the following prices (after the prices have been arranged in ascending order).

X_i
$1.68
1.89
1.89
1.89
1.94 ⎤ Middle Two
2.10 ⎦ Values
2.10
2.17
2.20
2.24

Then the median would be the average of the middle 2 values or

$$\text{Median} = \frac{1.94 + 2.10}{2} = \$2.02$$

The median is also referred to as the second quartile (Q_2) or the 50th percentile.

(e)   Assume in the above example of 9 gas stations that gas station number one's price was $2.94 per liter. Then would the mean or the median be a better measure of location?

Answer: Since the mean is influenced by extreme values and under the above assumption one gas station has an extreme price of $2.94, the median would be a better measure of location. Note that with the extreme price of $2.94 the mean changes from $2.00 to $2.11, while the median does not change and is still $1.94.

(f)   Compute the 25th percentile (i.e., the first quartile).

Answer: The 25th percentile for the above example is that price where at least 25% of the gas stations charge *equal to* or *less than* that price. To determine that price, we do the following step-by-step procedure

STEP 1: Arrange the prices of the 9 gas stations in ascending order.

Position	Price Per Liter (X_i)
1	$1.68
2	1.89
3	1.89 ⟵ 25th Percentile
4	1.89
5	1.94
6	2.10
7	2.17
8	2.20
9	2.24

STEP 2: Determine the position of the 25th percentile by computing an index "i" as follows.

$$i = (p/100)(n)$$

In the above formula, p represents the percentile of interest (in this case 25) and n is the number of data values (in this case 9). Thus, the index i is computed as follows.

$$i = (25/100)(9) = 2.25$$

STEP 3: If i is not an integer value, the next integer value greater than i will represent the position of the percentile of interest. In this exercise, i is not an integer value (2.25). Therefore, the position of the 25th percentile is the next integer value greater than 2.25 or the 3rd position. Now considering the data elements after they were arranged in ascending order (see Step 1), we note that the 3rd position has a value of $1.89

(highlighted in the above table), which is the 25th percentile. This indicates that at least 25% of gas stations have prices of $1.89 or less.

Note: In Step 3 above, if i was an integer, the pth percentile would have been the average of the data values in positions i and (i+1).

(g)   Compute the 75th percentile (i.e., the third quartile).

Answer: The 75th percentile or the third quartile (Q_3) for the above example is that price where at least 75% of the gas stations charge equal to or less than that price. The procedure for computing the 75th percentile is similar to that of computing the 25th percentile (as shown in Part f).

STEP 1: Arrange the prices of the 9 gas stations in ascending order.

Position	Price Per Liter (X_i)
1	$1.68
2	1.89
3	1.89
4	1.89
5	1.94
6	2.10
7	2.17 ← 75th Percentile
8	2.20
9	2.24

STEP 2: Determine the position of the 75th percentile by computing an index "i" as follows.

$$i = (75/100)(9) = 6.75$$

STEP 3: In this exercise, i is not an integer value (6.75). Therefore, the position of the 75th percentile is the next integer value greater than 6.75 or the 7th position. Now considering the data elements after they were arranged in ascending order (see Step 1), we note that the 7th position has a value of $2.17, which is the 75th percentile. This indicates that at least 75% of gas stations have prices of $2.17 or less.

(h)   Compute the interquartile range.

Answer: The interquartile range is the difference between the third and the first quartiles. In Parts f and g of this problem, we computed the first and the third quartiles as $Q_1 = 1.89$ and $Q_3 = 2.17$. Therefore, the interquartile range is

$$IQR = Q_3 - Q_1 = 2.17 - 1.89 = 0.28$$

2.   The price of a selected stock over a five day period is shown below.

$$17, \ 11, \ 13, \ 17, \ 16$$

Using the above data, compute the mean, the median, and the mode.

3.   The prices of a sample of eight selected men's colognes are shown below.

Product	Size of Container (Fl. Oz.)	Price Per Container
A	2	$4.00
B	4	12.00
C	3	12.00
D	4	20.00
E	2	10.00
F	5	30.00
G	6	42.00
H	2	16.00

(a)   Determine the median and the mode for the price *per ounce*.
        Hint: The prices shown above are not the price *per ounce*. They represent the prices of each container.

(b)   Determine the average of the per ounce prices for the eight colognes.

(c)   Compute the 85th percentile and explain its meaning.

4. A sample of 10 employees in the graphics department of Design, Inc. is selected. The employees' ages are given below:

Employee Number	Age
1	34
2	35
3	39
4	24
5	62
6	40
7	18
8	35
9	28
10	35

(a) What is the average age of the employees in the graphics department of Design, Inc.?

(b) Determine the mode.

(c) Determine the median.

(d) Compute the first and the third quartiles.

(e) Compute the interquartile range.

5.   You are given the following information regarding the number of hours of sick leave that a sample of the employees of Pecora, Inc. has taken during the first quarter of the year (rounded to the nearest hour). ***Use Excel or software available to you to solve this problem.***

19	22	27	24	28	12
23	47	11	55	25	42
36	25	34	16	45	49
12	20	28	29	21	10
59	39	48	32	40	31

(a)   Determine the average hours of sick leave.

(b)   Determine the mode and the median.

6.   The temperatures (in degrees Fahrenheit) for the month of June in a southern city are given below.

70	75	79	80	78	82
82	89	88	87	90	92
91	92	93	95	94	95
97	95	98	100	107	107
105	104	108	111	109	116

Determine the mean, median, and mode for the above data. *Use Excel or software available to you to solve this problem.*

Solved Problem

---

*7. In exercise *1 of this chapter, the gasoline prices for 9 selected gas stations were given. Refer to exercise *1 and answer the following questions.

(a) What is the range of the gasoline prices?

Answer: The range is a measure of variability (dispersion) whose value is equal to the difference between the largest and the smallest values of a data set. Hence, the range of gasoline prices is

Range = 2.24 - 1.68 = $0.56

(b) Calculate the sample variance.

Answer: The variance is a measure of variability that is defined as

$$S^2 = \frac{\Sigma\left(X_i - \overline{X}\right)^2}{n-1}$$

To calculate the variance, the first step will be to determine $\Sigma\left(X_i - \overline{X}\right)^2$. (Remember the sample mean $\overline{X}$ was calculated previously, and its value was $2.00.)

Station Number	X_i	$\left(X_i - \overline{X}\right)$	$\left(X_i - \overline{X}\right)^2$
1	$1.94	1.94 - 2.00 = - 0.06	0.0036
2	1.89	1.89 - 2.00 = - 0.11	0.0121
3	2.24	2.24 - 2.00 = 0.24	0.0576
4	2.10	2.10 - 2.00 = 0.10	0.0100
5	2.17	2.17 - 2.00 = 0.17	0.0289
6	1.89	1.89 - 2.00 = - 0.11	0.0121
7	2.20	2.20 - 2.00 = 0.20	0.0400
8	1.68	1.68 - 2.00 = - 0.32	0.1024
9	1.89	1.89 - 2.00 = - 0.11	0.0121

$$\Sigma\left(X_i - \overline{X}\right)^2 = 0.2788$$

Therefore, the variance is calculated as

$$S^2 = \frac{\Sigma\left(X_i - \overline{X}\right)^2}{n-1} = \frac{0.2788}{9-1} = 0.03485$$

(c)   If the above data represented a population, how would the variance be computed?

Answer: The variance of a population would be computed as follows.

$$\sigma^2 = \frac{\Sigma(X_i - \mu)^2}{N} = \frac{0.2788}{9} = 0.03098$$

(d)   Determine the sample's standard deviation.

Answer: The standard deviation is the square root of the variance. Therefore, it is

$$S = \sqrt{S^2} = \sqrt{0.03485} = 0.18668$$

(e)   Is there another approach for computing the sample variance?

Answer: Yes, the following formula may be easier to use and reduces rounding errors.

$$S^2 = \frac{\Sigma X_i^2 - n\overline{X}^2}{n-1}$$

We have already calculated the sample mean $\overline{X}$ to be 2.00 (see problem *1). The only other value in the above formula that needs to be calculated is ΣX_i^2.

X_i	X_i^2
1.94	3.7636
1.89	3.5721
2.24	5.0176
2.10	4.4100
2.17	4.7089
1.89	3.5721
2.20	4.8400
1.68	2.8224
1.89	3.5721
	$\Sigma X_i^2 = $ 36.2788

Then

$$S^2 = \frac{\Sigma X_i^2 - n\overline{X}^2}{n-1} = \frac{36.2788 - (9)(2.00)^2}{9-1} = \frac{0.2788}{8} = 0.03485$$

(f)   If a sample of gas stations in Paris, France shows a mean price of $2.17 with a standard deviation of $0.196, then which city's sample shows a more dispersed price distribution?

Answer: To compare the relative variability (dispersion) of two groups, we need to calculate the coefficient of variation, which is a measure of relative variability.

$$\text{Coefficient of Variation} = \left(\frac{S}{\overline{X}}\right)(100)$$

$$\text{Coefficient of Variation for London} = \left(\frac{0.18668}{2.00}\right)(100) = 9.334\%$$

$$\text{Coefficient of Variation for Paris} = \left(\frac{0.196}{2.17}\right)(100) = 9.032\%$$

Therefore, the sample in Paris shows a lesser degree of relative variability than London even though Paris had greater absolute variability (i.e., the standard deviation of Paris was larger than the standard deviation of London).

(g)   Compute the z-score for a gas station showing a price of $2.25 per liter.

Answer: The z-score represents the number of standard deviations a particular data element is from the mean. The mean and the standard deviation for this problem were computed previously, and their values were $2.00 and $0.18668, respectively. Thus, the z-score for the gas station with the price of $2.25 is

$$z = \frac{X_i - \overline{X}}{S} = \frac{2.25 - 2.00}{.18668} = 1.339 \text{ (Rounded)}$$

The above z-score indicates that the gas station with the price of $2.25 is approximately 1.339 standard deviations above the mean.

(h)   Excel provided a skewness measure of –0.2283 for this problem. What does this measure indicate?

Answer: Skewness is a measure of shape, or form of a distribution. If skewness is zero, it indicates the distribution is symmetrical; whereas, a positive value indicates that the distribution is skewed to the right. Since the skewness in this problem is negative (-0.2283), it indicates the distribution is skewed to the left.

8.   In exercise 3 of this chapter, the prices of a sample of eight selected men's colognes were given as shown below.

Product	Size of Container (Fl. Oz.)	Price
A	2	$4.00
B	4	12.00
C	3	12.00
D	4	20.00
E	2	10.00
F	5	30.00
G	6	42.00
H	2	16.00

(a)   Compute the range for the price *per ounce*.

(b)   Compute the variance and the standard deviation for the price *per ounce*.

(c)   Determine the coefficient of variation and explain its meaning.

9.   In 2011, the average donation to the United Help Organization was $500 with a standard deviation of $60. In 2012, the average donation was $650 with a standard deviation of $65. In which year do the donations show a more dispersed distribution?

10. Global Engineers hired the following number of Class 1 engineers during the first six months of the past year. (Assume the data represent a sample.)

Month	No. of Class 1 Engineers Hired
January	3
February	2
March	4
April	2
May	6
June	0

(a) Determine the mean, median, mode and range for the above data.

(b) Compute the variance (S^2) and the standard deviation (S).

(c) Compute the first and the third quartiles.

(d) Compute the z-scores for the months of May and June.

11.   A consumer product testing group tested the gas water heaters produced by 11 leading producers (all heaters were of the same size and the same specifications) and determined the following annual operating costs:

Manufacturer	Annual Operating Costs (in dollars)
A	$121
B	124
C	134
D	128
E	119
F	115
G	131
H	124
I	125
J	133
K	132

(a)   Find the average operating costs among the 11 producers.

(b)   Find the mode and median.

(c)   Determine the range.

(d)   Compute the variance and the standard deviation. (Assume the data represent a sample.)

Solved Problem

*12. The flashlight batteries produced by one of the northern manufacturers are known to have an average life of 60 hours with a standard deviation of 4 hours.

(a)   At least what percentage of flashlights will have a life of 54 to 66 hours?

Answer: Chebyshev's theorem states that for any data set, at least $(1 - 1/z^2)$ of the data elements fall within plus or minus z (for z > 1) standard deviations of the mean. In the above example, the distance from 54 to the mean of 60 is 6 hours. Since the standard deviation is 4 hours, the 6 hours represents 1.5 standard deviations (i.e., z = 1.5). Applying Chebyshev's theorem, we note that

$$[1 - (1/z^2)] = [1 - (1/(1.5)^2] = 0.56$$

indicating that at least 56% of the batteries will have a life of 54 to 66 hours.

(b)   At least what percentage of the batteries will have a life of 52 to 68 hours?

Answer: Again applying Chebyshev's theorem, with z = 2 standard deviations (note that there are 8 hours from the lower point of 52 to the mean of 60, which represents 2 standard deviations)

$$[1 - (1/z^2)] = [1 - (1/(2)^2] = 0.75$$

indicating that at least 75% of the batteries have a life of 52 to 68 hours.

(c)   Determine an interval for the batteries' lives that will be true for at least 80% of the batteries.

Answer: Once again, by using Chebyshev's theorem,

$$[1 - (1/z^2)] = 0.80$$

we can solve for z in the above equation by first subtracting 1 from both sides of the equation:

$$- 1/z^2 = - 0.20$$

then multiplying both sides by $- z^2$

$$1 = 0.2 \, z^2$$

and now solving for z^2

$$z^2 = 1/0.20 = 5$$

Hence, $z = \sqrt{5}$ or 2.236 standard deviations. Therefore, 80% of the values will be in the interval of the mean plus or minus 2.236 standard deviations or, $60 \pm (2.236)(4)$. This indicates that at least 80% of the batteries will have lives of 51.056 to 68.944 hours.

13. In a statistics class, the average grade on the final examination was 75 with a standard deviation of 5.

(a)   At least what percentage of the students received grades between 50 and 100?

(b)   Determine an interval for the grades that will be true for at least 70% of the students.

Solved Problem

---

*14. The weights of 12 individuals who enrolled in a fitness program are shown below.

Individual	Weight (Pounds)
1	100
2	105
3	110
4	130
5	135
6	138
7	142
8	145
9	150
10	170
11	240
12	300

(a)   Provide a five-number summary for the data.

Answer: A five-number summary is a method of summarizing data by means of the following five values.

1.   Smallest value
2.   First quartile (Q_1)
3.   Median
4.   Third quartile (Q_3)
5.   Largest value

For the above data, the smallest weight is 100 pounds; the first quartile $Q_1 = 120$ pounds (i.e., the average weight of individuals 3 and 4); the median weight is 140 pounds; the third quartile $Q_3 = 160$ pounds (i.e., the average weight of individuals 8 and 9); and the largest value is 300 pounds. Therefore, the five-number summary for the above data is

Smallest	Q_1	Q_2 (Median)	Q_3	Largest
100	120	140	160	300

This five-number summary indicates that approximately 25% of the data elements are located between adjacent values.

(b)   Show the box plot for the weight data.

Answer: A box plot is a visual presentation of the five-number summary. Figure 3.1 shows the box plot for the weight data.

Box Plot for the Weight Data

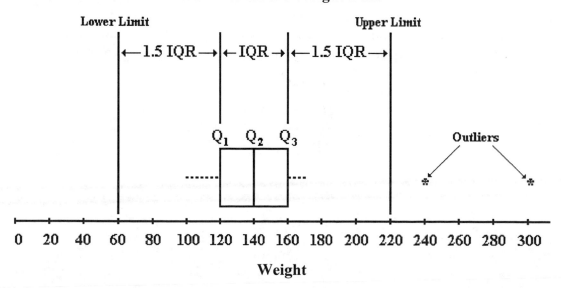

Weight

Figure 3.1

The following procedure is used for constructing the box plot.

1.   A box is drawn to contain the middle 50% of the data elements. Thus the ends of this box are located at the first and the third quartiles. In this example, the box begins at $Q_1 = 120$ and ends at $Q_3 = 160$. The width of the box shows the interquartile range.

2.   At the location of the median (in our case at 140) a vertical line is drawn in the box to show at what point data is divided into two equal parts.

3.   *The lower and the upper limits* are determined by using the interquartile range (IQR). Remember IQR $= Q_3 - Q_1 = 160 - 120 = 40$. The lower limit is drawn at 1.5 IQR below Q_1 or at $120 - (1.5)(40) = 60$, and the upper limit is drawn at 1.5 Q_3. Or at $160 + (1.5)(40) = 220$. The limits are used for identifying *outliers*. Data elements that fall outside the limits are considered to be *outliers*.

4.   Dashed lines, known as *whiskers*, are drawn from the ends of the box to the smallest and largest data values *inside the limits*, which were determined in Step 3. In our example, the whiskers end at weights of 100 and 170.

5.   The location of outliers are marked by the symbol "*." Thus, in our example, we note there are two outliers; (240) and (300). In Figure 3.1, for the purpose of demonstration, the limits and various distances and labels have been shown. Ordinarily, the box plot does not show the above but will simply appear as shown in Figure 3.2.

The Usual Appearance of the Box Plot for the Weight Data

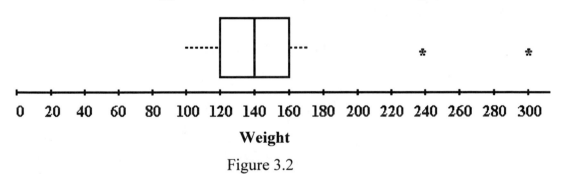

Weight

Figure 3.2

15. The annual salaries of the employees of MBS accounting firm are shown below.

Employee	Salary ($1,000s)
1	75
2	18
3	26
4	29
5	24
6	35
7	40
8	60
9	45
10	38
11	24
12	27
13	37
14	32
15	20

Provide a five-number summary for the above data.

Solved Problem

*16. The average grades of a sample of 8 students in statistics and the number of absences they had during the semester are given below.

Student	Number of Absences (X_i)	Average Grade (Y_i)
1	1	94
2	2	78
3	2	70
4	1	88
5	3	68
6	4	40
7	8	30
8	3	60

(a)   Compute the sample covariance.

Answer: The sample covariance, which is a measure of association between two variables, is defined as

$$S_{xy} = \frac{\Sigma(X_i - \overline{X})(Y_i - \overline{Y})}{n-1}$$

To calculate the covariance, we need to compute $\Sigma(X_i - \overline{X})(Y_i - \overline{Y})$, where $\overline{X}$ is the average of X values (24/8 = 3) and $\overline{Y}$ is the average of Y values (528/8 = 66). Thus, the numerator for the above formula can be computed by means of the following table.

(X_i)	(Y_i)	$(X_i - \overline{X})$	$(Y_i - \overline{Y})$	$(X_i - \overline{X})(Y_i - \overline{Y})$
1	94	-2	28	-56
2	78	-1	12	-12
2	70	-1	4	-4
1	88	-2	22	-44
3	68	0	2	0
4	40	1	-26	-26
8	30	5	-36	-180
3	60	0	-6	0
Totals 24	528	0	0	-322

Now the sample covariance can be computed as

$$S_{xy} = \frac{\Sigma(X_i - \overline{X})(Y_i - \overline{Y})}{n-1} = \frac{-322}{8-1} = -46$$

(b)   If the above data represented a population, how would the covariance be computed?

Answer: The covariance of the population is computed as follows.

$$\sigma_{xy} = \frac{\Sigma(X_i - \mu_X)(Y_i - \mu_Y)}{N} = \frac{-322}{8} = -40.25$$

(c)   Interpret the meaning of the sample covariance that was found in part (a).

Answer: Covariance is a measure of linear relationship between two variables. If the covariance is negative it indicates a negative, or if it is positive, a positive linear relationship between variables. In our case the sample covariance was computed to be 46. Thus, it indicates that there is a negative linear relationship between the number of absences and the average grade. This indicates that as the number of absences increase, the average grade tends to decrease.

(d)   Is there any problem in using sample covariance as a measure of strength of linear relationship between variables?

Answer: The problem with using the sample covariance as a measure of strength of association between variables is the fact that the magnitude of the covariance depends on the units of measurement. Assume we are interested in determining the association between the monthly income of individuals and their age. If the monthly income figures are given in dollars the magnitude of the covariance would be much smaller than if the figures were given in cents, where in fact the degree of association is the same.

(e)   Is there a measure of association that avoids the problem with units of measurement?

Answer: The Pearson Product Moment Correlation Coefficient (or, simply, the sample correlation coefficient) is a measure that overcomes the problem of units of measurement. The sample correlation coefficient is computed by dividing the sample covariance by the product of the standard deviations of the two variables. The sample coefficient of correlation is computed as

$$r_{XY} = \frac{S_{XY}}{S_X S_Y}$$

where

$$r_{XY} = \text{Sample correlation coefficient}$$
$$S_{XY} = \text{Sample covariance}$$
$$S_X = \text{Sample standard deviation of X}$$
$$S_Y = \text{Sample standard deviation of Y}$$

The sample covariance was computed in part (a). Its value was $S_{XY} = -46$. Now we need to compute the standard deviation of the X and Y values. The standard deviation of X values is computed as

$$S_X = \sqrt{\frac{\Sigma\left(X_i - \overline{X}\right)^2}{n-1}} = \sqrt{\frac{36}{8-1}} = 2.268$$

Similarly the standard deviation of Y values is computed as

$$S_Y = \sqrt{\frac{\Sigma\left(Y_i - \overline{Y}\right)^2}{n-1}} = \sqrt{\frac{3440}{8-1}} = 22.168$$

Now the coefficient of correlation can be computed as

$$r_{XY} = \frac{S_{XY}}{S_X S_Y} = \frac{-46}{(2.268)(22.168)} = -0.915$$

The coefficient of correlation ranges between -1 to +1. A value of -1 indicates a perfect negative, and a value of +1 indicates a perfect positive correlation. In our case the coefficient of correlation is -0.915, which shows a very strong negative relationship between the number of absences and the average grade, indicating that as the number of absences increases the average grade decreases.

17. You are given the following ten observations on two variables, x and y. Assume the data represent a sample.

x	y
1	8
5	15
6	20
4	12
2	10
8	20
9	26
1	5
6	18
8	26

(a)   Compute the sample covariance.

(b)   Interpret the meaning of the sample covariance that was found in Part a.

(c)   Compute the coefficient of correlation.

18. The following data represent the daily demand (y in thousands of units) and the unit price (x) for a product.

x	y
4	40
7	32
8	34
3	32
6	68
7	18
12	14
9	28

(a) Compute the sample covariance for the above data.

(b) Compute the sample correlation coefficient.

Solved Problem

*19. The mean of n observations is determined by summing the data values $(X_1 + X_2 + X_3 + \ldots X_n)$ and dividing the sum by the total number of observations (n). You were given the following equation for computing the mean of a sample.

$$\overline{X} = \frac{\sum X_i}{n}$$

When the above equation is used to compute the mean, it is assumed that each observation has the same weight or importance. There are situations where some data values have different weights or are more or less important than others. In these instances, a weighted mean is computed by assigning various weights to data values and then computing the weighted mean. The following table shows the weight (percent of final grade) assigned to each component of a course and the score (out of a possible 100) that a student has received for each component.

Component	Score X_i	Weight (%)w_i
Daily Assignments	80	10
Term Project	81	15
Mid-term Exam	87	30
Final Exam	94	45
Total	342	100

Compute the weighted mean score for this student.

Answer: The weighted mean is computed by

$$\overline{X} = \frac{\sum w_i X_i}{\sum w_i}$$

To compute $\sum w_i X_i$, we simply multiply the score of each component by its weight and sum the results as shown below.

Component	Score X_i	Weight (%)w_i	$w_i X_i$
Daily Assignments	80	10	800
Term Project	81	15	1215
Mid-term Exam	87	30	2610
Final Exam	94	45	4230
Total	342	100	8855

Thus, the weighted mean is computed as

$$\overline{X}_{wt} = \frac{\sum w_i X_i}{\sum w_i} = \frac{8855}{100} = 88.5$$

Therefore, the student's final score for the course is 88.5. Note that if we had computed the simple average, it would have been

$$\overline{X} = \frac{\sum X_i}{n} = \frac{342}{4} = 85.5, \text{ which, of course, is different from the weighted mean.}$$

20.   Compute the weighted mean of the following data.

X_i	Weight (w_i)
5	50
9	20
8	80
6	30
2	20
	200

21.   The Freeman Paint Company has purchased paint from several suppliers. The purchase price per gallon and the number of gallons purchased are shown below.

Supplier	Price Per Gallon ($)	Number of Gallons
A	17	4,000
B	19	3,000
C	18	9,000
D	16	20,000

Compute the weighted average price per Gallon.

Solved Problem

*22. The income distribution for a sample of 155 recent business school graduates is shown below.

Yearly Income (in thousands of dollars)	Frequency f_i	Class Midpoint M_i	f_iM_i
30-34	12	32	384
35-39	23	37	851
40-44	35	42	1470
45-49	40	47	1880
50-54	35	52	1820
55-59	10	57	570
	155		$\sum f_iM_i = \mathbf{6975}$

(a)   Compute the mean income for the above sample.

Answer: The procedure that was used for computing the weighted mean can be extended to approximate the mean of grouped data. The mean for grouped data is given by

$$\overline{X} = \frac{\sum f_iM_i}{n}$$

To calculate $\sum f_iM_i$, first the class midpoints (M_i) are determined. The class midpoints are located halfway between the class limits. For instance, the midpoint of the first class is $(30 + 34)/2 = 32$. The class midpoints for all classes are shown above. Next, the product of the class midpoints and their respective frequencies are determined (shown above in the last column). The sum of the values of the column of $\sum f_iM_i$ yields 6975. Therefore, the mean income will be

$$\overline{X} = \frac{\sum f_iM_i}{n} = \frac{6975}{155} = 45$$

Since the incomes were in thousands of dollars, the mean income is $45,000.

(b)   Compute the sample variance.

Answer: The variance of a sample for grouped data is

$$S^2 = \frac{\sum f_i(M_i - \overline{X})^2}{n-1}$$

To compute the numerator, first the difference between each midpoint and the sample mean (45) is determined. These values are shown below in the third column designated "deviation." Next, each deviation is squared, as shown in the fourth column. Then, each squared deviation is multiplied by its respective frequency, as shown in the last column. The sum of the values in the last column (7130) is the numerator for the computation of the variance.

Income	Midpoint (M_i)	Deviation $(M_i - \overline{X})$	Squared Deviation $(M_i - \overline{X})^2$	Frequency (f_i)	$f_i(M_i - \overline{X})^2$
30-34	32	-13	169	12	2028
35-39	37	-8	64	23	1472
40-44	42	-3	9	35	315
45-49	47	2	4	40	160
50-55	52	7	49	35	1715
55-59	57	12	144	10	1440

$$\sum f_i(M_i - \overline{X})^2 = 7130$$

Therefore, the sample variance is

$$S^2 = \frac{\sum f_i(M_i - \overline{X})^2}{n-1} = \frac{7130}{155 - 1} = 46.2987 \text{ (Rounded)}$$

The standard deviation is $\sqrt{46.2987} = 6.804$ (i.e., $6,804).

23.   The following frequency distribution shows the sale prices of cars and their respective frequencies: Assume the data represent a sample.

Sale Price (in thousands of dollars)	Number of Cars Sold
20 - 39	1
40 - 59	2
60 - 79	4
80 - 99	2
100 - 119	1

(a)   Determine the mean.

(b)   Determine the standard deviation.

24. The following frequency distribution has been formulated from a *sample*.

No. of Magazine Subscriptions Sold	No. of Students Who Sold in this Range
30 - 39	2
40 - 49	3
50 - 59	7
60 - 69	5
70 - 79	1

(a)   Determine the mean.

(b)   Compute the variance and the standard deviation.

25. The following frequency distribution has been developed from a *population*.

Temperature	Number of Days
70 - 79	4
80 - 89	6
90 - 99	11
100 - 109	7
110 - 119	2

(a)   Determine the mean.

(b)   Compute the standard deviation.

26. Compute the mean and the standard deviation for the following frequency distribution. Assume the data represent a *sample*.

Class	Frequency
45 - 47	3
48 - 50	6
51 - 53	8
54 - 56	2
57 - 59	1

SELF-TESTING QUESTIONS

In the following multiple choice questions, circle the correct answer. An answer key is provided following the questions.

1.   A numerical value used as a summary measure for a population of data is called a
a)   sample
b)   statistic
c)   range
d)   parameter

2.   The average value of a data set is called the
a)   mean
b)   median
c)   mode
d)   range

3.   The most frequently occurring data value in a data set is the
a)   median
b)   arithmetic mean
c)   population parameter
d)   mode

4.   A statistic is
a)   a descriptive measure of a population
b)   a descriptive measure of a sample
c)   always smaller than a parameter
d)   always larger than a parameter

5.   A measure of central location which splits the data set into two equal groups is called the
a)   mean
b)   mode
c)   median
d)   standard deviation

6.   The coefficient of variation is
a)   the same as the variance
b)   a measure of central tendency
c)   a measure of absolute variability
d)   a measure of relative variability

Exhibit 3.1
Assume the following data set represents a sample.

6, 8, 3, 7, 6, 0

7. Refer to Exhibit 3.1. The median of this data set is
a) 5
b) 6
c) 6.5
d) 3

8. Refer to Exhibit 3.1. The mode of this data set is
a) 8
b) 0
c) 3
d) 6

9. Refer to Exhibit 3.1. The mean of this data set is
a) 5
b) 6
c) 7
d) 8

10. Refer to Exhibit 3.1. The standard deviation of this data set is
a) 2.7
b) 8.8
c) 2.9
d) 0

11. Refer to Exhibit 3.1. The range of this data set is
a) 6
b) 8
c) 3
d) 5

Exhibit 3.2
The following frequency distribution shows the time (in minutes per week) that a sample of business students used the computer terminals.

Time	f
20 - 39	2
40 - 59	4
60 - 79	6
80 - 99	4
100 - 119	2

12.   Refer to Exhibit 3.2. The mean of the distribution is
a)   3.6
b)   5.2
c)   69.5
d)   80

13.   Refer to Exhibit 3.2. The standard deviation of the distribution is
a)   564.70
b)   312.72
c)   70
d)   23.76

14.   An exploratory data analysis which uses the lowest value, 25th percentile, median, 75th percentile and largest value is known as a
a)   median analysis
b)   box analysis
c)   5 - number summary
d)   4 - number summary

15.   A box plot is
a)   the same as an ogive
b)   a frequency distribution
c)   the same as a frequency polygon
d)   a visual presentation of a 5 - number summary

16.   The symbol μ is used to represent
a)   the mean of the sample
b)   the mean of the population
c)   the standard deviation of the sample
d)   the standard deviation of the population

17.   The symbol σ is used to represent
a)   the mean of the sample
b)   the mean of the population
c)   the standard deviation of the sample
d)   the standard deviation of the population

18.   The symbol $\overline{X}$ is used to represent
a)   the mean of the sample
b)   the mean of the population
c)   the standard deviation of the sample
d)   the standard deviation of the population

19. The symbol S is used to represent
a) the mean of the sample
b) the mean of the population
c) the standard deviation of the sample
d) the standard deviation of the population

20. The symbol N is used to represent
a) the mean of the sample
b) the mean of the population
c) the standard deviation of the sample
d) the size of the population

21. The sum of the deviation of the individual data elements from their mean is always
a) equal to zero
b) equal to one
c) negative
d) positive

22. The median is always the same as
a) the first quartile
b) the second quartile
c) the third quartile
d) the mean

23. The interquartile range
a) is a measure of location
b) is a measure of variability
c) is always equal to the median
d) is always equal to the mode

24. The ratio of the standard deviation to the mean is
a) the variance
b) the range
c) the coefficient of variation
d) always greater than 1

25. The value of the variance can never be
a) positive
b) zero
c) larger than the standard deviation
d) negative

26.   A numerical measure of linear association between two variables is
a)   the standard deviation
b)   the coefficient of variation
c)   the mean
d)   the covariance

27.   The range of the correlation coefficient is
a)   0 to +1
b)   -1 to +1
c)   -1 to infinity
d)   -1 to 0

ANSWERS TO THE SELF-TESTING QUESTIONS

1. d
2. a
3. d
4. b
5. c
6. d
7. b
8. d
9. a
10. c
11. b
12. c
13. d
14. c
15. d
16. b
17. d
18. a
19. c
20. d
21. a
22. b
23. b
24. c
25. d
26. d
27. b

ANSWERS TO CHAPTER THREE EXERCISES

2.   Mean = 14.8   Median = 16   Mode = 17

3.   Hint: first find the price per ounce.
   (a)   Median = $5.00   Mode = $5.00
   (b) $5.00
   (c) $7.00

4.   (a)   35
   (b)   Mode = 35
   (c)   Median = 35
   (d)   First quartile = 28
      Third quartile = 39
   (e)   IQR = 11

5.   (a)   30.3
   (b)   Median = 28   There are 3 modes: 12, 28, and 25

6.   Mean = 93.63   Mode = 95   Median = 93.5

8.   (a) $6.00
   (b) $S^2 = 4$ $S = 2$
   (c)   40%

9.   Coefficient of variation in 2011 = 12% *(more dispersed)*
   Coefficient of variation in 2012 = 10%

10. (a)   Mean = 2.833   Median = 2.5   Mode = 2.0   Range = 6
   (b) $S^2 = 4.166$ $S = 2.041$
   (c)   First quartile = 2
      Third quartile = 4
   (d)   Z-score for May = 1.55 (rounded)
      Z-score for June = -1.39 (rounded)

11. (a)   Mean = 126
   (b)   Mode = 124   Median = 125
   (c)   19
   (d) $S^2 = 38.203$ $S = 6.181$

13. (a)   96%
   (b) $75 \pm (1.826)(5) = 65.87$ to 84.13

15.   Lowest = 18
        Q_1 = 24 (i.e., the 25th percentile)
        Median (Q_2) = 32
        Q_3 = 40 (i.e., the 75th percentile)
        Highest = 75

17. (a) 20.67 (rounded)
     (b) Since the covariance is positive it indicates that there is a positive correlation between x and y. That means as x increases so does y.
     (c) 0.9673 (rounded)

18. (a) -22.2857 (rounded)
     (b) -0.4798 (rounded)

20. 6.45

21. $16.86

23. (a) Mean = 69.5 (in thousands of dollars)
     (b) S = 23.094 (in thousands of dollars)

24. (a) Mean − 54.5
     (b) Variance = 117.65 (rounded)   Standard deviation = 10.85 (rounded)

25. (a) Mean = 93.5
     (b) Standard deviation = 11.06 (rounded)

26. Mean = 50.8   Standard deviation = 3.14 (rounded)

CHAPTER FOUR

INTRODUCTION TO PROBABILITY

CHAPTER OUTLINE AND REVIEW

There are many situations in which someone must make decisions in an environment of future uncertainties. Therefore, the decision maker is faced with the "chance" or likelihood that a particular situation may prevail (or fail).

This chapter covers the concepts that deal with such uncertainties. The topics of study are the concept of probability, the terminology used in the study of probability, and the various laws governing probability. The following is a brief description of the main points involved in the study of probability.

Addition Law is the law of probability which is used to determine the probability of the union of events.

Basic Requirements of Assigning Probabilities are the following.

1. If E_i represents the ith outcome of an experiment, then the probability of each E_i, must have a value between 0 and 1. In other words, $0 \le P(E_i) \le 1$.

2 The sum of all the possible outcomes of an experiment must equal to 1. In other words, $P(E_1) + P(E_2) + \ldots + P(E_n) = 1$.

Bayes' Theorem is a method of determining posterior probabilities.

Classical Method is a method of assigning probabilities that assumes that if there are n possible outcomes to an experiment, each of the experimental outcomes has the same chance of occurring. Hence, the probability of the occurrence of each outcome is 1/n. In other words, the classical method assumes equal probabilities for various experimental outcomes.

Collectively Exhaustive Events are a group of events which contain all the sample points in the sample space.

Complement of an Event A is the collection of all the sample points that are not included in event A. The complement of A is denoted as A^c. The following Venn diagram shows events A and its complement.

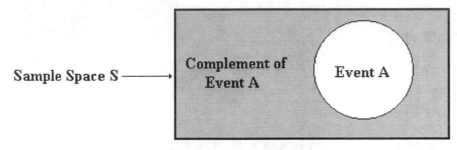

Conditional Probability is the probability of the occurrence of an event, given that another event has occurred.

Counting Rules are methods of identifying the number of experimental outcomes (sample points) in an experiment. There are three counting rule methods: (1) the counting rule for multiple step experiments; (2) *combination*, the counting rule that is used for counting the number of experimental outcomes when n objects are selected from a set of N objects where *order of selection* is not important; and (3) *permutation*, the counting rule that is used to determine the number of experimental outcomes when n objects are selected from a set of N objects where the *order of selection* is important. For more detail on these counting rules, refer to the section of chapter formulas.

Experiment is any process that results in well-defined outcomes. In any experiment, only one outcome is possible.

Event is any specific collection of sample points in an experiment.

Independent Events are two events are said to be independent if the occurrence of one does not affect the occurrence of the other.

Intersection of Two Events is the event that contains all the sample points that are in both events. The symbol " ∩ " denotes intersection of events. The shaded area in the following Venn diagram shows the intersection of events A and B.

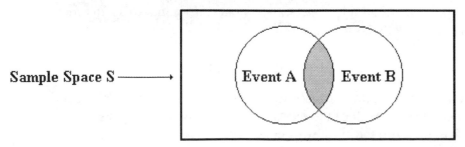

Joint Probability is the probability of two events both occurring, that is the probability of the intersection of two events.

Multiplication Law is the law of probability which is used to determine the probability of the intersection of events.

Mutually Exclusive Events are two events that are said to be mutually exclusive if they have no sample points in common (which means their intersection is not possible). Hence, if one event occurs, the other cannot occur.

Posterior Probabilities is the resulting probabilities after the probabilities are revised in the light of new information.

Prior Probabilities is the initial estimates of the probabilities of the occurrences of various events.

Probability is the numerical measure of the likelihood of the occurrence of an event. Probability ranges between 0 and 1.0, where 0 indicates the event will not occur and 1.0 indicates that the event will definitely occur. Furthermore, if there are k possible outcomes, then the sum of the probabilities of all k outcomes must be equal to 1.0.

Relative Frequency Method is the assignment of probabilities based on historical data.

Sample Point is each individual outcome of an experiment.

Sample Space is the collection of all possible sample points in an experiment.

Subjective Method is the assignment of probabilities based on the judgment of the experimenter.

Tree Diagram is a graphical method of presenting the sample points of an experiment.

Union of Two Events is that event that contains all the sample points, which are in one event or the other event or in both events. Hence, the union of events A and B is the event that contains all the sample points that are in both. The symbol " $\cup$ " is used to denote the union of two events. In the following Venn diagram the area that is shaded shows the union of events A and B.

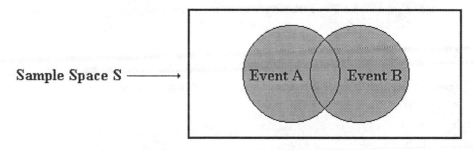

Venn diagram is a graphical method of showing the sample space, events, and the operations involving events.

CHAPTER FORMULAS

Counting Rules

A.   Number of Experimental Outcomes in Multiple-Step Experiments

Total number of outcomes = $(n_1)(n_2)...(n_k)$

where (n_1) = number of possible outcomes on the first step

(n_2) = number of possible outcomes on the second step

and   k = number of steps

B.   Combination

The number of experimental outcomes when n objects are selected from a set of N objects where the *order of selection is **not** important.*

$$C_n^N = \binom{N}{n} = \frac{N!}{n!(N-n)!} \tag{4.1}$$

where $N! = N(N-1)(N-2)...(2)(1)$
$n! = n(n-1)(n-2)...(2)(1)$

and $0! = 1$

C.   Permutation

The number of experimental outcomes when n objects are selected from a set of N objects where the *order of selection **is** important.*

$$P_n^N = n!\binom{N}{n} = \frac{N!}{(N-n)!} \tag{4.2}$$

Range of the Probability of each Outcome

$0 \le P(E_i) \le 1.0$ for all i's   (4.3)

Sum of all the Experimental Outcome Probabilities

$\sum P(E_i) = 1.0$ (4.4)

CHAPTER FORMULAS
(Continued)

Sum of the Probability of Event A and its Complement

$$P(A) + P(A^c) = 1.0$$

Computing Probability Using the Complement

$$P(A) = 1 - P(A^c) \tag{4.5}$$

Addition Law (the Probability of the Union of Two Events)

$$P(A \cup B) = P(A) + P(B) - P(A \cap B) \tag{4.6}$$

Conditional Probability

$$P(A|B) = \frac{P(A \cap B)}{P(B)} \tag{4.7}$$

or

$$P(B|A) = \frac{P(A \cap B)}{P(A)} \tag{4.8}$$

Two Events A and B are Independent if

$$P(A|B) = P(A) \tag{4.9}$$

or

$$P(B|A) = P(B) \tag{4.10}$$

Multiplication Law (the Probability of the Intersection of Two Events)

$$P(A \cap B) = P(B)\, P(A|B) \tag{4.11}$$

or

$$P(A \cap B) = P(A)\, P(B|A) \tag{4.12}$$

Multiplication Law for Independent Events

$$P(A \cap B) = P(A)\, P(B) \tag{4.13}$$

Because for independent events, $P(B|A) = P(B)$

CHAPTER FORMULAS
(Continued)

Bayes' Theorem (Two - Event Case)

$$P(A_1|B) = \frac{P(A_1)\,P(B|A_1)}{P(A_1)\,P(B|A_1) + P(A_2)\,P(B|A_2)} \tag{4.17}$$

and

$$P(A_2|B) = \frac{P(A_2)\,P(B|A_2)}{P(A_1)\,P(B|A_1) + P(A_2)\,P(B|A_2)} \tag{4.18}$$

Bayes' Theorem in General

$$P(A_i|B) = \frac{P(A_i)\,P(B|A_i)}{P(A_1)\,P(B|A_1) + P(A_2)\,P(B|A_2) + ... + P(A_n)\,P(B|A_n)} \tag{4.19}$$

for $A_i = A_1, A_2, \ldots, A_n$

where $P(A_i)$ = prior probability of event i
$P(B|A_i)$ = conditional probability of event B given A_i
$P(A_i|B)$ = posterior probability of A_i given B

EXERCISES

*1. Some of the flash drives produced by a manufacturer are defective. From the production line, 2 flash drives are selected and inspected.

(a) What constitutes an experiment for the above situation?

Answer: An experiment is any process which results in well-defined outcomes. In the above situation, the selection and classification of flash drives (as to being defective or non-defective) represent an experiment.

(b) How many sample points exist in the above experiment? List the sample points.

Answer: There are 2 possible outcomes in the selection of the first flash drive, that is, defective or non-defective ($n_1 = 2$) and 2 possible outcomes on the selection of the second flash drive ($n_2 = 2$). Hence, there are $(n_1)(n_2) = (2)(2) = 4$ distinct sample points or experimental outcomes. Letting E_i represent the experimental outcomes, then the sample points are as follows.

Sample Points	First Flash Drive	Second Flash Drive
E_1	defective	defective
E_2	defective	non-defective
E_3	non-defective	defective
E_4	non-defective	non-defective

(c) What constitutes the sample space? Use set notation to define the sample space.

Answer: The sample space refers to the collection of all possible sample points. Therefore, for the above experiment, the sample space is shown by the following set notation:

$$S = \{E_1, E_2, E_3, E_4\}$$

(d) Construct a tree diagram for the above experiment.

Answer: Figure 4.1 is a tree diagram for the previous experiment. The first step corresponds to the selection of the first flash drive, and the second step corresponds to the selection of the second flash drive. Note that the sample points are given on the right side of the diagram.

TREE DIAGRAM

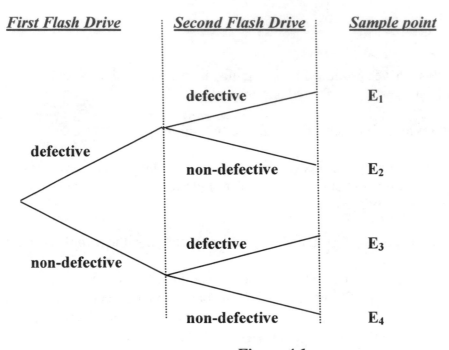

Figure 4.1

2. From nine cards numbered 1 through 9, two cards are drawn. Consider the selection and classification of the cards as odd or even as an experiment.

(a) How many sample points are there for this experiment?

(b) Use set notation to define the sample space.

3. Three applications for admission to a local university are checked, and the gender (male or female) of each applicant is determined.

(a) What represents the experiment?

(b) How many sample points exist in the above experiment?

(c) List the sample points and use set notation to show the sample space.

4. Assume your favorite soccer team has 2 games left to finish the season. The outcome of each game can be win, lose, or tie.

(a) How many possible outcomes exist?

(b) List the sample points.

5.   Each customer entering a department store will either buy or not buy some merchandise. An experiment consists of following 3 customers and determining whether or not they make a purchase. How many sample points exist in the above experiment? (Note that each customer is either a purchaser or non-purchaser.) List the sample points.

Solved Problem

*6.   A company plans to interview 10 recent graduates for possible employment. The company has three positions available. How many groups of three can the company select?

Answer: In this situation, we are interested in determining the number of combinations of 10 jobs (i.e., N = 10) taken three at a time (i.e., n = 3). In this situation, the order of selection is of no consequence; we are merely interested in determining how many groups of three can be selected. Therefore, we use the combinations formula as follows.

$$C_n^N = \binom{N}{n} = \frac{N!}{n!(N-n)!} = \frac{10!}{3!(10-3)!} = \frac{10!}{3!(7!)}$$

$$= \frac{(10)(9)(8)(7)(6)(5)(4)(3)(2)(1)}{[(3)(2)(1)][(7)(6)(5)(4)(3)(2)(1)]} = 120$$

7.   A student has to take 7 more courses before she can graduate. If none of the courses are prerequisite to others, how many groups of three courses can she select for the next semester?

8.   How many committees consisting of 3 female and 5 male students can be selected from a group of 5 female and 8 male students? (Hint: Find the possible groups for each gender and then multiply the results.)

Solved Problem

*9. From a group of three finalists (Nancy, Michael, and Sammie) for a privately endowed scholarship, two individuals are to be selected for the *first* and *second* places.

(a) Enumerate all of the possible selections.

Answer: In this situation, the order of selection is important. Thus, the possibilities can be listed as

Possibilities

First Place:	Nancy	Michael	Nancy	Sammie	Michael	Sammie
Second Place:	Michael	Nancy	Sammie	Nancy	Sammie	Michael

As you note, there are six possible outcomes without enumeration.

(b) Without enumerating all of the possibilities, compute the number of selections.

Answer: Since the order of selection is important, we are interested in the number of permutations of three finalists (N = 3) taken two at a time (n = 2). Hence, the permutation formula can be used as follows.

$$P_n^N = \frac{N!}{(N-n)!} = \frac{3!}{(3-2)!} = 6$$

10. Eight individuals are candidates for positions of president, vice president, and treasurer of an organization. How many possibilities of selections exist?

11. In a horse race, nine horses are running. Assume you have purchased a Trifecta ticket. (In Trifecta, the player selects three horses as first, second, and third place winners. To win, those three horses must finish the race in the precise order the player has selected.) How many possibilities of a Trifecta exist?

Solved Problem
---

*12. The sales records of an automobile dealer in Dallas indicate the following weekly sales volume over the last 200 weeks.

Number of Cars Sold	Number of Weeks
0	8
1	14
2	25
3	60
4	50
5	23
6	12
7	8
Total	200

(a)   Determine the probabilities associated with the various sales volumes.

Answer: Since historical data are available, the probabilities can be assigned based on the relative frequency method. For example, out of the 200 weeks, there were 8 weeks where the sales level was zero. Hence, the probability of zero sales is 8/200 = 0.04. Similarly, the probability of selling 1 automobile in any given week is 14/200 = 0.07. Then the probabilities associated with the various sales levels will be as follows:

Sales Level	Probability of the Sales Level
0	0.040
1	0.070
2	0.125
3	0.300
4	0.250
5	0.115
6	0.060
7	0.040
Total	1.000

(b)   Have the two basic requirements of the probability assignment been met?

Answer: The first requirement is that the range of probability for any experimental outcome be between zero and 1. As can be seen from the above probabilities, this requirement has been met. The second requirement is that the sum of the probabilities of all experimental outcomes be equal to 1. We note that the sum of the probabilities of the various sales levels is 1. Hence, the second requirement has also been met.

13.   A recent survey conducted among 800 married couples showed the following number of children per couple.

Number of Children	Number of Couples
None	40
1	100
2	480
3	120
4	40
≥ 5	20
Total	800

(a)   Which approach would you recommend for assigning probabilities to the sample points?

(b)   What is the probability of a couple having 5 or more children?

(c)   Assign probabilities to the sample points and verify that your assignment satisfies the two basic requirements of probability assignment.

*14. A market analyst assigns the following subjective probabilities for the Dow Jones Industrial Averages at the close of tomorrow's market.

Dow Jones Compared to Today		Probability
Higher	(E_1)	0.6
The Same	(E_2)	0.2
Lower	(E_3)	0.1

(a)   Are the above probability assignments valid?

Answer: One of the requirements of probability assignment is that the sum of the probabilities of all experimental outcomes be equal to 1. In the above example, all possible outcomes are given; but the sum of their probabilities does not add to 1. Hence, the assignment is ***not valid***.

(b)   Assume that in the previous example an analyst predicts that the chance of the market going up tomorrow is 10 times as large as the chance of the market going down. Furthermore, she feels that the chance of the market remaining the same is 9 times as large as the market going down. Assign valid probabilities to the market's outcome.

Answer: Assigning a weight of 1 to E_3, we note that E_1 is 10 times as likely as E_3, and E_2 is 9 times as likely as E_3. Hence, the probabilities can be calculated as follows:

Market Condition		Weights	Probability
Higher	(E_1)	10	$10/20 = 0.50$
The Same	(E_2)	9	$9/20 = 0.45$
Lower	(E_3)	1	$1/20 = \underline{0.05}$
Total		20	1.00

15.   A sportscaster assigned the following subjective probabilities to the outcome of the forthcoming game for the home team.

Experimental Outcome		Probability
E_1	(Win)	0.5
E_2	(Tie)	0.3
E_3	(Lose)	0.3

(a)   Are the above probability assignments valid? Why or why not? Explain fully.

(b)   Some local coaches feel that the home team's chance of winning the forthcoming game is 6 times as large as losing the game and 2 times as large as having a tie game. Assign valid probabilities for the win, loss, and tie game.

Solved Problem

*16. Your favorite professional soccer team (we shall refer to them as the "Favorites") has 2 games left to finish the season, which they will play in the next 2 weeks. If we define the experiment as playing the 2 games,

(a)   How many sample points are there in this experiment?

Answer: There are 3 possible outcomes (win, lose, and tie) for each game. Therefore, there is a total of 3 x 3 = 9 possible outcomes.

(b)   List all the experimental outcomes for the Favorites.

Answer: All the experimental outcomes (sample points) are

Experimental Outcome	First Game	Second Game
E_1	Win	Win
E_2	Win	Tie
E_3	Win	Lose
E_4	Tie	Win
E_5	Tie	Tie
E_6	Tie	Lose
E_7	Lose	Win
E_8	Lose	Tie
E_9	Lose	Lose

(c)   Use set notation to define the sample space for the Favorites.

Answer: $S = \{E_1, E_2, E_3, E_4, E_5, E_6, E_7, E_8, E_9\}$

(d)   Assume 200 soccer experts have given their opinions on the possible outcomes of the two forthcoming games. The following table shows the results of the experts' predictions.

	First Game			
	Win	Tie	Lose	Total
Second Game Win	80	15	5	100
Tie	30	20	10	60
Lose	10	25	5	40
Total	120	60	20	200

Based on the predictions of the 200 experts, assign probabilities for all the possible outcomes of the two future games.

Answer: Based on the experts' predictions, we note that 80 experts felt that the Favorites will win both games. Therefore, we can assign a probability of winning both games as $P(E_1) = 80/200 = 0.4$. In a similar fashion, we can determine the probability of winning the first game and tying the second as $P(E_2) = 30/200 = 0.15$. Continuing in a similar manner, the following probabilities can be assigned.

Experimental Outcome	**First Game**	**Second Game**	**Probabilities $P(E_i)$**
E_1	Win	Win	0.400
E_2	Win	Tie	0.150
E_3	Win	Lose	0.050
E_4	Tie	Win	0.075
E_5	Tie	Tie	0.100
E_6	Tie	Lose	0.125
E_7	Lose	Win	0.025
E_8	Lose	Tie	0.050
E_9	Lose	Lose	0.025
		Total	1.000

(e)   Assume the Favorites need to win at least one of the remaining games to qualify for playing in the World Cup competition. What is the probability of their going to the World Cup?

Answer: Let us define the following events.

W_1 = the event of winning the first game

W_2 = the event of winning the second game

W_p = the event of playing in the World Cup

Referring to the answer to Part "d" of the exercise, we note that sample points E_1, E_2 and E_3 correspond to event W_1; sample points E_1, E_4 and E_7 correspond to event W_2; and sample points E_1, E_2, E_3, E_4 and E_7 correspond to event W_p. In set notation, the events are

$W_1 = \{E_1, E_2, E_3\}$

$W_2 = \{E_1, E_4, E_7\}$

$W_p = \{E_1, E_2, E_3, E_4, E_7\}$

Since the probability of any event is equal to the sum of the probabilities of the sample points in the event, the probabilities of the above events will be

$P(W_1) = P(E_1) + P(E_2) + P(E_3) = 0.40 + 0.15 + 0.05 = 0.60$

Similarly,

$P(W_2) = P(E_1) + P(E_4) + P(E_7) = 0.4 + 0.075 + 0.025 = 0.50$

and

$P(W_p) = P(E_1) + P(E_2) + P(E_3) + P(E_4) + P(E_7)$
$= 0.400 + 0.150 + 0.050 + 0.075 + 0.0250 = 0.70$

Therefore, the probability of winning the first game is 0.6; the probability of winning the second game is 0.5; and the probability of playing in the World Cup is 0.70.

(f)   Find the probability of the union of events W_1 and W_2 (i.e., $P(W_1 \cup W_2)$) and explain what the union shows.

Answer: The union of two events refers to the sample points belonging to one or the other or both. In this case, the union of W_1 and W_2 refers to all the sample points belonging to W_1 or W_2 or both. From Part "e" of the exercise, we have

$W_1 = \{E_1, E_2, E_3\}$
and
$W_2 = \{E_1, E_4, E_7\}$

Therefore, the union of W_1 and W_2 is

$W_1 \cup W_2 = \{E_1, E_2, E_3, E_4, E_7\}$

Note that the sample points in $W_1 \cup W_2$ are situations in which at least one of the games is won and the Favorites qualify to play in the World Cup. Therefore,

$$P(W_1 \cup W_2) = P(E_1, E_2, E_3, E_4, E_7) = 0.70$$

This probability was actually calculated in part "e" of this exercise and was denoted as $P(W_p)$.

(g)   Find the probability of winning both games.

Answer: In this question, we are interested in the intersection of events W_1 and W_2. The intersection of W_1 and W_2 is that event which contains all the sample points belonging to both W_1 and W_2. Recall that

$$W_1 = \{E_1, E_2, E_3\}$$

and

$$W_2 = \{E_1, E_4, E_7\}$$

The only sample point which is in both W_1 and W_2 is E_1. Denoting the intersection of the two events as $W_1 \cap W_2$, we have

$$W_1 \cap W_2 = \{E_1\}$$

Therefore, the probability of winning both games is

$$P(W_1 \cap W_2) = P(E_1) = 0.4$$

(h)   Are the events W_1 and W_2 mutually exclusive? If they are not mutually exclusive, can you find the union of the two events?

Answer: Two or more events are said to be mutually exclusive if the events have no sample points in common. Recall that

$$W_1 = \{E_1, E_2, E_3\} \qquad \text{and} \qquad W_2 = \{E_1, E_4, E_7\}$$

In this case, we note that W_1 and W_2 have the sample point E_1 in common. Therefore, they are not mutually exclusive. When events are not mutually exclusive, we can find their union as follows.

$$P(W_1 \cup W_2) = P(W_1) + P(W_2) - P(W_1 \cap W_2)$$

In part (e), we determined

$$P(W_1) = 0.6$$

$$P(W_2) = 0.5$$

and in part (g), we calculated $P(W_1 \cap W_2) = 0.4$.

Therefore,

$$P(W_1 \cup W_2) = 0.6 + 0.5 - 0.4 = 0.70$$

Note that this is the same answer that we had found in parts (e) and (f).

(i)   Let L_1 represent the event that the Favorites lose the first game. Are the events W_1 and L_1 mutually exclusive? Find $P(W_1 \cup L_1)$.

Answer: The sample points that correspond to the loss of the first game are

$$L_1 = \{E_7, E_8, E_9\}$$

and we recall

$$W_1 = \{E_1, E_2, E_3\}$$

Since events L_1 and W_1 do not have any sample points in common, *they are mutually exclusive*. The probability of the union of mutually exclusive events is the sum of the probabilities of all the sample points in each event. Therefore,

$$P(W_1 \cup L_1) = P(W_1) + P(L_1)$$

$$= P(E_1) + P(E_2) + P(E_3) + P(E_7) + P(E_8) + P(E_9)$$

$$= 0.400 + 0.150 + 0.050 + 0.025 + 0.050 + 0.025 = 0.7$$

(j)   Define T_1 as the event that the Favorites tie the first game. Are the events W_1, T_1, and L_1 mutually exclusive and collectively exhaustive?

Answer: The sample points that correspond to each of the three events are

$$W_1 = \{E_1, E_2, E_3\}$$

$$T_1 = \{E_4, E_5, E_6\}$$

$$L_1 = \{E_7, E_8, E_9\}$$

Since the three events do not have any sample points in common, they are *mutually exclusive*. Furthermore, the union of the three events includes all the possible outcomes; hence, they are *collectively exhaustive*. This simply means that the events W_1, T_1, and L_1 are *mutually exclusive* and *collectively exhaustive*. Therefore,

$$P(W_1 \cup T_1 \cup L_1) = 1$$

(k)   If $P(W_1)$ is the probability of winning the first game, what is the probability of not winning the first game?

Answer: Since W_1 is the event of winning the first game, then its complement, or W_1^c is the event of not winning the first game. Recall

$$W_1 = \{E_1, E_2, E_3 \}$$

$$P(W_1) = 0.6$$

The complement of W_1 (denoted as W_1^c) must contain all the sample points which are not in W_1. Hence,

$$W_1^c = \{E_4, E_5, E_6, E_7, E_8, E_9\}$$

Therefore, the probability of W_1^c is

$$P(W_1^c) = P(E_4) + P(E_5) + P(E_6) + P(E_7) + P(E_8) + P(E_9)$$

$$= 0.075 + 0.100 + 0.125 + 0.025 + 0.050 + 0.025 = 0.4$$

A more direct approach to the above is to note that

$$P(W_1) + P(W_1^c) = 1$$

Since we had previously calculated the $P(W_1) = 0.6$, we can simply calculate $P(W_1^c)$ as

$$P(W_1^c) = 1 - P(W_1) = 1 - 0.60 = 0.40$$

17.   Assume a sample space is given as

$$S = \{E_1, E_2, E_3, E_4, E_5\}$$

and the following probabilities are assigned to the sample points.

$$P(E_1) = 0.01$$
$$P(E_2) = 0.19$$
$$P(E_3) = 0.40$$
$$P(E_4) = 0.30$$
$$P(E_5) = \underline{0.10}$$
Total   1.00

Let
$$A = \{E_1, E_3, E_5\}$$
$$B = \{E_2, E_3\}$$
$$C = \{E_1, E_2, E_4\}$$

(a)   Find P(A), P(B) and P(C).

(b)   Find (A ∩ C) and P(A ∩ C).

(c)   Are events A and C mutually exclusive? Why or why not?

(d)   Find $P(C^c)$.

(e)   Find (A ∪ B) and P(A ∪ B).

(f)   Let

$$X = \{E_1, E_3, E_5\}$$
$$Y = \{F_2, F_4\}$$

Are events X and Y mutually exclusive? Are they collectively exhaustive? Explain.

18.   Assume you have applied to two different universities (let's refer to them as universities A and B) for your graduate work. In the past, 25% of students (with similar credentials as yours) who applied to University A were accepted; while University B accepted 35% of the applicants. Assume that acceptance at the two universities are independent events.

(a)   What is the probability that you will be accepted into both universities?

(b)   What is the probability that you will be accepted into at least one graduate program?

(c)   What is the probability that one and only one of the universities will accept you?

(d)   What is the probability that neither university will accept you?

19.   The flash drive manufacturer (from exercise ***1**) has determined that 3% of his flash drives are defective. He has just sold 2 flash drives to a customer.

(a)   What is the probability that both of the flash drives purchased by the customer are defective?

(b)   What is the probability that one of the flash drives is defective?

(c)   What is the probability that neither one of the flash drives is defective?

(d)   Are the events described in a, b, and c of this exercise mutually exclusive and collectively exhaustive? Explain.

20.   In exercise 13 of this chapter, the results of a survey of 800 married couples and the number of children they had were given. Based on that data, the following probabilities were determined.

Number of Children	Probability
0	0.050
1	0.125
2	0.600
3	0.150
4	0.050
≥ 5	0.025
Total	1.000

If a couple is selected at random, what is the probability that the couple will have

(a)   Less than 4 children?

(b)   More than 2 children?

(c)   Either 2 or 3 children?

21.   Assume that in your hand you hold an ordinary six-sided die and a dime. You toss both the die and the dime onto a table.

(a)   What is the probability that a head appears on the dime and a six on the die?

(b)   What is the probability that a tail appears on the dime and any number more than 3 appears on the die?

(c)   What is the probability that a number larger than 2 appears on the die?

22.   On a very short quiz, there are two questions: one multiple choice question with 5 possible choices (a, b, c, d, e) and one true or false question. Assume you are taking the quiz but do not have any idea what the correct answer is to either question. You mark an answer to each question randomly. Assume that the events are independent of each other.

(a)   What is the probability that you have given the correct answer to both questions?

(b)   What is the probability that only one of the two answers is correct?

(c)   What is the probability that neither answer is correct?

(d)   What is the probability that only your answer to the multiple choice question is correct?

(e)   What is the probability that you have answered only the true or false question correctly?

23.   Each year the IRS randomly audits 10% of the tax returns. Assume a married couple has filed separate returns and the events of their being audited are independent of each other.

(a)   What is the probability that both the husband and the wife will be audited?

(b)   What is the probability that only one of them will be audited?

(c)   What is the probability that neither one of them will be audited?

(d)   What is the probability that at least one of them will be audited?

Solved Problem

*24. Assume $P(A) = 0.40$, $P(B) = 0.50$, and $P(A|B) = 0.3$

(a)   Are events A and B independent? Explain.

Answer: Two events, A and B, are independent if $P(A|B) = P(A)$. Since in this situation $P(A|B)$ and $P(A)$ are not equal, the two events are not independent.

(b)   Find $P(A \cap B)$ Hint: $P(A \cap B) = P(B \cap A)$

Answer: The multiplication law of probability states that

$$P(B \cap A) = P(B)P(A|B)$$

Therefore,

$$P(B \cap A) = (0.5)(0.3) = 0.15$$

(c)   Find $P(B|A)$.

Answer: Once again using the Multiplication Law, we note that

$$P(A \cap B) = P(A)P(B|A)$$

Solving for P(B|A), we have

$$P(B|A) = \frac{P(A \cap B)}{P(A)}$$

Substituting the values, we conclude

$$P(B|A) = \frac{0.15}{0.4} = 0.375$$

(d)   Find P(A $\cup$ B)

Answer: The addition law of probability states that

$$P(A \cup B) = P(A) + P(B) - P(A \cap B)$$

In part (b) we found P(B $\cap$ A) = (0.5)(0.3) = 0.15. Now we can find P(A $\cup$ B) as

$$P(A \cup B) = 0.4 + 0.5 - 0.15 = 0.75$$

25.   Assume that P(A) = 0.7, P(B) = 0.8, and P(B $\cap$ A) = 0.56.

(a)   Find P(A|B) and P(B|A).

(b)   Are events A and B independent? Explain.

26.   Assume that two events A and B are mutually exclusive; and furthermore, P(A) = 0.3 and P(B) = 0.4.

(a)   Explain what is meant by "mutually exclusive" events.

(b)   Find P(A $\cap$ B).

(c)   Find P(A $\cup$ B).

Solved Problem

*27. Sammie is a general contractor and has submitted two bids for two projects (A and B). The probability of getting project A is 0.65. The probability of getting project B is 0.77 . The probability of getting at least one of the two projects is 0.90.

(a)   What is the probability that she will get both projects?

Answer: We are interested in finding $P(A \cap B)$. The Addition Law states

$$P(A \cup B) = P(A) + P(B) - P(A \cap B)$$

In this problem $P(A \cup B) = 0.90$, $P(A) = 0.65$, and $P(B) = 0.77$. Substituting these values in the above equation, we will have

$$0.90 = 0.65 + 0.77 - P(A \cap B)$$

Now solving for $P(A \cap B)$, we have

$$P(A \cap B) = 0.65 + 0.77 - 0.90 = 0.52$$

(b)   Are the events of getting the two projects mutually exclusive?

Answer: If the events are mutually exclusive, their intersection must be zero. In Part a, we found that the intersection of these two events was $P(A \cap B) = 0.52$. Thus, the events are not mutually exclusive.

(c)   Are the two events independent? Explain, using probabilities.

Answer: The two events A and B are independent if $P(A|B) = P(A)$. For this problem, we can find $P(A|B)$ as

$$P(A|B) = \frac{P(A \cap B)}{P(B)} = \frac{0.52}{0.77} = 0.675$$

Since this value is not equal to the probability of A we conclude that the events are not independent.

28.   Assume you are taking two courses this semester (A and B). The probability that you will pass course A is 0.835, the probability that you will pass both courses is 0.276. The probability that you will pass at least one of the courses is 0.981.

(a)   What is the probability that you will pass course B?

(b)   Are the passing of the two courses independent events? Use probability information to justify your answer.

(c)   Are the events of passing the courses mutually exclusive? Fully explain.

Solved Problem

---

*29. Freeman Research Group is investigating the relationship between smoking and emphysema. Their research, involving a sample of 400 individuals, provided the following information.

Table 1

	Smoker	Nonsmoker	Total
Person *has* emphysema	80	32	112
Person *does not have* emphysema	40	248	288
Total	120	280	400

(a)   Show the joint probability table for the above data.

Answer: Let us define the following notations:
    S = Person is a smoker
    S^c = Person is a nonsmoker
    E = Person has emphysema
    E^c = Person does not have emphysema

The *joint probability* table is simply a table showing the intersection of the two events. For example, the probability that a person *is a smoker* and *has emphysema* is $P(S \cap E)$. Since the sample contains 400 individuals and 80 of these individuals are smokers who have emphysema, then $P(S \cap E) = 80/400 = 0.20$. The other probabilities can be computed in the same manner resulting in the following joint probability table.

Joint probabilities are shown in the body of the table	Smoker (S)	Nonsmoker (S^c)	Total
Person *has* emphysema (E)	0.20	0.08	0.28
Person *does not have* emphysema (E^c)	0.10	0.62	0.72
Total	0.30	0.70	1.00

Marginal Probabilities are shown in the margins of the table

The values in the margins of the above table are referred to as the *marginal probabilities,* and they represent the probability of each event separately. For instance, 0.70 in the bottom margin of the above table indicates that the probability of a person being a Nonsmoker is 0.70.

(b)   What is the probability that a randomly selected individual has emphysema?

Answer: In the sample of 400, there were 112 individuals who had emphysema. Therefore, the probability of an individual having emphysema is $P(E) = 112/400 = 0.28$.

(c)   Given that an individual is a smoker, what is the probability that this individual has emphysema?

Answer: Referring to Table 1, we note that there were 120 individuals who were smokers, 80 of whom had emphysema. Thus, $P(E|S) = 80/120 = 0.6667$. We could have determined this probability by using the joint probability table above and stating

$$P(E|S) = \frac{P(E \cap S)}{P(S)} = \frac{0.20}{0.30} = 0.6667$$

(d)   Does the research show that emphysema and smoking are independent events? Use probabilities to justify your answer.

Answer: If the events were independent, then $P(E|S) = P(E)$. In other words, if the events were independent, then being a smoker or a nonsmoker would not have any effect on the likelihood of having emphysema. In this problem, $P(E|S) = 0.6667$, which is not equal to $P(E) = 0.28$, indicating the events are not independent. The likelihood of *smokers* having emphysema is much larger than the probability of an individual in the entire sample having emphysema.

30.   A study was conducted to determine the relationship between gender and major field of study. The results of a survey of 900 students are shown below.

	Female	Male	Total
Arts and Sciences	180	90	270
Engineering	54	180	234
Business	198	198	396
Total	432	468	900

(a)   Show the joint probability table for the above data.

(b)   What is the probability that a randomly selected individual is majoring in Arts and Sciences?

(c)   Given that an individual is female, what is the probability that she is majoring in Arts and Sciences?

(d)   Does the research show that major field of study is independent of gender? Use probabilities to justify your answer.

Solved Problem

31. An automobile dealer has kept records on the customers who visited his showroom. Forty percent of the people who visited his dealership were female. Furthermore, his records show that 35% of the females who visited his dealership purchased an automobile, while 20% of the males who visited his dealership purchased an automobile. Let

A_1 = the event that the customer is female

A_2 = the event that the customer is male

(a)   What is the probability that a customer entering the showroom will buy an automobile?

Answer: In this case, we want to determine the probability that a customer, regardless of the gender of the customer, will buy a car. Let B = the event that the customer will buy a car. From the statement of the problem, we know the conditional probabilities. That is, the probability that a customer will buy a car under the condition that the customer is a female, is 0.35; and the probability that the customer will buy a car under the condition that the customer is male is 0.20. What was just said can be expressed as

$P(B|A_1) = 0.35$

$P(B|A_2) = 0.20$

Therefore, the probability that a customer will buy a car, that is P(B), can be computed as

$$P(B) = P(A_1)\,P(B|A_1) + P(A_2)\,P(B|A_2) = (0.4)\,(0.35) + (0.6)\,(0.2) = 0.26$$

This indicates that the probability of a customer purchasing a car (regardless of the customer's gender) is 0.26. For details see Figure 4.2.

(b)   A car salesperson has just informed us that he sold a car to a customer. What is the probability that the customer was female?

Answer: Based on the information that a purchase was made, we can revise the probability of a customer being a female. Bayes' theorem states

$$P(A_1|B) = \frac{P(A_1)\,P(B|A_1)}{P(A_1)\,P(B|A_1) + P(A_2)\,P(B|A_2)}$$

Substituting the values in the previous equation, we have

$$P(A_1|B) = \frac{(0.4)\,(0.35)}{(0.4)\,(0.35) + (0.6)\,(0.2)} = \frac{0.14}{0.26} = 0.538$$

Hence, the probability that the customer was a female has been revised from 0.4 to 0.538.

(c)   Prepare a table in order to calculate $P(A_1|B)$, $P(A_2|B)$ and $P(B)$.

Answer: The following table summarizes the Bayes' theorem calculations. The calculations are the same as those shown in Parts a and b. However, the tabular approach is clearer.

Event	Prior Probabilities $P(A_i)$	Conditional Probabilities $P(B|A_i)$	Joint Probabilities $P(A_i \cap B)$	Posterior Probabilities $P(A_i|B)$
A_1	0.4	0.35	0.14	$\frac{.14}{.26} = .538$
A_2	0.6	0.20	0.12	$\frac{.12}{.26} = .462$
			$P(B) = 0.26$	

You must note that the joint probability in the above table is the product of the prior and the conditional probabilities. Furthermore, you can see that the probability that a customer is female, given that she purchased a car is 0.538; while the probability that a customer is male, given that he purchased a car is 0.462.

(d) Draw a complete probability tree for the above problem.

PROBABILITY TREE

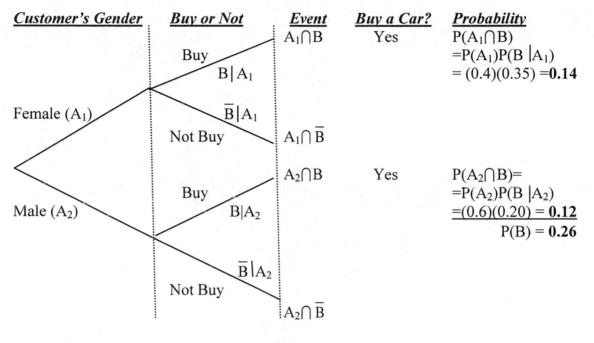

Figure 4.2

32. Refer to exercise 31 and let B^c = the event that the customer will not buy a car.

(a) A customer visited the store but did not purchase a car. What is the probability that the customer was male? Hint: You want to find $P(A_2|B^c)$.

(b) Prepare a table in order to calculate $P(A_1|B^c)$, $P(A_2|B^c)$ and $P(B^c)$.

33. The prior probabilities for events A_1 and A_2 are $P(A_1) = 0.1$ and $P(A_2) = 0.9$, and the conditional probabilities of event B given A_1 and A_2 are $P(B|A_1) = 0.8$ and $P(B|A_2) = 0.7$.

(a) Compute $P(B \cap A_1)$, $P(B \cap A_2)$, and $P(B)$.

(b) Apply Bayes' theorem to compute the posterior probabilities $P(A_1|B)$ and $P(A_2|B)$.

(c) Use a tabular approach to compute $P(B)$, $P(A_1|B)$, and $P(A_2|B)$.

(d) Use a tabular approach to compute $P(B^c)$, $P(A_1|B^c)$, and $P(A_2|B^c)$.

34. A local university offers a review course for those who are planning to take the GMAT exam. Thirty percent of the people who took the exam had attended the university's GMAT review course. The results of the test showed that 60% of those who attended the GMAT review course passed the exam; while among those who did not attend the course, only 20% passed the exam.

(a) An individual has passed the exam. What is the probability that he attended the GMAT review course?

(b) Let

A$_1$ = the event that the individual attended the GMAT review course
A$_2$ = the event that the individual did not attend the GMAT review
 course
B = the event that the individual passed the exam

Use a tabular approach to compute P(B), P(A$_1$|B), and P(A$_2$|B).

(c) Use a tabular approach to compute P(B^c), P(A$_1$|B^c), and P(A$_2$|B^c).

35. The table below shows part of the results of applying Bayes' theorem to a situation.

Events	$P(A_i)$	$P(B|A_i)$	$P(A_i \cap B)$	$P(A_i|B)$
A_1	.3	.8		
A_2	.2	.4		
A_3	.5	.6		

(a)   Identify the prior, conditional, joint, and posterior probabilities.

(b)   Complete the above table and find $P(A_1 \cap B)$, $P(A_2 \cap B)$, $P(B)$, $P(A_1|B)$, and $P(A_2|B)$.

36. The prior probabilities for events A_1, A_2, A_3 and A_4 are $P(A_1) = 0.1$, $P(A_2) = 0.6$, $P(A_3) = 0.25$, and $P(A_4) = .05$. The conditional probabilities of event B are $P(B|A_1) = .7$, $P(B|A_2) = 0.5$, $P(B|A_3) = 0.4$, and $P(B|A_4) = 0.9$.

(a)   Use the tabular approach to find $P(B)$, $P(A_1|B)$, $P(A_2|B)$, $P(A_3|B)$, and $P(A_4|B)$.

(b)   Use the tabular approach to find $P(B^c)$, $P(A_1|B^c)$, $P(A_2|B^c)$, $P(A_3|B^c)$, and $P(A_4|B^c)$.

37.   A survey of business students who had taken the Graduate Management Admission Test (GMAT) indicated that students who had spent at least five hours studying GMAT review guides had a probability of 0.85 of scoring above 500. Students who did not review had a probability of 0.65 of scoring above 500. It has been determined that 70% of the business students had reviewed for the test.

(a)   Find the probability of scoring above 500.

(b)   Given that a student scored above 500, what is the probability that he/she had reviewed for the test?

38.   Michael O. Ahmadi has applied for scholarships to two universities. The probability that he will receive a scholarship from University A is 0.55; the probability that he will receive a scholarship from University B is 0.65. The probability that he will receive scholarships from both universities is 0.4.

(a)   What is the probability that he will receive at least one scholarship? (Hint: find the probability of A or B or both.)

(b)   What is the probability that he will not receive a scholarship from either university?

Solved Problem

*39. What is the probability that in a group of three people, at least 2 of them will have the same birth dates (i.e., the same date and not necessarily the same year)? **Do not consider leap years and assume there are 365 days in every year**.

Answer: First let us compute the probability that none of them have the same birth dates and then subtract the results from one, thus arriving at the probability that at least two of them have the same birth dates. The probability that the first individual has a birth date is 365/365; the probability that the second person was not born on the same day of the year is 364/365; and the probability that the third person was not born on any of the other two person's birth date is 363/365. Now we can compute the probability that none of them have the same birth date as

$$\frac{365}{365} \cdot \frac{364}{365} \cdot \frac{363}{365} = 0.9917958$$

Finally, the probability that at least 2 of them were born on the same day is

$$1 - 0.9917958 = 0.0082042$$

40. What is the probability that in a group of four people, at least 2 of them will have the same birth dates (i.e., the same date and not necessarily the same year)?

SELF-TESTING QUESTIONS

In the following multiple choice questions, circle the correct answer. An answer key is provided following the questions.

1.   The set of all possible sample points (experimental outcomes) is called
a)   a sample
b)   an event
c)   the sample space
d)   the union

2.   A method of assigning probabilities which assumes that the experimental outcomes are equally likely is referred to as the
a)   objective method
b)   classical method
c)   subjective method
d)   control method

3.   A method of assigning probabilities based on historical data is called the
a)   classical method
b)   subjective method
c)   relative frequency method
d)   objective method

4.   The probability assigned to each experimental outcome must be
a)   any value larger than zero
b)   smaller than zero
c)   at least one
d)   between zero and one

5.   If two events are mutually exclusive, then their intersection
a)   will always be equal to zero
b)   can have any value larger than zero
c)   must be larger than zero, but less than one
d)   can be any value

6.   The union of events A and B is
a)   the same as the intersection of events A and B
b)   always equal to zero
c)   that event which contains all sample points belonging to A and B
d)   that event which contains all sample points belonging to A or B or both

7.   Given that an event E has a probability of 0.25, then the probability of the complement of event E
a)   cannot be determined with the information given
b)   can have any value between zero and one
c)   must be 0.75
d)   must be 1.25

8.   Two events X and Y are independent if
a) $P(Y|X) = P(X)$
b) $P(Y|X) = P(Y)$
c) $P(X|Y) = 1$
d) $P(X) = P(X|Y) = 0$

9.   If $P(A) = 0.2$, $P(B) = 0.6$, and $P(A|B) = 0.4$, then $P(A \cap B)$ is
a)   0.80
b)   0.08
c)   0.12
d)   0.24

10.   If $P(A) = 0.5$, $P(B) = 0.3$, and $P(A \cap B) = 0.1$, then $P(B|A)$ is
a)   0.33
b)   0.20
c)   0.15
d)   0.05

11.   Of five letters (A, B, C, D, and E), two letters are to be selected at random. How many possible selections are there?
a)   20
b)   7
c)   5!
d)   10

12.   An experiment consists of three steps. There are three possible outcomes on the first step, four possible outcomes on the second step, and five possible outcomes on the third step. The total number of experimental outcomes is
a)   (3!)(4!)(5!)
b)   60
c)   20
d)   10

13.   The range of probability is
a)   any value larger than zero
b)   any value between minus infinity to plus infinity
c)   zero to one
d)   any value between -1 to 1

14.   If a penny is tossed six times and comes up heads all six times, the probability of heads on the seventh trial is
a)   less than the probability of tails
b)   1/64
c)   0.5
d)   larger than the probability of tails

15.   If X and Y are independent events with P(X) = 0.3 and P(Y) = 0.5, then P(X ∪ Y) is
a)   0.80
b)   0.15
c)   0.20
d)   0.65

16.   From a group of seven people, three individuals are to be selected at random. How many possible selections are there?
a)   21
b)   49
c)   35
d)   3

17.   If A and B are independent events with P(A)= 0.65 and P(A ∩ B)=0.26, then, P(B)=
a)   0.400
b)   0.169
c)   0.390
d)   0.650

18.   Given that event E has a probability of 0.31, the probability of the complement of event E
a)   cannot be determined with the above information
b)   can have any value between zero and one
c)   0.69
d)   is 0.31

19.   Each individual outcome of an experiment is called
a.   the sample space
b.   a sample point
c.   an experiment
d.   an individual

20.   An experiment consists of selecting a student body president and vice president. All undergraduate students (freshmen through seniors) are eligible for these offices. How many sample points (possible outcomes as to the classifications) exist?
a.   4
b.   16
c.   8
d.   32

ANSWERS TO THE SELF-TESTING QUESTIONS

1. c
2. b
3. c
4. d
5. a
6. d
7. c
8. b
9. d
10. b
11. d
12. b
13. c
14. c
15. d
16. c
17. a
18. c
19. b
20. b

ANSWERS TO CHAPTER FOUR EXERCISES

2. (a) $(2)(2) = 4$

    (b) Let   0 = odd

    E = even

    S = {00, 0E, E0, EE}

3. (a) The selection and classification by gender

    (b) $(2)(2)(2) = 8$

    (c)
MMM	FMM	FFM	FFF
	MFM	FMF	
	MMF	MFF	

    Let E_i represent each of the above sample points.

    Then:

    S = {E_1, . . . ,E_8}

4. (a) $(3)(3) = 9$

    (b) (Let Win = W, Lose = L, Tie = T

    Sample points are

WW	LW	TW
WL	LL	TL
WT	LT	TT

5. $(2)(2)(2) = 8$

    Let P = purchaser

    N = non-purchaser

PPP	PPN	PNN	NNN
	PNP	NPN	
	NPP	NNP	

7. 35

8. 560

10. 336

11. 504

13. (a) Relative frequency
    (b) 0.025
    (c)

Number of Children	**P**
0	0.050
1	0.125
2	0.600
3	0.150
4	0.050
5	0.025
	1.000

15. (a) No. Sum of probabilities is greater than 1.
    (b) 0.6, 0.3, 0.1

17. (a) $P(A) = P(E_1) + P(E_3) + P(E_5) = 0.01 + 0.4 + 0.1 = 0.51$
        $P(B) = 0.59$
        $P(C) = 0.50$
    (b) $(A \cap C) = \{E_1\}$
        $P(A \cap C) = P(E_1) = 0.01$
    (c) A and C are not mutually exclusive because they have E_1 in common.
    (d) $P(C^c) = 1 - P(C) = 1 - 0.5 = 0.5$
    (e) $(A \cup B) = \{E_1, E_2, E_3, E_5\}$
        $P(A \cup B) = 0.7$
    (f) X and Y are mutually exclusive and collectively exhaustive because they do not have any sample points in common and the sum of their probabilities is equal to 1.

18. (a) 0.0875
    (b) 0.5125
    (c) 0.425
    (d) 0.4875

19. (a) 0.0009
    (b) 0.0582
    (c) 0.9409
    (d) Yes, they do not have any sample points in common, and the sum of their probabilities is equal to 1.

20. (a) 0.925
    (b) 0.225
    (c) 0.750

21. (a) 1/12
    (b) 3/12
    (c) 8/12

22. (a) 1/10
    (b) 5/10
    (c) 4/10
    (d) 1/10
    (e) 4/10

23. (a) 0.01
    (b) 0.18
    (c) 0.81
    (d) 0.19

25. (a) 0.7, 0.8
    (b) Yes, P(A|B) = P(A)

26. (a) Two events are said to be mutually exclusive if they have no sample points in common (which means their intersection is not possible). Hence, if one event occurs, the other cannot occur.
    (b) 0
    (c) 0.7

28. (a) 0.422
    (b) No, P(A|B) = 0.276/0.422 = 0.654 which is not equal to P(A) = 0.835
    (c) No, the intersection is not zero.

30. (a)

	Female	Male	Total
Arts and Sciences	0.20	0.10	0.30
Engineering	0.06	0.20	0.26
Business	0.22	0.22	0.44
Total	0.48	0.52	1.00

    (b) P(Art and Science) = 0.30
    (c) P(Art and Science | Female) = 0.4167 (that is 0.20/0.48 or 180/432)
    (d) Field of study is not independent of gender. P(Art and Science) is not equal P(Art and Science | Female)

32. (a) 0.6486

    (b)

Event	$P(A_i)$	$P(B^c|A_i)$	$P(A_i \cap B^c)$	$P(A_i|B^c)$
A_1	.4	.65	.26	.26/.74 = .3514
A_2	.6	.80	.48	.48/.74 = .6486
			$P(B^c) = .74$	

33.

                                              (a) $P(B \cap A_1) = 0.08$

$P(B \cap A_2) = 0.63$

$P(B) = 0.71$

(b) $P(A_1|B) = 0.08/.71 = 0.1127$

$P(A_2|B) = 0.63/0.71 = 0.8873$

(c)

Event	$P(A_i)$	$P(B\|A_i)$	$P(B \cap A_i)$	$P(A_i\|B)$
A_1	.1	.8	.08	.08/.71 = .1127
A_2	.9	.7	.63	.63/.71 = .8873
			$P(B) = .71$	

(d)

Event	$P(A_i)$	$P(B^c\|A_i)$	$P(B^c \cap A_i)$	$P(A_i\|B^c)$
A_1	.1	.2	.02	.02/.29 = .069
A_2	.9	.3	.27	.27/.29 = .931
			$P(B^c) = .29$	

34. (a)   .18/.32 = .5625

(b)

Event	$P(A_i)$	$P(B\|A_i)$	$P(B \cap A_i)$	$P(A_i\|B)$
A_1	.3	.60	.18	.18/.32 = .5625
A_2	.7	.20	.14	.14/.32 = .4375
			$P(B) = .32$	

(c)

Event	$P(A_i)$	$P(B^c\|A_i)$	$P(B^c \cap A_i)$	$P(A_i\|B^c)$
A_1	.3	.40	.12	.12/.68 = .1765
A_2	.7	.80	.56	.56/.68 = .8235
			$P(B^c) = .68$	

35. (a) and (b)

Event	Prior $P(A_i)$	Conditional $P(B\|A_i)$	Joint $P(A_i \cap B)$	Posterior $P(A_i\|B)$
A_1	.3	.8	.24	.24/.62 = .3871
A_2	.2	.4	.08	.08/.62 = .1290
A_3	.5	.6	.30	.30/.62 = .4839
			$P(B) = .62$	

36. (a)

Event	$P(A_i)$	$P(B\|A_i)$	$P(A_i \cap B)$	$P(A_i\|B)$
A_1	0.10	.7	.070	.07/.515 = .1359
A_2	0.60	.5	.300	.30/.515 = .5825
A_3	0.25	.4	.100	.10/.515 = .1942
A_4	0.05	.9	.045	.045/.515 = .0874
			$P(B) = .515$	

(b)

Event	$P(A_i)$	$P(B^c|A_i)$	$P(A_i \cap B^c)$	$P(A_i|B^c)$
A_1	0.10	.3	.030	.03/.485 = .0618
A_2	0.60	.5	.300	.31/.485 = .6186
A_3	0.25	.6	.150	.15/.485 = 3093
A_4	0.05	.1	.005	.005/.485 = .0103

$$P(B^c) = .485$$

37.

Event	$P(A_i)$	$P(B|A_i)$	$P(A_i \cap B)$	$P(A_i|B)$
A_1	.70	.85	.595	.595/.79 = .7532
A_2	.30	.65	.195	.195/.79 = .2468

$$P(B) = .790$$

(a) .79
(b) .595/.790 = 0.7532

38. (a) 0.8
(b) 0.2

40. $1 - \left(\dfrac{365}{365} \cdot \dfrac{364}{365} \cdot \dfrac{363}{365} \cdot \dfrac{362}{365} \right) = 0.01635$

CHAPTER FIVE

DISCRETE PROBABILITY DISTRIBUTIONS

CHAPTER OUTLINE AND REVIEW

In Chapter 4, you learned what is meant by an experiment, how one determines the probability of the outcome of an experiment, and various laws of probability. Chapter 5 introduces you to the concept of a random variable and the probability distribution of a discrete random variable. You are also introduced to three major discrete probability distributions: *Binomial*, *Poisson*, and *Hypergeometric* distributions. The main concepts covered in Chapter 5 are as follows.

Binomial Probability Distribution is a distribution which is applied to discrete random variables and is used for determining the probability of x successes in n trials. For the binomial distribution to be applicable, all of the following assumptions must be satisfied.

1. The experiment consists of a sequence of n identical trials.
2. For each trial, there are two possible outcomes (one called success, the other failure).
3. The probabilities of success (or failure) remain the same as successive trials are made.
4. The trials are independent of each other.

Binomial Probability Function is a function used to determine probabilities in a binomial experiment.

Continuous Random Variable is a variable that can assume any value in an interval. For example, if a random variable is the weight of an item, which may weigh from 5 to 7 ounces, the random variable weight is a continuous random variable because it can take any value in the interval of 5 to 7 ounces (such as 5.1, 6.22, etc.).

Discrete Probability Distribution is a description of how the probabilities of a discrete random variable are distributed over various values of the random variable by means of a probability function denoted by f(x).

Discrete Random Variable is a random variable that can assume only a countable number of values. For example, if the random variable is the number of defective tires in a group of 10 tires, the variable under consideration is a discrete random variable because it can take only values of 0 or 1 or 2 or 3 or . . . 10 (i.e., we cannot have 1.7 or 2.2 defective tires).

Discrete Uniform Probability Distribution is a probability distribution for which each possible value of the random variable has the same probability.

Expected Value occurs when the values of the random variable are multiplied by their respective probabilities and the results are summed, this summation is known as the expected value. Hence, the expected value is actually a weighted average of the values of the random variable, where the probabilities are the weights. The expected value can be viewed as a long run average.

Hypergeometric Probability Function the function used to compute the probability of x successes in n trials when the trials are not independent.

Poisson Probability Distribution is a distribution (like the binomial distribution) which is applied to discrete random variables. It is used to determine the probability of x occurrences of an event over a designated interval. For the Poisson distribution to be applicable, both of the following assumptions must be satisfied.

1. The probability of the occurrence of an event is the same for any two intervals of the same length.
2. The occurrence of an event in any interval is independent of the occurrence in any other interval.

Poisson Probability Function is a function used to compute Poisson probabilities.

Probability Distribution is a description of how the probabilities are distributed over the values the random variable can assume.

Probability Function is a function such as f(x) that gives the probability that x can assume a particular value.

Random Variable is a numerical description of the outcome of an experiment. For instance, if an experiment consists of inspecting 10 tires produced by a manufacturer, then the random variable is the number of defective tires whose value could be any number from zero to 10.

Standard Deviation is the positive square root of the variance.

Variance is a measure of dispersion or variability of a random variable.

CHAPTER FORMULAS

Required Conditions for a Discrete Probability Function

$$f(x) \geq 0 \tag{5.1}$$

$$\sum f(x) = 1 \tag{5.2}$$

Discrete Uniform Probability Function

$$f(x) = 1/n \tag{5.3}$$

where n = the number of values the random variable may assume

Expected Value of a Discrete Random Variable

$$E(x) = \mu = \sum (x \, f(x)) \tag{5.4}$$

Variance of a Discrete Random Variable

$$\text{Variance } (x) = \sigma^2 = \sum (x - \mu)^2 \, f(x) \tag{5.5}$$

Number of Experimental Outcomes Providing Exactly x Successes in n Trials

$$\binom{n}{x} = \frac{n!}{x!(n - x)!} \tag{5.6}$$

where $n! = n\,(n - 1)\,(n - 2) \ldots (2)(1)$ (Remember: $0! = 1$)

Probability of a Particular Sequence of Outcomes (in a Binomial Experiment) Resulting in Exactly x Successes in n Trials

$$p^x (1 - p)^{n - x} \tag{5.7}$$

where p = probability of success
x = number of successes
n = number of trials

Chapter Formulas
(Continued)

Binomial Probability Function

$$f(x) = \frac{n!}{x!(n-x)!}\, p^x (1-p)^{n-x} \tag{5.8}$$

where $x = 0, 1, 2, ..., n$

The Mean of a Binomial Distribution

$$\mu = n\,p \tag{5.9}$$

The Variance of a Binomial Distribution

$$\sigma^2 = n\,p\,(1-p) \tag{5.10}$$

Poisson Probability Function

$$f(x) = \frac{\mu^x e^{-\mu}}{x!} \qquad \text{for } x = 0, 1, 2, ... \tag{5.11}$$

where μ = average number of occurrences in an interval
$e = 2.71828$
$x = 0, 1, 2, ..., n$

Hypergeometric Probability Function

$$f(x) = \frac{\binom{r}{x}\binom{N-r}{n-x}}{\binom{N}{n}} \qquad \text{for } 0 \le x \le r \tag{5.12}$$

where $f(x)$ = probability of x successes
N = number of elements in the population
r = number of elements in the population labeled success
n = number of elements in the sample

EXERCISES

Solved Problem

*1.   An experiment consists of counting the number of bad checks received by a grocery store in a given day.

(a)   Identify the random variable.

Answer: A random variable is a numerical description of the outcome of an experiment. In this case, the random variable is the number of bad checks received in a given day.

(b)   What is the value that the random variable can take?

Answer: The value that the random variable can take ranges between zero and the number of checks written in a given day.

(c)   Is the random variable discrete or continuous?

Answer: Our random variable (the number of bad checks) can take only a countable number of values. That is, the number of bad checks could be 1, 2, 3, etc. Therefore, the random variable is a discrete random variable.

2.   An experiment consists of making 80 telephone calls in order to sell a particular insurance policy.

(a)   What is the random variable?

(b)   What values can the random variable take?

(c)   Is the random variable discrete or continuous?

*3.   Ziba Corporation has kept a record of the number of grievances filed per week for the last 50 weeks. The results are shown below.

Number of Grievances	Number of Weeks
0	2
1	18
2	25
3	4
4	1
Total	50

(a)   Develop a probability distribution for the above data.

Answer: A probability distribution describes the distribution of random variables and their corresponding probabilities. In the above situation, we note that the probability of no grievance is 2/50 or symbolically, f(0) = 2/50 = 0.04. Similarly, the probability of 1 grievance or f(1) = 18/50 = 0.36. Continuing in the same manner, the probability distribution can be shown as follows, where x represents the number of grievances and f(x) is the probability of that number of grievances.

x	f(x)
0	0.04
1	0.36
2	0.50
3	0.08
4	0.02
Total	1.00

(b)   Is the above a proper probability distribution?

Answer: We note that both required conditions for a discrete probability distribution have been met. First, f(x) ≥ 0, which means the probability for each event is greater than or equal to zero; and in this case, each probability is greater than zero. The second required condition is that $\sum$ f(x) = 1, which means the sum of all the probabilities must be equal to one. In the above situation, this second condition is also satisfied. Hence, the distribution which was determined in part (a) is a proper probability distribution.

(c)   Determine the cumulative probability distribution for the above problem.

Answer: The cumulative probability distribution F(x), gives the probability that a random variable can take on a certain value or less. In this case, we note that the probability of zero grievances is 0.04; and the probability of one or less grievance is 0.04 + 0.036 = 0.40. Symbolically, we can write the sum of the probability of zero grievances and one grievance as F(1) = f(0) + f(1) = 0.04 + 0.36 = 0.40. Similarly, we can compute the cumulative probability for the entire distribution:

x	F(x)
0	0.04
1	0.40
2	0.90
3	0.98
4	1.00

4.   The management of the grocery store mentioned in exercise 1, has kept a record of bad checks received per day for a period of 200 days. The data is shown below.

Number of Bad Checks Received	Number of Days
0	8
1	12
2	20
3	60
4	40
5	30
6	20
7	10

(a)   Develop a probability distribution for the above data.

(b)   Is the probability distribution that you found in part (a) a proper probability distribution? Explain.

(c)   Determine the cumulative probability distribution F(x).

(d)   What is the probability that in a given day the store receives four or less bad checks?

(e)   What is the probability that in a given day the store receives more than 3 bad checks?

5.   The police records of a metropolitan area kept over the past 300 days show the following number of fatal accidents.

Number of Fatal Accidents x	Number of Days f(x)
0	45
1	75
2	120
3	45
4	15

(a)   Develop a probability distribution for the daily fatal accidents.

(b)   Determine the cumulative probability F(x).

(c)   What is the probability that in a given day there will be less than 3 accidents?

(d)   What is the probability that in a given day there will be at least 1 accident?

Solved Problem

6. Referring to exercise *3 of this chapter, we note the following probability distribution existed for the number of grievances filed with the Ziba Corporation.

x	f(x)
0	0.04
1	0.36
2	0.50
3	0.08
4	0.02

(a) Determine the expected value of the number of grievances and explain its meaning.

Answer: The expected value of a discrete random variable is a weighted average of all possible values of the random variable, where the probabilities are the weights. In other words, the expected value of a discrete random variable x is as follows.

$$E(x) = \mu = \sum (x\, f(x))$$

Hence, the expected value can be calculated as follows.

x	f(x)	x f(x)
0	0.04	(0)(0.04) = 0.00
1	0.36	(1)(0.36) = 0.36
2	0.50	(2)(0.50) = 1.00
3	0.08	(3)(0.08) = 0.24
4	0.02	(4)(0.02) = 0.08

$$E(x) = \mu = \sum (x\, f(x)) = 1.68$$

The expected value of the number of grievances is 1.68. This figure represents the mean or the average value of the random variable. Obviously, the Ziba Corporation will never have 1.68 grievances, but this figure shows the "long run" average value of the number of grievances.

(b) Determine the variance and the standard deviation.

Answer: The variance of a discrete random variable is as follows.

$$\text{Variance }(x) = \sigma^2 = \sum ((x - \mu)^2\, f(x))$$

We have already calculated the mean to be $\mu = 1.68$. Hence, the variance can be calculated as shown below.

x	x - μ	$(x - \mu)^2$	f(x)	$(x - \mu)^2$ f(x)
0	-1.68	2.8224	0.04	0.1129
1	-0.68	0.4624	0.36	0.1665
2	0.32	0.1024	0.50	0.0512
3	1.32	1.7424	0.08	0.1394
4	2.32	5.3824	0.02	0.1076

$$\sigma^2 = \sum (x - \mu)^2 \, f(x) = 0.5776$$

Since the standard deviation is the square root of the variance, the standard deviation can be determined as

$$\sigma = \sqrt{\sigma^2} = \sqrt{0.5776} = 0.76$$

7.   Referring to exercise 4, we note that the number of bad checks received per day and their respective probabilities are as follows:

Number of Bad Checks Received Per Day	Probability
0	0.04
1	0.06
2	0.10
3	0.30
4	0.20
5	0.15
6	0.10
7	0.05

(a)   What is the expected number of bad checks received per day?

(b)   Determine the variance in the number of bad checks received per day.

(c)   What is the standard deviation?

8.   The number of electrical outages in a city varies from day to day. Assume that the number of electrical outages in the city (x) has the following probability distribution.

x	f(x)
0	0.80
1	0.15
2	0.04
3	0.01

(a)   Determine the mean and the standard deviation for the number of electrical outages.

(b)   If each outage costs the power company $1500, what is the expected daily cost?

9.   Oriental Reproductions, Inc. is a company that produces handmade carpets with oriental designs. The production records show that the monthly production has ranged from 1 to 5 carpets. The production levels and their respective probabilities are shown below.

Production Per Month x	Probability f(x)
1	0.01
2	0.04
3	0.10
4	0.80
5	0.05

(a)   Determine the expected monthly production level.

(b)   Determine the standard deviation for the production.

Solved Problem

*10. A production process has been producing 10% defective items. A random sample of four items is selected from the production line.

(a)   What is the probability that the first 3 selected items are non-defective and the last item is defective?

Answer: If we let D represent the outcome where the selected item is defective and N represent the selection of a non-defective item, then the outcome whose probability we want to find is

(N, N, N, D)

Since these events are independent, the probability of their joint occurrence is equal to the product of their individual probabilities. Therefore, the probability of 3 non-defectives followed by a defective item is $(0.9)(0.9)(0.9)(0.1) = 0.0729$. Now let us view the above situation in a more generalized form. Recall that when an experiment involves n trials, the probability of obtaining any one sequence of outcomes that result in exactly x successes, as given by chapter formula 5.7, is

$$p^x (1 - p)^{n - x}$$

where p = probability of success (in the above situation $p = 0.9$)
            x = number of successes (in our case, the number of non-defective items, which is 3)
            n = number of trials (in our situation, $n = 4$)

Hence, the probability of the above sequence of outcomes is as follows.

$$(0.9)^3 (1 - 0.9)^{4 - 3} = (0.9)^3 (.1)^1 = 0.0729$$

(b)   If a sample of 4 items is selected, how many outcomes contain exactly 3 non-defective items?

Answer: In part (a) of this exercise, we looked at one possible outcome which contained exactly 3 non-defective items. We can enumerate all the outcomes that contain exactly 3 non-defective items.

(N, N, N, D)
(N, N, D, N)
(N, D, N, N)
(D, N, N, N)

As you can see, there are 4 possible outcomes that contain exactly 3 non-defective items. Now let us look at the situation posed in part (b) in a more generalized form. Using equation 5.5, we can determine the number of experimental outcomes providing exactly x successes in n trials.

$$\binom{n}{x} = \frac{n!}{x!(n-x)!} = \frac{4!}{3!(4-3)!} = 4$$

(c)   What is the probability that a random sample of 4 contains 3 non-defective items?

Answer: In part (a), we determined the probability of 3 non-defective items (in a specific sequence) to be 0.0729; and in part (b), we determined that there were 4 possible sequences. Hence, the probability of 3 non-defective items (in any sequence) is

(4) (0.0729) = 0.2916

In general, we can use the binomial probability function to determine the probability of x successes in n trials. This equation states

$$f(x) = \frac{n!}{x!(n-x)!} \, p^x (1-p)^{n-x}$$

where   x = 0, 1, 2, . . . n

Therefore, for our example,

$$f(3) = \frac{4!}{3!(4-3)!} (0.9)^3 (.1)^1 = 0.2916$$

(d)   Determine the probability distribution for the number of non-defective items in a sample of four.

Answer: In a sample of four, the number of non-defectives can be 0, 1, 2, 3, or 4. We can determine the probability distribution as

x	f(x)
0	$\frac{4!}{0!4!} (0.9)^0 (0.1)^4 = 0.0001$
1	$\frac{4!}{1!3!} (0.9)^1 (0.1)^3 = 0.0036$
2	$\frac{4!}{2!2!} (0.9)^2 (0.1)^2 = 0.0486$
3	$\frac{4!}{3!1!} (0.9)^3 (0.1)^1 = 0.2916$
4	$\frac{4!}{4!0!} (0.9)^4 (0.1)^0 = \underline{0.6561}$

1.0000

(e)   Are there tables available where one can readily read the probabilities?

Answer: Yes, Table 5 of the Appendix provides us with probabilities for various values of p, n, and x. In part (c) of this problem, we computed the probability that a sample of four (n = 4) contains three non-defective (x = 3) elements, where the probability of a non-defective element was 0.9. The probability was determined to be 0.2916. Now let us determine this probability by using the table of binomial probabilities. Refer to Table 5 of the Appendix. At the top of the page, you are given the probability of success (p). Locate the p of 0.9. On the left, you are given the sample size. Locate a sample size of 4. Now you can read the binomial probability for x = 3, n = 4, and p = 0.9 as f(3) = 0.2916. As you note, this is the same value that was determined in part (c).

11.   Forty percent of all registered voters in a national election are female. If a random sample of 5 voters is selected,

(a)   What is the probability that the sample contains 2 female voters?

(b)   What is the probability that there are no females in the sample?

(c)   What is the probability that every member of the selected sample is female?

12.   The records of a department store show that 20% of their customers who make a purchase return the merchandise in order to exchange it. What is the probability that in the next 6 transactions

(a)   Three customers return the merchandise for exchange?

(b)   Four customers return the merchandise for exchange?

(c)   None of the customers return the merchandise for exchange?

13.   A cosmetics salesperson, who calls potential customers to sell her products, has determined that 30% of her telephone calls result in a sale. Determine the probability distribution for her next three calls. Note that the next three calls could result in 0, 1, 2, or 3 sales.

Solved Problem

*14. Refer to exercise *10 of this chapter.

(a)   Determine the expected number of non-defective items in a sample of four.

Answer: We know that the expected number of non-defectives can be calculated as shown below.

$$\mu = \sum (x\, f(x))$$

In part (d) of exercise 10, we determined the probability distribution for the number of non-defectives in a sample of four. Hence, the expected number of non-defective items can be calculated as

x	f(x)	x f(x)
0	0.0001	0.0000
1	0.0036	0.0036
2	0.0486	0.0972
3	0.2916	0.8748
4	0.6561	2.6244
		E(x) = 3.6000

(b)   Is there another approach for determining the expected number of non-defectives? If yes, explain.

Answer: In the case of a binomial distribution, the expected value of a random variable can be determined by

$$E(x) = n\, p$$

Therefore, in our example where $n = 4$ and $p = 0.9$, we can determine the expected number of non-defective items as $E(x) = (4)\,(0.9) = 3.6$

(c)   Find the standard deviation for the number of non-defectives.

Answer: In the case of a binomial distribution, the variance of a random variable is given by the following.

$$\sigma^2 = n\,p\,(1 - p)$$

Therefore, the variance is

$$\sigma^2 = (4)(.9)(1 - .9) = 0.36$$

and the standard deviation is

$$\sigma = \sqrt{\sigma^2} = \sqrt{0.36} = 0.6$$

15.   In exercise 13, you were asked to determine the probability distribution for the number of telephone calls resulting in a sale (from a sample of three), where past data indicated that 30% of the calls resulted in a sale. The following table gives this probability distribution.

x	f(x)	x f(x)
0	0.343	
1	0.441	
2	0.189	
3	0.027	

(a)   Find the expected number of sales and show that $np = \sum x\, f(x)$.

(b)   Find the standard deviation for the number of sales.

IN EXERCISES 16 THROUGH 18, USE THE BINOMIAL PROBABILITY TABLES. (TABLE 5 OF THE APPENDIX)

16. In a large western university, 15% of the students are graduate students. If a random sample of 20 students is selected, what is the probability that the sample contains

(a) Exactly four graduate students?

(b) No graduate students?

(c) Exactly twenty graduate students?

(d) More than nine graduate students?

(e) Less than five graduate students?

(f) What is the expected number of graduate students?

17. In a southern state, it was revealed that 5% of all automobiles in the state did not pass inspection. What is the probability that of the next ten automobiles entering the inspection station

(a) None will pass inspection?

(b) All will pass inspection?

(c) Exactly two will not pass inspection?

(d)   More than three will not pass inspection?

(e)   Less than two will not pass inspection?

(f)   Find the expected number of automobiles not passing inspection.

(g)   Determine the standard deviation for the number of cars not passing inspection.

18.   Twenty percent of the applications received for a particular credit card are rejected. What is the probability that among the next fifteen applications

(a)   None will be rejected?

(b)   All will be rejected?

(c)   Less than 2 will be rejected?

(d)   More than four will be rejected?

(e)   Determine the expected number of rejected applications and its variance.

Solved Problem

*19. During the registration period (of a local college), students consult their advisors about course selection. A particular advisor noted that during each half hour an average of eight students came to see her for advising.

(a)   What is the probability that during a half hour period exactly four students will consult her?

Answer: If we assume that the probability of a student consulting his/her advisor is the same for any two time periods of equal length and, furthermore, if we assume that consulting or not consulting the advisor in any time period is independent of consulting or not consulting the advisor in any other time period, we can conclude that the Poisson probability distribution is applicable. The Poisson probability function is

$$f(x) = \frac{\mu^x e^{-\mu}}{x!} \qquad \text{for } x = 0, 1, 2, \dots$$

where μ is the average number of occurrences in an interval and e is a constant whose value is 2.7182818. . . Therefore, we can find the probability of four students consulting their advisor as

$$f(4) = \frac{(8)^4 (e)^{-8}}{4!} = \frac{(4096)(0.0003355)}{24} = 0.0573$$

(b)   Are there tables available where one can readily read probabilities for specific values of x and μ?

Answer: Yes, there are tables that give probabilities for specific values of x and μ. Refer to Table 7 of the Appendix (the Poisson probability table). At the top of the table, you are given the values of the mean; and on the left, you are given the values of the number of occurrences in an interval (x). Locate $\mu = 8$ and $x = 4$. By looking in the body of the table at the intersection of $\mu = 8$ and $x = 4$, the probability can be read as $f(4) = 0.0573$, which is the same value which we found in part (a).

(c)   What is the probability that less than three students will consult their advisor?

Answer: In this question, we are interested in determining the probability that 0, 1, or 2 students will consult their advisor. We can read the individual probabilities from the Poisson probability tables and sum the individual probabilities in order to find the probability of $x \leq 2$. In other words,

$$f(x \leq 2) = f(2) + f(1) + f(0) = 0.0107 + 0.0027 + 0.0003 = 0.0137$$

20.   An insurance company has determined that each week an average of nine claims are filed in their Atlanta branch. What is the probability that during the next week

(a)   Exactly seven claims will be filed?

(b)   No claims will be filed?

(c)   Less than four claims will be filed?

(d)   At least eighteen claims will be filed?

21.   *Use the Poisson probability table (Table 7 of the Appendix) for this problem.*
Only 0.02% of credit card holders of a company report the loss or theft of their credit cards each month. The company has 15,000 credit cards in the city of Memphis. What is the probability that during the next month in the city of Memphis

(a)   No one reports the loss or theft of his/her credit cards?

(b)   Every credit card is lost or stolen?

(c)   Six people report the loss or theft of their cards?

(d)   At least nine people report the loss or theft of their cards?

(e)   Determine the expected number of reported lost or stolen credit cards.

(f)   Determine the standard deviation for the number of reported lost or stolen cards.

Solved Problem

*22. A retailer of electronic equipment received six DVDs from the manufacturer. Three of the DVDs were damaged during shipment. The retailer sold two DVDs to two customers.

(a)   What is the probability that both customers received damaged DVDs?

Answer: Let us denote "D" as damaged and "G" as good in the population of the six DVDs as

   D D D G G G

The probability that the first customer received a damaged DVD is 3/6. Once the first customer has received a damaged one, then the population will consist of five:

   D D G G G

Now, the probability that the second customer received a damaged one is 2/5. Therefore, the probability that both customers received damaged DVDs is the product of the two probabilities or (3/6) (2/5) = 6/30 = 0.2.

(b)   Can a binomial formula be used for the solution of the above problem?

Answer: No, in a binomial experiment, trials are independent of each other. Hence, the probability remains the same as successive trials are made. In the above problem, the probability of having purchased a defective DVD changes from customer to customer.

(c)   What kind of probability distribution does the above satisfy, and is there a function for solving such problems?

Answer: This problem represents a hypergeometric probability distribution, which is closely related to the binomial distribution. The only difference between the two distributions is that in a hypergeometric distribution the probability of outcomes changes from trial to trial. The hypergeometric probability function, as shown below, yields the probability of x successes in n trials when the trials are not independent.

$$f(x) = \frac{\binom{r}{x}\binom{N-r}{n-x}}{\binom{N}{n}} \qquad \text{for } 0 \le x \le r$$

where   f(x) = probability of x successes
         N = number of elements in the population
         r = number of elements in the population labeled success
         n = number of elements in the sample

In the case of the above problem

      N = 6 (total number of elements)
      r = 3 (number of defective parts)
      n = 2 (number of elements in the sample)

The hypergeometric function for x = 2 is shown below.
(Remember N - r = 6 - 3 = 3 and n - x = 2 - 2 = 0.)

$$f(2) = \frac{\binom{3}{2}\binom{3}{0}}{\binom{6}{2}} = \frac{\left(\frac{3!}{2!\,1!}\right)\left(\frac{3!}{0!\,3!}\right)}{\left(\frac{6!}{2!\,4!}\right)} = \frac{3}{15} = 0.2$$

Note, this is the same answer that was obtained in part (a) of this problem.

(d)   What is the probability that one of the two customers received a defective DVD?

Answer: The hypergeometric function can be solved for the following values.

      N = 6
      r = 3
      n = 2
      x = 1
      N - r = 6 - 3 = 3
      n - x = 2 - 1 = 1

as

$$f(1) = \frac{\binom{3}{1}\binom{3}{1}}{\binom{6}{2}} = \frac{\left(\frac{3!}{1!\,2!}\right)\left(\frac{3!}{1!\,2!}\right)}{\left(\frac{6!}{2!\,4!}\right)} = \frac{9}{15} = 0.6$$

23. Compute the hypergeometric probabilities for the following values of n and x. Assume N = 8 and r = 5.

(a) n = 5, x = 2

(b) n = 6, x = 4

(c) n = 3, x = 0

(d) n = 3, x = 3

24. Seven students have applied for merit scholarships. This year 3 merit scholarships were awarded. If a random sample of 3 applications (from the population of seven) is selected, what is the probability that

(a) Two students received scholarships?

(b) Not any of the students received scholarships?

25. Determine the probability of being dealt 4 aces in a 5-card poker hand.

SELF-TESTING QUESTIONS

In the following multiple choice questions, circle the correct answer. An answer key is provided following the questions.

1. The variance is a measure of dispersion or variability in the random variable. It is a weighted average of the
   a) square root of the deviations from the mean
   b) square root of the deviations from the median
   c) squared deviations from the median
   d) squared deviations from the mean

2. A numerical description of the outcome of an experiment is a random
   a) description
   b) outcome
   c) number
   d) variable

3. A random variable that can take on only a finite or countable number of values is known as a
   a) continuous random variable
   b) discrete random variable
   c) discrete probability function
   d) finite probability function

4. A random variable that may take on any value in an interval or collection of intervals is known as a
   a) continuous random variable
   b) discrete random variable
   c) continuous probability function
   d) finite probability function

5. A weighted average of the value of a random variable where the probability function provides weights is known as
   a) a probability function
   b) a random variable
   c) the expected value
   d) the variance

Exhibit 5-1
The following represents the probability distribution for the daily demand of microcomputers at a local store.

Demand	Probability
0	0.1
1	0.2
2	0.3
3	0.2
4	0.2

6.   Refer to Exhibit 5-1. The expected daily demand is
a)   1.0
b)   2.2
c)   2, since it has the highest probability
d)   of course 4, since it is the largest demand level

7.   Refer to Exhibit 5-1. The probability of having a demand for at least two microcomputers is
a)   0.7
b)   0.3
c)   0.4
d)   1.0

8.   The probability distribution for a discrete random variable which is used to compute the probability of x successes in n trials is known as the
a)   normal probability distribution
b)   standard normal distribution
c)   binomial probability distribution
d)   a discrete random variable

9.   The probability distribution for a discrete random variable that is used to compute the probability of x occurrences of an event over a specified interval is known as
a)   the normal probability distribution
b)   the standard normal distribution
c)   a discrete random variable
d)   the Poisson probability distribution

Exhibit 5-2
The student body of a large university consists of 60% female students. A random sample of 8 students is selected.

10.   Refer to Exhibit 5-2. What is the probability that among the students in the sample exactly two are female?
a)   0.0896
b)   0.2936
c)   0.0413
d)   0.0007

11.   Refer to Exhibit 5-2. What is the probability that among the students in the sample at least 7 are female?
a)   0.1064
b)   0.0896
c)   0.0168
d)   0.8936

12.   Refer to Exhibit 5-2. What is the probability that among the students in the sample at least 6 are male?
a)   0.0413
b)   0.0079
c)   0.0007
d)   0.0499

13.   Which of the following is a required condition for a discrete probability function?
a) $\sum f(x) = 0$
b) $\sum f(x) = 1$
c) $f(x) < 0$
d) $f(x) > 0$

14.   Which of the following is **not** a characteristic of a binomial experiment?
a)   the experiment consists of a sequence of n identical trials
b)   at least 2 outcomes are possible
c)   probabilities remain the same as successive trials are made
d)   the trials are independent of each other

15.   The expected value of a binomial probability distribution is
a) $E(x) = pn(1 - n)$
b) $E(x) = np(1 - p)$
c) $E(x) = np$
d) $E(x) = p(1 - n)$

ANSWERS TO THE SELF-TESTING QUESTIONS

1. d
2. d
3. b
4. a
5. c
6. b
7. a
8. c
9. d
10. c
11. a
12. d
13. b
14. b
15. c

ANSWERS TO CHAPTER FIVE EXERCISES

2. (a) Number of sales
   (b) 0 to 80
   (c) Discrete

4.

Number of Bad Checks	(a) Probability	(c) F(x)
0	.04	.04
1	.06	.10
2	.10	.20
3	.30	.50
4	.20	.70
5	.15	.85
6	.10	.95
7	.05	1.00

   (b) Yes, the sum of the probabilities is equal to 1.
   (d) 0.7
   (e) 0.5

5.

x	(a) p(x)	(b) F(x)
0	0.15	0.15
1	0.25	0.40
2	0.40	0.80
3	0.15	0.95
4	0.05	1.00

   (c) 0.80
   (d) 0.85

7. (a) 3.66
   (b) 2.7644
   (c) 1.6626

8. (a) 0.26, 0.577
   (b) $390

9. (a) 3.84
   (b) 0.61196

11. (a) 0.3456
    (b) 0.0778
    (c) 0.0102

12. (a) 0.0819
    (b) 0.0154
    (c) 0.2621

13.

x	p
0	0.3430
1	0.4410
2	0.1890
3	0.0270

15. (a) 0.9
    (b) 0.794

16. (a) 0.1821
    (b) 0.0388
    (c) 0.0000
    (d) 0.0002
    (e) 0.8298
    (f) 3

17. (a) 0.0000
    (b) 0.5987
    (c) 0.0746
    (d) 0.0011
    (e) 0.9138
    (f) 0.5000
    (g) 0.6892

18. (a) 0.0352
    (b) 0.0000
    (c) 0.1671
    (d) 0.1643
    (e) 3, 2.4

20. (a) 0.1171
    (b) 0.0001
    (c) 0.0212
    (d) 0.0053

21. (a) 0.0498
    (b) 0.0000
    (c) 0.0504
    (d) 0.0038
    (e) 3
    (f) 1.73

23.   (a)   10/56 = 0.1786
       (b)   15/28 = 0.5357
       (c)   1/56 = 0.01786
       (d)   10/56 = 0.1786

24.   (a)   12/35=0.3428571
       (b)   4/35 = 0.1143

25.   120/6,497,400 = 0.00001847

CHAPTER SIX

CONTINUOUS PROBABILITY DISTRIBUTIONS

CHAPTER OUTLINE AND REVIEW

This chapter focuses on probability distributions of continuous random variables. Three major continuous probability distributions, the *uniform*, *normal*, and *exponential* distributions are introduced. More specifically, you will learn the following concepts.

Continuity Correction Factor is a value of 0.5 that is added and/or subtracted from a value of x when the continuous normal distribution is used to approximate the discrete binomial distribution.

Exponential Probability Distribution is a continuous probability distribution that is useful in computing probabilities for the time it takes to complete a task.

Normal Probability Distribution is a continuous probability distribution. The normal distribution is a symmetrical distribution with a mean, μ, and a standard deviation, σ.

Probability Density Function is a function used to compute probabilities for a continuous random variable. The area under the graph of a probability density function over an interval represents probability.

Standard Normal Distribution is a normal distribution with a mean of zero ($\mu = 0$) and a standard deviation of one ($\sigma = 1$).

Uniform Probability Distribution is a probability distribution of a continuous random variable, where the probability that the random variable will take on a value in any interval of equal length, is the same for each interval.

CHAPTER FORMULAS

Uniform Probability Density Function for a Random Variable x

$$f(x) = \begin{cases} \dfrac{1}{b-a} & \text{for } a \le x \le b \\ \\ 0 & \text{elsewhere} \end{cases} \tag{6.1}$$

Mean and Variance of a Uniform Continuous Probability Distribution

$$\mu = \frac{a+b}{2}$$

$$\sigma^2 = \frac{(b-a)^2}{12}$$

Normal Probability Density Function

$$f(x) = \frac{1}{\sigma\sqrt{2\pi}} e^{-(x-\mu)^2/2\sigma^2} \qquad \text{for} \quad -\infty \le x \le \infty \tag{6.2}$$

where μ = mean of the random variable x

σ^2 = variance of the random variable x
π = 3.14159...
e = 2.71828...

The transformation of any Random Variable x with Mean μ and Standard Deviation σ to the Standard Normal Distribution

$$z = \frac{(x-\mu)}{\sigma} \tag{6.3}$$

where   z = the number of standard deviations

Exponential Probability Density function

$$f(x) = \frac{1}{\mu} e^{-x/\mu} \tag{6.4}$$

Exponential Distribution Probabilities

$$p(x \le x_0) = 1 - e^{-x_0/\mu} \tag{6.5}$$

EXERCISES

Solved Problem

*1.   The driving time for an individual from his home to his work is uniformly distributed between 300 to 480 seconds.

(a)   Give a mathematical expression for the probability density function.

Answer: The probability density function of a uniform probability distribution is given in chapter formula 6.1 as

$$f(x) = \begin{cases} \dfrac{1}{b-a} & \text{for } a \le x \le b \\[2ex] 0 & \text{elsewhere} \end{cases}$$

In our example, b = 480 and a = 300. Therefore, the probability density function is

$$f(x) = \frac{1}{480 - 300} = \frac{1}{180}$$

This figure indicates that for any value of x (from 300 to 480), the f(x) is constant and its value is equal to 1/180.

(b)   Compute the probability that the driving time will be less than or equal to 435 seconds.

Answer: In this part, we are interested in determining the p(300 ≤ x ≤ 435) . This probability is the area under a uniform distribution with a height of 1/180 and a width of 135 seconds (i.e., 435 - 300 = 135). Hence, the area is (135)(1/180)= 0.75. This indicates that p(300 ≤ x ≤ 435) = 0.75. The shaded area in Figure 6.1 represents this probability.

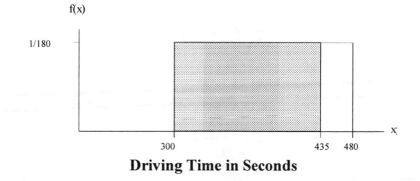

Driving Time in Seconds

Figure 6.1

(c)   Determine the expected driving time and its standard deviation.

Answer: The expected value of a uniform continuous random variable is

$$E(x) = \frac{a + b}{2}$$

Hence, in our example, the expected value of x is

$$E(x) = \frac{480 + 300}{2} = 390$$

Furthermore, the variance is given by

$$Variance\ (x) = \frac{(b - a)^2}{12}$$

Therefore

$$Variance\ (x) = \frac{(480 - 300)^2}{12} = 2700$$

Hence, the standard deviation is

$$\sigma = \sqrt{2700} = 51.96$$

2.   The Body Paint, an automobile body paint shop, has determined that the painting time of automobiles is uniformly distributed and that the required time ranges between 45 minutes to 1 ½ hours.

(a)   Give a mathematical expression for the probability density function.

(b)   What is the probability that the painting time will be less than or equal to one hour?

(c)   What is the probability that the painting time will be more than 50 minutes?

(d)   Determine the expected painting time and its standard deviation.

3.   The length of time patients must wait to see a doctor in a local clinic is uniformly distributed between 15 minutes and 2 ½ hours.

(a)   Give a mathematical expression for the probability density function.

(b)   What is the probability that a patient would have to wait between 45 minutes and 2 hours?

(c)   Compute the probability that a patient would have to wait over 2 hours.

(d)   Determine the expected waiting time and its standard deviation.

*4.   The *standard normal distribution* represents the probability distribution of a random variable that is normally distributed and has a mean of zero ($\mu = 0$) and a standard deviation of one ($\sigma = 1$). Let z represent the number of standard deviations from the mean.

(a)   What is the probability that z will be less than or equal to 1.21 (i.e., find $p(z \leq 1.21)$?

Answer: Table 1 of the Appendix (the table of cumulative probabilities for the standard normal distribution) provides us with the probabilities associated with a specified value for z. It gives the probability of z being less than or equal to a value. In this particular example, the shaded area in Figure 6.2 shows the desired area.

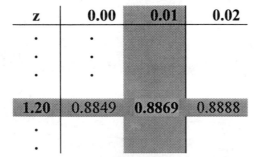

0   z = 1.21

Figure 6.2

Referring to Table 1 of the Appendix, we note that the areas under the curve are shown in the body of the table and the values of z are given in the left column and the top row. For example for a z of 1.21, we locate 1.20 on the left column, and the next digit of 0.01 is found in the top row. The following is part of the table showing the design of the table.

z	0.00	0.01	0.02
.	.		
.	.		
.	.		
1.20	0.8849	0.8869	0.8888
.			
.			

Therefore, the desired area is found at the intersection of shaded row and column. Hence, the probability that z is less than or equal to 1.21 is **0.8869**.

(b)   What is the probability that z will be between -1.2 and +1.2?

Answer: Again we use Table 1 of the Appendix. In Figure 6.3, the shaded area represents the probability that z will fall between -1.2 and +1.2.

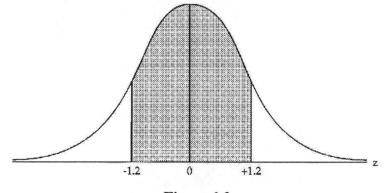

Figure 6.3

First we find the area to the left of 1.2. This area is 0.8849. Then we read the area to the left of -1.2 (Note that z is negative), which is 0.1151. Finally, we subtract the smaller area from the larger area as 0.8849-0.1151 = 0.7698. Therefore, $p(-1.2 \leq z \leq 1.2) =$ 0.7698.

(c)   What is the probability that a z value will be between z = -2.5 and z = 1.8?

Answer: The shaded area in Figure 6.4 shows the desired area.

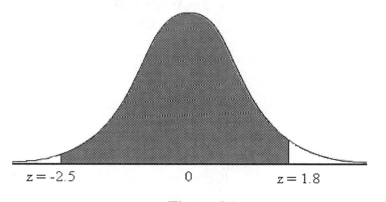

Figure 6.4

Referring to the table of areas under the normal curve (Table 1 of the Appendix), we note that the area to the left of 1.8 is 0.9641 and the area to the left of z = -2.5 (Note that z is negative) is 0.0062. Once again, subtracting the smaller area from the larger area gives us the desired probability. Hence, $p(-2.5 \leq z \leq 1.8) = 0.9641 - 0.0062 = 0.9579$.

(d)   What is the probability that z will have a value larger than 1.8?

Answer: Referring to Figure 6.4, you will note that the requested area is the area to the right of z = 1.8. In part (c), we determined the area to the left of z = 1.8 to be 0.9641. Subtracting this value from 1.0 (the area under the entire normal distribution is 1.0) results in the requested area. Therefore, $p(z \leq 1.80) = 1.0 - 0.9641 = 0.0359$.

(e)   What is the probability that z will have a value between z = 1.4 and z = 1.9?

Answer: The shaded area in Figure 6.5 shows the required area.

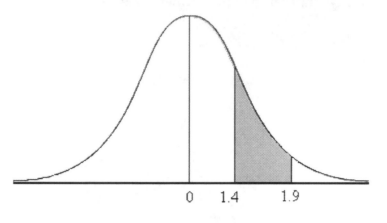

0   1.4   1.9

Figure 6.5

To determine this probability, we first determine the area to the left of z = 1.9, which is 0.9713. Then find the area to the left of z = 1.4, which is 0.9192. Finally, to obtain the desired probability, we subtract the smaller area from the larger area. Therefore, $p(1.4 \leq z \leq 1.9) = 0.9713 - 0.9192 = 0.0521$.

5.   For a standard normal distribution, determine the probabilities of obtaining the following z values. It is helpful to draw a normal distribution for each case and show the corresponding area.

(a)   Greater than zero.

(b)   Between -2.4 and -2.0

(c)   Less than 1.6.

(d)   Between -1.9 to 1.7.

(e)   Between 1.5 and 1.75.

6.   Given that Z is a standard normal random variable, determine the following probabilities:

(a)   P (-2.51 ≤ Z ≤ -1.53) = _____?

(b)   P (Z ≥ -2.12) = _____?

(c)   P (-2.08 ≤ Z ≤ 1.46) = _____?

7.   Given that Z is a standard normal random variable, determine Z for each of the following:

(a)   The area to the right of Z is 0.9834. Z = _____?

(b)   The area to the left of Z is 0.119. Z = _____?

(c)   The area between -Z and Z is 0.901. Z = _____?

*8. Sun Love grapefruit growers have determined that the diameters of their grapefruits are normally distributed with a mean of 4.5 inches and a standard deviation of 0.3 inches.

(a)   What is the probability that a randomly selected grapefruit will have a diameter of at least 4.14 inches?

Answer: The required area is shown by the shaded area in Figure 6.6.

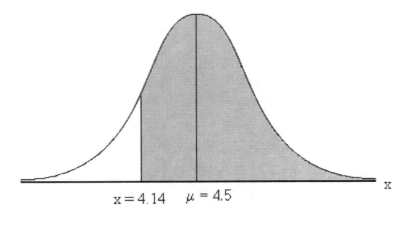

$$x = 4.14 \quad \mu = 4.5$$

Figure 6.6

To determine this area, we first need to find the number of standard deviations from the point of x = 4.14 to the mean. The number of standard deviations is computed as

$$z = \frac{(x - \mu)}{\sigma} = \frac{4.14 - 4.5}{0.3} = -1.2$$

Looking in the table of areas under the normal curve (Table 1 of the Appendix), we note that the area to the left of z = -1.2 is 0.1151. Therefore, the probability of a grapefruit having a diameter greater than 4.14, is the area to the right of z = -1.2. Therefore, the desired are is 1.0 -0.1151 = 0.8849.

(b)   What percentage of the grapefruits has a diameter between 4.8 and 5.04 inches?

Answer: You should realize that the entire area under the normal curve represents 100% of the grapefruits. The percentage of the area that falls between 4.8 and 5.04 inches is shown in Figure 6.7 by the shaded area.

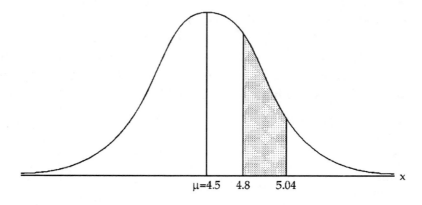

Figure 6.7

To find this area, we first need to determine the number of standard deviations from the mean to x = 5.04 as

$$z = \frac{(x - \mu)}{\sigma} = \frac{5.04 - 4.5}{0.3} = 1.8$$

Then read the area to the left of z = 1.8. From the Table 1 of the Appendix, we read this area to be 0.9641. Then we need to determine the number of standard deviations from the mean to x = 4.8 as

$$z = \frac{(x - \mu)}{\sigma} = \frac{4.8 - 4.5}{0.3} = 1.0$$

From the table of areas under the normal curve (Table 1 of the Appendix), the area to the left of z = 1.0 is determined to be 0.8413. Subtracting the smaller area from the larger area we obtain 0.9641 − 0.8413 = 0.1228. Hence, we can conclude that 12.28% of the grapefruits have diameters between 4.8 and 5.04 inches.

(c)   Sun Love packs their largest grapefruits in special packages called the *super pack*. If 5% of all their grapefruits are packed as *super packs*, what is the smallest diameter of the grapefruits that are in the *super packs*?

Answer: The shaded area in Figure 6.8 represents the percentage of the area representing the *super pack* grapefruits, which is 5%.

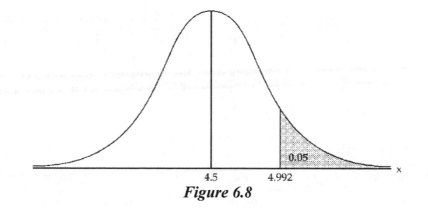

Figure 6.8

Therefore, the area to the left of this point is 0.95 of the entire area. Now looking in the body of the table of areas under the normal curve, we see that the area of 0.95 (the closest value to 0.95 is 0.9495) actually occurs approximately 1.64 standard deviations above the mean. Hence, to find the smallest diameter of the grapefruits in the *super pack* corresponding to z = 1.64, we calculate x as follows.

$$z = \frac{(x - \mu)}{\sigma}$$

$$1.64 = \frac{x - 4.5}{0.3}$$

$$x = 4.5 + (1.64)(0.3) = 4.992$$

This figure indicates that the smallest grapefruit in the *super pack* will have a diameter of 4.992 inches.

(d)   In this year's harvest, there were 111,500 grapefruits that had a diameter over 5.01 inches. How many grapefruits has Sun Love harvested this year?

Answer: The shaded area in Figure 6.9 represents the portion of the entire area that satisfies the above condition.

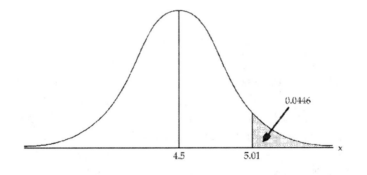

Figure 6.9

To find this area, we will first find the area to the left of 5.01 inches and then subtract the result from 1.0.

$$z = \frac{(x - \mu)}{\sigma} = \frac{5.01 - 4.5}{0.3} = 1.7$$

Therefore, there are 1.7 standard deviations from the mean to the point x = 5.01. Now referring to the table of areas under the normal curve (Table 1 of the Appendix), we note that an area of 0.9554 corresponds to 1.7 standard deviations from the mean. Therefore, the shaded area is 1.0 - 0.9554 = 0.0446. This value indicates that 0.0446 of the entire harvest is represented by 111,500 grapefruits. Letting N represent the total harvest, we can then write:

0.0446 N = 111,500

Solving for N, we have: $N = \dfrac{111,500}{0.0446} = 2,500,000$

Therefore, Sun Love has harvested 2,500,000 grapefruits this year.

9.   The life expectancy of a particular brand of hair dryer is normally distributed with a mean of four years and a standard deviation of eight months.

(a)   What is the probability that a hair dryer will be in working condition for more than five years?

(b)   The company has a three year warranty period on its hair dryers. What percentage of its hair dryers will be in operating condition after the warranty period?

(c)   What are the minimum and the maximum life expectancies of the middle 90% of the hair dryers?

(d)   Ninety-five percent of the hair dryers will have a life expectancy of at least how many months?

10.   Duckworth Drug Company is a large manufacturer of various kinds of liquid vitamins. The quality control department has noted that the bottles of vitamins marked 6 ounces vary in content with a standard deviation of 0.3 ounces. Assume the contents of the bottles are normally distributed.

(a)   What percentage of all bottles produced contains more than 6.51 ounces of vitamins?

(b)   What percentage of all bottles produced contains less than 5.415 ounces?

(c)   What percentage of bottles produced contains between 5.46 and 6.495 ounces?

(d)   Ninety-five percent of the bottles will contain at least how many ounces?

(e)   What percentage of the bottles contains between 6.3 and 6.6 ounces?

11.   A professor at a local community college noted that the grades of his students were normally distributed with a mean of 74 and a standard deviation of 10. The professor has informed us that 6.3 percent of his students received A's while only 2.5 percent of his students failed the course and received F's.

(a)   What is the minimum score needed to make an A?

(b)   What is the maximum score among those who received an F?

(c)   If there were 5 students who did not pass the course, how many students took the course?

12. In grading shrimp into small, medium, and large, the Globe Fishery packs the shrimp that weigh more than 2 ounces each in packages marked *large* and the shrimp that weigh less than 0.75 ounces each into packages marked *small*; the remainder are packed in *medium* size packages. If a day's catch showed that 15.87 percent of the shrimp were *large* and 6.68 percent were *small*, determine the mean and the standard deviation for the shrimp weights. Assume that the shrimps' weights are normally distributed.

13. The average price of personal computers manufactured by Ahmadi Company is $1,200 with a standard deviation of $220. Furthermore, it is known that the computer prices manufactured by Ahmadi are normally distributed.

(a) What is the probability that a randomly selected computer will have a price of at least $1,530?

(b) Computers with prices of more than $1,750 receive a discount. What **percentage** of the computers will receive the discount?

(c) What are the **minimum** and the **maximum** values of the middle 95% of computer prices?

(d) If 513 of the Ahmadi computers were priced at or below $647.80, how many computers were produced by Ahmadi?

Solved Problem

*14. The First National Mortgage Company has noted that 6% of their customers pay their mortgage payments past the due date.

(a)   What is the probability that in a random sample of 150 mortgages, 7 will be late on their payments?

Answer: In this situation, we are interested in determining the binomial probability of exactly 7 successes in 150 trials, where the probability of each success is 0.06. That is, we want to find

$$P(x = 7, \ n = 150, \ p = 0.06)$$

Since n is greater than 20, we are unable to use the binomial tables (note that the binomial tables in your text give probabilities for sample sizes up to 20). However, we can approximate this binomial probability by the use of a normal distribution with a mean of

$$\mu = n \, p = (150)\,(.06) = 9$$

and a standard deviation of

$$\sigma = \sqrt{n \, p \, (1 - p)} \ - \ \sqrt{(150)\,(.06)\,(.94)} \ = 2.91$$

Then to approximate the binomial probability of exactly 7 successes, we need to find the area under the normal curve between 6.5 and 7.5, which is shown by the shaded area in Figure 6.10. Note that a continuity correction factor of 0.5 is added to and subtracted from 7 in order to approximate a discrete distribution using a continuous probability distribution.

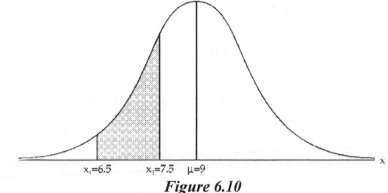

$x_1 = 6.5$ $x_2 = 7.5$ $\mu = 9$

Figure 6.10

In order to find this area, we first determine the number of standard deviations from each point to the mean as

$$z_1 = \frac{x_1 - \mu}{\sigma} = \frac{6.5 - 9}{2.91} = -0.86$$

$$z_2 = \frac{x_2 - \mu}{\sigma} = \frac{7.5 - 9}{2.91} = -0.52$$

Now referring to the table of areas under the normal curve, we see that an area to the left of -0.86 is 0.1949 and the area to the left of -0.52 is 0.3015. Subtracting the smaller area from the larger area yields:

0.3015 - 0.1949 = 0.1066

Thus, the normal approximation to the 7 successes in 150 trials is 0.1066.

(b)   What is the probability that in a random sample of 150 mortgages at least 10 will be late on their payments?

Answer: In this case, we need to determine the shaded area in Figure 6.11.

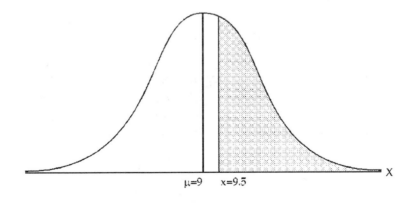

Figure 6.11

Note that the continuity correction factor has been subtracted from 10. Hence, the desired probability is represented by the area to the right of 9.5. To determine this probability, we first determine the z value between 9 and 9.5.

$$z = \frac{(x - \mu)}{\sigma} = \frac{9.5 - 9}{2.91} = 0.17$$

From the table of areas under the normal curve, we determine that the area to the left of 0.17 to be 0.5675. Therefore, the area to the right of 9.5 is: 1.0 - 0.5675 = 0.4325 Therefore, the probability that in a random sample of 150 mortgages at least 10 will be late on their payments is 0.4325.

15.   The records show that 8% of the items produced by a machine do not meet the specifications. Use the normal approximation to the binomial distribution to answer the following questions. What is the probability that a sample of 100 units contains

(a)   exactly 6 defective units?

(b)   exactly 11 defective units?

(c)   six or fewer defective units?

16.   Approximate the following binomial probabilities by the use of normal approximation.

(a) $P(x = 18, \ n = 50, \ p = 0.3)$

(b) $P(x \geq 15, \ n = 50, \ p = 0.3)$

17.   An airline has determined that 20% of its international flights are not on time. Use the normal approximation to the binomial distribution to answer the following questions. What is the probability that of the next 80 international flights

(a)   exactly 16 will not be on time?

(b)   fourteen or more will not be on time?

Solved Problem

*18. The time required to assemble a part of a machine follows an exponential probability distribution. The average time of assembling the part is 10 minutes.

(a)   Give the appropriate probability density function.

Answer: The probability density function for an exponential distribution is given by

$$f(x) = \frac{1}{\mu} e^{-x/\mu}$$

where μ is the mean and $e = 2.71828$. Thus, the probability density functions for our example is

$$f(x) = \frac{1}{10} e^{-x/10}$$

(b)   What is the probability that the part can be assembled in 7 minutes or less?

Answer: The probability that x is less than or equal to a specific value x_o is given by

$$p(x \leq x_o) = 1 - e^{-x_o/\mu}$$

Thus, the probability of x being less than or equal to 7 minutes is computed as

$$p(x \leq 7) = 1 - e^{-7/10} = 1 - 0.4966 = 0.5034$$

(c)   Find the probability of completing the assembly in 3 to 7 minutes.

Answer: The probability of this interval (3 to 7) can be computed by $p(x \leq 7) - p(x \leq 3)$. In part (b), we computed $p(x \leq 7) = 0.5034$.

Now let us compute $p(x \leq 3)$:

$$p(x \leq 3) = 1 - e^{-3/10} = 1 - 0.7408 = 0.2592$$

Therefore, the probability of completing the assembly in 3 to 7 minutes is

$$p(x \leq 7) - p(x \leq 3) = 0.5034 - 0.2592 = 0.2442$$

19. The time between arrivals of customers at the drive-up window of a bank follows an exponential probability distribution with a mean of 14 minutes.

(a) Give the appropriate probability density function.

(b) What is the probability that the arrival time between customers is 7 minutes or less?

(c) What is the probability that the arrival time between customers is 3.5 to 7 minutes?

20. The time it takes to complete an examination follows an exponential distribution with a mean of 40 minutes.

(a) What is the probability of completing the examination in 30 minutes or less?

(b) What is the probability of completing the examination in 30 to 35 minutes?

SELF-TESTING QUESTIONS

In the following multiple choice questions, circle the correct answer. An answer key is provided following the questions.

1. For the standard normal probability distribution, the area to the left of the mean is
a) greater than 0.5
b) -0.5
c) one
d) 0.5

2. In a standard normal distribution, the range of z values is
a) 0 to 1
b) -1 to 1
c) $-\infty$ to ∞
d) -3.09 to 3.09

3. If a z value is to the left of the mean, then its value is
a) negative
b) positive
c) any value between $-\infty$ to ∞
d) zero

4. Assume z is a standard normal random variable, the $p(-1.50 \le z \le 1.90)$ equals
a) 0.0381
b) 0.9045
c) -0.0381
d) 0.4

5. Assume z is a standard normal random variable, the $p(-2.0 \le z \le -1.0)$ equals
a) 0.8185
b) 0.1469
c) 1.0000
d) 0.1359

6. Assume z is a standard normal random variable, the $p(2.0 \le z \le 2.5)$ equals
a) 0.9710
b) 0.0166
c) 0.5000
d) 4.5000

7. Assume z is a standard normal random variable, the $p(-2.54 \le z \le 2.54)$ equals
a) 0.4945
b) 0.0000
c) 0.5400
d) 0.9890

8.   Assume z is a standard normal random variable, the $p(2.32 \leq z \leq 3.05)$ equals
a)   0.4989
b)   0.9887
c)   0.0091
d)   0.7300

9.   Assume z is the standard normal random variable. If the area between zero and z is 0.4115, then the z value is
a)   2.70
b)   1.35
c)   1.00
d)   0.2077

10.   Assume z is the standard normal random variable. If the area to the right of z is 0.8413, then z is
a)   -1.0
b)   1.0
c)   2.0
d)   -2.0

11.   Assume z is the standard normal random variable. If the area to the right of z is 0.0668, then z is
a)   0.17
b)   2.00
c)   1.50
d)   1.00

Exhibit 6-1
The travel time for a businesswoman traveling between Dallas and Fort Worth is uniformly distributed between 40 and 90 minutes.

12.   Refer to Exhibit 6-1. The probability that she will finish her trip in 80 minutes or less is
a)   0.02
b)   0.2
c)   0.8
d)   1.0

13.   Refer to Exhibit 6-1. The probability that her trip will take longer than 60 minutes is
a)   0.4
b)   0.6
c)   0.02
d)   1.00

14. Refer to Exhibit 6-1. The probability that her trip will take exactly 50 minutes is
a) 1.0
b) 0.02
c) 0.06
d) almost zero

15. A standard normal distribution is a normal distribution
a) with a mean of 1 and a standard deviation of 0
b) with any mean and any standard deviation
c) with a mean of 0 and any standard deviation
d) with a mean of 0 and a standard deviation of 1

16. A normal probability distribution
a) is a discrete probability distribution
b) is a continuous probability distribution
c) can be either continuous or discrete
d) must always have a mean of zero

Exhibit 6-2
The life expectancy of a particular brand of tire is normally distributed with a mean of 40,000 miles and a standard deviation of 5,000 miles.

17. Refer to Exhibit 6-2. What is the probability that a randomly selected tire will have a life of at least 30,000 miles?
a) 0.4772
b) 0.9772
c) 0.0228
d) 1.9772

18. Refer to Exhibit 6-2. What is the probability that a randomly selected tire will have a life of at least 47,500 miles?
a) 0.4332
b) 0.9332
c) 0.0668
d) 0.5668

19. Refer to Exhibit 6-2. What percentage of tires will have a life of 34,000 to 46,000 miles?
a) 38.49%
b) 76.98%
c) 50%
d) 26.98%

20. An exponential probability distribution
a) is a continuous distribution
b) is a discrete distribution
c) can be either continuous or discrete
d) is an example of a normal distribution

ANSWERS TO THE SELF-TESTING QUESTIONS

1. d
2. c
3. a
4. b
5. d
6. b
7. d
8. c
9. b
10. a
11. c
12. c
13. b
14. d
15. d
16. b
17. b
18. c
19. b
20. a

ANSWERS TO CHAPTER SIX EXERCISES

2. (a) $f(x) = \begin{cases} \dfrac{1}{45} & \text{for } 45 \leq x \leq 90 \\ \\ 0 & \text{elsewhere} \end{cases}$

   (b) 0.333
   (c) 0.889
   (d) 67.5, 12.99

3. (a) $f(x) = \begin{cases} \dfrac{1}{135} & \text{for } 15 \leq x \leq 150 \\ \\ 0 & \text{elsewhere} \end{cases}$

   (b) 0.556
   (c) 0.222
   (d) 82.5, 38.97

5. (a) 0.5
   (b) 0.0146
   (c) 0.9452
   (d) 0.9267
   (e) 0.0267

6. (a) 0.0570
   (b) 0.9830
   (c) 0.9091

7. (a) -2.13
   (b) -1.18
   (c) ±1.65

9. (a) 0.0668
   (b) 93.32%
   (c) 34.88 to 61.12 months
   (d) 34.88

10. (a) 4.46%
    (b) 2.56%
    (c) 91.46%
    (d) 5.508 ounces
    (e) 13.59%

11. (a)   89.3
     (b)   54.4
     (c)   200

12. Mean = 1.5   Standard deviation = 0.5

13. (a)   0.0668
     (b)   0.62%
     (c)   Minimum = 768.80   Maximum = 1631.20
     (d)   85,500

15. (a)   0.1124
     (b)   0.0803
     (c)   0.2912

16. (a)   0.0805
     (b)   0.5596

17. (a)   0.1114
     (b)   0.7580

19. (a) $f(x) = \dfrac{1}{14}\, e^{-X/14}$
     (b)   0.3935
     (c)   0.1723

20. (a)   0.5276
     (b)   0.0555

CHAPTER SEVEN

SAMPLING AND SAMPLING DISTRIBUTIONS

CHAPTER OUTLINE AND REVIEW

In Chapter 1, you were informed that one could make inferences about the characteristics of a population based on the sample information. This chapter covers the concept of sampling, how samples can be taken, and the characteristics of various sampling distributions. The objective of this chapter is to prepare you for future chapters where you will learn how to use these sampling distributions in order to make inferences about a population's characteristics. The following is an outline of the main points that you will learn.

Central Limit Theorem is a theorem which states that when samples of size n are selected from a population with mean μ and standard deviation σ. The distribution of sample means ($\overline{X}$) will approach a normal distribution with mean μ and standard deviation $\sigma / \sqrt{n}$ as the sample size increases.

Cluster Sampling is a probabilistic method of sampling in which the population is first divided into clusters and then one or more clusters are selected for sampling. In single-stage cluster sampling, every element in each selected cluster is sampled; in two-stage cluster sampling, a sample of the elements in each selected cluster is collected.

Convenience Sampling is a nonprobability method of sampling in which elements are selected on the basis of convenience.

Finite Population Correction Factor is the multiplier $\sqrt{(N - n)/(N - 1)}$ that is used to estimate $\sigma_{\bar{x}}$ and $\sigma_{\bar{p}}$. The population is considered finite when the sample size is more than or equal to 5% of the population, i.e., $n/N \geq 0.05$.

Judgment Sampling is a nonprobability method of sampling whereby the element selected is based on the judgment of the person doing the study.

Nonprobability Sample refers to a sample selected in a manner that the probability of each element being included in the sample is ***unknown*** (such as convenience and judgment samples).

Parameter is a descriptive measure of a population, such as a population mean (μ), a population standard deviation (σ), and a population proportion (p).

Point Estimate is a single numerical value used for estimating a population parameter.

Point Estimator is a sample statistic, such as a sample mean ($\overline{X}$), a sample standard deviation (S), or a sample proportion ($\bar{p}$), which is used to estimate a population parameter.

Probability Sample is a sample selected under any method of sampling (stratified random sampling, cluster sampling, systematic sampling, or simple random sampling), where each element in the population has a known probability of being included in the sample.

Sampling Distribution is a probability distribution showing all possible values that a sample statistic (such as a sample mean, a sample standard deviation, or a sample proportion) can assume.

Simple Random Sampling is the process of selecting a sample from a population in which each individual element of the population has an equal chance of being selected.

Sample Statistic is a descriptive measure of a sample, such as a sample mean ($\overline{X}$), a sample standard deviation (S), or a sample proportion ($\bar{p}$). Each descriptive measure from the sample is used to estimate the value of the population parameter.

Sampling without Replacement is the process of selecting items for a sample from a population and not returning them to the population.

Sampling with Replacement is the process of selecting items for a sample from a population and returning them to the population so that the same item may be selected again.

Standard Error is the standard deviation of a point estimator, such as the standard error of the mean ($\sigma_{\bar{x}}$) and the standard error of the proportion ($\sigma_{\bar{p}}$).

Stratified Simple Random Sampling is a method of selecting a sample in which the population is first divided into strata and a simple random sample is then taken from each stratum.

Systematic Sampling is a method of choosing a sample by randomly selecting the first element and then selecting every k^{th} element thereafter.

Unbiased is a property of a point estimator, where the expected value of a point estimator is equal to the population parameter that it is estimating. The point estimator is known as an unbiased estimator and the point estimate as an unbiased estimate.

CHAPTER FORMULAS

The number of different simple random samples of size n that can be selected from a finite population of size N

$$\frac{N!}{n!(N-n)!}$$

FINITE POPULATION   *INFINITE POPULATION*

Expected Value of $\overline{X}$

$$E(\overline{X}) = \mu \qquad\qquad\qquad\qquad E(\overline{X}) = \mu \qquad\qquad (7.1)$$

where $E(\overline{X})$ = the expected value of the random variable $\overline{X}$
μ = the population mean

Standard Deviation of the Distribution of $\overline{X}$ Values
(The Standard Error of the Mean)

$$\sigma_{\overline{x}} = \sqrt{\frac{N-n}{N-1}} \cdot \frac{\sigma}{\sqrt{n}} \qquad\qquad\qquad \sigma_{\overline{x}} = \frac{\sigma}{\sqrt{n}} \qquad\qquad (7.2)$$

Expected Value of $\overline{p}$

$$E(\overline{p}) = p \qquad\qquad\qquad\qquad E(\overline{p}) = p \qquad\qquad (7.4)$$

where $E(\overline{p})$ = the expected value of the random variable $\overline{p}$
p = the population proportion

Standard Deviation of the Distribution of $\overline{p}$ Values
(The Standard Error of the Proportion)

$$\sigma_{\overline{p}} = \sqrt{\frac{N-n}{N-1}} \cdot \sqrt{\frac{p(1-p)}{n}} \qquad\qquad \sigma_{\overline{p}} = \sqrt{\frac{p(1-p)}{n}} \qquad\qquad (7.5)$$

EXERCISES

Solved Problem

*1. From a group of 12 students, we want to select a random sample of 4 students to serve on a university committee.

(a) How many different random samples of 4 students can be selected?

Answer: The number of different random samples of size n (in this example, n = 4) that can be selected from a population of size N (in this example, N = 12) is given by

$$\frac{N!}{n!(N-n)!} = \frac{12!}{4!(12-4)!} = \frac{12!}{4!8!} = 495$$

Therefore, there are 495 different samples of size 4 that can be selected from a population of size 12.

(b) Explain how we can select a random sample of size 4.

Answer: Various computer software packages, such as Minitab and Excel, can be used for selecting random samples. In our example, we can assign numbers 1 through 12 to our students, then use Excel and generate 4 random numbers. The function for generating random numbers between two values is

    =RANDBETWEEN (Bottom, Top)

Thus, we generate 4 random numbers by

    =RANDBETWEEN (1, 12)

Solved Problem

*2. A simple random sample of 6 system analysts in Chattanooga, Tennessee revealed the following information about the daily incomes and the gender of the analysts.

System Analyst	Daily Income	Gender
A	$250	M
B	270	M
C	285	F
D	240	M
E	255	M
F	290	F

(a)   What is the point estimate for the average daily income of all the system analysts in Chattanooga?

Answer: Recall that a point estimate is a single numerical value used for estimating the population parameter. In this case, we are interested in the average. Hence, we need to find the average income of the individuals in the sample:

$$\overline{X} = \frac{\Sigma X_i}{n} = \frac{250 + 270 + 285 + 240 + 255 + 290}{6} = 265$$

Therefore, the point estimate for the average daily income of all the system analysts in Chattanooga is $265.

(b)   What is the point estimate for the standard deviation of the population?

Answer: The point estimate for the standard deviation of the population is determined by finding the standard deviation of the sample:

$$S = \sqrt{\frac{\Sigma(X_i - \overline{X})^2}{n-1}}$$

The $\Sigma(X_i - \overline{X})^2$ is calculated as

X_i	$(X_i - \overline{X})^2$
250	225
270	25
285	400
240	625
255	100
290	625

$$\Sigma(X_i - \overline{X})^2 = 2000$$

Therefore, the standard deviation of the sample is

$$S = \sqrt{\frac{\Sigma(X_i - \overline{X})^2}{n-1}} = \sqrt{\frac{2000}{6-1}} = 20$$

Hence, the point estimate for the standard deviation of the population is $20.

(c)   Determine a point estimate for the proportion of all analysts in Chattanooga who are female.

Answer: In the sample, there are 2 female analysts. Therefore, the proportion of female analysts in the sample is

$$\bar{p} = \frac{2}{6} = 0.33$$

The above figure (0.33) is used as a point estimate for the population proportion.

3.   A random sample of 15 telephone calls in an office showed the duration of each call and whether it was a local or a long distance call.

Call Number	Duration (In Minutes)	Type of Call
1	2	local
2	12	long distance
3	10	local
4	3	local
5	5	long distance
6	6	local
7	3	local
8	5	local
9	8	local
10	4	local
11	5	local
12	4	local
13	5	local
14	4	local
15	9	long distance

(a)   What is the point estimate for the average duration of all calls?

(b)   What is the point estimate for the standard deviation of the population?

(c)   What is the point estimate for the proportion of all calls that were long distance?

4.   A random sample of 10 examination papers in a course, which was given on a pass or fail basis, showed the following scores.

Paper Number	Grade	Status
1	65	Pass
2	87	Pass
3	92	Pass
4	35	Fail
5	79	Pass
6	100	Pass
7	48	Fail
8	74	Pass
9	79	Pass
10	91	Pass

(a)   What is the point estimate for the mean of the population?

(b)   What is the point estimate for the standard deviation of the population?

(c)   What is the point estimate for the proportion of all students who passed the course?

Solved Problem

*5. Consider a population of four weights identical in appearance but weighing 2, 4, 6, and 8 grams. If we select samples of size 2 **with replacement**, there will be a total of 16 different samples.

(a)   List all the possible samples of size 2 and determine the mean weight of each sample.

Answer: The 16 possible samples of size 2, and the average weight of each sample is shown below.

Possible Sample	Sample Mean ($\overline{X}$)
2 and 2	2
2 and 4	3
2 and 6	4
2 and 8	5
4 and 2	3
4 and 4	4
4 and 6	5
4 and 8	6
6 and 2	4
6 and 4	5
6 and 6	6
6 and 8	7
8 and 2	5
8 and 4	6
8 and 6	7
8 and 8	8

(b)   List all possible sample means, determine the frequency of the appearance of each mean, and draw a histogram of the sampling distribution of $\overline{X}$.

Answer: From part (a) of this exercise, we can determine the frequency of each mean as follows:

Possible Sample Mean	Frequency
2	1
3	2
4	3
5	4
6	3
7	2
8	1

Therefore, the histogram of the sampling distribution can be shown as follows.

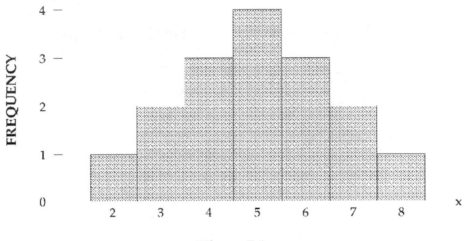

Figure 7.1

As you note, the sampling distribution of the sample means ($\overline{X}$), as shown in Figure 7.1, is approximately normally distributed.

Solved Problem

*6.   Now let us consider a situation where sampling is done **without replacement**. Assume a population consists of 5 weights identical in appearance but weighing 1, 3, 5, 7, and 9 ounces. If we select samples of size 2 **without replacement**, there will be a total of 10 different samples.

(a)   List all the possible samples of size 2 and determine the mean weight of each sample.

Answer: The 10 possible samples of size 2, and the average weight of each sample is shown below.

Possible Sample	Sample Mean ($\overline{X}$)
1 and 3	2
1 and 5	3
1 and 7	4
1 and 9	5
3 and 5	4
3 and 7	5
3 and 9	6
5 and 7	6
5 and 9	7
7 and 9	8

(b)   List all possible sample means; determine the frequency of the appearance of each mean, and draw a histogram of the sampling distribution of $\overline{X}$.

Answer: From part (a) of this exercise, we can determine the frequency of each mean:

Possible Sample Mean	Frequency
2	1
3	1
4	2
5	2
6	2
7	1
8	1

Therefore, the histogram of the sampling distribution can be shown as presented in Figure 7.2.

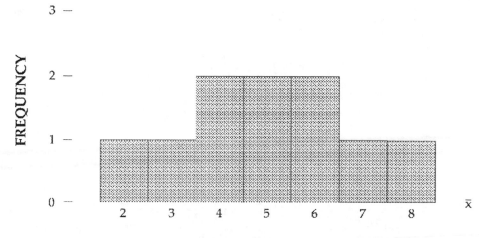

Figure 7.2

As you note, the sampling distribution of the sample means ($\overline{X}$), as shown in Figure 7.2, is approximately normally distributed.

7.   Consider a population of five families with the following data representing the number of children in each family.

Family	Number of Children
A	2
B	6
C	4
D	3
E	1

(a)   There are ten possible samples of size 2 (**sampling without replacement**). List the 10 possible samples of size 2, and determine the mean of each sample.

(b)   List all the possible sample means and determine the frequency of the appearance of each mean.

8.   Refer to exercise 7. Sampling **without replacement** with a sample size of 3 results in a total of 10 possible samples.

(a)   List the 10 possible samples of size 3.

(b)   Determine the mean of each sample.

Solved Problem

*9.   Refer to exercise *5 in which a population consisted of 4 weights of 2, 4, 6, and 8 grams.

(a)   Determine the mean and the variance of the population.

Answer: The mean of the population is

$$\mu = \frac{\sum X_i}{N} = \frac{2+4+6+8}{4} = 5$$

and the variance of the population can be determined as

$$\sigma^2 = \frac{\sum (X_i - \mu)^2}{N}$$

Then, calculating the value of the numerator, we have

X_i	$(X_i - \mu)^2$
2	9
4	1
6	1
8	9

$$\sum (X_i - \mu)^2 = 20$$

Therefore, the variance of the population is

$$\sigma^2 = \frac{\sum (X_i - \mu)^2}{N} = \frac{20}{4} = 5$$

(b)   Sampling **with replacement** from the above population with a sample size of 2 produces sixteen possible samples, which have been shown in part (a) of exercise 8. Using the sixteen $\overline{X}$ values, determine the mean and the variance of $\overline{X}$.

Answer: The sixteen sample means as previously shown are

Possible Means ($\overline{X}$)	$\left(\overline{X} - \mu\right)^2$
2	9
3	4
4	1
5	0
3	4
4	1
5	0
6	1
4	1
5	0
6	1
7	4
5	0
6	1
7	4
8	9
$\Sigma \overline{X} = 80$	$\Sigma(\overline{X} - \mu)^2 = 40$

Then, the mean of the above sixteen sample means is

$$E(\overline{X}) = \frac{80}{16} = 5$$

As you will note, the mean of the sample means is 5, which is equal to the mean of the population (as shown in part (a)). In other words, we have just seen that $E(\overline{X}) = \mu$. To determine the variance of $\overline{X}$, we need to determine $\Sigma(\overline{X} - \mu)^2$; the calculation of which is shown in the second column above. Therefore, the variance of the 16 sample means is

$$\sigma_{\overline{x}}^2 = \frac{\Sigma\left(\overline{X} - \mu\right)^2}{N} = \frac{40}{16} = 2.5$$

(c)   Use equation 7.2 to determine the variance of $\overline{X}$.

Answer: Since sampling is done **with replacement** the following form of equation 7.2 is used

$$\sigma_{\overline{x}} = \frac{\sigma}{\sqrt{n}}$$

Therefore,

$$\sigma_{\bar{x}}^2 = \frac{\sigma^2}{n}$$

In part (a) of this exercise, we calculated the variance of the population. The value of which was equal to 5. Now using equation 7.2, we can determine the variance of $\bar{X}$ as

$$\sigma_{\bar{x}}^2 = \frac{\sigma^2}{n} = \frac{5}{2} = 2.5$$

As you can see, we can determine the variance of $\bar{X}$ by direct computation as shown in part (b) or simply use equation 7.2 to arrive at the same value.

Solved Problem

*10. Now let us apply the above procedure to sampling **without replacement.** Refer to exercise *9 in which a population consisted of 5 weights of 1, 3, 5, 7, and 9 ounces.

(a) Determine the mean and the variance of the population.

Answer: The mean of the population is

$$\mu = \frac{\Sigma X}{N} = \frac{1+3+5+7+9}{5} = 5$$

and the variance of the population can be determined as

$$\sigma^2 = \frac{\Sigma(X-\mu)^2}{N}$$

Then, calculating the value of the numerator, we have

X	$X-\mu$	$(X-\mu)^2$
1	-4	16
3	-2	4
5	0	0
7	2	4
9	4	16
		$\Sigma(X-\mu)^2 = 40$

Therefore, the variance of the population is

$$\sigma^2 = \frac{\Sigma(X-\mu)^2}{N} = \frac{40}{5} = 8$$

(b)   Sampling **without replacement** from the above population with a sample size of 2 produces ten possible samples, which have been shown in part (a) of exercise *9. Using the ten $\overline{X}$ values, determine the mean and the variance of $\overline{X}$.

Answer: The ten sample means, as previously shown, are

Possible Means ($\overline{X}$)	$\left(\overline{X}-\mu\right)^2$
2	9
3	4
4	1
5	0
4	1
5	0
6	1
6	1
7	4
8	9
$\Sigma\overline{X} = 50$	$\Sigma\left(\overline{X}-\mu\right)^2 = 30$

Then, the mean of the above ten sample means is

$$E(\overline{X}) = \frac{50}{10} = 5$$

As you will note, the mean of the sample means is 5, which is equal to the mean of the population (as shown in part (a)). In other words, we have just seen that $E(\overline{X}) = \mu$.

To determine the variance of $\overline{X}$, we need to compute $\Sigma\left(\overline{X}-\mu\right)^2$; the calculation of which is shown in the second column on the previous page. Therefore, the variance of the 10 sample means is

$$\sigma_{\overline{x}}^2 = \frac{\Sigma\left(\overline{X}-\mu\right)^2}{n} = \frac{30}{10} = 3$$

(c)   Use equation 7.2 to determine the variance of $\overline{X}$.

Answer: Equation 7.2 states

$$\sigma_{\overline{x}} = \sqrt{\frac{N-n}{N-1}} \cdot \frac{\sigma}{\sqrt{n}}$$

Therefore, by squaring both sides of the equation, we get

$$\sigma_{\bar{x}}^2 = \frac{N-n}{N-1} \cdot \frac{\sigma^2}{n}$$

In part (a) of this exercise, we calculated the variance (σ^2) of the population, the value of which was equal to 8. Now using equation 7.2, we can determine the variance of $\overline{X}$ as

$$\sigma_{\bar{x}}^2 = \frac{N-n}{N-1} \cdot \frac{\sigma^2}{n} = \frac{5-2}{5-1} \cdot \frac{8}{2} = 3$$

As you can see, we can determine the variance of $\overline{X}$ by direct computation as shown in part (b) or by simply using equation 7.2 to arrive at the same value.

11. In exercise 7, you were given the following information regarding a population of five families and the number of children in each family, replicated below.

Family	Number of Children
A	2
B	6
C	4
D	3
E	1

(a) Determine the mean and the variance of the population.

(b) Using the ten $\overline{X}$ values (computed in exercise *10), compute the mean and the variance of $\overline{X}$.

(c) Using equations 7.1 and 7.2, determine the mean and the variance of the sample means ($\overline{X}$). Compare your values to those that you determined in part (b).

*12. The average weekly starting salary of bus drivers in a city is \$750 (that is μ) with a standard deviation of \$40 (that is σ). Assume that we select a random sample of 64 bus drivers.

(a)   Show the sampling distribution of the sample means ($\overline{X}$).

Answer: From the central limit theorem, we know that the distribution of $\overline{X}$ is normal with a mean equal to μ and a standard deviation equal to $\sigma_{\overline{x}}$. Therefore, the mean of the distribution is

$$E(\overline{X}) = \mu = 750$$

and the standard deviation of the sampling distribution (i.e., the standard error of the mean) is calculated as

$$\sigma_{\overline{x}} = \frac{\sigma}{\sqrt{n}} = \frac{40}{\sqrt{64}} = 5$$

(b)   What is the probability that the sample mean will be greater than \$740?

Answer: The shaded area of the sampling distribution in Figure 7.3 shows this desired probability.

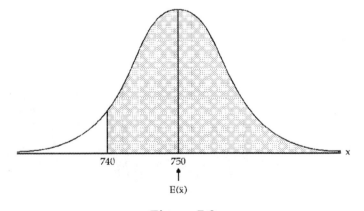

Figure 7.3

Since the sampling distribution is normal with a mean of \$750 and a standard deviation of \$5, we calculate the number of standard errors of the mean (z-score) to be between 740 to 750 as

$$Z = \frac{740 - 750}{5} = -2.0$$

Then from the table of cumulative probability under the normal curve (Table 1 of the Appendix), we read the area to the left of -2.0 as 0.0228. Hence, the area to the right of 740 is 1.0-0.0228 = 0.9772. Therefore, there is a 0.9772 probability that the sample mean will be greater than $740.

(c)   If the population consisted of 320 bus drivers, what would be the standard error of the mean?

Answer: With such a population, we note that n/N = 64/320 = 0.2. (This means that the sample represents 20% of the population.) Since n/N is greater than 0.05, we consider the population to be a finite population. Hence, we use equation 7.2 to determine the standard error of the mean.

$$\sigma_{\bar{x}} = \sqrt{\frac{N-n}{N-1}} \cdot \frac{\sigma}{\sqrt{n}}$$

$$\sigma_{\bar{x}} = \sqrt{\frac{320 - 64}{320 - 1}} \cdot \frac{40}{\sqrt{64}} = (0.896)(5) = 4.48$$

13.   An automotive repair shop has determined that the average service time on an automobile is 130 minutes with a standard deviation of 26 minutes. A random sample of 40 automotive services is selected.

(a)   Show the sampling distribution of $\bar{X}$.

(b)   What is the probability that the sample of 40 automotive services will have a mean service time greater than 136 minutes?

(c)   Assume the population consists of 400 automotive services. Determine the standard error of the mean.

14.   There are 8,000 students at the University of Tennessee at Chattanooga. The average age of all the students is 24 years with a standard deviation of 9 years. A random sample of 36 students is selected.

(a)   Determine the standard error of the mean.

(b)   What is the probability that the sample mean will be larger than 25.5?

(c)   What is the probability that the sample mean will be between 21.6 and 27 years?

Solved Problem

*15. In a local university, 40% of the students live in the dormitories. A random sample of 96 students is selected for a particular study.

(a)   What is the sampling distribution of $\overline{p}$?

Answer: The distribution of the sample proportion is normal with an expected value of $\overline{p}$ as

$$E(\overline{p}) = p$$

where p is the population proportion. In this case, since 40% of the students live in the dormitories, p = 0.4. Therefore, $E(\overline{p}) = 0.4$. The standard deviation of $\overline{p}$, known as the standard error of the proportion, is determined as

$$\sigma_{\overline{p}} = \sqrt{\frac{p(1-p)}{n}} = \sqrt{\frac{.4(1-.4)}{96}} = 0.05$$

(b)   What is the probability that the sample proportion (the proportion living in the dormitories) is between 0.30 and 0.50?

Answer: The shaded area shown in Figure 7.4 represents the desired probability.

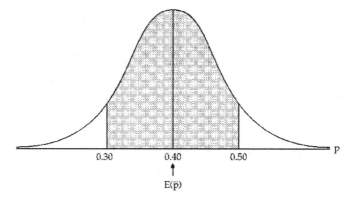

Figure 7.4

To find this area, first we compute the z-score between 0.5 and 0.4 as

$$Z = \frac{0.5 - 0.4}{0.05} = 2.0$$

From Table 1 of the Appendix (cumulative probability under the normal curve), we read the area to the left of z = 2.0 as 0.9772. Then we compute the z-score between 0.3 and 0.4 as

$$Z = \frac{0.3 - 0.4}{0.05} = -2.0$$

Then from Table 1, we read the area to the left of -2.0 as 0.0228. Subtracting the area to the left of z = -2.0 from the area to the left of z = 2.0 yields 0.9772-0.0228 = 0.9544. Therefore the probability that the sample proportion is between 0.30 and 0.50 would be 0.9544.

16.   A department store has determined that 25% of all their sales are credit sales. A random sample of 60 sales is selected.

(a)   What is the sampling distribution of $\bar{p}$?

(b)   What is the probability that the sample proportion will be greater than 0.30?

(c)   What is the probability that the sample proportion will be between 0.20 to 0.30?

17.   Only 4% of the items produced by a machine are defective. A random sample of 200 items is selected and checked for defects.

(a)   Determine the standard error of the proportion.

(b)   What is the probability that the sample contains more than 7% defective units?

SELF-TESTING QUESTIONS

In the following multiple-choice questions, circle the correct answer. An answer key is provided following the questions.

1. A probability distribution for all possible values of a sample statistic is known as
a) a sample statistic
b) a parameter
c) simple random sampling
d) a sampling distribution

2. A population characteristic, such as a population mean, is called
a) a statistic
b) a parameter
c) a sample
d) a normal distribution

3. A measure from a sample, such as a sample mean, is known as
a) a statistic
b) a parameter
c) consistency
d) efficiency

4. The standard deviation of a point estimator is called the
a) standard mean
b) standard error
c) point estimator
d) mean error

5. A single numerical value used as an estimate of a population parameter is known as
a) sample statistic
b) sample parameter
c) a sample size
d) a point estimate

6. The sample statistic, such as $\overline{X}$, S, and $\overline{p}$, that provides the point estimate of the population parameter is known as the
a) point estimator
b) parameter
c) population parameter
d) sample parameter

7.   A theorem that allows us to use the normal probability distribution to approximate the sampling distribution of $\overline{X}$ and $\overline{p}$ whenever the sample size is large is known as the
a)   approximation theorem
b)   normal probability theorem
c)   central limit theorem
d)   consistency theorem

8.   Cluster sampling is an example of
a)   nonprobability sampling
b)   stratified sampling
c)   probability sampling
d)   judgment sampling

9.   The number of different simple random samples of size 4 that can be selected from a population of size 6 is
a)   24
b)   30
c)   15
d)   4

10.   Since the sample size is always smaller than the size of the population, then the sample mean
a)   must always be smaller than the population mean
b)   must be larger than the population mean
c)   must be equal to the population mean
d)   could be larger, smaller, or equal to the mean of the population

11.   As the sample size increases
a)   the standard deviation of the population decreases
b)   the population mean increases
c)   the standard error of the mean increases
d)   the standard error of the mean decreases

12.   The point estimator of μ is
a)   S
b) $\overline{X}$
c)   p
d) σ

13. The point estimator of σ is
a) S
b) $\overline{X}$
c) X
d) μ

14. Which of the following is a point estimator?
a) σ
b) $\overline{X}$
c) μ
d) $\propto$

15. In computing the standard error of the mean, the finite population correction factor is used when
a) n/N > 30
b) N/n ≤ 0.05
c) n/N ≤ 0.05
d) n/N ≥ 0.05

16. As the sample size becomes larger, the sampling distribution of the sample mean approaches a
a) binomial distribution
b) normal distribution
c) hypergeometric distribution
d) chi-square distribution

ANSWERS TO THE SELF-TESTING QUESTIONS

1. d
2. b
3. a
4. b
5. d
6. a
7. c
8. c
9. c
10. d
11. d
12. b
13. a
14. b
15. d
16. b

ANSWERS TO CHAPTER SEVEN EXERCISES

3. (a) 5.67
   (b) 2.85
   (c) 0.20

4. (a) 75
   (b) 20.48
   (c) 0.8

7. (a) AB, AC, AD, AE
      BC, BD, BE
      CD, CE
      DE

   (b)
Possible Sample Mean	Frequency
1.5	1
2.0	1
2.5	2
3.0	1
3.5	2
4.0	1
4.5	1
5.0	1

8. (a) ABC, ABD, ABE, ACD, ACE, ADE
      BCD, BCE, BDE
      CDE

   (b)
Sample	Sample Mean
ABC	4
ABD	3.667
ABE	3
ACD	3
ACE	2.33
ADE	2
BCD	4.33
BCE	3.67
BDE	3.33
CDE	2.67

11. (a) 3.2, 2.96
    (b) 3.2, 1.11
    (c) 3.2, 1.11

13. (a) E($\overline{X}$) = 130   Standard Error = 4.11
    (b) 0.0721
    (c) 3.9

14. (a) 1.5
    (b) 0.1587
    (c) 0.9224

16. (a) E($\overline{p}$) = 0.25   Standard Error = .056 (rounded)
    (b) 0.1867
    (c) 0.6266

17. (a) 0.0139 (rounded)
    (b) 0.0154

CHAPTER EIGHT

INTERVAL ESTIMATION

CHAPTER OUTLINE AND REVIEW

In Chapter 7 you were introduced to the concept of point estimation. As you learned in that chapter, a point estimate is a single numerical value used for estimating a population parameter. Therefore, one cannot expect a point estimate to be exactly equal to the population parameter. Furthermore, a point estimate does not give us information about how close the point estimate is to the true value of the population parameter.

In Chapter 8, you are introduced to the concept of interval estimation, which is the determination of an interval for the population parameter based on sample information. More specifically, you will learn the following concepts.

Confidence Coefficient is the confidence level expressed as a decimal value. For example, for a 90% confidence level, the confidence coefficient is 0.90.

Confidence Interval is another name for an interval estimate.

Confidence Level is the confidence that is placed on the ability of an interval estimate to contain the true value of the population parameter is called the confidence level.

Degrees of Freedom is when the t distribution is used to develop an interval estimate of the population mean, the appropriate t distribution has $(n - 1)$ degrees of freedom, where n is the sample size.

Interval Estimate is an estimate of a population parameter that provides an interval of values believed to contain the value of the parameter. The interval has the form:

Point estimate ± margin of error.

The general form of an interval estimate of a ***population mean*** is $\bar{x}$ ± margin of error; and similarly, the general form of an interval estimate of a population proportion is $\bar{p}$ ± margin of error.

Margin of Error is the value added and subtracted from a point estimate in order to develop an interval estimate of a population parameter.

σ Known is a situation in which the historical data or some other existing information can provide a good estimate of the standard deviation of the population (σ). This value (σ) is used for computing the margin of error in determining the interval estimation.

σ Unknown is a situation in which there is no good available information for estimating the standard deviation of the population (σ). The sample standard deviation (S) is used for computing the margin of error.

t Distribution is a family of probability distributions. This probability distribution is used to estimate an interval for the mean of the population when the standard deviation of the population is not known. The standard deviation of the sample, "S", is used to estimate the standard deviation of the population "σ." The number of degrees of freedom for computing an interval estimate for the mean is (n − 1), where n is the sample size.

CHAPTER FORMULAS

Interval Estimation of a Population Mean (μ)

A. **When the standard deviation of the population σ is known,**

$$\mu = \bar{x} \pm Z_{\alpha/2}\,\frac{\sigma}{\sqrt{n}} \qquad (8.1)$$

where the standard error of the mean is $\sigma_{\bar{x}} = \dfrac{\sigma}{\sqrt{n}}$

and the margin of error $= Z_{\alpha/2}\,\dfrac{\sigma}{\sqrt{n}}$

B. **When the standard deviation σ is unknown,**

$$\mu = \bar{x} \pm t_{\alpha/2}\,\frac{S}{\sqrt{n}} \qquad (8.2)$$

where the standard error of the mean is $S_{\bar{x}} = \dfrac{S}{\sqrt{n}}$

and the margin of error $= t_{\alpha/2}\,\dfrac{S}{\sqrt{n}}$

Sample Size for an Interval Estimate of a Population Mean

$$n = \frac{\left(Z_{\alpha/2}\right)^2 \sigma^2}{E^2} \qquad (8.3)$$

where E = the desired margin of error

Interval Estimation of a Population Proportion (P)

$$p = \bar{p} \pm Z_{\alpha/2} \cdot \sqrt{\frac{\bar{p}\left(1-\bar{p}\right)}{n}} \qquad (8.6)$$

where the standard error of proportion is $S_{\bar{p}} = \sqrt{\dfrac{\bar{p}\left(1-\bar{p}\right)}{n}}$

and the margin of error $= Z_{\alpha/2}\sqrt{\dfrac{\bar{p}\left(1-\bar{p}\right)}{n}}$

Sample Size for an Interval Estimate of a Population Proportion

$$n = \frac{\left(Z_{\alpha/2}\right)^2 p^*\left(1-p^*\right)}{E^2} \qquad (8.7)$$

If the value of p^* in equation 8.7 is not known and a good estimate of p^* is not available, use $p^* = 0.50$.

EXERCISES

Solved Problem

*1.   In order to estimate the average electric usage per month, a sample of 81 houses was selected, and the electric usage was determined.

(a)   Assume a population standard deviation of 450-kilowatt hours. Determine the standard error of the mean.

Answer: When the ***standard deviation of the population*** is known, the standard error of the mean is

$$\sigma_{\bar{x}} = \frac{\sigma}{\sqrt{n}} = \frac{450}{\sqrt{81}} = 50$$

(b)   With a 0.95 probability (i.e., 95% confidence), what can be said about the size of the margin of error?

Answer: The probability of 0.95 indicates that $\alpha = 0.05$, which means that the area in each tail of the normal distribution as shown in Figure 8.1 is $\alpha/2 = 0.025$.

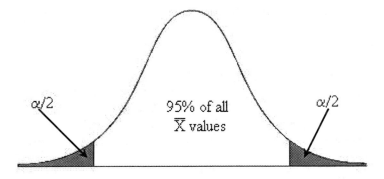

Figure 8.1

Thus, the area to the left of the upper tail is 0.975. Now looking in the body of Table 1 of the Appendix (the table of cumulative probabilities for the standard normal distribution), we note that the Z value corresponding to an area of 0.975 is 1.96. Similarly, on the left of the distribution, the area is $\alpha/2 = 0.025$. Looking in the body of Table 1, we can read the Z scores corresponding to 0.025 to be 1.96. Therefore, we can state that 95% of the sample means will lie within plus or minus 1.96 standard deviations of the mean. Since $1.96\,\sigma_{\bar{x}} = (1.96)(50) = 98$, we can state that there is a 0.95 probability that the value of the sample mean will result in a margin of error of 98 KWH or less.

(c)   If the sample mean is 1858 KWH, what is the 95% confidence interval estimate of the population mean?

Answer: We have already determined that $\sigma_{\bar{x}} = 50$ and $Z_{.025} = 1.96$. When the standard deviation of the population is known, the interval estimate of the population mean is

$$\mu = \bar{x} \pm Z_{\alpha/2} \cdot \sigma_{\bar{x}} = 1858 \pm (1.96)\,(50)$$

$$= 1{,}858 \pm 98$$

Therefore, the confidence interval of the mean is from 1,760 to 1,956 KWH.

2.   A random sample of 81 credit sales in a department store showed an average sale of $68.00. From past data, it is known that the ***standard deviation of the population*** is $27.00.

(a)   Determine the standard error of the mean.

(b)   With a 0.95 probability (95% confidence), what can be said about the size of the margin of error?

(c)   What is the 95% confidence interval of the population mean?

3.   Lyon brokerage firm wants to determine the average daily sales (in dollars) of stocks to their clients. A sample of the sales for 36 days revealed average sales of $139,000. Assume that the ***standard deviation of the population*** is known to be $12,000.

(a)   Provide a 95% confidence interval estimate for the average daily sales.

(b)   Provide a 97% confidence interval estimate for the average daily sales.

*4.   A random sample of 64 SAT scores of students applying for merit scholarships showed an average of 1400 with a standard deviation of 240. Provide a 95% confidence interval for the SAT scores of all the students who applied for the merit scholarships.

Answer: When the standard deviation of the population is not known, the sample standard deviation is used. Therefore, in this situation (since the standard deviation of the population is not known) the sample standard deviation (S = 240) is used for interval estimation. The interval estimate for the mean is

$$\mu = \bar{x} \pm t_{\alpha/2} \frac{S}{\sqrt{n}}$$

A 95% confidence indicates that $\alpha = 0.05$, which means $\alpha/2 = 0.025$. Thus, the area in the upper tail of the t-distribution is 0.025. To read the appropriate "t" value, we note that the sample size is 64. Therefore, there are 63 degrees of freedom (n – 1 = 64 – 1 = 63). Thus, we can read the "t" value at 63 degrees of freedom from Table 2 of the Appendix
(t Distribution) as $t_{.025} = 1.998$. Therefore, the interval estimate will be

$$\mu = \bar{x} \pm t_{\alpha/2} \frac{S}{\sqrt{n}} = 1400 \pm (1.998) \frac{240}{\sqrt{64}} = 1400 \pm (1.998)(30) = 1400 \pm 59.94$$

Hence, the 95% confidence interval estimate for the population mean is 1340.06 to 1459.94.

5.   The Highway Safety Department wants to study the driving habits of individuals. A sample of 81 cars traveling on the highway revealed an average speed of 67 miles per hour with a standard deviation of 9 miles per hour.

(a)   Compute the standard error of the mean.

(b)   Determine a 99% confidence interval estimate for the speed of all cars.

6.   To determine how many hours per week freshmen college students watch television, a random sample of 85 students was selected. It was determined that the students in the sample spent an average of 35 hours with a standard deviation of 12 hours watching TV per week. Provide a 95% confidence interval estimate for the average number of hours that all college freshmen spend watching TV per week.

7.   Lauren Computer Services, Inc. wants to determine a confidence interval for the average CPU time of their teleprocessing transactions. A sample of 64 transactions yielded a mean of 0.20 seconds with a standard deviation of 0.05. Determine a 90% confidence interval for the average CPU time.

8.   A sample of 91 patients in Doctor Lyon's office showed that they had to wait an average of 43 minutes, with a standard deviation of 8 minutes, before they could see the doctor.

(a)   Provide a 95% confidence interval estimate for the average waiting time of all the patients who visit Dr. Lyon.

(b)   Provide a 90% confidence interval estimate for the average waiting time of all the patients who visit Dr. Lyon.

9.   A random sample of 87 airline pilots had an average yearly income of $99,400 with a standard deviation of $12,000.

(a)   If we want to determine a 95% confidence interval for the average yearly income, what is the value of t?

(b)   Develop a 95% confidence interval for the average yearly income of all pilots.

10. The owner of a restaurant wants to determine the average number of customers who eat lunch at his restaurant each day. A sample of 64 days showed that an average of 130 lunches were served daily. The standard deviation of the sample was 12.

(a)   If we want to determine a 90% confidence interval, what is the value of t?

(b)   Determine the margin of error at 90% confidence.

(c)   Determine a 90% confidence interval estimate for the average number of lunches served per day.

Solved Problem

*11. In order to determine the life expectancy of a particular brand of computer tablets, a sample of 6 tablets was selected randomly. The sample revealed the following life expectancies.

Tablets	Life Expectancy x_i (1000 Hours)	$(x_i - \bar{x})$	$(x_i - \bar{x})^2$
1	8.2	0.2	0.04
2	7.5	-0.5	0.25
3	9.5	1.5	2.25
4	6.5	-1.5	2.25
5	8.5	0.5	0.25
6	7.8	-0.2	0.04
	$\sum x_i = 48$		$\sum(x_i - \bar{x})^2 = 5.08$

Provide a 90% confidence interval estimate for the life expectancy of all tablets for this brand. Assume the life expectancy of the population is normally distributed.

Answer: From the above data, we first must determine the mean of the sample as

$$\bar{x} = \frac{\sum x_i}{n} = \frac{48}{6} = 8$$

Since we do not know the standard deviation of the population, we calculate the standard deviation of the sample (S) and use it as a point estimator for the standard deviation of the population (σ).

$$S = \sqrt{\frac{\sum\left(x_i - \bar{x}\right)^2}{n-1}} = \sqrt{\frac{5.08}{6-1}} = 1.008$$

Since the standard deviation of the population is not known, we determine an interval estimate by

$$\mu = \bar{x} \pm t_{\alpha/2}\frac{S}{\sqrt{n}}$$

From Table 2 of the Appendix (t Distribution), at 90% confidence and 5 degrees of freedom (n - 1), we read

$$t_{\alpha/2} = t_{.05} = 2.015$$

Hence, the interval estimate becomes

$$\mu = \bar{x} \pm t_{\alpha/2}\frac{S}{\sqrt{n}} = 8 \pm (2.015)\left(\frac{1.008}{\sqrt{6}}\right)$$

$$= 8 \pm (2.015)\,(0.4115) = 8 \pm 0.829$$

The above yields an interval of 7.171 to 8.829. Since the units were in thousands of hours, the 90% confidence interval estimate of the population mean is from 7,171 hours to 8,829.

12.   A compact fluorescent light bulb manufacturer selected a sample of 10 fluorescent bulbs and gathered the following data.

Light Bulbs	Life Expectancy (In Hundreds of Hours)
1	39
2	42
3	41
4	38
5	40
6	43
7	36
8	37
9	43
10	41

(a) Compute the mean and the standard deviation.

(b)   Determine the margin of error at 98% confidence.

(c)   Determine a 98% confidence interval estimate for the life expectancy of all the bulbs produced by this manufacturer. Assume the population is normally distributed.

13.   A local university administers a comprehensive examination to the candidates for B.S. degrees in Business Administration. Five examinations are selected at random and scored. The scores are shown below.

Grade

94
72
93
54
77

Develop a 98% confidence interval estimate for the mean of the population. Assume the population is normally distributed.

*14. The monthly starting salaries of students who receive business degrees have a standard deviation of $600. What size sample should be selected so that there is 0.95 probability of estimating the mean monthly income within $150 or less?

Answer: From the above, it is indicated that the margin of error E = $150. Furthermore, $\alpha = 0.05$ and $\alpha/2 = 0.025$ (note that $1 - \alpha$ is 0.95). Thus, we read the $Z_{\alpha/2} = Z_{.025} = 1.96$. Then we determine the sample size as

$$n = \frac{(Z_{\alpha/2})^2 \sigma^2}{E^2} = \frac{(1.96)^2 (600)^2}{(150)^2} = 61.4656$$

The sample size must be at least 61.4656 in order to satisfy the margin of error requirements. Since the computed n is not an integer, we **round up** to the next integer value and conclude that the desired sample size is 62 students.

15. LML, a coal company wants to determine a 95% confidence interval estimate for the average daily tonnage of coal that they mine. Assuming that the company reports that the standard deviation of daily output is 80 tons, how many days should they sample so that the margin of error is 20 tons or less?

16. If the standard deviation for lifetimes of vacuum cleaners is estimated to be 400 hours, how large a sample must be taken in order to be 93% confident that the margin of error will not exceed 50 hours?

Solved Problem

---

*17. In the last election, a sample of 800 registered voters in Tennessee showed that 200 of them voted for the incumbent governor. Develop a 95% confidence interval estimate for the proportion of all Tennessee registered voters who voted for the incumbent governor.

Answer: In the sample of 800 registered voters, there were 200 who voted for the incumbent governor. Thus, the point estimate of the proportion of voters who voted for the incumbent governor is $\bar{p}$ = 200/800 = 0.25. Now we can estimate the standard error of the proportion using this sample proportion as

$$S_{\bar{p}} = \sqrt{\frac{\bar{p}\left(1-\bar{p}\right)}{n}} = \sqrt{\frac{0.25\left(1-0.25\right)}{800}} = 0.0153$$

At 95% confidence, $Z_{\alpha/2} = Z_{.025} = 1.96$. Therefore, the interval estimate can be determined as

$$p = \bar{p} \pm Z_{\alpha/2}S_{\bar{p}} = 0.25 \pm (1.96)\,(0.0153) = 0.25 \pm 0.03$$

Hence, we note that at 95% confidence the interval estimate for the proportion of all Tennessee registered voters who voted for the incumbent governor is from 0.22 to 0.28. In other words, we are 95% confident that between 22% to 28% of the Tennessee registered voters voted for the incumbent governor.

18. A local health care facility noted that in a sample of 200 patients, 180 were referred to them by the local hospital.

(a) Compute the standard error of proportion.

(b) At 99% confidence, determine the margin of error.

(c) Provide a 99% confidence interval for all the patients who were referred to this facility by the hospital.

19. In a random sample of 150 residents of Soddy Daisy, 90 residents indicated that they voted for the Democratic candidate in the last presidential election.

(a) Compute the standard error of proportion.

(b) At 95% confidence, determine the margin of error.

(c) Develop a 95% confidence interval estimate for the proportion of all Soddy Daisy residents who voted for the Democratic candidate.

Solved Problem

*20. In order to determine the summer unemployment rate among college students, a pilot sample was taken and it was determined that ten percent of the individuals in the sample were unemployed. Using the results of the pilot study and a 95% confidence, what size sample would be required to estimate the proportion of unemployed college students if we want the margin of error not to exceed 3 percent?

Answer: To determine this sample size, we use

$$n = \frac{\left(Z_{\alpha/2}\right)^2 p^*\left(1 - p^*\right)}{E^2}$$

Using the pilot study result of $\overline{P} = 0.10$ as the planning value of P^*, we can compute the required sample size:

$$n = \frac{\left(Z_{\alpha/2}\right)^2 p^*\left(1 - p^*\right)}{E^2} = \frac{(1.96)^2 (0.1)(0.9)}{(0.03)^2} = 384.16$$

According to our computations, the sample size must be at least 384.16 in order to satisfy the 3% margin of error requirement. Since the required sample size is not an integer, we **round up** to the next integer, indicating the required sample size is 385.

21. The manager of a grocery store wants to determine what proportion of people who enter his store are his regular customers. What size sample should he take so that at 95% confidence the margin of error will not be more than 0.1? Hint: Since p is not known, you need to determine the sample size by using p = 0.5.

22. A local weight loss clinic is interested in the effectiveness of its weight reduction program. In a random sample of 50 participants, 35 lost weight. How large a sample size is necessary for the margin of error to be no more than 10% at 95% confidence?

SELF-TESTING QUESTIONS

In the following multiple-choice questions, circle the correct answer. An answer key is provided following the questions.

1.   An estimate of a population parameter that provides an interval of values believed to contain the value of the parameter is known as the
a)   confidence level
b)   interval estimate
c)   parameter value
d)   population estimate

2.   When s is used to estimate σ, the margin of error is computed by using
a)   normal distribution
b)   t distribution
c)   the mean of the sample
d)   the mean of the population

3.   If an interval estimate is said to be constructed at the 90% confidence level, the confidence coefficient would be
a)   0.1
b)   0.95
c)   0.9
d)   0.05

4.   Whenever the population standard deviation is unknown and the population has a normal or near-normal distribution, which distribution is used in developing an interval estimation?
a)   standard distribution
b)   chi-square distribution
c)   beta distribution
d)   t distribution

5.   As the number of degrees of freedom in a t distribution increases, the difference between the t distribution and the standard normal distribution
a)   becomes larger
b)   becomes smaller
c)   varies according to the confidence coefficient
d)   gets closer to 0.05

6.   From a population with a standard deviation of 20, a sample of 100 items is selected. At 95% confidence, the margin of error is
a)   10
b)   2
c)   3.92
d)   5

7.   In order to determine an interval for the mean of a population with unknown standard deviation, a sample of 87 items is selected. The mean of the sample is determined to be 30. The number of degrees of freedom for reading the t value is
a)   29
b)   30
c)   86
d)   87

Exhibit 8-1

In order to estimate the average time spent on the computer terminals per student at a local university, data were collected from a sample of 81 business students over a one-week period. Assume the population standard deviation is 1.2 hours.

8.   Refer to Exhibit 8.1. The standard error of the mean is
a)   7.5
b)   0.014
c)   0.160
d)   0.133

9.   Refer to Exhibit 8.1. With a 0.95 probability, the margin of error is approximately
a)   0.26
b)   1.96
c)   0.21
d)   1.64

10.   Refer to Exhibit 8-1. If the sample mean is 9 hours, then the 95% confidence interval is
a)   7.04 to 110.96 hours
b)   7.36 to 10.64 hours
c)   7.80 to 10.20 hours
d)   8.74 to 9.26 hours

11.   The absolute value of the difference between the point estimate and the population parameter it estimates is
a)   the standard error
b)   the sampling error
c)   precision
d)   the error of confidence

12.   If we want to provide a 95% confidence interval for the proportion of a population, the Z value is
a)   0.45
b)   0.90
c)   1.96
d)   1.645

13. The Z value for a 97% confidence interval estimation is
a) 1.88
b) 1.96
c) 2.00
d) 2.17

14. The t value for a 95% confidence interval estimation with 28 degrees of freedom is
a) 2.467
b) 2.052
c) 2.048
d) 2.473

15. A 90% confidence interval for a population mean is determined to be 800 to 900. If the confidence coefficient is increased to 0.95, the interval for μ
a) becomes narrower
b) becomes 0.05
c) does not change
d) becomes wider

ANSWERS TO THE SELF-TESTING QUESTIONS

1. b
2. b
3. c
4. d
5. b
6. c
7. c
8. d
9. a
10. d
11. b
12. c
13. d
14. c
15. d

ANSWERS TO CHAPTER EIGHT EXERCISES

2. (a) 3.0
    (b) 5.88
    (c) $62.12 to $73.88

3. (a) $135,080 to $142,920
    (b) $134,660 to $143,340

5. (a) $S_{\bar{x}} = 1$
    (b) 64.36 to 69.64

6. 32.411 to 37.589

7. 0.1896 to 0.2104

8. (a) 41.333 to 44.667
    (b) 41.606 to 44.394

9. (a) 1.988
    (b) $96,842.37 to $101,957.60

10. (a) 1.669
    (b) 2.504
    (c) 127.50 to 132.50 (round to 127 to 133))

12. (a) 40, 2.45 (rounded)
    (b) 2.185
    (c) 37.815 to 42.185

13. 50.29 to 105.71

15. 62 (rounded)

16. 210 (rounded)

18. (a) 0.0212
    (b) 0.0546
    (c) 0.8454 to 0.9546

19. (a) 0.04
    (b) 0.0784
    (c) 0.5216 to 0.6784

21. 96.04 (round to 97)

22. 80.67 (round to 81)

CHAPTER NINE

HYPOTHESIS TESTING

CHAPTER OUTLINE AND REVIEW

This chapter introduces another form of statistical inference, namely, testing of a hypothesis. You will learn that one can state a hypothesis about the characteristic of a population and then, based on the sample information, decide whether or not the hypothesis is rejected. The main topics covered in this chapter are the following.

Alternative Hypothesis is the hypothesis that is assumed to be true when the null hypothesis is rejected. It can be directional (one-tailed) or non-directional (two-tailed).

Critical Value is a value that is compared with the test statistic in order to determine whether or not the null hypothesis is to be rejected.

Hypothesis is an assumption made about the value of a population parameter.

Level of Significance is the probability of committing a Type I error when the null hypothesis is true.

Null Hypothesis is the hypothesis that is tentatively assumed to be true in hypothesis testing. Based on sample information, we can decide whether to *reject* or *not reject* the null hypothesis.

One-Tailed Test is a testing situation in which the null hypothesis is rejected for the values of the point estimator only on one side (tail) of the sampling distribution.

Power is the probability of rejecting the null hypothesis (H_0) when it is false.

Power Curve is a graph of the probability of the rejection of the null hypothesis (H_0) for all possible values of the population parameter not satisfying the null hypothesis. The power curve provides the probability of correctly rejecting the null hypothesis.

P-Value is the probability that measures the support (or lack of support) provided by the sample for the null hypothesis. This probability is computed by the use of the test statistic. The null hypothesis is rejected if the *p*-value is less than or equal to the level of significance for the test. That is, reject H_0 if *p*-value $\leq \alpha$.

Test Statistic is a statistic whose value helps to determine whether the null hypothesis can be rejected.

Two-Tailed Test is a testing situation in which the null hypothesis is rejected for values of the point estimator in either tail of the sampling distribution.

Type I Error refers to the error of ***rejecting*** the null hypothesis when in fact it is actually true, because the sample information has resulted in the erroneous rejection of the true null hypothesis.

Type II Error refers to the error of ***not rejecting*** the null hypothesis when in fact it has been false, because the sample information has resulted in not rejecting a false null hypothesis.

Population Condition

	H_o *is True*	H_a *is True*
Do not Reject H_o	*Correct Conclusion*	Type II Error
Reject H_o	Type I Error	*Correct Conclusion*

Conclusion

Probability of Type I Error = α
Probability of Type II Error = β

CHAPTER FORMULAS

Steps of Hypothesis Testing

Step 1:   Develop the null and the alternative hypotheses.

Step 2:   Specify the level of significance.

Step 3:   Compute the test statistic (*t* or *Z*) from the sample data.

Rejection Rule: *p*-Value Approach

Step 4:   Compute the *p*-value by using the test statistic (*t* or *Z*) from step 3.

Step 5:   Reject H_o if *p*-value $\leq \alpha$.

Rejection Rule: Critical Value Approach

Step 4:   Determine the critical value(s) of *t* or *Z* at the specified level of significance α and set up the rejection rule.

Step 5:   Compare the test statistic from step 3 to that of the critical value(s) from step 4. If the test statistic is beyond the critical value(s), reject the null hypothesis.

$$\boxed{\text{Hypothesis Test Situations}}$$

I.   **Hypothesis Tests about a Population Mean: σ known**

Test Statistic: $Z = \dfrac{\overline{X} - \mu_0}{\sigma/\sqrt{n}}$ (9.1)

Decision Rules for *P*-Value Approach

$$\boxed{\textbf{When Using the \textit{P}-Value Approach, In All Cases Reject } H_0 \textbf{ if \textit{P}-Value} \leq \alpha}$$

CHAPTER FORMULAS
(Continued)

Decision Rule for Critical Value Approach

Lower One-Tailed Test of the Form	Upper One-Tailed Test of the Form	Two-Tailed Test of the Form
$H_o: \mu \geq \mu_o$ $H_a: \mu < \mu_o$ Reject H_o if: $Z \leq -Z_\alpha$	$H_o: \mu \leq \mu_o$ $H_a: \mu > \mu_o$ Reject H_o if: $Z \geq Z_\alpha$	$H_o: \mu = \mu_o$ $H_a: \mu \neq \mu_o$ Reject H_o if: $Z \leq -Z_{\alpha/2}$ or $Z \geq Z_{\alpha/2}$

II. Hypothesis Tests about a Population Mean: σ Unknown

$$\text{Test Statistic:} \quad t = \frac{\overline{X} - \mu_o}{S/\sqrt{n}} \tag{9.4}$$

> The decision rules are the same as those shown in **Part I** with the *t* statistic substituted for the *Z* statistic.

III. Hypothesis Tests about a Population Proportion

$$\text{Standardized Test Statistic:} \quad Z = \frac{\overline{p} - p_o}{\sigma_{\overline{p}}} \quad \text{where } \sigma_{\overline{p}} = \sqrt{\frac{p_o(1 - p_o)}{n}} \tag{9.5}$$

Thus Z will have the form:

$$Z = \frac{\overline{p} - p_o}{\sqrt{\dfrac{p_o(1 - p_o)}{n}}} \tag{9.6}$$

CHAPTER FORMULAS
(Continued)

Decision Rule for Critical Value Approach

Lower One-Tailed Test of the Form	Upper One-Tailed Test of the Form	Two-Tailed Test of the Form
$H_o: p \geq p_o$	$H_o: p \leq p_o$	$H_o: p = p_o$
$H_a: p < p_o$	$H_a: p > p_o$	$H_a: p \neq p_o$
Reject H_o if: $Z \leq -Z_\alpha$	Reject H_o if: $Z \geq Z_\alpha$	Reject H_o if: $Z \leq -Z_{\alpha/2}$ or $Z \geq Z_{\alpha/2}$

EXERCISES

*1.   The average gasoline price of one of the major oil companies in Europe has been $1.25 per liter. Recently, the company has undertaken several efficiency measures in order to reduce prices. Management is interested in determining whether their efficiency measures have actually **reduced** prices. That is, they are interested in determining whether or not the current average price is significantly less than $1.25 per liter. A random sample of 49 of their gas stations is selected and the average price is determined to be $1.20 per liter. Furthermore, assume that the standard deviation of the *population* (σ) is $0.14.

(a)   Develop appropriate hypotheses for this situation.

Answer: Since we are interested in determining if there has been a significant *reduction* in the average price, the null and the alternative hypotheses are stated as

H_o: $\mu \geq 1.25$

H_a: $\mu < 1.25$ (There was a reduction in the average price.)

(b)   Compute the value of the test statistic for this hypothesis test.

Answer: In this case, since the *standard deviation of the population is known*, the test statistic Z will be computed as

$$Z = \frac{\overline{X} - \mu_o}{\sigma_{\overline{X}}} = \frac{\overline{X} - \mu_o}{\sigma/\sqrt{n}} = \frac{1.20 - 1.25}{0.14/\sqrt{49}} = \frac{-0.05}{.02} = -2.5$$

(c)   Compute the *p*-value for this problem and explain its meaning.

Answer: The *p*-value is computed by using the test statistic, in this case the value of Z. The *p*-value is the probability that measures the support (or lack of support) provided by the sample information for the null hypothesis. In this problem, the *p*-value, as shown in Figure 9.1, is the area under the normal curve to the left of the test statistic $Z = -2.5$. From Table 1 of the appendix (the table of standard normal distribution.), the area corresponding to $Z = -2.5$ is determined to be 0.0062. This indicates that the probability of obtaining a sample mean of $\overline{X} = 1.20$ or smaller from a population with a mean $\mu = 1.25$ is only 0.0062.

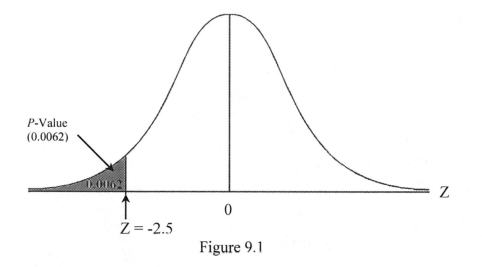

P-Value
(0.0062)

Z = -2.5

0

Z

Figure 9.1

(d)   Using the *p*-value, at 95% confidence, test to determine whether the measures were effective in reducing the average price.

Answer: ***The null hypothesis is rejected if the p-value ≤ α.*** In this problem, since the *p*-value is 0.0062, which is smaller than α of 0.05; the null hypothesis is rejected. Thus, it can be concluded that the average price is significantly less than $1.25, indicating that the measures were effective in reducing the average price.

(e)   Using the critical value approach, at 95% confidence, test to determine whether the measures were effective in reducing the average price.

Answer: Since this case is a lower one-tailed hypothesis testing situation, the null hypothesis is rejected if the test statistic $Z \le -Z_\alpha$. In part (b), the value of the test statistic was determined to be $Z = -2.5$. At a 0.05 level of significance, the area to the left of the critical value of Z is 0.05 (See Figure 9.2). ***Since the exact value of 0.05 is not in the table, the closest value corresponding to an area of 0.05 (which is 0.0505) is selected and we read the value of*** Z_α ***as*** $Z_{.05} = -1.64$***.*** The following is part of the normal distribution table showing this value.

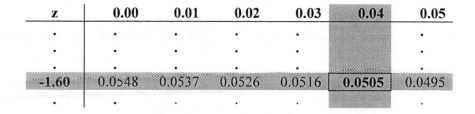

z	0.00	0.01	0.02	0.03	0.04	0.05
.	.	.	.	.		.
.	.	.	.	.		.
.	.	.	.	.		.
-1.60	0.0548	0.0537	0.0526	0.0516	0.0505	0.0495
.	.	.	.	.		.

As you can see in Figure 9.2 for any value of $Z \le -1.64$, the null hypothesis is rejected. In this case, since $Z = -2.5$ is less than $Z_{.05} = -1.64$, the null hypothesis is rejected, and it can be concluded that the efficiency measures were effective in reducing the average price. As you note, both the *p*-value approach and the critical value approach result in the same conclusion.

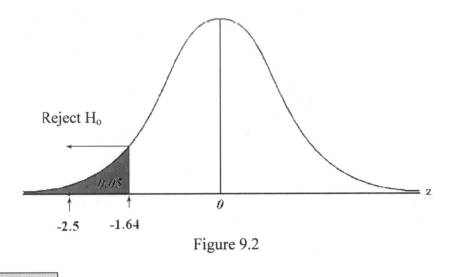

Figure 9.2

Solved Problem

*2.   The sales of a grocery store had an average of $8,000 per day. The store introduced several advertising campaigns in order to *increase* sales. To determine whether or not the advertising campaigns have been effective in increasing sales, a sample of 64 days of sales was selected. It was found that the average was $8,250 per day. From past information, it is known that the standard deviation of the *population* is $1,200.

(a)   Develop appropriate hypotheses to test for the effectiveness of advertising campaigns.

Answer: Since we want to determine if there has been an *increase* in the average sales, the null and the alternative hypotheses are stated as

H_0: $\mu \leq 8000$

H_a: $\mu > 8000$ (Average has increased)

(b)   Compute the value of the test statistic.

Answer: Since the *standard deviation of the population is known*, the test statistic Z is computed

$$Z = \frac{\overline{X} - \mu_0}{\sigma/\sqrt{n}} = \frac{8250 - 8000}{1200/\sqrt{64}} = 1.67$$

(c)   Compute the *p*-value and use it to test the above hypotheses at 99% confidence. ($\alpha = 0.01$)

Answer: Since this is a one-tailed (upper-tailed) testing situation, the *p*-value is the area under the normal curve to the right of the test statistic. The area to the left of the test statistic $Z = 1.67$ is read from the table of normal distribution as 0.9525. Therefore, the *p*-value $= 1.0 - 0.9525 = 0.0475$. Since the *p*-value is greater than $\alpha = 0.01$, the null hypothesis is not rejected. Thus, there is not sufficient evidence to conclude that there has been an increase in the average sales.

(d)   Using the critical value approach at 99% confidence ($\alpha = 0.01$), test the hypotheses.

Answer: In this case, we have an upper one-tailed hypothesis testing situation, and the null hypothesis will be rejected if $Z \geq Z_\alpha$. For a one-tailed test at 99% confidence, we read the Z_α corresponding to an area of 0.99 (See Figure 9.3). Since the exact value of 0.99 is not in the table of areas under the normal curve, we read the Z corresponding to 0.9901, which is $Z_{.01} = 2.33$. In part (b), the value of the test statistic Z was determined to be 1.67. Since the test statistic $Z = 1.67$ is less than $Z_{.01} = 2.33$, the null hypothesis is not rejected. Therefore, there is not sufficient evidence to conclude that sales have increased. The region where the null hypothesis is rejected is shown in Figure 9.3.

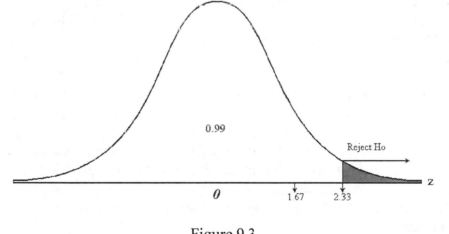

0.99

Reject Ho

Z

0   1.67   2.33

Figure 9.3

Solved Problem

*3.   A sample of 64 account balances from a credit company showed an average daily balance of $1,040. The standard deviation of the ***population*** is known to be $200. We are interested in determining if the mean of all account balances (i.e., population mean) is significantly different from $1,000.

(a)   Develop appropriate hypotheses for this problem.

Answer: Since in this situation we are interested in determining whether the average balance is significantly *different* (larger or smaller) from $1,000, a two-tailed test is required. The null and the alternative hypotheses are formulated as

$$H_o: \mu = 1000$$

$$H_a: \mu \neq 1000$$

(b)   Compute the test statistic.

Answer: Since the *standard deviation of the population is known*, the test statistic Z is computed as

$$Z = \frac{\overline{X} - \mu_o}{\sigma / \sqrt{n}} = \frac{1040 - 1000}{200 / \sqrt{64}} = 1.60$$

(c)   Compute the *p*-value.

Answer: For a two-tailed test, values of the test statistic in either tail will lead to the rejection of the null hypothesis. In part (b), we determined that the test statistic $Z = 1.60$. From the standard normal distribution, we read the area to the left of 1.60 to be 0.9452. Hence, the area to the right of our test statistic is $1.0 - 0.9452 = 0.0548$. Since this is a two-tailed test, we simply double the area that we found above and arrive at the *p*-value. Hence, the *p*-value $= 2(0.0548) = 0.1096$.

(d)   Using the *p*-value approach at 95% confidence ($\alpha = 0.05$), test the above hypotheses.

Answer: The general rule for hypothesis testing using the *p*-value approach is to *reject the null hypothesis if the p-value $\leq \alpha$.* In our situation, the *p*-value $= 0.1096$, which is larger than $\alpha = 0.05$ (95% confidence). Hence, the null hypothesis is not rejected; and we conclude that there is not sufficient evidence to indicate that the advertising campaigns have been effective.

(e)   Using the critical value approach at 95% confidence, test the hypotheses.

Answer: The level of significance, which is the probability of a Type I error (i.e., the probability of rejecting the null hypothesis when, in fact, it is true), is given as 0.05 (95% confidence). In the situation of a two-tailed test, half of the level of significance or, in this case, half of 0.05, or 0.025, will be in each tail of the sampling distribution. The area to the left of the critical value of Z is 0.975. Now, looking in the table of areas under the normal distribution, we read the Z corresponding to an area of 0.975 as $Z = 1.96$. Since we are dealing with a two-tailed test, there will be a corresponding $Z_{.025} = -1.96$ in the lower tail. (See Figure 9.4)

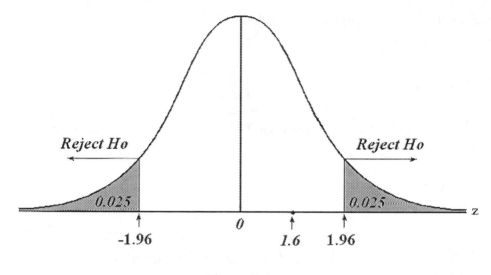

Figure 9.4

Now the decision rule can be stated:

Reject H_o if $Z \leq -1.96$ or $Z \geq 1.96$

In part (b), the Z statistic was computed and its value was 1.60. Since 1.60 is between -1.96 and 1.96, the null hypothesis cannot be rejected; and we conclude that there is no evidence that the mean is significantly different from $1,000.

4.   The Bureau of Labor Statistics reported that the average yearly income of dentists in the year 2006 was $110,000. A sample of 81 dentists, which was taken in 2007, showed an average yearly income of $120,000. Assume the standard deviation of the **population** of dentists in 2007 is $36,000.

(a)   We want to test to determine if there has been a significant **increase** in the average yearly income of dentists. Provide the null and the alternative hypotheses.

(b)   Compute the test statistic.

(c)   Determine the *p*-value; and at 95% confidence, test the hypotheses.

5.   Consider the following hypotheses test.

H_o: $\mu \geq 80$

H_a: $\mu < 80$

A sample of 121 provided a sample mean of 77.3. The ***population standard deviation*** is known to be 16.5.

(a)   Compute the value of the test statistic.

(b)   Determine the *p*-value; and at 93.7% confidence, test the above hypotheses.

(c)   Using the critical value approach at 93.7% confidence, test the hypotheses.

6.   College freshmen orientation fees in the year 2012 had an average fee of $58. In 2013, a sample of 64 colleges showed an average of $54.10. Assume the standard deviation of the ***population*** is $12. We want to test to see if there has been a ***significant change*** in the average fee.

(a)   Provide the null and the alternative hypotheses.

(b)   Compute the test statistic.

(c)   Determine the *p*-value; and at 97% confidence, test the hypotheses.

(d)   Using the critical value approach at 97% confidence, test the hypotheses.

Solved Problem

*7.   From a population of cereal boxes marked "12 ounces," a sample of 64 boxes is selected and the content of each box is weighed. The sample revealed a mean of 11.7 ounces with a standard deviation of 1.6 ounces.

(a)   Using the critical value approach, test to see if the mean of the population is significantly less than 12 ounces. Use a 0.05 level of significance.

Answer: The null and the alternative hypotheses are formulated as

$$H_o: \mu \geq 12$$

$$H_a: \mu < 12$$

Since the **standard deviation of the population is not known,** the *t* distribution is used for the hypothesis test. The rejection region for this test is located in the lower tail of the sampling distribution. The value of *t* with n - 1 = 64 - 1 = 63 degrees of freedom can be read from Table 2 of the Appendix as $t_{.05}$ = -1.669. *(Note that the actual value that is read from the table is 1.669; but since we are dealing with the lower tail of the distribution, t is -1.669.)* Now the decision rule is to reject H_o if *t* < -1.669, where the *t* statistic is computed as

$$t = \frac{\overline{X} - \mu_o}{S / \sqrt{n}} = \frac{11.7 - 12}{1.6 / \sqrt{64}} = -1.5$$

Since -1.5 is greater than -1.669, the null hypothesis is not rejected. (See Figure 9.5.) Therefore, at 95% confidence there is not sufficient evidence to conclude that the mean is significantly less than 12 ounces.

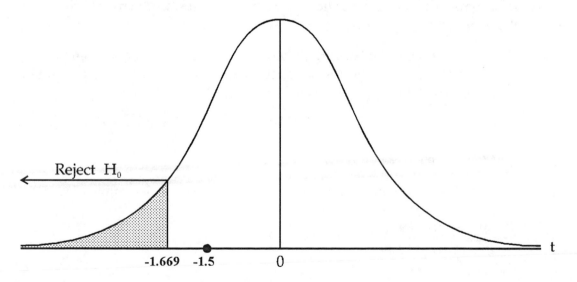

Figure 9.5

(b)   Using the *p*-value approach, test to see if the mean of the population is significantly less than 12 ounces. Use a 0.05 level of significance.

Answer: In part (a), the test statistic *t* was computed to be *t* = -1.5. With a lower-tail test, the *p*-value is the area in the lower tail to the left of -1.5. *(Note that the t distribution table only contains positive values of t; but since the t distribution is symmetrical, we can use the absolute value of the test statistic.)* Now, looking in the *t* table in the 63 degrees of freedom row, we note the following.

Area in the Upper Tail	0.20	0.10	0.05	0.025	0.01	0.005
t value (63 df)	0.847	1.295	1.669	1.998	2.387	2.656

$$t = 1.5$$

From the above results, we note that *t* = 1.5 is between 1.295 and 1.669, which indicates the *p*-value is between 0.1 and 0.05. Since the *p*-value is greater than α = 0.05, the null hypothesis is not rejected; and at 95% confidence, there is not sufficient evidence to conclude that the mean is significantly less than 12 ounces.

Solved Problem

*8.   A lathe is set to cut steel bars into lengths of 6 centimeters. The lathe is considered to be in perfect adjustment if the average length of the bars it cuts is 6 centimeters. A sample of 49 bars is selected randomly, and the lengths are measured. It is determined that the average length of the bars in the sample is 6.125 centimeters with a standard deviation of 0.35 centimeters.

(a)   At 95% confidence using the critical value approach, test to determine whether or not the lathe is in perfect adjustment.

Answer: In this situation, if the bars are cut too large or too small, the machine is considered not to be in perfect adjustment. Therefore, we have a two-tailed hypothesis testing situation in which the hypotheses are

H_o: $\mu = 6$

H_a: $\mu \neq 6$ (The lathe is not in perfect adjustment)

Since the **standard deviation of the population is not known**, we determine the *t* statistic:

$$t = \frac{\overline{X} - \mu_o}{S/\sqrt{n}} = \frac{6.125 - 6}{0.35/\sqrt{49}} = 2.5$$

The null hypothesis will be rejected if the test statistic $t > t_{\alpha/2}$ or if $t < - t_{\alpha/2}$. The value of $t_{\alpha/2}$ with 48 degrees of freedom (n - 1) = (49-1) = 48 can be read from Table 2 of the

---

Appendix as $t_{.025} = 2.011$. Since 2.5 is larger than 2.011, the null hypothesis is rejected; and we conclude that the machine is not perfectly adjusted. Figure 9.6 shows the value of $t = 2.5$, where the null hypothesis is rejected.

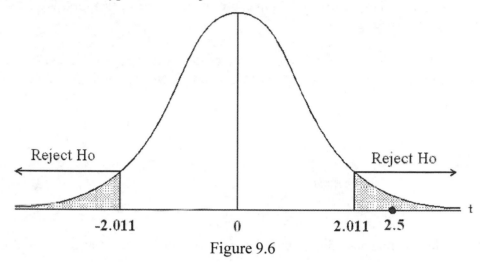

Figure 9.6

(a)   At 95% confidence, using the *p*-value value approach, test to determine whether or not the lathe is in perfect adjustment.

Answer: In part (a), the t statistic was determined to be $t = 2.5$. Since this situation represents a two-tailed test, the *p*-value is the sum of the area to the left of $t = -2.5$ and to the right of $t = 2.5$. Using the t distribution table for 48 degrees of freedom, we note the following.

Area in the upper tail	0.20	0.10	0.05	0.025	0.01	0.005
t value (48 df)	0.849	1.299	1.677	2.011	2.407	2.682

t = 2.5

In the above, we note that $t = 2.5$ is between 2.407 and 2.682. Hence, the area to the right of $t = 2.5$ is between 0.01 and 0.005. Since this is a two-tailed test, we double the values and conclude that the *p*-value is between 0.02 and .01. Since the *p*-value is less than $\alpha = 0.05$, the null hypothesis is rejected; and it is concluded that the machine is not adjusted properly.

9.   Automobiles manufactured by the Efficiency Company have been averaging 42 miles per gallon of gasoline in highway driving. It is believed that its new automobiles average **more** than 42 miles per gallon. An independent testing service road-tested 36 of the automobiles. The sample showed an average of 42.8 miles per gallon with a standard deviation of 1.2 miles per gallon.

(a)   With a 0.05 level of significance using the critical value approach, test to determine whether or not the new automobiles actually do average **more** than 42 miles per gallon.

(b)   What is the p-value associated with the sample results? What is your conclusion based on the p-value?

10.   A soft drink filling machine, when in perfect adjustment, fills bottles with 12 ounces of soft drink. A random sample of 49 bottles is selected, and the contents are measured. The sample yielded a mean content of 11.9 ounces with a standard deviation of 0.28 ounces.

(a)   With a 0.05 level of significance using the critical value approach, test to see if the machine is in perfect adjustment.

(b)   Repeat the test using the p-value approach.

11. A producer of various kinds of batteries has been producing "D" size batteries with a life expectancy of 87 hours. Due to an improved production process, management believes that there has been an increase in the life expectancy of their "D" size batteries. A sample of 36 batteries showed an average life of 88.5 hours. Assume from past information that it is known that the *standard deviation of the population* is 9 hours.

(a)   At 99% confidence using the critical value approach, test management's belief.

(b)   What is the *p*-value associated with the sample results? What is your conclusion based on the *p*-value?

12. In the past, the average age of evening students at a local college has been 21. A sample of 49 evening students was selected in order to determine whether the average age of the evening students has increased. The average age of the students in the sample was 23 with a standard deviation of 3.5.

(a)   At 90% confidence using the critical value approach, determine whether or not there has been an increase in the average age of the evening students.

(b)   Repeat the test using the *p*-value approach.

13.   A tire manufacturer has been producing tires with an average life expectancy of 26,000 miles. Now the company is advertising that its **new** tires' life expectancy has increased. In order to test the legitimacy of the advertising campaign, an independent testing agency tested a sample of 6 of their tires and has provided the following data.

**Life Expectancy
(In Thousands of Miles)**

28
27
25
28
29
25

(a)   Determine the mean and the standard deviation.

(b)   At 99% confidence using the critical value approach, test to determine whether or not the tire company is using legitimate advertising. Assume the population is normally distributed.

(c)   Repeat the test using the p-value approach.

14. The Department of Economic and Community Development (DECD) reported that in 2013 the average number of new jobs created per county was 450. The department also provided the following information regarding a sample of 5 counties in 2014.

County	New Jobs Created In 2014
Bradley	410
Rhea	480
Marion	407
Grundy	428
Sequatchie	400

(a)   Compute the sample average and the standard deviation for 2014.

(b)   We want to determine whether there has been a **significant decrease** in the average number of jobs created. Provide the null and the alternative hypotheses.

(c)   Compute the test statistic.

(d)   Compute the *p*-value and at 95% confidence, test the hypotheses. Assume the population is normally distributed.

Solved Problem

*15.   There have been indications that less than 12% of all CEO's have advanced college degrees. In a sample of 800 CEO's, 80 had advanced college degrees.

(a)   At 95% confidence using the critical value approach, test to determine whether or not the percentage of CEO's who have advanced degrees is ***significantly less*** than 12%.

Answer: The null and the alternative hypotheses are

$$H_o: \ p_o \geq 0.12$$
$$H_a: \ p_o < 0.12 \ \text{(The proportion is significantly less than 12\%)}$$

The standard error of the proportion can be determined as

$$\sigma_{\bar{p}} = \sqrt{\frac{p_o\,(1 - p_o)}{n}} = \sqrt{\frac{0.12\,(1 - 0.12)}{800}} = 0.0115 \ \text{(rounded)}$$

The null hypothesis will be rejected if the test statistic $Z < -Z_\alpha$, where

$$Z = \frac{\bar{p} - p}{\sigma_{\bar{p}}}$$

In the sample of 800 CEO's, only 80 had advanced degrees. Therefore, the sample proportion is

$$\bar{p} = \frac{80}{800} = 0.10$$

Now we can compute the test statistic Z as

$$Z = \frac{\bar{p} - p}{\sigma_{\bar{p}}} = \frac{0.10 - 0.12}{0.0115} = -1.74$$

From Table 1 of the Appendix, we read $Z_\alpha = Z_{.05} = -1.64$. Since $-1.74 < -1.64$, the null hypothesis is rejected. Therefore, we conclude that there is sufficient evidence to indicate that the percentage of the CEO's who have advanced degrees is significantly less than 12%. Figure 9.7 shows the region where the null hypothesis is rejected.

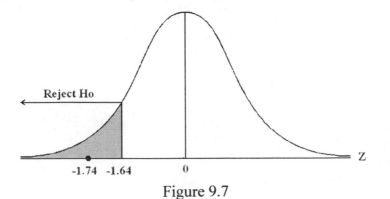

Figure 9.7

(b)　At 95% confidence using the *p*-value approach, test the hypotheses given above in part (a).

Answer:　The test statistic Z was computed in part (a) as $Z = -1.74$.　The *p*-value is the probability that Z is less than $Z = -1.74$.　Using the table of areas under the normal distribution, the area to the left of $Z = -1.74$ is 0.0409, which is the *p*-value.　Since the *p*-value $= 0.0409 < \alpha = 0.05$, the null hypothesis is rejected and it is concluded that the proportion is significantly less than 12%.

16.　An insurance company that currently only carries automobile insurance is planning to introduce homeowners' insurance to its customers.　Management has decided that it will introduce the homeowners' insurance if *more* than 85% of its current customers indicate that they will purchase the new insurance.　A random sample of 400 customers was selected and 348 customers indicated that they would purchase the homeowners' insurance.

(a)　Using $\alpha = .02$, do you recommend that the company introduce the homeowners' insurance?　Use the critical value approach.

(b)　Compute the *p*-value.

17.　One thousand numbers are selected randomly; 440 were odd numbers.　At 95% confidence using the critical value approach, determine whether the proportion of odd numbers is significantly different from 50%.

18.   In the last presidential election, a national survey company claimed that more than 56% of all registered voters voted for the Republican candidate. In a random sample of 200 registered voters, 116 voted for the Republican candidate.

(a)   Use $\alpha = 0.05$ and the critical value approach to test the survey company's claim.

(b)   Compute the p-value.

19.   An automobile manufacturer stated that it would be willing to mass produce electrically powered cars if more than 30% of potential buyers indicate they would purchase the newly designed electric cars. In a sample of 500 potential buyers, 160 indicated that they would buy such a product. Should the manufacturer produce the new electrically powered cars? Use the critical value approach, and let $\alpha = 0.05$.

20.   On graduation day at a large university, among a random sample of 60 graduates, 12 indicated that they had changed their major at least one time during their course of study. The records office believes that less than 25% of all its graduates change their major.

(a)   Do the sample results support the records office's belief? Use a 0.01 level of significance and the critical value approach.

(b)   Compute the p-value.

SELF-TESTING QUESTIONS

In the following multiple choice questions, circle the correct answer. An answer key is provided following the questions.

1.   In hypothesis testing, the hypothesis which is tentatively assumed to be true is called the
a)   correct hypothesis
b)   null hypothesis
c)   alternative hypothesis
d)   level of significance

2.   When the null hypothesis has been true, but the sample information has resulted in the rejection of the null, a _____ has been made.
a)   level of significance
b)   Type II error
c)   critical value
d)   Type I error

3.   The maximum probability of a Type I error that the decision maker will tolerate is called the
a)   level of significance
b)   critical value
c)   decision value
d)   probability value

4.   Which notation is used to represent the null hypothesis?
a) H_1
b) H_a
c) H_o
d) H_n

5.   A Type II error is the error of
a)   accepting H_o when it is false
b)   accepting H_o when it is true
c)   rejecting H_o when it is false
d)   rejecting H_o when it is true

6.   For setting the decision rule when the standard deviation of the sample is known and the sample is very small and if it is reasonable to assume that the population is normal, we use the
a)   t distribution with $n - 2$ degrees of freedom
b)   t distribution with $n - 1$ degrees of freedom
c)   t distribution with $n + 1$ degrees of freedom
d)   t distribution with n degrees of freedom

7.   A hypothesis test in which rejection of the null hypothesis occurs for values of the point estimator in either tail of the sampling distribution is called
a)   the null hypothesis
b)   the alternative hypothesis
c)   a one-tailed test
d)   a two-tailed test

Exhibit 9-1
The ABC Company claims that the batteries it produces have useful lives of more than 100 hours, with a known standard deviation (of the population) of 20 hours. A test is undertaken to test the validity of this claim.

8.   The correct set of hypotheses for this test is
a) H_o: $\mu = 100$
      H_a: $\mu \neq 100$

b) H_o: $\mu \geq 100$
      H_a: $\mu < 100$

c) H_o: $\mu \leq 100$
      H_a: $\mu > 100$

d) H_o: $\mu > 100$
      H_a: $\mu \leq 100$

9.   Refer to Exhibit 9-1. A sample of 64 batteries had an average useful life of 110 hours. The test statistic has a value of
a)   -4
b)   32
c)   4
d)   10

10.   Refer to Exhibit 9-1. With a 0.05 level of significance, the proper decision is
a)   do not reject H_o and conclude the claim is correct
b)   do not reject H_o and conclude the claim is false
c)   reject H_o and conclude the claim is correct
d)   reject H_o and conclude the claim is false

11. The average monthly income of recent business major graduates was reported to be $2,800. It is hypothesized that a recession has **reduced** the average income. The correct set of hypotheses is

a) H_0: $\mu < 2800$
   H_a: $\mu \geq 2800$

b) H_0: $\mu \geq 2800$
   H_a: $\mu < 2800$

c) H_0: $\mu > 2800$
   H_a: $\mu \leq 2800$

d) H_0: $\mu \leq 2800$
   H_a: $\mu \geq 2800$

12. The average life expectancy of Strong tires has been 30,000 miles. Because of improved processing, it is believed that the average life has **increased**. The correct set of hypotheses for testing this belief is

a) H_0: $\mu \leq 30,000$
   H_a: $\mu > 30,000$

b) H_0: $\mu \geq 30,000$
   H_a: $\mu < 30,000$

c) H_0: $\mu < 30,000$
   H_a: $\mu \geq 30,000$

d) H_0: $\mu > 30,000$
   H_a: $\mu \leq 30,000$

13. The level of significance is the
a) maximum allowable probability of Type II error
b) maximum allowable probability of Type I error
c) same as the confidence coefficient
d) same as the *p*-value

14. A Type II error is committed when
a) a true alternative hypothesis is mistakenly rejected
b) a true null hypothesis is mistakenly rejected
c) the sample size has been too small
d) a *t* distribution has been used instead of Z

15.   The error of rejecting a true null hypothesis is
a)   a Type I error
b)   a Type II error
c)   can be either a or b, depending on the situation
d)   committed when not enough information is available

16.   In hypothesis testing, α is
a)   the probability of committing a Type II error
b)   the probability of committing a Type I error
c)   the probability of either a Type I or Type II, depending on the hypothesis to be tested
d) $1 - \beta$

17.   In hypothesis testing, β is
a)   the probability of committing a Type II error
b)   the probability of committing a Type I error
c)   the probability of either a Type I or Type II, depending on the hypothesis to be tested
d) $1 - \alpha$

18.   When testing the following hypotheses at an α level of significance,
      H_o: $p \leq 0.7$
      H_a: $p > 0.7$
the null hypothesis will be rejected if the test statistic Z is
a) $Z > Z_\alpha$
b) $Z < Z_\alpha$
c) $Z < -Z_\alpha$
d) $Z < 0$

19.   Which of the following does **not** need to be known in order to compute the *p*-value?
a)   knowledge of whether the test is one-tailed or two-tailed
b)   the value of the test statistic
c)   the level of significance
d)   sample size

20.   If the level of significance of a hypothesis test is raised from .01 to .1, the probability of a Type II error
a)   will increase from .01 to .05
b)   will not change
c)   will decrease
d)   will increase

ANSWERS TO THE SELF-TESTING QUESTIONS

1. b
2. d
3. a
4. c
5. a
6. b
7. d
8. c
9. c
10. c
11. b
12. a
13. b
14. a
15. a
16. b
17. a
18. a
19. c
20. c

ANSWERS TO CHAPTER NINE EXERCISES

4.   (a) H_o: $\mu \leq \$110,000$

        H_a: $\mu > \$110,000$

  (b) $Z = 2.5$

  (c)   *p*-value = 0.0062

        Since the *p*-value = 0.0062 < 0.05, reject H_o. Therefore, there has been a significant increase.

5.   (a) $Z = -1.8$

  (b)   *p*-value = 0.0359 < 0.063, reject H_o

  (c)   test statistic $Z = -1.8 < Z_{.063} = -1.53$, reject H_o

6.   (a) H_o: $\mu = 58$

        H_a: $\mu \neq 58$

  (b) $Z = -2.6$

  (c)   *p*-value = 0.0094 (Hint: 2 tail) < $\alpha = 0.03$, reject H_o. There has been a significant change in the average fee.

  (d) $Z = -2.6 < Z_{.03} = -2.17$, reject H_o

9.   (a) H_o: $\mu \leq 42$

        H_a: $\mu > 42$

        Since $t = 4.0 > 1.690$, reject H_o and conclude that the new cars average more than 42 miles per gallon.

  (b)   *p*-value < 0.005, therefore reject H_o (area to the right of $t = 4.0$ is almost zero)

10.   (a) H_o: $\mu = 12$

        H_a: $\mu \neq 12$

        Since $t = -2.5 < -2.011$, reject H_o and conclude that the machine is not perfectly adjusted.

  (b)   *p*-value is between .01 and .02 (two-tailed); reject H_o

11.   (a) H_o: $\mu \leq 87$

        H_a: $\mu > 87$

        Since $Z = 1 < 2.33$, do not reject H_o and conclude that there is insufficient evidence to support the corporation's claim.

  (b)   *p*-value > 0.1587; therefore do not reject H_o

12. (a) H_o: $\mu \leq 21$

   H_a: $\mu > 21$

   Since $t = 4 > 1.299$, reject H_o and conclude that there has been an increase in the evening students' average age. (Hint: The standard deviation of the *population* is *not* known.)

   (b) *p*-value is almost zero ($< .005$); reject H_o

13. (a) $\bar{x} = 27$, s $= 1.67$

   (b) H_o: $\mu \leq 26000$

   H_a: $\mu > 26000$

   Since $t = 1.47 < 3.365$, do not reject H_o and conclude that there is insufficient evidence to support the manufacturer's claim.

   (c) *p*-value $> .1$; do not reject H_o

14 (a) $\bar{x} = 425$ and s $= 32.44$ (rounded)

   (b) H_o: $\mu \geq 450$

   H_a: $\mu < 450$

   (c) Test statistic $t = -1.724$

   (d) *P*-value is between 0.05 and 0.1; do not reject H_o. There is no evidence of significant decrease.

16. (a) H_o: $p \leq 0.85$

   H_a: $p > 0.85$

   Since $Z = 1.12 < 2.05$, do not reject H_o. Therefore, you should not recommend introducing homeowners insurance.

   (b) *p*-value $= 0.1314$

17. H_o: $p = 0.5$

   H_a: $p \neq 0.5$

   Since $Z = -3.79 < -1.96$, reject H_o and conclude that the proportion of odd numbers is significantly different from 50%.

18. (a) H_o: $p \leq 0.56$

   H_a: $p > 0.56$

   Since $Z = 0.57 < 1.64$, do not reject H_o and conclude that there is insufficient evidence to support the survey company's claim.

   (b) *p*-value $= 0.2843$

19. H_o: $p \le 0.3$
      H_a: $p > 0.3$
      Since Z = 0.98 < 1.64, do not reject H_o and conclude that there is insufficient
      evidence to support the production of the electric cars.

20.   (a) H_o: $p \ge 0.25$
            H_a: $p < 0.25$
            Since Z = -0.89 > -2.33, do not reject H_o and, therefore, there is insufficient
            evidence to support the records office's belief.
      (b)   0.1867

CHAPTER TEN

STATISTICAL INFERENCE ABOUT MEANS AND PROPORTIONS WITH TWO POPULATIONS

CHAPTER OUTLINE AND REVIEW

This chapter discusses the determination of an interval estimate and the testing of a hypothesis where two populations are involved. The main topics of study are inferences about the differences between means and also the differences between proportions of two populations. Some of the new terminology for these topics includes the following.

Independent Samples are samples in which the elements of the sample from one population are selected independently of the elements of a second sample from a second population.

Matched Samples (Paired samples) are samples in which the data value in one sample is matched with a corresponding data value in the second sample. In other words, subjects under study are the same in both samples.

Pooled Estimator of p is a weighted average of the two sample proportions that is obtained by averaging (pooling) the two sample proportions $\bar{p}_1$ and $\bar{p}_2$.

CHAPTER FORMULAS

> **Inferences About the Difference Between Two Population Means**
> **(μ_1 - μ_2): σ_1 and σ_2 Known**

Point Estimator of the Difference Between the Means of Two Populations

$$\bar{x}_1 - \bar{x}_2 \tag{10.1}$$

Standard Error of $\bar{x}_1 - \bar{x}_2$

(The Standard Deviation of the sampling distribution of $\bar{x}_1 - \bar{x}_2$)

$$\sigma_{\bar{x}_1-\bar{x}_2} = \sqrt{\frac{\sigma_1^2}{n_1} + \frac{\sigma_2^2}{n_2}} \tag{10.2}$$

I. **Interval Estimate of the Difference Between the Means of Two Populations**

$$\bar{x}_1 - \bar{x}_2 \pm Z_{\alpha/2} \sqrt{\frac{\sigma_1^2}{n_1} + \frac{\sigma_2^2}{n_2}} \tag{10.4}$$

Margin of Error = $Z_{\alpha/2} \cdot \sigma_{\bar{x}_1-\bar{x}_2} = Z_{\alpha/2} \sqrt{\frac{\sigma_1^2}{n_1} + \frac{\sigma_2^2}{n_2}}$ (10.3)

II. **Hypothesis Testing (Means), Independent Samples**

Test Statistic $Z = \dfrac{(\bar{x}_1 - \bar{x}_2) - D_0}{\sigma_{\bar{x}_1-\bar{x}_2}} = \dfrac{(\bar{x}_1 - \bar{x}_2) - D_0}{\sqrt{\dfrac{\sigma_1^2}{n_1} + \dfrac{\sigma_2^2}{n_2}}}$ (10.5)

D_0 is the hypothesized difference between μ_1 and μ_2. In most situations, $D_0 = 0$.

Decision Rules for *P*-Value Approach

> **When Using the *P*-Value Approach, In All Cases Reject H₀ if *P*-Value $\leq \alpha$**

CHAPTER FORMULAS
(Continued)

Decision Rules for Critical Value Approach

Lower one-tailed test of the form	Upper one-tailed test of the form	Two-tailed test of the form
H_O: $\mu_1 - \mu_2 \geq D_0$ H_a: $\mu_1 - \mu_2 < D_0$	H_O: $\mu_1 - \mu_2 \leq D_0$ H_a: $\mu_1 - \mu_2 > D_0$	H_O: $\mu_1 - \mu_2 = D_0$ H_a: $\mu_1 - \mu_2 \neq D_0$
Reject H_O if: $Z \leq -Z_\alpha$	Reject H_O if: $Z \geq Z_\alpha$	Reject H_O if: $Z \leq -Z_{\alpha/2}$ or $Z \geq Z_{\alpha/2}$

Inferences About the Difference Between Two Population Means
(μ_1 - μ_2): σ_1 and σ_2 Unknown

I.   **Interval Estimate of the Difference Between the Means of Two Populations**

$$(\bar{x}_1 - \bar{x}_2) \pm t_{\alpha/2}\sqrt{\frac{S_1^2}{n_1} + \frac{S_2^2}{n_2}} \tag{10.6}$$

II. **Hypothesis Testing (Means), Independent Samples**

$$\textbf{Test Statistic } t = \frac{(\bar{x}_1 - \bar{x}_2) - D_0}{\sqrt{\frac{S_1^2}{n_1} + \frac{S_2^2}{n_2}}} \tag{10.8}$$

The degrees of freedom for t are given by (10.7)

$$df = \frac{\left(\frac{S_1^2}{n_1} + \frac{S_2^2}{n_2}\right)^2}{\frac{1}{n_1-1}\left(\frac{S_1^2}{n_1}\right)^2 + \frac{1}{n_2-1}\left(\frac{S_2^2}{n_2}\right)^2} \tag{10.7}$$

Decision rules are the same as those given above, substituting t for Z.

CHAPTER FORMULAS
(Continued)

If it can be assumed that the variances of the two populations are equal, then

Test Statistic $t = \dfrac{(\bar{x}_1 - \bar{x}_2) - D_0}{S_p \sqrt{\dfrac{1}{n_1} + \dfrac{1}{n_2}}}$

Where the *pooled sample variance* $S_p^2 = \dfrac{(n_1 - 1)S_1^2 + (n_2 - 1)S_2^2}{n_1 + n_2 - 2}$

**Inferences About the Difference Between Two Population Means:
Matched Samples**

I.   **Interval Estimate**

$$\bar{d} \pm t_{\alpha/2} \frac{S_d}{\sqrt{n}}$$

II.   **Hypothesis Test**

Test statistic $t = \dfrac{\bar{d} - \mu_d}{s_d / \sqrt{n}}$ (10.9)

where $S_d = \sqrt{\dfrac{\Sigma(d_i - \bar{d})^2}{n - 1}}$

**Inferences About the Difference Between Two Population
Proportions**

Point Estimate for the Difference Between the Proportions of Two Populations:

$$\bar{p}_1 - \bar{p}_2$$ (10.10)

Standard deviation: $\sigma_{\bar{p}_1 - \bar{p}_2} = \sqrt{\dfrac{p_1(1 - p_1)}{n_1} + \dfrac{p_2(1 - p_2)}{n_2}}$ (10.11)

CHAPTER FORMULAS
(Continued)

$$\text{Margin of Error} = Z_{\alpha/2}\sqrt{\frac{\overline{p}_1(1-\overline{p}_1)}{n_1} + \frac{\overline{p}_2(1-\overline{p}_2)}{n_2}} \tag{10.12}$$

I.   Interval Estimate of the Difference Between the Proportions of Two Populations

$$\overline{p}_1 - \overline{p}_2 \pm Z_{\alpha/2}\sqrt{\frac{\overline{p}_1(1-\overline{p}_1)}{n_1} + \frac{\overline{p}_2(1-\overline{p}_2)}{n_2}} \tag{10.13}$$

II.   Hypothesis Tests about $p_1 - p_2$

$$\text{Test Statistic} \quad Z = \frac{\left(\overline{p}_1 - \overline{p}_2\right)}{\sqrt{\overline{p}(1-\overline{p})\left(\dfrac{1}{n_1} + \dfrac{1}{n_2}\right)}} \tag{10.16}$$

and assuming $p_1 = p_2$, the pooled proportion $\overline{p}$ is computed as

$$\text{where} \quad \overline{p} = \frac{n_1\overline{p}_1 + n_2\overline{p}_2}{n_1 + n_2} \tag{10.15}$$

The Three Forms of Hypothesis Tests

Lower one-tailed test of the form	Upper one-tailed test of the form	Two-tailed test of the form
H_O: $p_1 - p_2 \geq 0$	H_O: $p_1 - p_2 \leq 0$	H_O: $p_1 - p_2 = 0$
H_a: $p_1 - p_2 < 0$	H_a: $p_1 - p_2 > 0$	H_a: $p_1 - p_2 \neq 0$
Reject H_O if: $Z \leq -Z_\alpha$	Reject H_O if: $Z \geq Z_\alpha$	Reject H_O if: $Z \leq -Z_{\alpha/2}$ or $Z \geq Z_{\alpha/2}$

EXERCISES

Solved Problem

*1.   The management of a department store is interested in estimating the difference between the mean credit purchases made by customers using the store's credit card versus those customers using a national major credit card. Information regarding credit sales is shown below.

Store's Card	Major Credit Card
$n_1 = 64$	$n_2 = 49$
$\bar{x}_1 = \$140$	$\bar{x}_2 = \$125$
$\sigma_1 = \$10$	$\sigma_2 = \$8$

(a)   Develop a point estimate for the difference between the mean purchases of the users of the two credit cards.

Answer: The point estimate for the difference between the means of the two populations is $\bar{x}_1 - \bar{x}_2 = 140 - 125 = \$15$.

(b)   Provide a 95% confidence interval for the difference between the average purchases of the customers using the two different credit cards.

Answer: The interval estimate for the difference between the means of the two populations when σ_1 and σ_2 are known is given by

$$\bar{x}_1 - \bar{x}_2 \pm Z_{\alpha/2} \sqrt{\frac{\sigma_1^2}{n_1} + \frac{\sigma_2^2}{n_2}}$$

At 95% confidence, $z_{\alpha/2} = z_{.025} = 1.96$. Thus, the interval estimate is

$$\bar{x}_1 - \bar{x}_2 \pm Z_{\alpha/2} \sqrt{\frac{\sigma_1^2}{n_1} + \frac{\sigma_2^2}{n_2}} = (140 - 125) \pm (1.96) \sqrt{\frac{10^2}{64} + \frac{8^2}{49}} = 15 \pm 3.32$$

Therefore, at 95% confidence, the interval estimate for the difference in the mean purchases is from $11.68 to $18.32. Another way to denote this interval is shown below:

$$\$11.68 < \mu_1 - \mu_2 < \$18.32$$

2. A potential investor conducted a 144 day survey in each theater in order to determine the difference between the average daily attendance at the North Mall and South Mall theaters. The North Mall Theater averaged 630 patrons per day; while the South Mall Theater averaged 598 patrons per day. From past information, it is known that the variance for North Mall is 1,000; while the variance for the South Mall is 1304. Develop a 95% confidence interval for the difference between the average daily attendance at the two theaters.

3. The business manager of a local health clinic is interested in estimating the difference between the fees for extended office visits in their center and the fees of a newly opened group practice. She gathered the following information regarding the two offices.

Health Clinic	Group Practice
$n_1 = 70$ visits	$n_2 = 60$ visits
$\bar{x}_1 = \$35$	$\bar{x}_2 = \$30$
$\sigma_1 = \$8$	$\sigma_2 = \$9$

Develop a 95% confidence interval for the difference between the average fees of the two offices.

Solved Problem

*4.   In order to determine whether or not there is a significant difference between the hourly wages of two companies, the following data have been accumulated.

Company 1	**Company 2**
$n_1 = 80$	$n_2 = 60$
$\bar{x}_1 = \$10.80$	$\bar{x}_2 = \$10.00$
$\sigma_1 = \$2.00$	$\sigma_2 = \$1.50$

Is there any significant difference between the hourly wages of the two companies? Let $\alpha = 0.05$.

Answer: The hypotheses of interest are

H_o: $\mu_1 - \mu_2 = 0$

H_a: $\mu_1 - \mu_2 \neq 0$

These hypotheses reflect a two-tailed test because we are looking for a difference between groups.

The test statistic for this situation is

$$Z = \frac{(\bar{x}_1 - \bar{x}_2) - D_o}{\sqrt{\dfrac{\sigma_1^2}{n_1} + \dfrac{\sigma_2^2}{n_2}}} = \frac{(10.80 - 10.00) - 0}{\sqrt{\dfrac{(2.0)^2}{80} + \dfrac{(1.50)^2}{60}}} = 2.7$$

Now with the above test statistic ($Z = 2.7$), we can compute the *p*-value. The area to the left of $Z = 2.7$ (from the standard normal distribution table) is 0.9965. Therefore, the area in the upper end of the distribution is $1.0 - 0.9965 = 0.0035$. Since this situation represents a two-tailed test, the area in the upper tail of the distribution is doubled yielding *p*-value $= 2(0.0035) = 0.007$. Now we can use the decision rule for a two-tailed hypothesis test, which is reject H_o if the *p*-value $\leq \alpha$. Since the *p*-value of 0.007 is less than α of 0.05, the null hypothesis is rejected and it can be concluded that there is a significant difference between the hourly wages of the two companies.

5. The Commonwealth of the Bahamas is a collection of many islands lying in the Atlantic Ocean. Tourism has become the most important industry of the islands. Two of the most visited islands are New Province and Grand Bahamas. A random sample of 36 tourists in Grand Bahamas showed that they spent an average of $1,860 (in a week), and a sample of 64 tourists in New Province showed that they spent an average of $1,935 (in a week). From past information, it is known that the standard deviation for Grand Bahamas is $126 and the standard deviation for New Province is $138. Is there any significant difference between the average expenditures of those who visited the two islands? Let $\alpha = 0.05$.

6. Two universities in your state decided to administer a comprehensive examination to the recipients of M.B.A. degrees. A random sample of M.B.A. recipients was selected from each institution and they were given the test. The sample sizes, the average test scores, and the standard deviations of the scores for each institution are shown below.

Central University	**Northern University**
$n_1 = 32$	$n_2 = 32$
$\bar{x}_1 = 83$	$\bar{x}_2 = 77$
$\sigma_1 = 13$	$\sigma_2 = 14$

Test at a 0.05 level of significance to determine if there is a significant difference in the average test scores of the students from the two universities.

7.   A random sample of 90 days in Tennessee and Georgia revealed the following information about the rainfall.

Tennessee	Georgia
$\bar{x}_1 = 5.6$ inches	$\bar{x}_2 = 4.9$ inches
$\sigma_1 = 0.5$ inches	$\sigma_2 = 0.4$ inches

Test at a 0.1 level of significance to determine if there is a significant difference in the average rainfall of the two states.

Solved Problem

*8. In order to estimate the difference between the average daily sales of two branches of a department store, the following data has been gathered.

	Downtown Store	**North Mall Store**
Sample size	$n_1 = 23$ days	$n_2 = 26$ days
Sample mean (in $1,000)	$\overline{x}_1 = 37$	$\overline{x}_2 = 34$
Sample standard deviation (in $1,000)	$S_1 = 4$	$S_2 = 5$

(a) Develop a 95% confidence interval for the difference between the two population means.

Answer: Since the standard deviations of the two populations (σ_1 and σ_2) are unknown, the interval estimate for the difference between the means of the two populations is determined by the following expression.

$$\left(\overline{x}_1 - \overline{x}_2\right) \pm t_{\alpha/2} \sqrt{\frac{S_1^2}{n_1} + \frac{S_2^2}{n_2}}$$

The degrees of freedom for $t_{\alpha/2}$ in the above expression are determined as

$$df = \frac{\left(\dfrac{S_1^2}{n_1} + \dfrac{S_2^2}{n_2}\right)^2}{\dfrac{1}{n_1 - 1}\left(\dfrac{S_1^2}{n_1}\right)^2 + \dfrac{1}{n_2 - 1}\left(\dfrac{S_2^2}{n_2}\right)^2} = \frac{\left(\dfrac{4^2}{23} + \dfrac{5^2}{26}\right)^2}{\dfrac{1}{23 - 1}\left(\dfrac{4^2}{23}\right)^2 + \dfrac{1}{26 - 1}\left(\dfrac{5^2}{26}\right)^2} = 46.56$$

The non-integer value of the degrees of freedom (46.56) is rounded to the lower integer value of 46. Now, we can look up the t value, at 46 degrees of freedom, which is $t_{\alpha/2} = t_{.025} = 2.013$. Thus, the interval estimate becomes

$$\left(\overline{x}_1 - \overline{x}_2\right) \pm t_{\alpha/2} \sqrt{\frac{S_1^2}{n_1} + \frac{S_2^2}{n_2}} = (37 - 34) \pm (2.013)\sqrt{\frac{4^2}{23} + \frac{5^2}{26}} = 3 \pm 2.591$$

The point estimate of the difference is 3 and the margin of error is 2.591, indicating the interval will be from 3 - 2.591 = 0.409 to 3 + 2.591 = 5.591. The above indicates that at 95% confidence the interval estimate for the difference in the average sales of the two stores is from $409 to $5,591. This may also be written as $409 \le \mu_1 - \mu_2 \le $5,591$.

(b)   At 95% confidence test to determine if the average daily sales of the Downtown Store (μ_1) is significantly **more** than the average sales of the North Mall Store (μ_2).

Answer: The hypotheses of interest are

$$H_o: \ \mu_1 - \mu_2 \leq 0$$

$$H_a: \ \mu_1 - \mu_2 > 0$$

Since the standard deviations of the two populations (σ_1 and σ_2) are unknown, the t statistic is computed as follows.

$$t = \frac{(\bar{x}_1 - \bar{x}_2) - D_0}{\sqrt{\dfrac{S_1^2}{n_1} + \dfrac{S_2^2}{n_2}}} = \frac{(37 - 34) - 0}{\sqrt{\dfrac{4^2}{23} + \dfrac{5^2}{26}}} = 2.33$$

In part a of this problem, it was determined that we have 46 degrees of freedom. Now, looking in the t table in the 46 degrees of freedom row, we note the following.

Area in the upper tail	0.20	0.10	0.05	0.025	0.01	0.005
t value (46 df)	0.850	1.300	1.679	2.013	2.410	2.687

$$t = 2.33$$

With an upper-tail test, the *p*-value is the area in the upper tail to the right of 2.33. From the above results, we note that the *p*-value is between .025 and .01. Since the *p*-value is less than $\alpha = 0.05$, the null hypothesis is rejected; and, therefore, we conclude that the average daily sales of the Downtown Store is significantly more than the average daily sales of the North Mall Store.

9.   In order to estimate the difference between the yearly incomes of marketing managers in the East and West of the United States, the following information was gathered.

East	West
East	**West**

$n_1 = 40$ $n_2 = 45$

$\bar{x}_1 = 72$ (in \$1,000) $\bar{x}_2 = 78$ (in \$1,000)

$s_1 = 6$ (in \$1,000) $s_2 = 8$ (in \$1,000)

(a)   Develop an interval estimate for the difference between the average yearly incomes of the marketing managers in the East and West. Let $\alpha = 0.05$.

(b)   At 95% confidence, use the *p*-value approach and test to determine if the average yearly income of marketing managers in the East is significantly different from the West.

*10. Two of the major automobile manufacturers have produced compact cars with the same size engines. We are interested in determining whether or not there is a significant difference in the MPG (miles per gallon) of the two models of automobiles. A random sample of 8 cars from each manufacturer is selected, and 8 drivers are selected to drive each automobile for a specified distance. The following data show the results of the test.

Driver	MPG Model A	MPG Model B	Difference in MPG d_i	$(d_i - \bar{d})^2$
1	29	24	5	16
2	24	22	2	1
3	26	28	-2	9
4	24	23	1	0
5	25	24	1	0
6	27	26	1	0
7	30	28	2	1
8	25	27	-2	9
			$\Sigma d_i = 8$	$\Sigma(d_i - \bar{d})^2 = 36$

(a)   At 95% confidence, test to determine if there is a difference in the average MPG of the two models.

Answer: In this situation, we have a matched sample design, where each driver provides a pair of data values, one value for the MPG of model A and another value for the MPG of model B. Thus, we have 8 data values, namely, the differences between the MPG's of the two models, to analyze. (These differences are shown above in the fourth column marked d_i.) Now, we set our hypotheses:

$H_0: \mu_d = 0$ There is no difference between the MPG's of the two models.

$H_a: \mu_d \neq 0$ There is a difference between the MPG's of the two models.

Then, we calculate the mean for the differences as

$$\bar{d} = \frac{\Sigma d_i}{n} = \frac{8}{8} = 1.0$$

The standard deviation for the differences is determined as

$$s_d = \sqrt{\frac{\Sigma(d_i - \bar{d})^2}{n-1}}$$

The value of $\Sigma(d_i - \bar{d})^2 = 36$ is shown above on the bottom of the last column. Thus, the value of the standard deviation is

$$s_d = \sqrt{\frac{36}{8-1}} = 2.268$$

The test statistic is computed as

$$t = \frac{\bar{d} - \mu_d}{s_d/\sqrt{n}} = \frac{1.0 - 0}{2.268/\sqrt{8}} = 1.247$$

Now we can use this t value of 1.247 with $n - 1 = 8 - 1 = 7$ degrees of freedom to compute the *p*-value. From the t distribution table from the 7 degrees of freedom row, we have the following.

Area in the upper tail	0.20	0.10	0.05	0.025	0.01	0.005
t value (7 df)	0.896	1.415	1.895	2.365	2.998	3.499

t=1.247

Therefore, the area in the upper tail is between 0.1 and 0.2. Since this is a two-tailed test, we double these values and conclude that the *p*-value is between 0.2 and 0.4. Since the *p*-value is greater than $\alpha = 0.05$, the null hypothesis is not rejected; and therefore, we conclude that there is not sufficient evidence to indicate that there is any difference between the MPG's of the two models.

(b)   Provide a 95% confidence interval for μ_d.

Answer: The interval is computed as

$$\bar{d} \pm t_{\alpha/2} \frac{s_d}{\sqrt{n}} = 1 \pm (2.365) \frac{2.268}{\sqrt{8}} = 1 \pm 1.896$$

This indicates that the interval will be from -0.896 to 2.896, or $-0.896 \le \mu_1 - \mu_2 \le 2.896$

11.   A large corporation wants to determine whether or not the "typing efficiency" course given at a local college can increase the typing speeds of its word processing personnel. A sample of 6 typists is selected, and are sent to take the course. The typing speeds of the typists in words per minute (WPM) are shown below.

Typist	WPM Before the Course	WPM After the Course
1	65	68
2	60	62
3	61	66
4	63	66
5	64	67
6	65	67

(a)   Use $\alpha = 0.05$ and test to see if it can be concluded that taking the course will actually increase the average typing speeds of the typists. (Hint: This is a one-tailed test.)

(b)   Compute a 95% confidence interval for μ_d .

Solved Problem

*12. In a sample of 500 Chattanooga residents, 90 indicated they refinanced their home mortgages this year; while of a sample of 400 Atlanta residents, 44 indicated they refinanced this year. Determine a 95% confidence interval estimate for the difference between the **proportions** of the two populations.

Answer: The interval estimate for the difference between the proportion of the two populations is

$$\bar{p}_1 - \bar{p}_2 \pm Z_{\alpha/2}\sqrt{\frac{\bar{p}_1(1-\bar{p}_1)}{n_1} + \frac{\bar{p}_2(1-\bar{p}_2)}{n_2}}$$

First we need to calculate $\bar{p}_1 = \dfrac{90}{500} = 0.18$ and $\bar{p}_2 = \dfrac{44}{400} = 0.11$. Therefore, we determine the confidence interval as

$$\bar{p}_1 - \bar{p}_2 \pm Z_{\alpha/2}\sqrt{\frac{\bar{p}_1(1-\bar{p}_1)}{n_1} + \frac{\bar{p}_2(1-\bar{p}_2)}{n_2}} =$$

$$(0.18 - 0.11) \pm 1.96\sqrt{\frac{0.18(1-0.18)}{500} + \frac{0.11(1-0.11)}{400}} = 0.07 \pm (0.046)$$

Thus, the 95% confidence interval estimate for the difference in the proportion of the individuals who refinanced their mortgages in the two cities is 0.024 to 0.116.

13. From production line A, a sample of 200 items is selected at random; and it is determined that 16 items are defective. While in a sample of 300 items from production process B (which produces identical items to line A), there are 21 defective items. Determine a 95% confidence interval estimate for the difference between the proportions of defectives in the two lines.

14. Among a sample of 600 M.D.s (medical doctors) in Montana, there were 48 who indicated they make house calls. While among a sample of 500 M.D.s in Idaho, 25 said they make house calls. Determine a 95% interval estimate for the difference between the proportions of doctors who make house calls in the two states.

Solved Problem

*15. Refer to exercise *12. Use $\alpha = 0.1$ and test the hypothesis that claims that the proportion of the individuals who refinanced their home mortgages is the same for the two cities.

Answer: The hypotheses to be tested are

$$H_o: p_1 - p_2 = 0$$
$$H_a: p_1 - p_2 \neq 0$$

The pooled proportion is computed as

$$\bar{p} = \frac{n_1 \bar{p}_1 + n_2 \bar{p}_2}{n_1 + n_2} = \frac{(500)(0.18) + (400)(0.11)}{500 + 400} = 0.149$$

Then the test statistic Z is computed as

$$Z = \frac{(\bar{p}_1 - \bar{p}_2)}{\sqrt{\bar{p}(1-\bar{p})\left(\frac{1}{n_1} + \frac{1}{n_2}\right)}} = \frac{(0.18 - 0.11)}{\sqrt{(0.149)((1-0.149)\left(\frac{1}{500} + \frac{1}{400}\right)}} = 2.93$$

Now with the test statistic $Z = 2.93$, we can compute the *p*-value. Referring to the table of normal distribution, we note that the area to the left of $Z = 2.93$ is 0.9983. Therefore, the area in the upper tail of the distribution is $1.00 - 0.9983 = 0.0017$. Since this situation represents *a two-tailed test*, we double the area in the upper tail, which is 0.0017, hence obtaining a *p*-value = $2(.0017) = 0.0034$. Since this *p*-value (0.0034) is less than α of 0.1, *the null hypothesis is rejected*; and we conclude that there is a significant difference between the proportions of the individuals who refinanced their mortgages in the two cities.

16.   Refer to exercise 13. Use the *p*-value approach and test the hypothesis that the proportions of defectives in both lines are the same. Let $\alpha = 0.05$.

17.   Refer to exercise 14. Use the *p*-value approach and test the hypothesis that the proportions of house calls for the two states are the same. Let $\alpha = 0.05$.

SELF-TESTING QUESTIONS

In the following multiple choice questions, circle the correct answer. An answer key is provided following the questions.

1. An estimate of a population's variance that is based on the combination of two sample results is known as the
a) pooled standard deviation
b) matched variance
c) pooled variance estimate
d) pooled mean

2. If a hypothesis is rejected at the 3% level of significance,
a) it must also be rejected at the 2% level of significance
b) it must also be rejected at the 5% level of significance
c) it will sometimes be rejected and sometimes not be rejected at the 5% level of significance
d) an error has been made

3. To construct an interval estimate for matched samples, we must use a t distribution with
a) n degrees of freedom
b) n + 1 degrees of freedom
c) n + 2 degrees of freedom
d) n - 1 degrees of freedom

4. The null hypothesis that states that there is no significant difference between the means of two populations can be stated as
a) $\mu_1 - \mu_2 = 0$
b) $\mu_1 \geq \mu_2$
c) $\mu_1 - \mu_2 \leq 0$
d) $\mu_1 \neq \mu_2$

5. When each data value in one sample is matched with a corresponding data value in the other sample, the samples are known as
a) corresponding samples
b) matched samples
c) independent samples
d) matched means

6.   Assume we are interested in determining whether the proportion of voters planning to vote for Candidate A (P_A) is significantly **less** than the proportion of voters planning to vote for Candidate B (P_B). The correct set of hypotheses for testing the above is

a) H_0: $P_A - P_B \leq 0$
       H_a: $P_A - P_B > 0$

b) H_0: $P_A - P_B = 0$
       H_a: $P_A - P_B > 0$

c) H_0: $P_A - P_B \neq 0$
       H_a: $P_A - P_B = 0$

d) H_0: $P_A - P_B \geq 0$
       H_a: $P_A - P_B < 0$

7.   We want to test whether the average life expectancy of nonsmokers (μ_n) is significantly **more** than that of smokers (μ_s). The correct set of hypotheses for testing the above is

a) H_0: $\mu_n - \mu_s > 0$
       H_a: $\mu_n - \mu_s \leq 0$

b) H_0: $\mu_n - \mu_s \geq 0$
       H_a: $\mu_n - \mu_s < 0$

c) H_0: $\mu_n - \mu_s \leq 0$
       H_a: $\mu_n - \mu_s > 0$

d) H_0: $\mu_n - \mu_s < 0$
       H_a: $\mu_n - \mu_s \geq 0$

8.   If we are interested in testing whether the proportion of items in population 1 is larger than the proportion of items in population 2, the
a)   null hypothesis should state $P_1 - P_2 < 0$
b)   null hypothesis should state $P_1 - P_2 \geq 0$
c)   alternative hypothesis should state $P_1 - P_2 > 0$
d)   alternative hypothesis should state $P_1 - P_2 < 0$

9.   When developing an interval estimate for the difference between two sample means, with sample sizes of n_1 and n_2,
a) n_1 must be equal to n_2
b) n_1 must be smaller than n_2
c) n_1 must be larger than n_2
d) n_1 and n_2 can be of different sizes,

Exhibit 10-1
Salary information regarding male and female employees of a large company is shown below.

	Male	Female
Sample Size	64	36
Sample Mean Salary (in $1,000)	44	41
Population Variance (σ^2)	128	72

10.   Refer to Exhibit 10-1. The point estimate of the difference between the means of the two populations is
a)   -28
b)   3
c)   4
d)   -4

11.   Refer to Exhibit 10-1. The standard error for the difference between the two means is
a)   4
b)   7.46
c)   4.24
d)   2.0

12.   Refer to Exhibit 10-1. At 95% confidence, the margin of error is
a)   1.96
b)   1.645
c)   3.920
d)   2.000

13.   Refer to Exhibit 10-1. The 95% confidence interval for the difference between the means of the two populations is
a)   0 to 6.92
b)   -2 to 2
c)   -1.96 to 1.96
d)   -0.92 to 6.92

14. Refer to Exhibit 10-1. If you are interested in testing whether or not the average salary of males is significantly greater than that of females, the test statistic is
a) 2.0
b) 1.5
c) 1.96
d) 1.645

15. Refer to Exhibit 10-1. The *p*-value is
a) 0.0668
b) 0.0334
c) 1.336
d) 1.96

ANSWERS TO THE SELF-TESTING QUESTIONS

1. c
2. b
3. d
4. a
5. b
6. d
7. c
8. c
9. d
10. b
11. d
12. c
13. d
14. b
15. a

ANSWERS TO CHAPTER TEN EXERCISES

2. 24.16 to 39.84   (rounding: 24 to 40)

3. 2.051 to 7.949

5. H_o: $\mu_1 - \mu_2 = 0$
H_a: $\mu_1 - \mu_2 \neq 0$
$Z = -2.76$, p-value $= 2(.0029) = 0.0058 < \alpha = .05$, reject H_o and conclude that there is a significant difference between the average expenditures of those who visited the two islands.

6. H_o: $\mu_1 - \mu_2 = 0$
H_a: $\mu_1 - \mu_2 \neq 0$
$Z = 1.78$, p-value $= 2(1.0 - .9625) = 0.075 > \alpha = .05$, do not reject H_o and conclude that there is not sufficient evidence to indicate that there is a significant difference in the average test scores from the two universities.

7. H_o: $\mu_1 - \mu_2 = 0$
H_a: $\mu_1 - \mu_2 \neq 0$
$Z = 10.37$, p-value $= 0.0000 < \alpha - 0.1$, reject H_o and conclude that there is a significant difference in the average rainfall of the two states.

9. (a) -9.084 to -2.916
   (b) Test statistic $t = -3.937$ (df $= 80$), p-value $< .005$, reject H_o and conclude that there is a significant difference.

11. (a) H_o: $\mu_d \leq 0$
   H_a: $\mu_d > 0$
   $t = -6.708$, p-value $< .005$ which is less than $\alpha = .05$, reject H_o and conclude that taking the course will increase the typists' average typing speeds.
   (b) -4.15 to -1.85

13. -0.037 to 0.057

14. 0.001 to 0.059

16. H_o: $p_1 - p_2 = 0$
H_a: $p_1 - p_2 \neq 0$
Since $Z = 0.42$, p-value $= 2(1.0 - 0.6628) = 0.6744$, do not reject H_o and conclude that there is not sufficient evidence to indicate that there is a significant difference in the proportions of defectives in the two lines.

17. H_o: $p_1 - p_2 = 0$

H_a: $p_1 - p_2 \neq 0$

Since $Z = 1.99$, p-value $= 2(1.0 - 0.9767) = 0.0466 < \alpha = 0.05$, reject H_o and conclude that there is a significant difference in the proportions of house calls in the two states.

CHAPTER ELEVEN

INFERENCES ABOUT POPULATION VARIANCES

CHAPTER OUTLINE AND REVIEW

This chapter discusses how to make inferences about population variances. You will be introduced to two new distributions, namely, the "chi-square (χ^2)" distribution and the "F" distribution. For interval estimation and hypothesis testing concerning the variance of a single normal population, the chi-square distribution is used. When testing a hypothesis concerning the variance of two normal populations, the F distribution is used.

CHAPTER FORMULAS

Interval Estimate for a Population Variance

$$\frac{(n-1)S^2}{\chi^2_{\alpha/2}} \leq \sigma^2 \leq \frac{(n-1)S^2}{\chi^2_{(1-\alpha/2)}} \tag{11.7}$$

where χ^2 values are based on a chi-square distribution with (n - 1) degrees of freedom.

Tests of Hypothesis Regarding the Variance of a Single Population

---

Test Statistic: $\chi^2 = \dfrac{(n-1)S^2}{\sigma_o^2}$ $\tag{11.8}$

Decision Rules

Lower Tailed Test of the Form	Upper Tailed Test of the Form	Two-Tailed Test of the Form
$H_o:\ \sigma^2 \geq \sigma_o^2$ $H_a:\ \sigma^2 < \sigma_o^2$ Reject H_o if $\chi^2 \leq \chi^2_{(1-\alpha)}$	$H_o:\ \sigma^2 \leq \sigma_o^2$ $H_a:\ \sigma^2 > \sigma_o^2$ Reject H_o if $\chi^2 \geq \chi^2_\alpha$	$H_o:\ \sigma^2 = \sigma_o^2$ $H_a:\ \sigma^2 \neq \sigma_o^2$ Reject H_o if $\chi^2 \leq \chi^2_{(1-\alpha/2)}$ or $\quad$ if $\chi^2 \geq \chi^2_{\alpha/2}$
When Using the *P*-Value Approach, In All Cases Reject H_o if *P*-Value $\leq \alpha$		

CHAPTER FORMULAS
(Continued)

Tests of Hypothesis Regarding Variances of Two Populations

Test Statistic: $F = \dfrac{S_1^2}{S_2^2}$ (11.10)

Denote the population providing the larger sample variance as population 1.

The critical value of F is based on an F distribution with $(n_1 - 1)$ degrees of freedom for the numerator and $(n_2 - 1)$ degrees of freedom for the denominator.

Decision Rules

Lower Tailed Test of the Form	Two-Tailed Test of the Form
$H_o: \sigma_1^2 \le \sigma_2^2$ $H_a: \sigma_1^2 > \sigma_2^2$ Reject H_o if $F \ge F_\alpha$	$H_o: \sigma_1^2 = \sigma_2^2$ $H_a: \sigma_1^2 \ne \sigma_2^2$ Reject H_o if $F \ge F_{\alpha/2}$
When Using the *P*-Value Approach, In All Cases Reject H_o if *P*-Value $\le \alpha$	

EXERCISES

Solved Problem

*1. The manager of the service department of a local car dealership has noted that the service times for a sample of 15 new automobiles had a standard deviation of 4 minutes. Provide a 95% confidence interval estimate for the standard deviation of service times for all their new automobiles.

Answer: The interval estimate for a population variance is determined by

$$\frac{(n-1)S^2}{\chi^2_{\alpha/2}} \leq \sigma^2 \leq \frac{(n-1)S^2}{\chi^2_{(1-\alpha/2)}}$$

With a sample of 15, there are $(n - 1) = (15 - 1) = 14$ degrees of freedom. Thus, we can read the chi-square values from Table 3 of the Appendix as

$$\chi^2_{\alpha/2} = \chi^2_{.025} = 26.119$$

$$\chi^2_{(1-\alpha/2)} = \chi^2_{.975} = 5.629$$

Hence, the interval estimate is determined by using the following equation.

$$\frac{(n-1)S^2}{\chi^2_{\alpha/2}} \leq \sigma^2 \leq \frac{(n-1)S^2}{\chi^2_{(1-\alpha/2)}}$$

$$\frac{(15-1)(4)^2}{26.119} \leq \sigma^2 \leq \frac{(15-1)(4)^2}{5.629}$$

Computing the above yields the following interval for the variance of the population.

$$8.58 \leq \sigma^2 \leq 39.79 \text{ (rounded)}$$

Taking the square root of the above terms, we find the following 95% confidence interval estimate for the standard deviation of the population.

$$2.93 \leq \sigma < 6.31$$

2.   A random sample of 25 employees of a local utility firm showed that their monthly incomes had a sample standard deviation of $112. Provide a 90% confidence interval estimate for the standard deviation of the incomes for all the firm's employees.

3.   A random sample of 41 scores of students taking the ACT test showed a standard deviation of 8 points. Provide a 98% confidence interval estimate for the standard deviation of all the ACT test scores.

> **Solved Problem**

*4.   The producer of a certain medicine claims that its bottling equipment is very accurate and that the standard deviation of all its filled bottles is 0.1 ounce or less. A sample of 20 bottles showed a standard deviation of 0.11.

(a)   Does this sample result confirm the claim of the manufacturer? Use the critical value approach for this test. Use $\alpha = 0.05$.

Answer: The hypotheses to be tested are shown below. *Note:* $\sigma^2 = (0.1)^2 = 0.01$.

$$H_0: \; \sigma^2 \le 0.01$$
$$H_a: \; \sigma^2 > 0.01 \quad \text{(Claim is not true)}$$

For an upper one-tailed test about a population variance, the null hypothesis is rejected if the test statistic:

$$\chi^2 = \frac{(n-1)S^2}{\sigma_0^2} > \chi_\alpha^2$$

From Table 3 of the Appendix, we read χ_α^2 with $n - 1 = 20 - 1 = 19$ degrees of freedom as $\chi_{.05}^2 = 30.144$. With this as the critical value for the test, then the decision rule will be

Do not reject H_0 if $\chi^2 \le 30.144$
Reject H_0 if $\chi^2 > 30.144$

The test statistic χ^2 based on the sample information is computed as follows.

$$\chi^2 = \frac{(n-1)S^2}{\sigma_0^2} = \frac{(20-1)(0.11)^2}{(0.1)^2} = 22.99$$

Since $22.99 < 30.144$, the null hypothesis is not rejected; and we conclude that there is not sufficient evidence to reject the company's claim.

(b)   Use the *p*-value approach at 95% confidence to test the manufacturer's claim.

Answer: Since the chi-square distribution table does not contain sufficient detail, we will not be able to determine the exact value of the *p*-value. However, we can approximate its value with the same method we used for the t values. From the chi-square table in the Appendix for 19 degrees of freedom, we have the following.

Area in the Upper Tail	0.9	0.1	0.05	0.025	0.01
χ^2 values (19 df)	11.651	27.204	30.144	32.852	36.191

$\chi^2 = 22.9$

In part (a), the value of the test statistic chi-square was determined to be $\chi^2 = 22.99$. As you note in the above table, this value falls between 11.651 and 27.204 indicating the *p*-value is between 0.90 and 0.10. Since the *p*-value $> \alpha = 0.05$, the null hypothesis is not rejected, and we conclude that there is not sufficient evidence to reject the company's claim.

(c)   Use Excel to determine the *p*-value.

Answer: As you noted in part (b), the χ^2 tables can provide us with an approximation of the *p*-value. However, we can use Excel's "**CHIDIST**" function to determine the *p*-value. Using Excel, in statistical function, select "**CHIDIST**." The syntax of this function is in the form of

    = CHIDIST(X, degrees_freedom)

where X is the value of χ^2 that we computed in part (a) as 22.99, and degrees of freedom is n – 1 = 20 – 1 = 19. Substituting these values in the "**CHIDIST**" function will look like = CHIDIST (22.99, 19). This entry results in a *p*-value = 0.2378 $> \alpha = 0.05$. Thus, the null hypothesis cannot be rejected.

5.   A lumber company has claimed that the standard deviation for the lengths of their six-foot boards is 0.5 inches or less. To test their claim, a random sample of 17 six-foot boards is selected; and it is determined that the standard deviation of the sample is 0.43.

(a)   Do the results of the sample support the company's claim? Use the critical value approach and let $\alpha = 0.1$.

(b)   Use the *p*-value approach to test the hypotheses.

(c)   Using Excel, determine the *p*-value and show that you arrive at the same conclusion that you arrived at in parts (a) and (b).

6.   An egg packing company has stated that the standard deviation of the weights of its grade A large eggs is 0.07 ounces or less. The sample variance for 51 eggs was 0.0065 ounces.

(a)   Can this sample result confirm the company's claim? Use the critical value approach and let $\alpha = 0.1$.

(b)   Use the *p*-value approach to test the company's claim. Let $\alpha = 0.1$.

(c)   Using Excel, determine the *p*-value and test the company's claim.

Solved Problem

---

*7.   Last year, the standard deviation of the ages of the students at the University of Tennessee at Chattanooga (UTC) was 1.81 years. Recently, a sample of 61 students had a standard deviation of 2.1 years.

(a)   At 95% confidence, using the critical value approach and $\alpha = 0.05$, test to see if there has been a significant change in the standard deviation of the ages of the students at UTC.

Answer: In this case, we are interested in testing for a change in the variance. Thus, we have a two-tailed test concerning the population variance, where the hypotheses can be stated:

$$H_o: \sigma^2 = (1.81)^2$$
$$H_a: \sigma^2 \neq (1.81)^2 \quad \text{(There has been a change in the variance.)}$$

For a two-tailed test, the null hypothesis is rejected if

$$\chi^2 < \chi^2_{(1-\alpha/2)} \quad \text{or if} \quad \chi^2 > \chi^2_{\alpha/2}$$

First, we can read the chi-square values from Table 3 of the Appendix (with $n - 1 = 61 - 1 = 60$ degrees of freedom) as

$$\chi^2_{(1-\alpha/2)} = \chi^2_{.975} = 40.482 \text{ and } \chi^2_{\alpha/2} = \chi^2_{.025} = 83.298$$

Then, we calculate chi-square from the sample information:

$$\chi^2 = \frac{(n-1)S^2}{\sigma_0^2} = \frac{(61-1)(2.1)^2}{(1.81)^2} = 80.767$$

Since this value (80.767) is in the range of 40.482 to 83.298, the null hypothesis is not rejected. Thus, we conclude that there is not sufficient evidence to confirm that there has been any change in the standard deviation of the ages of the students at UTC.

(b)   Compute the p-value.

Answer: From the chi-square table with $n - 1 = 61 - 1 = 60$ degrees of freedom, we have the following information.

Area in the Upper Tail	**0.05**	**0.025**	**0.01**
χ^2 values (60 df)	79.082	83.298	88.379

$$\chi^2 = 80.767$$

The test statistic $\chi^2 = 80.767$ is between 79.082 and 83.298. Therefore, the area in the upper tail is between 0.05 and 0.025. Since this is a two-tailed test, we double these values and conclude the p-value is between 0.1 and 0.05. This may be denoted as $0.05 \leq p\text{-}value \leq 0.10$.

8.   The standard deviation of the daily temperatures in Honolulu last year was $\sigma = 3.2$ degrees Fahrenheit. A random sample of 41 days resulted in a standard deviation of 4 degrees Fahrenheit.

(a)   Has there been a significant change in the variance of the temperatures? Use the critical value approach and let $\alpha = 0.05$.

(b)   Determine the p-value.

9. Do the following data indicate that the variance of the population from which this sample has been drawn is $\sigma^2 = 17$? Use $\alpha = 0.05$.

$$
\begin{array}{c}
\mathbf{X} \\
12 \\
5 \\
9 \\
14 \\
10
\end{array}
$$

Solved Problem

---

*10. We are interested in determining whether or not the variances of the sales at two small grocery stores are equal. A sample of 21 days of sales at Store A and a sample of 16 days of sales at Store B indicated the following.

	Store A	Store B
	$n_1 = 21$	$n_2 = 16$
	$S_1^2 = 800$	$S_2^2 = 400$

(a) Are the variances of the populations (from which these samples came) equal? Use the critical value approach and let $\alpha = 0.05$.

Answer: The hypotheses to be tested are

$$
H_o: \sigma_1^2 = \sigma_2^2
$$
$$
H_a: \sigma_1^2 \neq \sigma_2^2
$$

The sample information results in an F value of

$$
F = \frac{S_1^2}{S_2^2} = \frac{800}{400} = 2.0
$$

Note that the population with the larger sample variance is denoted as population 1.

For a two-tailed test regarding the variances of two populations, the null hypothesis is rejected if $F > F_{\alpha/2}$. From Table 4 of the Appendix with $\alpha = 0.05$ and

$(n_1 - 1) = (21 - 1) = 20$ numerator degrees of freedom and $(n_2 - 1) = (16 - 1) = 15$ denominator degrees of freedom, we read $F_{\alpha/2} = F_{.025} = 2.76$. Since $2.0 < 2.76$, the null hypothesis is not rejected; and we conclude that there is not sufficient evidence to confirm that the variances of the two populations are different.

(b) Compute the *p*-value and use it to test the above hypotheses.

Answer: The F table of the Appendix provides the following information for 20 numerator and 15 denominator degrees of freedom.

Area in the Upper Tail	0.1	0.05	0.025	0.01
F values (df$_1$ = 20, df$_2$ = 15)	1.92	2.33	2.76	3.37

$$F = 2.0$$

Similar to other hypotheses testing procedures, we can approximate the *p*-value. In the above table, we note that 2.0 is between 1.92 and 2.33. Hence, the area in the upper tail is between 0.1 and 0.05. Since this situation represents a two-tail test, we double the values and conclude the *p*-value is between 0.2 and 0.1. Since the *p*-value is larger than $\alpha = 0.05$, the null hypothesis is not rejected. This may also be denoted as $0.10 \leq p\text{-}value \leq 0.20$.

11. You are given the following information.

Group 1	Group 2
$n_1 = 21$	$n_2 = 19$
$S_1 = 18$	$S_2 = 16$

(a) At $\alpha = 0.1$ using the critical value approach, test to see if the population variances from which the above samples were drawn are equal.

(b) Compute the *p*-value.

12.   The standard deviation of the ages of a sample of 16 executives from northern states was 8.2 years; while the standard deviation of the ages of a sample of 25 executives from southern states was 12.8 years. At $\alpha = 0.1$, test to see if there is any difference in the standard deviations of the ages of all northern and southern executives.

13.   Student advisors are interested in determining if the variances of the grades of day students and night students are the same. The following samples are drawn.

Day	Night
$n_1 = 25$	$n_2 = 31$
$S_1 = 9.8$	$S_2 = 14.7$

Test the equality of the variances of the populations at $\alpha = 0.05$.

SELF-TESTING QUESTIONS

In the following multiple choice questions, circle the correct answer. An answer key is provided following the questions.

1. The sampling distribution used when making inferences about a single population variance is the
a) t distribution with (n - 1) degrees of freedom
b) chi-square distribution with (n - 1) degrees of freedom
c) F distribution with (n - 1) degrees of freedom for the numerator and (n - 1) degrees of freedom for the denominator
d) chi-square distribution with (n - 2) degrees of freedom

2. The sampling distribution of the ratio of two independent sample variances extracted from normal populations with equal variances is the
a) t distribution
b) chi-square distribution
c) F distribution
d) normal distribution

3. $\chi^2_{.90}$ with 20 degrees of freedom is
a) 28.4120
b) 27.2036
c) 11.6509
d) 12.4426

4. To avoid the problem of not having access to tables of F distribution with values given for the lower tail when a two-tailed test is required, let the sample with the smaller sample variance be
a) the numerator of the test statistic
b) the denominator of the test statistic
c) It makes no difference how the ratio is set up.
d) equal to one

5. A sample of 20 cans of tomato juice showed a standard deviation of 0.4 ounces. A 95% confidence interval estimate for the variance of the population is
a) 0.2313 to 0.8533
b) 0.2224 to 0.7924
c) 0.0889 to 0.3169
d) 0.0925 to 0.3413

Exhibit 11-1
A bottler of a certain soft drink claims its equipment is accurate and that the variance of all filled bottles is less than 0.05 ounces. A sample of 26 bottles had a standard deviation of 0.2.

6.   Refer to Exhibit 11-1. The null hypothesis to test the claim would be written

a) H_o: $\sigma^2 \geq 0.05$

b) H_o: $\sigma^2 > 0.05$

c) H_o: $\sigma^2 < 0.05$

d) H_o: $\sigma^2 \leq 0.05$

7.   Refer to Exhibit 11-1. The value of the test statistic is

a)   104

b)   20.80

c)   37.65

d)   26.00

8.   Refer to Exhibit 11-1. The critical value of χ^2 at 95% confidence is

a)   14.6114

b)   15.3791

c)   37.6525

d)   38.8852

9.   The $F_{.05}$ value with 20 numerator degrees of freedom and 30 denominator degrees of freedom is

a)   1.93

b)   1.94

c)   2.20

d)   2.55

10.   A sample of 40 items from population 1 has a sample variance of 8 while a sample of 60 items from population 2 has a sample variance of 10. If we test whether the variances of the two populations are equal, the test statistic will have a value of

a)   0.8

b)   1.56

c)   1.5

d)   1.25

ANSWERS TO THE SELF-TESTING QUESTIONS

1. b
2. c
3. d
4. b
5. d
6. d
7. b
8. c
9. a
10. d

ANSWERS TO CHAPTER ELEVEN EXERCISES

2. 90.93 to 147.44 (rounded)

3. 6.34 to 10.75 (rounded)

5. (a) H_o: $\sigma^2 \le 0.25$
    H_a: $\sigma^2 > 0.25$
    Since $\chi^2 = 11.834 < 23.542$, do not reject H_o and conclude that there is not sufficient evidence to reject the company's claim.
    (b) *p*-value is between 0.1 and 0.9; do not reject H_o
    (c) *p*-value $= 0.7553 > \alpha = 0.1$, do not reject H_o

6. (a) H_o: $\sigma^2 \le 0.0049$
    H_a: $\sigma^2 > 0.0049$
    Since $\chi^2 = 66.327 > 63.167$, reject H_o and conclude that the sample results do not support the company's claim.
    (b) *p*-value is between 0.1 and 0.05; reject H_o
    (c) *p*-value $= 0.0608 < \alpha = 0.1$, reject H_o

8. (a) H_o: $\sigma^2 = 10.24$
    H_a: $\sigma^2 \ne 10.24$
    $\chi^2_{.01} = 59.342$ $\chi^2_{.99} = 24.433$
    The test statistic $\chi^2 = 62.5$; thus, reject H_o and conclude that there is sufficient evidence to show a change in the variance of the temperature.
    (b) *p*-value is between .01 and .05 (two-tailed)

9. H_o: $\sigma^2 = 17$
    H_a: $\sigma^2 \ne 17$
    $\chi^2_{.025} = 11.143$ $\chi^2_{.975} = 0.484$
    Calculated $\chi^2 = 2.706$; thus, do not reject H_o and conclude that there is not sufficient evidence to indicate that the variance of the population is significantly different from 17.

11. (a) H_o: $\sigma_1^2 = \sigma_2^2$
    H_a: $\sigma_1^2 \ne \sigma_2^2$
    Since $F = 1.26 < 2.19$, do not reject H_o; therefore, there is not sufficient evidence to conclude that the population variances are unequal.
    (b) *p*-value is greater than 0.1

12. H_o: $\sigma_1^2 = \sigma_2^2$

    H_a: $\sigma_1^2 \neq \sigma_2^2$

    Since F = 2.44 > 2.29, reject H_o and conclude that there is a difference in the standard deviation of the ages of northern and southern executives.

13. H_o: $\sigma_1^2 = \sigma_2^2$

    H_a: $\sigma_1^2 \neq \sigma_2^2$

    Since F = 2.25 > 2.21, reject H_o and conclude that the variances of the two populations are not equal.

CHAPTER TWELVE

TESTS OF GOODNESS OF FIT AND INDEPENDENCE

CHAPTER OUTLINE AND REVIEW

This chapter introduces the tests for goodness of fit and independence. You will learn how to use the chi-square distribution for determining whether or not an observed frequency distribution can be considered a hypothesized probability distribution. The goodness of fit is demonstrated for multinomial, Poisson, and normal distributions. As an extension of the goodness of fit test, the test for independence is another major topic of this chapter. The major topics of this chapter are listed below.

Contingency Table is a table that is used to summarize the observed and the expected frequencies for a test of the independence of the population characteristics.

Goodness of Fit Test is a statistical testing procedure for determining whether or not to reject a hypothesized probability distribution for a population.

Multinomial Population is a population in which each element is assigned to one and only one of several categories.

CHAPTER FORMULAS

Goodness of Fit Test

Test Statistic: $\chi^2 = \sum\limits_{i=1}^{k} \dfrac{\left(f_i - e_i\right)^2}{e_i}$ (12.1)

where f_i = the observed frequency for category i
        e_i = the expected frequency for category i based on the assumption that the null
              hypothesis is true
        k = the number of categories
        degrees of freedom = k − 1

Note: The expected frequencies should be *5 or more* for all categories.

When using the critical value approach, reject H₀ if $\chi^2 \ge \chi^2_\alpha$

When using the *p*-value criterion, reject H₀ if the *p*-value ≤ α

Test of Independence

Test Statistic: $\chi^2 = \sum\limits_{i}\sum\limits_{j} \dfrac{\left(f_{ij} - e_{ij}\right)^2}{e_{ij}}$ (12.3)

where f_{ij} = the observed frequencies for contingency tables in row i and
               column j
        e_{ij} = the expected frequencies for contingency tables in row i and
               column j (Under the assumption of independence)
        degrees of freedom = (number of rows - 1) (number of columns - 1)

Note: $e_{ij} = \dfrac{(\text{Row i total})(\text{Column j total})}{\text{Sample size}}$ (12.2)

When using the critical value approach, reject H₀ if $\chi^2 \ge \chi^2_\alpha$

When using the *p*-value criterion, reject H₀ if the *p*-value ≤ α

EXERCISES

Solved Problem

*1.   Last school year, the student body of a local college consisted of 30% freshmen, 24% sophomores, 26% juniors, and 20% seniors. A sample of 300 students taken from this year's student body showed the following number of students in each classification.

Freshmen	83
Sophomores	68
Juniors	85
Seniors	64
Total	300

(a)   Has there been any significant change in the number of students in each classification between the last school year and this school year? Use the *p*-value approach and let $\alpha = 0.05$.

Answer: The null and the alternative hypotheses can be stated as

H_0: P(Freshmen) = 0.3, P(Sophomores) = 0.24, P(Juniors) = 0.26, and
        P(Seniors) = 0.20

H_a: The population proportions are not as stated in H_0.

If the sample results lead to the rejection of H_0, we can conclude that there has been a significant change in the number of students in each classification. However, if there has not been a significant change, we would expect the following number of students to fall into each classification.

		e_i
Freshmen	(300)(0.3) =	90
Sophomores	(300)(0.24) =	72
Juniors	(300)(0.26) =	78
Seniors	(300)(0.20) =	60
		300

The test statistic is chi-square whose value is computed:

$$\chi^2 = \sum_{i=1}^{k} \frac{\left(f_i - e_i\right)^2}{e_i}$$

Then, to compute the value of chi-square, we can write the observed (f_i) and the expected frequencies (e_i) and complete the calculations shown below.

f_i	e_i	$(f_i - e_i)^2$	$(f_i - e_i)^2/e_i$
83	90	49	0.5444
68	72	16	0.2222
85	78	49	0.6282
64	60	16	0.2667

$$\chi^2 = 1.6615$$

From the chi-square table of the Appendix at $\alpha = 0.05$ with $(k - 1) = (4 - 1) = 3$ degrees of freedom, we have the following information.

Area in the Upper Tail	0.900	0.100	0.050	0.025
χ^2 Values (3 df)	0.584	6.251	7.815	9.348

$$\chi^2 = 1.6615$$

Since large differences between the observed and expected frequencies result in large values of chi-square, the test of goodness of fit is always a one-tail (upper tail) test. In the above, 1.6615 is between 0.584 and 6.251, which indicates that the p-value is between 0.1 and 0.9. The null hypothesis would be rejected if the p-value $\leq \alpha$. In this case, the p-value $> \alpha = .05$; thus, the null hypothesis is not rejected. Therefore, we conclude that there is not sufficient evidence to indicate that there has been a significant change from last year in the number of students in each classification.

(b)   Use Excel to determine the p-value for this problem and answer the question given in part (a).

Answer: In Excel's functions (f_x) under "Function category," select **statistical**; then under "Function name," select **CHITEST**. Define the "Actual_Range" (i.e., observed frequencies) and the "Expected_range" (i.e., expected frequencies) and click OK. The formula result is the p-value of 0.6455. Since the p-value $= 0.6455 > \alpha = 0.05$, the null hypothesis cannot be rejected.

(c)   Use the critical value approach and at 95% confidence test the above hypotheses.

Answer: The null hypothesis will be rejected if the test statistic (chi-square) determined from the data is larger than χ^2_α. (That is, reject H_o if $\chi^2 \geq \chi^2_\alpha$.) The test statistic chi-square was determined in part (a) as $\chi^2 = 1.6615$. Now from Table 3 of the Appendix, we read the value of chi-square at $\alpha = 0.05$ with $(k - 1) = (4 - 1) = 3$ degrees of freedom as $\chi^2_{.05} = 7.815$. Since the test statistic ($\chi^2 = 1.6615$) is less than the critical value of 7.815, the null hypothesis is not rejected.

2.   Before the candidates started their major campaigns in the last presidential election, the percentages of registered voters who favored the various candidates were as follows.

Candidates	Percentages
Republicans	34%
Democrats	43%
Independents	23%

After the major campaigns began, a random sample of 400 voters showed that 172 favored the Republican candidate; 164 were in favor of the Democratic candidate; and 64 favored the Independent candidate. We are interested in determining whether the proportion of voters who favored the various candidates had changed.

(a)   Compute the test statistic.

(b)   Using the *p*-value approach, test to see if the proportions have changed.

(c)   Using the critical value approach, test the hypotheses.

(d)   Using **CHITEST** in Excel, determine the *p*-value.

3.   Before the Christmas shopping rush began, the manager of Brock Department Store noted that one-third of the customers paid for their purchases with the store's credit card; one-third used a major credit card; and one-third paid cash (that is, $P_1 = P_2 = P_3 = 1/3$). In a sample of 150 customers shopping during the Christmas rush, 46 used the store's credit card, 43 used a major credit card, and 61 paid cash.

(a)   Compute the test statistic.

(b)   With $\alpha = 0.05$, test to see if the customers have changed their methods of payment during the Christmas rush. Use the *p*-value approach.

(c)   Use the critical value approach at 95% confidence and test the hypotheses.

(d)   Using Excel and the CHITEST function, determine the *p*-value and test the hypotheses.

4.   A major automobile manufacturer claimed that the frequencies of repair on all of their five models of cars are the same. A sample of 200 repair service receipts showed the following frequencies on the various models of cars.

Model of Car	Frequency
A	32
B	45
C	43
D	34
E	46

(a)   State the hypotheses for this test.

(b)   Compute the test statistic.

(c)   At $\alpha = 0.05$, test the manufacturer's claim.

(d)   Use the *p*-value approach at 95% confidence and test the hypotheses.

(e)   Using Excel and the CHITEST function, determine the *p*-value and answer part (a).

Solved Problem

*5. A group of 500 individuals were asked to cast their votes regarding a particular issue in the Equal Rights Amendment. The following contingency table shows the results of the votes.

Sex	Favor	Undecided	Oppose	Total
Female	180	80	40	300
Male	150	20	30	200
TOTAL	330	100	70	500

We want to determine if the votes cast were ***independent*** of the sex of the individuals.

(a) State the hypotheses for this problem.

Answer: The null and the alternative hypotheses are

H_0: Casting of the vote is independent of the sex of the voter.

H_a: Casting of the vote is not independent of the sex of the voter.

(b) Determine the table of expected frequencies (contingency table).

Answer: The expected frequencies under the assumption of independence between the votes cast and the sex of the individuals are computed as follows. We note that 330/500 = 0.66 of all the voters voted in favor of the issue; 100/500 = 0.2 of the voters were undecided; and 70/500 = 0.14 opposed the issue. Therefore, if the independence assumption is valid, the same fractions must be applicable to both male and female voters. Since there were 300 female and 200 male voters, we expect the following frequencies to exist.

Sex	Favor	Undecided	Oppose
Female	(0.66)(300) = 198	(0.2)(300) = 60	(0.14)(300) = 42
Male	(0.66)(200) = 132	(0.2)(200) = 40	(0.14)(200) = 28

The above table shows the expected frequencies under the assumption of independence.

(c) Compute the test statistic.

Answer: The test statistic χ^2 is computed by

$$\chi^2 = \sum_i \sum_j \frac{\left(f_{ij} - e_{ij}\right)^2}{e_{ij}}$$

Thus, chi-square value will be calculated:

$$\chi^2 = \frac{(180 - 198)^2}{198} + \frac{(80 - 60)^2}{60} + \ldots + \frac{(30 - 28)^2}{28} = 20.976$$

(d)   Use the critical value approach and test the hypotheses.

Answer: Now we can read the critical chi-square value from the chi-square table in the Appendix with (number of rows - 1) x (number of columns - 1) = (2 - 1)(3 - 1) = 2 degrees of freedom as $\chi^2_{.05}$ = 5.991. Since the test statistic χ^2 = 20.976 > 5.991, we reject the null hypothesis and conclude that the votes cast were not independent of the sex of the voters.

To determine the actual value of the *p*-value, we can use the CHITEST function in Excel and define the "actual_range" and the "expected_range" and obtain a *p*-value of 0.0000276.

(e)   Use the *p*-value approach and test the hypotheses.

Answer: From the chi-square table under 2 degrees of freedom, we have the following information.

Area in the Upper Tail	0.05	0.025	0.01	0.005
χ^2 values (2 df)	5.991	7.378	9.210	10.597

$$\chi^2 = 20.976$$

Since the test statistic χ^2 = 20.976 is larger than 10.597, the *p*-value is less than 0.005. Hence, the null hypothesis is rejected.

6.   Among 1,000 managers with degrees in business administration, the following data have been accumulated as to their fields of concentration.

Major	Top Management	Middle Management	TOTAL
Management	280	220	500
Marketing	120	80	200
Accounting	150	150	300
TOTAL	550	450	1000

We want to determine if the position in management is independent of field (major) of concentration.

(a)   Compute the test statistic.

(b)   Using the *p*-value approach at 90% confidence, test to determine if management position is independent of major.

(c)   Using the critical value approach, test the hypotheses. Let $\alpha = 0.10$.

(d)   Using Excel (or other software), determine the *p*-value.

7.   From a poll of 800 television viewers, the following data have been accumulated as to their levels of education and their preference of television stations.

Educational Level

	High School	Bachelor	Graduate	TOTAL
Public Broadcasting	50	150	80	280
Commercial Stations	150	250	120	520
TOTAL	200	400	200	800

(a)   At 95% confidence using the critical value approach, test to determine if the selection of a TV station is independent of the level of education.

(b)   Use the *p*-value approach and test the hypotheses. Let $\alpha = 0.05$.

Solved Problem

*8. The number of emergency calls per day at a hospital over a period of 120 days are shown below.

Number of Emergency Calls (x)	Observed Frequency (f)	f · x
0	9	0
1	12	12
2	30	60
3	27	81
4	22	88
5	13	65
6	7	42
	$n = \Sigma f - 120$	$\Sigma f \cdot x = 348$

(a) At 95% confidence using the critical value approach, test to see if the data have a Poisson probability distribution.

Answer: The null and the alternative hypotheses are

H_0: The number of emergency calls have a Poisson distribution.

H_a: The number of emergency calls do not have a Poisson distribution.

The first step is to determine the mean of the distribution:

$$\mu = \frac{\Sigma f \cdot x}{n}$$

The calculation of $\Sigma f \cdot x$ is shown above in the last column. Thus, the mean is

$$\mu = \frac{348}{120} = 2.9$$

Now, from Table 7 of the Appendix, we can read the Poisson probabilities with a mean $\mu = 2.9$ as shown below.

Number of Emergency Calls (x)	Poisson Probability f (x)	Expected Number of Emergency Calls
0	0.0550	6.600
1	0.1596	19.152
2	0.2314	27.768
3	0.2237	26.844
4	0.1622	19.464
5	0.0940	11.280
6	0.0455	5.460
7 or more	0.0286	3.432

The expected frequencies can be determined by multiplying the Poisson probability values by 120. The expected frequencies are shown above in the last column. Since the expected frequency of the last category is less than 5, we combine the last two categories into a single category. Thus, the observed and the expected frequencies can be written as shown below.

Number of Emergency Calls	Observed Freq. (f_i)	Expected Freq. (e_i)	Difference $(f_i - e_i)$	$(f_i - e_i)^2/e_i$
0	9	6.600	2.400	0.873
1	12	19.152	-7.152	2.671
2	30	27.768	2.232	0.179
3	27	26.844	0.156	0.001
4	22	19.464	2.536	0.330
5	13	11.280	1.720	0.262
6 or more	7	8.892	-1.892	0.403

Then, the value of chi-square is determined by summing the values of the last column shown above.

$$\chi^2 = \sum \frac{(f_i - e_i)^2}{e_i} = 0.873 + 2.671 + ... + 0.403 = 4.719$$

From Table 3 of the Appendix, we can now read the value of chi-square to be 11.07. Note that there are k - p - 1 = 7 - 1 - 1 = 5 degrees of freedom, where k is the number of categories, (in this case 7), and p is the number of population parameters estimated from the sample data. In this case, the sample was used to estimate the mean, therefore, p = 1. Since the chi-square that was calculated above (4.719) is less than $\chi^2_{.05} = 11.07$, the null hypothesis is not rejected; and we conclude that the number of emergency calls have a Poisson distribution.

(b)   Determine the *p*-value.

Answer: Referring to the chi-square table (5 degrees of freedom), we note that the test statistic $\chi^2 = 4.719$ is between 1.610 and 9.236. Therefore, the *p*-value is between 0.1 and 0.90.

9.   An insurance company has gathered the following information regarding the number of accidents reported per day over a period of 100 days.

Accidents Per Day	Number of Days (f_i)
0	5
1	18
2	25
3	24
4	20
5	8

We want to determine if the above data have a Poisson distribution.

(a)   Compute the mean of the above distribution.

(b)   At 95% confidence, test to see if the above data have a Poisson distribution.

(c)   Test the above hypotheses using the *p*-value approach. Let $\alpha = 0.05$.

Solved Problem

*10. The following data show the grades of a sample of 40 students who have taken statistics.

98	64	96	69
45	94	58	59
63	49	88	83
85	87	68	77
56	63	86	89
84	73	52	63
64	80	69	68
79	73	78	79
72	82	78	88
83	76	66	76

(a)   At 90% confidence conduct a goodness of fit test to determine if the sample comes from a population that has a normal distribution. Use the critical value approach.

Answer: The mean and the standard deviation for the above data can be determined as

$$\bar{x} = \frac{\sum x_i}{n} = \frac{2960}{40} = 74$$

$$S = \sqrt{\frac{\sum(x_i - \bar{x})^2}{n - 1}} = \sqrt{\frac{6409}{40 - 1}} = 12.82$$

Then, the hypotheses are stated:

H_0: The population of the examination scores has a normal distribution with a mean of 74 and a standard deviation of 12.82.

H_a: The population of the examination scores does not have a normal distribution with a mean of 74 and a standard deviation of 12.82.

Now, we divide the sample of 40 into 8 categories, and each category will contain 5 test scores, or 12.5% of the test scores. (Recall that the rule of thumb requires that at least 5 elements be included in each expected frequency category.) We can determine the boundaries of each 12.5% of the test scores. For example, the lowest 12.5% of the test scores will have an upper limit of

$$x = 74 - (1.15)(12.82) = 59.26 \text{ (rounded)}$$

where the z value of 1.15 is read from Table 1 of the Appendix and corresponds to an area of 0.375. Working through the normal distribution in a similar manner, we can determine the following category limits.

$$(74) - (0.67)(12.82) = 65.41$$
$$(74) - (0.31)(12.82) = 70.02$$
$$(74) - (0.00)(12.82) = 74.00$$
$$(74) + (0.31)(12.82) = 77.97$$
$$(74) + (0.67)(12.82) = 82.59$$
$$(74) + (1.15)(12.82) = 88.74$$

Thus, we determine the observed and the expected frequencies as

Interval of Examination Scores	Observed Frequency (f_i)	Expected Frequency (e_i)	$(f_i - e_i)$	$(f_i - e_i)^2/e_i$
less than 59.26	6	5	1	0.2
59.26 to 65.41	5	5	0	0.0
65.41 to 70.02	5	5	0	0.0
70.02 to 74.00	3	5	-2	0.8
74.00 to 77.97	3	5	-2	0.8
77.97 to 82.59	6	5	1	0.2
82.59 to 88.74	8	5	3	1.8
over 88.74	4	5	-1	0.2
				4.0

Therefore, the value of the test statistic χ^2 calculated from the sample as shown at the bottom of the last column is 4. Now, we can read the chi-square value with $k - p - 1 = 8 - 2 - 1 = 5$ degrees of freedom, where there are $k = 8$ categories and $p = 2$ parameters (the mean and the standard deviation) as $\chi^2_{0.10} = 9.236$. Since $4 < 9.236$, the null hypothesis is not rejected; and, therefore, there is insufficient evidence to conclude that the examination scores do **not** have a normal distribution with a mean of 74 and a standard deviation of 12.82.

(b)   Compute the *p*-value.

Answer: The test statistic $\chi^2 = 4$ (with 5 degrees of freedom) is between 1.610 and 9.236. Therefore, the *p*-value is between 0.9 and 0.1.

11. We want to determine if the following sample comes from a normal distribution:

105	260	314	400	520
300	306	115	200	208
418	110	410	312	360
310	314	418	316	412
516	480	490	504	518
280	270	516	419	520
420	438	511	708	300
420	519	702	690	518
510	700	650	670	612
460	600	680	692	600

(a)   Compute the mean and the standard deviation.

(b)   Compute the test statistic. Hint: divide the distribution into 10 equal intervals.

(c)   At 95% confidence using the critical value approach, test to determine if the sample comes from a normal population.

(d)   Compute the p-value.

SELF-TESTING QUESTIONS

In the following multiple choice questions, circle the correct answer. An answer key is provided following the questions.

1. A population where each element of the population is assigned to one and only one of several classes or categories is a
a) multinomial population
b) Poisson population
c) normal population
d) class population

2. The sampling distribution for a goodness of fit test is the
a) Poisson distribution
b) t distribution
c) normal distribution
d) chi-square distribution

3. A goodness of fit test is always conducted as
a) a lower tail test
b) an upper tail test
c) either a lower or an upper test
d) a t-test

4. Which of the following is **not** an application of the chi-square distribution?
a) making inferences about a single population variance
b) testing for goodness of fit
c) testing for the independence of two variables
d) making inferences about the interval of a mean

5. The number of degrees of freedom for the appropriate chi-square distribution in a test of independence is
a) n - 1
b) k - 1
c) the number of rows minus 1 times number of columns minus 1
d) the number of rows times the number of columns

6. In order not to violate the requirements necessary to use the chi-square distribution, each expected frequency in a goodness of fit test must be
a) at least 5
b) at least 10
c) no more than 5
d) at least 30

7.   A statistical test conducted to determine whether to reject or not reject a hypothesized probability distribution for a population is known as a
a)   contingency test
b)   probability test
c)   goodness of fit test
d)   alpha test

8.   The degrees of freedom for a contingency table with 21 rows and 7 columns is
a)   20
b)   27
c)   26
d)   120

ANSWERS TO THE SELF-TESTING QUESTIONS

1. a
2. d
3. b
4. d
5. c
6. a
7. c
8. d

ANSWERS TO CHAPTER TWELVE EXERCISES

2. (a) $\chi^2 = 18.42$
    (b) p-value $< .005$, reject H_0, the proportions have changed
    (c) $\chi^2 = 18.42 > 9.210$; reject H_0, the proportions have changed
    (d) p-value $= 0.00036 < \alpha = .01$, reject H_0

3. (a) $\chi^2 = 3.72$
    (b) p-value is between 0.1 and 0.9, do not reject H_0, method of payment has not changed
    (c) $\chi^2 = 3.72 < 5.991$; do not reject H_0; the method of payment has not changed
    (d) p-value $= 0.1557 > \alpha = 0.05$, do not reject H_0

4. (a) H_0: $p_A = p_B = p_C = p_D = p_E = 0.2$
          H_a: proportions are not as stated in H_0
    (b) $\chi^2 = 4.25$
    (c) $\chi^2 = 4.25 < 9.488$; do not reject H_0, there is no difference in the frequencies of repair
    (d) p-value is between 0.1 and 0.9, which is greater than $\alpha = 0.05$; do not reject H_0
    (e) p-value $= 0.3732 > \alpha = 0.05$, do not reject H_0

6. (a) $\chi^2 = 5.253$
    (b) p-value is between $.05$ and 0.10, reject H_0, position is not independent of major
    (c) $\chi^2 = 5.253 > 4.605$; reject H_0, the position is not independent of the major
    (d) p-value $= 0.0723$

7. (a) $\chi^2 = 12.088 > 5.991$; reject H_0, the selection of a TV station is not independent of the level of education
    (b) p-value is much less than $.005$ (Excel's result 0.00237); reject H_0

9. (a)   Mean $= 2.6$
    (b) $\chi^2 = 5.018 < 9.488$; do not reject H_0, the data have a Poisson distribution
    (c)   The test statistic (5.018) is between 1.064 and 7.779; therefore, the p-value is between 0.1 and 0.9. Do not reject H_0.

11. (a) $\bar{x} = 440.42$
           $S = 163.21$
     (b) $\chi^2 = 23.2$
     (c)   Since the test statistic ($\chi^2 = 23.2$) is greater than $\chi^2_{.05} = 14.067$ (df $= 7$), the null hypothesis is rejected, thus, concluding that the distribution is not normal.
     (d) p-value is less than 0.005

CHAPTER THIRTEEN

ANALYSIS OF VARIANCE AND EXPERIMENTAL DESIGN

CHAPTER OUTLINE AND REVIEW

Chapter 10 explained how to test whether or not the means of two populations are equal. This chapter introduces the analysis of variance (ANOVA) procedure. You will learn this procedure (ANOVA) for determining whether or not the means of more than two populations are equal. The specific concepts that you will learn in this chapter are listed below.

Analysis of Variance (ANOVA) Procedure is a statistical approach for determining whether or not the means of several different populations are equal.

ANOVA Table is a table used to summarize the analysis of variance computations and results. It contains columns showing the source of variation, the degrees of freedom, the sum of squares, the mean squares, and the F value.

Blocking is the process of using the same, or similar, experimental units for all treatments. The purpose of blocking is to remove a source of variation from the error term and, hence, provide a sharper test of the difference in population or treatment means.

Comparisonwise Type I Error Rate is the probability of a Type I error associated with a single pairwise comparison.

Completely Randomized Design is an experimental design where the experimental units are randomly assigned to the treatments.

Experimental Units are the objects of interest in the experiment.

Experimentwise Type I Error Rate is the probability of making a Type I error on at least one of several pairwise comparisons.

Factor is another word for the independent variable of interest in an ANOVA procedure.

Factorial Experiments is an experimental design that permits statistical conclusions about two or more factors. All levels of each factor are considered with all levels of the other factors in order to specify the experimental conditions for the experiment.

Interaction is the response produced when the treatments of one factor interact with the treatments of another in influencing the response variable.

Main Effect is the response produced by the different factors in factorial design.

Mean Square is the sum of squares divided by its corresponding degrees of freedom. This quantity is used in the F ratio to determine if significant differences in means exist or not.

Multiple Comparison Procedure is a statistical procedure that can be used for conducting statistical comparisons between pairs of population means.

Partitioning is the process of allocating the total sums of squares and degrees of freedom into the various components.

Randomized Block Design is an experimental design employing blocking. The experimental unit(s) within a block is (are) assigned randomly or ordered for the treatments.

Replication is the number of times each experimental condition is observed in a factorial design. It is the sample size associated with each treatment combination.

Single-Factor Experiment is an experiment involving only one factor with k populations or treatments.

Treatments are the different levels of a factor.

CHAPTER FORMULAS

Sample Mean for Treatment j

$$\bar{x}_j = \frac{\sum_{i=1}^{n_j} x_{ij}}{n_j} \tag{13.1}$$

Sample Variance for Treatment j

$$S_j^2 = \frac{\sum_{i=1}^{n_j} \left(x_{ij} - \bar{x}_j \right)^2}{n_j - 1} \tag{13.2}$$

where

x_{ij} = the value of observation i for Treatment j

n_j = the number of observations for treatment j

The Overall Sample Mean

$$\bar{\bar{x}} = \frac{\sum_{j=1}^{k} \sum_{i=1}^{n_j} x_{ij}}{n_T} \tag{13.3}$$

where: $\quad n_T = n_1 + n_2 + ... + n_k \tag{13.4}$

The Overall Sample Mean When Sample Sizes Are Equal

$$\bar{\bar{x}} = \frac{\sum_{j=1}^{k} \bar{x}_j}{k} \tag{13.5}$$

Mean Square due to (between) Treatments

$$MSTR = \frac{SSTR}{k-1} \tag{13.7}$$

where: $\quad SSTR = \sum_{j=1}^{k} n_j \left(\bar{x}_j - \bar{\bar{x}} \right)^2 \tag{13.8}$

then $MSTR = \dfrac{\sum_{j=1}^{k} n_j \left(\bar{x}_j - \bar{\bar{x}} \right)^2}{k-1}$

CHAPTER FORMULAS
(Continued)

Mean Square due to Error (within) Treatments

$$MSE = \frac{SSE}{n_T - k} \qquad\qquad (13.10)$$

$$\text{where:} \quad SSE = \sum_{j=1}^{k} (n_j - 1) S_j^2 \qquad\qquad (13.11)$$

$$\text{then } MSE = \frac{\displaystyle\sum_{j=1}^{k} (n_j - 1) S_j^2}{n_T - K} \qquad\qquad (13.9)$$

CHAPTER FORMULAS
(Continued)

I.   Analysis of Variance for Testing the Equality of the Means of K Populations (General Form)

H_o: $\mu_1 = \mu_2 = \ldots = \mu_k$

H_a: Not all the population means are equal

where

μ_j = the mean of the jth population
k   = the number of populations or treatments

Decision rules:

When using the *p*-value approach, reject H_o if the p-value $\leq \alpha$

When using the critical value approach, reject H_o if F = $\dfrac{MSTR}{MSE} \geq F_\alpha$ (13.12)

Note: The procedure for computing MSTR and MSE are given above in equations 13.7 and 13.10.

Total Sum of Squares

$$SST = \sum_{j=1}^{k} \sum_{i=1}^{n_j} \left(x_{ij} - \overline{\overline{x}} \right)^2$$ (13.13)

or

$$SST = SSTR + SSE$$ (13.14)

CHAPTER FORMULAS
(Continued)

MULTIPLE COMPARISON

Fisher's LSD (Least Significance Difference) Procedure

H_o: $\mu_i = \mu_j$

H_a: $\mu_i \neq \mu_j$

Test Statistic

$$t = \frac{\bar{x}_1 - \bar{x}_2}{\sqrt{MSE\left(\dfrac{1}{n_i} + \dfrac{1}{n_j}\right)}} \tag{13.16}$$

Decision rules:

When using the *p*-value approach, reject H_o if the p-value $\leq \alpha$

When using the critical value approach, reject H_o if $t \leq -t_{\alpha/2}$ or $t \geq t_{\alpha/2}$
(Degrees of freedom = n_T - k)

Fisher's LSD Procedure Based Upon the Test Statistic ($\bar{x}_1 - \bar{x}_2$)

Test Statistic

$\bar{x}_i - \bar{x}_j$

Reject H_o if $\left|\bar{x}_i - \bar{x}_j\right| > LSD$

where $LSD = t_{\alpha/2}\sqrt{MSE\left(\dfrac{1}{n_i} + \dfrac{1}{n_j}\right)}$ $\tag{13.17}$

Confidence Interval Estimate of the Difference between Two Population Means Using Fisher's LSD Procedure

$(\bar{x}_i - \bar{x}_j) \pm LSD$ $\tag{13.18}$

where $LSD = t_{\alpha/2}\sqrt{MSE\left(\dfrac{1}{n_i} + \dfrac{1}{n_j}\right)}$ $\tag{13.19}$

Degrees of freedom = $n_T - k$

CHAPTER FORMULAS
(Continued)

II. Analysis of Variance for Completely Randomized Designs

H_0: $\mu_1 = \mu_2 = \ldots = \mu_k$

H_a: Not all the population means are equal

where

μ_j = the mean of the jth population

k = the number of populations or treatments

Decision rules:

when using the *p*-value approach, reject H_0 if the p-value $\leq \alpha$

when using the critical value approach, reject H_0 if F $= \dfrac{MSTR}{MSE} \geq F_\alpha$

The Sum of Squares Due to (between) Treatments

$$SSTR = \sum_{j=1}^{k} n_j \left(\overline{x}_j - \overline{\overline{x}} \right)^2$$

where, n_j = the number of observations for treatment j

$\overline{x}_j$ = the sample mean for treatment j

Mean Square due to (between) Treatments

$$MSTR = \frac{SSTR}{k-1} = \frac{\sum_{j=1}^{k} n_j \left(\overline{x}_j - \overline{\overline{x}} \right)}{k-1} \tag{13.20}$$

The Sum of Squares due to Error (within) Treatments

$$SSE = \sum_{j=1}^{k} \left(n_j - 1 \right) s_j^2$$

Mean Square due to Error (within) Treatments

$$MSE = \frac{SSE}{n_T - k} = \frac{\sum_{j=1}^{k} \left(n_j - 1 \right) s_j^2}{n_T - k} \tag{13.21}$$

The Total Sum of Squares

$$SST = SSTR + SSE \tag{13.22}$$

The F Ratio

$$F = \frac{MSTR}{MSE} \tag{13.23}$$

CHAPTER FORMULAS
(Continued)

III. Analysis of Variance for the Randomized Block Design

The Total Sum of Squares

The following notations are used for the *randomized block design*:

x_{ij} = the value of the observation under treatment i in block j
$T_{i.}$ = the total of all observations in treatment i
$T_{.j}$ = the total of all observations in block j
T = the total of all observations
k = the number of treatments
b = the number of blocks
n_T = the total sample size, $n_T = k\,b$
$\bar{x}_{.j}$ = the sample mean of the jth treatment
$\bar{x}_{i.}$ = the sample mean for the jth block
$\bar{\bar{X}}$ = the overall sample mean

The Total Sum of Squares

$$SST = SSTR + SSBL + SSE \qquad (13.24)$$

where

SST = Sum of squares total
SSTR = Sum of squares due to treatments
SSBL = Sum of squares due to blocks
SSE = Sum of squares due to error

SST is computed as

$$SST = \sum_{i=1}^{b}\sum_{j=1}^{k}\left(x_{ij} - \bar{\bar{x}}\right)^2 \qquad (13.25)$$

The Sum of Squares due to (between) Treatments

$$SSTR = b\sum_{j=1}^{k}(\bar{x}_{.j} - \bar{\bar{x}})^2 \qquad (13.26)$$

CHAPTER FORMULAS
(Continued)

The Sum of Squares due to Blocks

$$SSBL = k \sum_{i=1}^{b} \left(\overline{x}_{i.} - \overline{\overline{x}} \right)^2 \qquad (13.27)$$

The Sum of Squares due to Error

$$SSE = SST - SSTR - SSBL \qquad (13.28)$$

Degrees of freedom $= (k - 1)(b - 1)$

IV. Analysis of Variance for Factorial Experiments

The following notations are used for *factorial experiments*:

a = the number of levels of factor A
b = the number of levels of factor B
r = the number of replications
n_T = the total number of observations taken in the experiment
x_{ijk} = the observation corresponding to the kth replicate taken from treatment i of factor A and treatment j of factor B
$T_{i.}$ = the total of all observations in treatment i (factor A)
$T_{.j}$ = the total of all observations in treatment j (factor B)
T_{ij} = the total of all observations in the combination of treatment i (factor A) and treatment j (factor B)
T = the total of all observations
$\overline{x}_{i.}$ = the sample mean for the observations in treatment i (factor A)
$\overline{x}_{.j}$ = the sample mean for the observations in treatment j (factor B)
$\overline{x}_{ij}$ = the sample mean for the observations in the combination of treatment i (factor A) and treatment j (factor B)
$\overline{\overline{x}}$ = the overall sample mean

CHAPTER FORMULAS
(Continued)

The Total Sum of Squares

$$SST = SSA + SSB + SSAB + SSE \qquad (13.29)$$

or

$$SST = \sum_{i=1}^{a}\sum_{j=1}^{b}\sum_{k=1}^{r}(x_{ijk} - \overline{\overline{x}})^2 \qquad (13.30)$$

Degrees of freedom = $n_T - 1$

The Sum of Squares for Factor A

$$SSA = br\sum_{i=1}^{a}(\overline{x}_{i.} - \overline{\overline{x}})^2 \qquad (13.31)$$

Degrees of freedom = a - 1

The Sum of Squares for Factor B

$$SSB = ar\sum_{j=1}^{b}(\overline{x}_{.j} - \overline{\overline{x}})^2 \qquad (13.32)$$

Degrees of freedom = b - 1

The Sum of Squares for the Interaction

$$SSAB = r\sum_{i=1}^{a}\sum_{j=1}^{b}\left(\overline{x}_{ij} - \overline{x}_{i.} - \overline{x}_{.j} + \overline{\overline{x}}\right)^2 \qquad (13.33)$$

Degrees of freedom = (a - 1) (b - 1)

The Sum of Squares due to Error

$$SSE = SST - SSA - SSB - SSAB \qquad (13.34)$$

Degrees of freedom = a b (r - 1)

EXERCISES

Solved Problem

*1.   M. B. Shultz, a manufacturer of foam rubber sofas, wants to determine whether or not the type of work schedule her employees have has any effect on their productivity. She has selected 12 production employees at random and has randomly assigned 4 employees to each of the 3 proposed work schedules. The proposed work schedules are explained below.

1. 4 days - 40 hours per week
2. flexible time - 40 hours per week
3. standard 5 days - 40 hours per week

The following table shows the units of production (per week) under each of the work schedules.

Work Schedule
(Treatment)

4-Day Program	Flexible Time	5-Day Program
32	33	26
30	35	34
26	30	28
28	38	32

(a)   The analysis of variance procedure is based on two major assumptions. Fully explain these assumptions.

Answer: The two assumptions are stated below.

1.   The variable of interest for each population has a normal probability distribution. In this example, we assume that the variable of interest, that is, units of production is normally distributed for each of the 3 work schedules.

2.   The variance associated with the variable must be the same for each population. In this example, we assume that the variance of the units of production is the same for the employees in each of the 3 types of work schedules.

(b)   Use the analysis of variance (completely randomized design) procedure with $\alpha = 0.05$ to determine if there is a significant difference in the mean weekly units of production for the three types of work schedules.

Answer: The analysis of variance (ANOVA) procedure tests the following hypotheses.

H_0: $\mu_1 = \mu_2 = \ldots = \mu_k$

H_a: Not all the population means are equal

where μ_j = the mean of the jth population

  k = the number of populations or treatments

The means of each of the three random samples are computed by

$$\bar{x}_j = \frac{\sum\limits_{i=1}^{n_j} x_{ij}}{n_j}$$

resulting in the following sample means.

$\bar{x}_1 = 29$
$\bar{x}_2 = 34$
$\bar{x}_3 = 30$

Then an overall sample mean, $\bar{\bar{x}}$, is computed as the estimate of μ.

$$\bar{\bar{x}} = \frac{\sum\limits_{j=1}^{k}\sum\limits_{i=1}^{n_j} x_{ij}}{n_T}$$

where x_{ij} = the value of observation i for treatment j

  n_T = the total sample size for the experiment.

Thus, the overall sample mean becomes

$$\bar{\bar{x}} = \frac{32 + 30 + 26 + \ldots + 28 + 32}{12} = 31$$

Then, we need to determine two independent estimates of the variance of the population σ^2. The first estimate is based upon the differences **between** the treatment means and the overall sample mean and is termed *mean square due to (between) treatments* (MSTR). The second estimate is based upon the differences of observations **within** each treatment from the corresponding treatment mean and is termed *mean square within treatments* or *mean square due to error* (MSE). By comparing these two estimates of the population variance, we will be able to conclude whether or not the population means are equal.

The first estimate of σ^2 or MSTR can be written as

$$MSTR = \frac{SSTR}{k-1}$$

where $SSTR = \sum_{j=1}^{k} n_j \left(\bar{x}_j - \bar{\bar{x}} \right)^2$

Thus, SSTR can be computed as

$$SSTR = 4\,[(29 - 31)^2 + (34 - 31)^2 + (30 - 31)^2] = 4\,(4 + 9 + 1) = 56$$

Now we can compute MSTR as

$$MSTR = \frac{SSTR}{k-1} = \frac{56}{3-1} = 28$$

The second estimate of σ^2 (MSE) is given by

$$MSE = \frac{SSE}{n_T - k}$$

where $SSE = \sum_{j=1}^{k} \left(n_j - 1 \right) S_j^2$

SSE is referred to as the sum of squares within treatments or sum of squares due to error. First we need to compute the variance of each sample as

$$S_j^2 = \frac{\sum_{i=1}^{n_j} \left(x_{ij} - \bar{x}_j \right)^2}{n_{j-1}}$$

The variance for the first sample (4 day program) is computed as

$$S_1^2 = \frac{(32-29)^2 + (30-29)^2 + (26-29)^2 + (28-29)^2}{4-1} = \frac{20}{3} = 6.67$$

Similarly, the variances of the other two samples are computed, and their values are

$$S_2^2 = \frac{34}{4-1} = 11.33$$

$$S_3^2 = \frac{40}{4-1} = 13.33$$

Now that the variances have been computed, we can compute SSE as

$$SSE = \sum_{j=1}^{k}(n_j - 1)S_j^2 = (4 - 1)(6.67) + (4 - 1)(11.34) + (4 - 1)(13.33) = 94$$

Then MSE is computed as

$$MSE = \frac{SSE}{n_T - k} = \frac{94}{12 - 3} = 10.44$$

Now we compute an F value as

$$F = \frac{MSTR}{MSE} = \frac{28}{10.44} = 2.68$$

As with any other test, now we can use the *p*-value procedure to test our hypotheses. From the F distribution table of the Appendix with k - 1 = 3 - 1 = 2 numerator degrees of freedom and n_T - k = 12 - 3 = 9 denominator degrees of freedom, we have the following information.

Area in the Upper Tail	0.1	0.05	0.025	0.01
F values ($df_1 = 2$, $df_2 = 9$)	3.01	4.26	5.71	8.02

F = 2.68

From the above, we note that the test statistic F = 2.68 is less than 3.01, indicating the *p*-value is greater than 0.1. Since the *p*-value of 0.1 is greater than $\alpha = 0.05$, the null hypothesis is not rejected and it is concluded that there is not sufficient evidence to indicate that there is a significant difference in the means of the three populations. The F table of the Appendix provides limited values of α (0.1, .05, .025, and .01). Hence, our *p*-value is only an estimation. If we had used the ANOVA procedure of Excel, the exact *p*-value would have been determined to be 0.1221.

(c)   Use the critical value approach and test the above hypotheses. Let $\alpha = 0.05$.

Answer: The decision rule for the critical value approach is to reject H_0 if the test statistic $F \geq F_\alpha$

From Table 4 of the Appendix, we read the critical value of $F_{.05}$ with 2 numerator degrees of freedom and 9 denominator degrees of freedom as $F_{.05} = 4.26$. (Recall our computed value of the test statistic $F = MSTR/MSE = 2.68$.) Since $2.68 < 4.26$, the null hypothesis is not rejected, thus, indicating that there is not sufficient evidence to conclude that there exists a statistically significant difference in the three population means at the 0.05 level.

2.   A random sample of six automobile tires from each of the three major manufacturers showed the following life expectancies. All of the figures are in thousands of miles.

Manufacturer A	Manufacturer B	Manufacturer C
41	47	47
38	42	41
44	44	42
42	34	49
36	42	40
39	43	45

(a)   Test at $\alpha = 0.05$ to determine if there is a significant difference in the average lives of the three brands of tires. Use the *p*-value approach.

(b)   Use the critical value approach. Let $\alpha = .05$.

(c)   Use ANOVA in Excel (or another software available to you) and solve this problem.

*3.   Use the results of exercise *1 and set up a complete ANOVA table.

Answer: The general from of the ANOVA table is shown below.

Source of Variation	Sum of Squares	Degrees of Freedom	Mean Square	F
Between Treatments	SSTR	K - 1	MSTR	
				$\dfrac{\text{MSTR}}{\text{MSE}}$
Error (Within Treatments)	SSE	n_t - K	MSE	
Total	SST	n_t - 1		

Referring to exercise *1 and filling in the required information, the ANOVA table will be as follows.

Source of Variation	Sum of Squares	Degrees of Freedom	Mean Square	F
Between Treatments	56	2	28	
				2.68
Error (Within Treatments)	94	9	10.44	
Total	150	11		

4.   The heating bills for a selected sample of houses using various forms of heating are given below. (Values are in dollars.)

Natural Gas	Central Electric	Heat Pump
84	95	85
64	60	93
93	89	90
88	96	92
71	90	80

(a)   At $\alpha = 0.05$, test to see if there is a significant difference among the average heating bills of the homes. Use the p-value approach.

(b)   Test the above hypotheses using the critical value approach. Let $\alpha = .05$.

5.   Use the results of exercise 4 and fill in the blanks in the following ANOVA table. Use the space below to show your work.

Source of Variation	Sum of Squares	Degrees of Freedom	Mean Square	F
Between Treatments	____?	____?	____?	
				____?
Error (Within Treatments)	____?	____?	____?	
Total	____?	____?		

Solved Problem

---

6.   Three universities in your state have decided to administer the same comprehensive examination to the recipients of MBA degrees from the three institutions. From each institution, a random sample of MBA recipients has been selected and given the test. The following table shows the scores of the students from each university.

	Northern University	Central University	Southern University
	56	62	94
	85	97	72
	65	91	93
	86	82	78
	93		54
			77
Sample Mean ($\bar{x}_j$)	77.0	83.0	78.0
Sample Variance (s_j^2)	246.5	234.0	218.8

(a)   Using the *p*-value approach, test to see if there is any significant difference in the average scores of the students from the three universities. Let $\alpha = 0.01$. **Note that the sample sizes are not equal.**

Answer: The hypotheses to be tested are

$$H_0: \mu_1 = \mu_2 = \ldots = \mu_k$$

H_a: Not all means are equal.

First we compute the overall sample mean, $\overline{\overline{x}}$, as

$$\overline{\overline{x}} = \frac{\sum\limits_{j=1}^{k}\sum\limits_{i=1}^{n_j} x_{ij}}{n_T} = \frac{56 + 85 + 65 + \ldots + 78 + 54 + 77}{15} = 79$$

Note: Since the sample sizes are unequal we **could not** average the sample means to obtain the overall mean.

Since the individual means are given, SSTR can simply be computed as

$$SSTR = \sum\limits_{j=1}^{k} n_j \left(\overline{x}_j - \overline{\overline{x}}\right)^2 = 5(77 - 79)^2 + 4(83 - 79)^2 + 6(78 - 79)^2 = 90$$

Now we can compute MSTR as

$$MSTR = \frac{SSTR}{k-1} = \frac{90}{3-1} = 45$$

Since the variances of the individual treatments are given, SSE can be computed as

$$SSE = \sum\limits_{j=1}^{k}\left(n_j - 1\right)s_j^2 = (5-1)(246.5) + (4-1)(234.0) + (6-1)(218.8) = 2782$$

Then MSE is computed as

$$MSE = \frac{SSE}{n_T - k} = \frac{2782}{15-3} = 231.83$$

Now we compute the test statistic F as

$$\text{Test Statistic } F = \frac{MSTR}{MSE} = \frac{45}{231.83} = 0.194$$

From the F distribution table of the Appendix with $k - 1 = 3 - 1 = 2$ numerator and $n_T - k = 15 - 3 = 12$ denominator degrees of freedom, we have the following information.

Area in the Upper Tail	0.1	0.05	0.025	0.01
F values ($df_1 = 2$, $df_2 = 12$)	2.81	3.89	5.10	6.93

$$F = 0.194$$

Since the F statistic (0.194) is less than 2.81, it implies that the *p*-value is greater than 0.1. Since the *p*-value $> \alpha = 0.01$, the null hypothesis is not rejected. Thus, we conclude that there is not sufficient evidence to indicate that the average scores of the students from the three universities are significantly different.

We could have used the critical value approach to test the above hypotheses. The decision rule for the critical value approach would be as follows.

Do not reject H_0 if $F < F_\alpha$

Reject H_0 if $F \geq F_\alpha$

From Table 4 of the Appendix, we read the critical value of F_α with 2 numerator and 12 denominator degrees of freedom as $F_{.01} = 6.93$. Since 0.194 is less than 6.93, the null hypothesis is not rejected.

7. The three major automobile manufacturers have entered their cars in the Indianapolis 500 race. The speeds of the tested cars are given below.

	G	F	C
	185	173	162
	182	176	176
	179	160	184
	188	171	
	206		
Sample Mean ($\bar{x}_j$)	188	170	174
Sample Variance (s_j^2)	112.5	48.67	124.0

(a) Using the *p*-value approach, test to see if there is a significant difference in the average speeds of the cars of the three auto manufacturers. Let $\alpha = 0.05$.

(b) Using the critical value approach, test the above hypotheses. Let $\alpha = .05$.

Solved Problem

*8. Refer to exercise *6. Part of the ANOVA table for exercise *6 is shown below.

Source of Variation	Sum of Squares	Degrees of Freedom	Mean Square	F
Between Treatments	90	2	____?	____?
Error (Within Treatments)	2782	12	____?	

Compute the missing values and use $\alpha = 0.01$ to determine if there is any significant difference among the means. Use the critical value approach.

Answer: As you can see, the above results are the same as those calculated in exercise 1. The MSTR and MSE can be calculated as

$$MSTR = \frac{SSTR}{DF(Between)} = \frac{90}{2} = 45$$

$$MSE = \frac{SSE}{DF(Within)} = \frac{2,782}{12} = 231.83$$

Thus, we can calculate the F value as

$$F = \frac{MSTR}{MSE} = \frac{45}{231.83} = 0.194$$

Since $0.194 < 6.93$, the null hypothesis is not rejected; therefore, we conclude that there is no significant difference between the average scores of the students from the three universities.

9. Refer to exercise 7. Part of the ANOVA table for exercise 7 is shown below.

Source of Variation	Sum of Squares	Degrees of Freedom	Mean Square	F
Between Treatments	801	____?	____?	
				____?
Within Treatments (Error)	844	____?	____?	

Complete all the missing values in the above table and use $\alpha = 0.05$ to determine if there is any significant difference among the means.

*10. A test of general knowledge was administered to students in the fields of (1) engineering, (2) education, and (3) business (treatments).

In each of the three treatments, 11 students took the test. An analysis of variance was performed on the test scores. Part of the ANOVA table for this study is shown below.

Source of Variation	Sum of Squares	Degrees of Freedom	Mean Square	F
Between Treatments	491.7	_____?	_____?	
				_____?
Within Treatments (Error)	1165.3	_____?	_____?	
Total	1657			

(a)   Complete the ANOVA table; and at $\alpha = 0.05$, test to determine if there is a significant difference in the means of the three populations (treatments).

Answer: The degrees of freedom associated with *due to (between) Treatments* are $K - 1 = 3 - 1 = 2$, where K represents the number of treatments. The degrees of freedom associated with *Error (Within Treatments)* are given by n_T - K. Since there were 11 observations in each treatment, $n_T = 11 \times 3 = 33$. Therefore, the degrees of freedom is $n_T - K = 33 - 3 = 30$.

Next, we compute MSTR as

$$MSTR = \frac{SSTR}{K-1} = \frac{491.7}{3-1} = 245.85$$

and MSE is computed as

$$MSE = \frac{SSE}{n_T - K} = \frac{1165.3}{33-3} = 38.84$$

Finally, the test statistic F is calculated as

$$F = \frac{MSTR}{MSE} = \frac{245.85}{38.84} = 6.33$$

Thus, the complete ANOVA table will be as follows.

Source of Variation	Sum of Squares	Degrees of Freedom	Mean Square	F
Between Treatments	491.7	2	245.85	
				6.33
Error (Within Treatments)	1165.3	30	38.84	
Total	1657	32		

The hypotheses to be tested are

$$H_o: \mu_1 = \mu_2 = \mu_3$$

$$H_a: \text{ Not all the population means are equal}$$

From the F table with 2 numerator and 30 denominator degrees of freedom, we read $F_{.05} = 3.32$.

Since $F = 6.33 > 3.32$, the null hypothesis is rejected, and we conclude that at least one mean is different from the others.

(b)   Now that we have determined that at least one mean is different from the others, determine which mean(s) is (are) different. The sample means for this study are shown below.

Treatment	Sample Mean
(1) Engineering	84.0
(2) Education	87.5
(3) Business	93.4

Answer: Probably the most widely used method for making pair wise comparison of population means is Fisher's least-significant-difference (LSD). First, let us test to determine if the means of Population 1 (Engineering) and Population 2 (Education) are different. The hypotheses to be tested are

$$H_o: \mu_1 = \mu_2$$

$$H_a: \mu_1 \neq \mu_2$$

The null hypothesis will be rejected if $\left|\bar{x}_1 - \bar{x}_2\right| > LSD$, where LSD is, according to chapter formula (13.16):

$$LSD = t_{\alpha/2}\sqrt{MSE\left(\frac{1}{n_1} + \frac{1}{n_2}\right)}$$

The value of MSE was computed in part (a) and is shown in the ANOVA table as 38.84. The value of $t_{\alpha/2}$ is read from the t table at 30 degrees of freedom as $t_{.025} = 2.042$. Thus, LSD is computed as

$$LSD = t_{\alpha/2}\sqrt{MSE\left(\frac{1}{n_1} + \frac{1}{n_2}\right)} = (2.042)\sqrt{38.84\left(\frac{1}{11} + \frac{1}{11}\right)} = 5.42$$

Now, we find the absolute value of the difference between the means of Sample 1 and Sample 2 as

$$\left|\bar{x}_1 - \bar{x}_2\right| = \left|84.0 - 87.5\right| = 3.5$$

Since 3.5 is not greater than the LSD value of 5.42, the null hypothesis is not rejected. Hence, we cannot conclude that there is a significant difference between the means of Population 1 (Engineering) and Population 2 (Education). Once the LSD is computed, we simply find the absolute value of the difference between any pair of sample means; and if this difference is greater than LSD, the null hypothesis will be rejected.

For instance, to test for the significant difference between the means of Population 1 (Engineering) and Population 3 (Business), simply compute the following

$$\left|\bar{x}_1 - \bar{x}_3\right| = \left|84.0 - 93.4\right| = 9.4$$

Since 9.4 > 5.42, the null hypothesis (i.e., H_0: $\mu_1 = \mu_3$) is rejected. We can then conclude that there is a significant difference between the means of Population 1 (Engineering) and Population 3 (Business).

We can also test to see if there is a significant difference between the means of Population 2 (Education) and Population 3 (Business) by computing the following.

$$\left|\bar{x}_2 - \bar{x}_3\right| = \left|87.5 - 93.4\right| = 5.9$$

Since 5.9 > 5.42, the null hypothesis (i.e., H_0: $\mu_2 = \mu_3$) is rejected; therefore, we conclude that there is a significant difference between the means of population 2 (Education) and population 3 (Business).

11. Eight observations were selected from each of 3 populations, and an analysis of variance was performed on the data. The following are part of the results.

Source of Variation	Sum of Squares	Degrees of Freedom	Mean Square	F
Between Treatments	?	?	34.67	
				?
Error (Within Treatments)	?	?	?	
Total	189.33			

(a) Using $\alpha = .05$, test to see if there is a significant difference among the means of the three populations. Show the complete ANOVA table.

(b) If in part (a) you concluded that at least one mean is different from the others, determine which mean is different. The three sample means are $\bar{x}_1 = 28$, $\bar{x}_2 = 27$, and $\bar{x}_3 = 31$. Use Fisher's LSD procedure and let $\alpha = .05$.

12. Ten observations were selected from each of 3 populations, and an analysis of variance was performed on the data. The following information was obtained.

$\overline{x}_1 = 147.1 \qquad \overline{x}_2 = 180.0 \qquad \overline{x}_3 = 196.8$

MSB = 614.83   (Also referred to as MSE)

At the $\alpha = 0.05$ level of significance, use Fisher's LSD procedure and determine which mean(s) is (are) different from the others (if any).

*13. Mary Beth is an instructor in the statistics laboratory. She has noted that some statistics professors give objective examinations (i.e., true or false and multiple choice questions), while other professors give subjective examinations (i.e., short-answer questions and problems). In order to evaluate the two types of examinations, she has randomly selected 4 students who have just finished the statistics course and has asked them to take two types of examinations, one objective and another subjective. Table 13.1 shows the scores of the 4 students on the two types of examinations.

Type of Examination Treatment	Student (Blocks)				Row or Treatment Totals	Treatment Means $\left(\bar{x}_{.j}\right)$
	1	2	3	4		
Objective	90	70	60	80	300	$\bar{x}_{.1} = \dfrac{300}{4} = 75$
Subjective	80	90	80	70	320	$\bar{x}_{.2} = \dfrac{320}{4} = 80$
Column or Block Totals	170	160	140	150	$\sum_i \sum_j x_{ij}$ 620 = Overall sum	
Block Means $\left(\bar{x}_{i.}\right)$	$\bar{x}_{1.} = \dfrac{170}{2}$ = 85	$\bar{x}_{2.} = \dfrac{160}{2}$ = 80	$\bar{x}_{3.} = \dfrac{140}{2}$ = 70	$\bar{x}_{4.} = \dfrac{150}{2}$ = 75	$\bar{\bar{x}} = \dfrac{620}{8} = 77.5$	

Table 13.1

Treating the students as *blocks*, at $\alpha = 0.05$, test to see if there is any difference in the scores of the two types of examinations. Use the procedure as explained in section 13.6 of your textbook.

Answer: The ANOVA procedure for the *randomized block design* partitions the sum of squares total (SST) into three sums of squares as follows.

$$\begin{array}{ccccccc} \text{SST} & = & \text{SSTR} & + & \text{SSBL} & + & \text{SSE} \\ \uparrow & & \uparrow & & \uparrow & & \uparrow \\ \begin{array}{c}\text{Sum of Squares}\\ \text{Total}\end{array} & & \text{Treatment} & & \text{Block} & & \text{Error} \end{array}$$

Thus, we need to compute each of the sums of squares as shown in the following step-by-step procedure.

STEP 1: Compute the total sum of squares (SST) with chapter formula (13.21).

$$SST = \sum_{i=1}^{b}\sum_{j=1}^{k}\left(x_{ij} - \overline{\overline{x}}\right)^2 = (90 - 77.5)^2 + (70 - 77.5)^2 + \ldots + (70 - 77.5)^2 = 750$$

STEP 2: Compute SSTR as

$$SSTR = b\sum_{j=1}^{k}(\overline{x}_{.j} - \overline{\overline{x}})^2 = 4[(75 - 77.5)^2 + (80 - 77.5)^2] = 50$$

STEP 3: Compute SSBL as

$$SSBL = k\sum_{i=1}^{b}\left(\overline{x}_{i.} - \overline{\overline{x}}\right)^2$$

$$= 2[(85 - 77.5)^2 + (80 - 77.5)^2 + (70 - 77.5)^2 + (75 - 77.5)^2] = 250$$

STEP 4: Compute SSE as

$$SSE = SST - SSTR - SSB = 750 - 50 - 250 = 450$$

The above sums of squares divided by their corresponding degrees of freedom provide the mean square values. The mean square values are computed below.

$$MSTR = \frac{SSTR}{k-1} = \frac{50}{2-1} = 50$$

$$MSB = \frac{SSB}{b-1} = \frac{250}{4-1} = 83.33$$

$$MSE = \frac{SSE}{(k-1)(b-1)} = \frac{450}{(2-1)(4-1)} = 150$$

Now we can complete the ANOVA table as shown in Table 13.2.

Source of Variation	Sum of Squares	Degrees of Freedom	Mean Square	F
Between Treatments	50	1	50.00	0.33
Between Blocks	250	3	83.33	
Error	450	3	150.00	
Total	750	7		

Table 13.2

The test statistic F is computed as MSTR/MSE = 50/150 = 0.33. From the F table in the Appendix with k - 1 = 2 - 1 = 1 numerator and (k - 1)(b - 1) = (2 - 1)(4 - 1) = 3 denominator degrees of freedom, we have the following.

Area in the Upper Tail	0.1	0.05	0.025	0.01
F values (df$_1$ = 1, df$_2$ = 3)	5.54	10.13	17.44	34.12

F = 0.33

Since the test statistic F = 0.33 is less than 5.54, the *p*-value is greater than 0.1. With the *p*-value > 0.1, the null hypothesis is not rejected. Therefore, we do not have sufficient evidence to conclude that the means of the two types of examinations are different.

We could also have used the critical value approach to test the hypotheses. The critical F value in Table 4 of the Appendix at α = 0.05 is 10.13 (1 numerator degrees of freedom and 3 denominator degrees of freedom). Since 0.33 < 10.13, we do not reject the null hypothesis.

14. Five drivers were selected to test drive 2 makes of automobiles. The following table shows the number of miles per gallon for each driver driving both cars.

Automobile	Drivers (Blocks)				
A	30	31	30	27	32
B	36	35	28	31	30

At $\alpha = 0.05$, test to see if there is any difference in the miles per gallon of the two makes of automobiles.

*15. In exercise *6, you were introduced to a situation where only one factor (the universities) existed. Let us expand that situation to a two factor problem. Assume that as a second factor we are considering the sex of the students taking the examination. The first factor has 3 treatments (the preparation program at the 3 universities), and the second factor has two treatments (male or female). Thus, there are a total of 3 x 2 = 6 treatment combinations. A sample of two students is selected corresponding to each of the 6 treatments. The scores of the students on the examination are shown in Table 13.4.

Factor B: Sex of the Students

		Male	Female
	Northern	79	83
		81	91
Factor A: University	Central	92	84
		86	94
	Southern	90	86
		86	94

Table 13.4

Use the procedure as explained in section 13.7 of your textbook to answer the following questions: (Let $\alpha = 0.05$.)

1.   Do the universities' preparation programs differ in terms of effect on the examination scores (Main effect, Factor A)?

2.   Do the male and female students differ in terms of their ability to perform on the examination (Main effect, Factor B)?

3.   Do students of one sex do better in one university while students of the other sex do better in a different university (Interaction effect, Factors A and B)?

Answer: The analysis of variance for the two-factor factorial experiment partitions the SST as follows.

	SST	=	SSA	+	SSB	+	SSAB	+	SSE
Sum of	↑		↑		↑		↑		↑
Squares	Total		Factor A		Factor B		Interaction Of Factors A and B		Error

First, let us compute a summary of the data as presented in Table 13.5.

FACTOR B: SEX OF THE STUDENTS

Treatment Combination Totals	Male	Female	Row Totals	Factor A Means
	79	83		
	80	91		
Northern	160	174	334	$\bar{x}_{1.} = \dfrac{334}{4}$ $= 83.5$
	$\bar{x}_{11} = \dfrac{160}{2} = 80$	$\bar{x}_{12} = \dfrac{174}{2} = 87$		
	92	84		
	86	94		
Central	178	178	356	$\bar{x}_{2.} = \dfrac{356}{4}$ $= 89$
FACTOR A: **UNIVERSITY**	$\bar{x}_{21} = \dfrac{178}{2} = 89$	$\bar{x}_{22} = \dfrac{178}{2} = 89$		
	90	86		
	86	94		
Southern	176	180	356	$\bar{x}_{3.} = \dfrac{356}{4}$ $= 89$
	$\bar{x}_{31} = \dfrac{176}{2} = 88$	$\bar{x}_{32} = \dfrac{180}{2} = 90$		
Column Totals	514	532	1046 = Overall Total $\bar{\bar{x}} = \dfrac{1046}{12} = 87.17$	
Factor B Means	$\bar{x}_{.1} = \dfrac{514}{6} = 85.67$	$\bar{x}_{.2} = \dfrac{532}{6} = 88.67$		

Table 13.5

Then, we can compute each of the sums of squares by the following step-by-step procedure.

STEP 1: Compute SST as

$$SST = \sum_{i=1}^{a}\sum_{j=1}^{b}\sum_{k=1}^{r}(x_{ijk} - \overline{\overline{x}})^2$$

$$= (79 - 87.17)^2 + (81 - 87.17)^2 + \ldots + (86 - 87.17)^2 + (94 - 87.17)^2 = 275.67$$

STEP 2: Compute SSA as

$$SSA = br\sum_{i=1}^{a}(\overline{x}_{i.} - \overline{\overline{x}})^2$$

$$= (2)(2)[(83.5 - 87.17)^2 + (89 - 87.17)^2 + (89 - 87.17)^2] = 80.67$$

STEP 3: Compute SSB as

$$SSB = ar\sum_{j=1}^{b}(\overline{x}_{.j} - \overline{\overline{x}})^2$$

$$= (3)(2)[(85.67 - 87.17)^2 + (88.67 - 87.17)^2] = 27$$

STEP 4: Compute SSAB as

$$SSAB = r\sum_{i=1}^{a}\sum_{j=1}^{b}\left(\overline{x}_{ij} - \overline{x}_{i.} - \overline{x}_{.j} + \overline{\overline{x}}\right)^2$$

$$= 2[(80 - 83.5 - 85.67 + 87.17)^2 + \ldots + (90 - 89 - 88.67 + 87.17)^2] = 26$$

STEP 5: Compute SSE as

SSE = SST - SSA - SSB - SSAB

$$= 275.67 - 80.67 - 27 - 26 = 142$$

Now that we have computed all the sums of squares, we can compute the mean squares by dividing each sum of square by its corresponding degrees of freedom, where degrees of freedom are as follows.

Source of Variation	Degrees of Freedom
Factor A treatment	$a - 1 = 3 - 1 = 2$
Factor B treatment	$b - 1 = 2 - 1 = 1$
Interaction	$(a - 1)(b - 1) = (2)(1) = 2$
Error	$a\,b\,(r - 1) = (3)(2)(2 - 1) = 6$

With this information, we can set up the ANOVA table as shown in Table 13.6.

Source of Variation	Sum of Squares	Degrees of Freedom	Mean Square	F
Factor A Treatment	80.67	2	40.33	$\dfrac{40.33}{23.67} = 1.70$
Factor B Treatment	27.00	1	27.00	$\dfrac{27.00}{23.67} = 1.14$
Interaction (AB)	26.00	2	13.00	$\dfrac{13.00}{23.67} = 0.55$
Error	142.00	6	23.67	
Total	275.67	11		

Table 13.6

Now we are in a position to answer the questions set forth at the beginning of the exercise. The F ratio used to test for a difference among the universities' preparation programs is 1.70. The critical F value at $\alpha = 0.05$ (with 2 numerator degrees of freedom and 6 denominator degrees of freedom) is 5.14. Since $1.70 < 5.14$, we cannot reject the null hypothesis. Therefore, we conclude that there is no difference in the preparation provided by the three universities.

The F ratio for the sex of the students is 1.14. The critical F value with 1 numerator and 6 denominator degrees of freedom is 5.99. Since $1.14 < 5.99$, we cannot reject the null hypothesis. Therefore, we conclude that there is no difference in the performance of male and female students.

Finally, the interaction F value is 0.55. The critical F value with 2 numerator and 6 denominator degrees of freedom is 5.14. Since $0.55 < 5.14$, no significant interaction can be identified. Thus, we conclude that there is no reason to believe that the three universities differ in their ability to prepare male and female students.

If we had used the *p*-value approach, the *p*-value would have been greater than 0.1 leading to the same conclusions as those above.

16. A factorial experiment involving 2 levels of Factor A and 2 levels of Factor B resulted in the following.

		Factor B	
		Level 1	Level 2
Factor A	Level 1	14	18
		16	12
	Level 2	18	16
		20	14

Test for any significant main effect and any interaction effect. Use $\alpha = 0.05$.

SELF-TESTING QUESTIONS

In the following multiple choice questions, circle the correct answer. An answer key is provided following the questions.

1.   The F ratio in a completely randomized ANOVA is the ratio of
a)   MST/MSE
b)   MSE/MSTR
c)   MSE/MST
d)   MSTR/MSE

2.   The critical F value with 8 numerator and 6 denominator degrees of freedom at $\alpha = .05$ is
a)   3.58
b)   4.88
c)   4.15
d)   8, 6

3.   The ANOVA procedure is a statistical approach for determining whether or not the
a)   means of two samples are equal
b)   means of more than two samples are equal
c)   means of two or more populations are equal
d)   medians of two samples are equal

4.   The variable of interest in an ANOVA procedure is called
a)   a factor
b)   a treatment
c)   interaction
d)   variance

5.   An ANOVA procedure is applied to data obtained from 5 samples, where each sample contains 9 observations. The degrees of freedom for the critical value of F are
a)   5 numerator and 9 denominator degrees of freedom
b)   4 numerator and 8 denominator degrees of freedom
c)   45 degrees of freedom
d)   4 numerator and 40 denominator degrees of freedom

6.   In the ANOVA, treatment refers to
a)   experimental units
b)   different levels of a factor
c)   a factor
d)   levels of experimental units

7. The mean square is the sum of squares divided by
a) the total number of observations
b) its corresponding degrees of freedom - 1
c) its corresponding degrees of freedom
d) 100

8. In factorial designs, the response produced when the treatments of one factor interact with the treatments of another in influencing the response variable is known as
a) the main effect
b) interaction
c) replication
d) main replication

9. An experimental design where the experimental units are randomly assigned to the treatments is known as
a) factor block design
b) random factor design
c) completely randomized design
d) block randomized

10. The number of times each experimental condition is observed in a factorial design is known as
a) replication
b) the experimental condition
c) a factor
d) treatments

11. When analysis of variance is performed on samples drawn from K populations, the mean square between treatments (MSTR) is SSTR divided by
a) n_T
b) $n_T - 1$
c) K
d) K - 1

12. In analysis of variance, where the total sample size for the experiment is n_T and the number of populations is K, the mean square within treatments is computed by dividing SSE by
a) n_T
b) $n_T - K$
c) $n_T - 1$
d) $n_T + K$

Exhibit 13-1
In a completely randomized experimental design involving four treatments, a total of 10 observations were recorded for **each** of the four treatments. The following information is provided.

SSTR = 300 (Sum Square Between Treatments)
SST = 1200 (Total Sum Square)

13. Refer to Exhibit 13-1. The sum of squares within treatments (SSE) is
a)   1500
b)   900
c)   300
d)   1200

14. Refer to Exhibit 13-1. The mean square between treatments (MSTR) is
a)   75
b)   25
c)   100
d)   36

15. Refer to Exhibit 13-1. The computed F statistic is
a)   3
b)   4
c)   5
d)   6

Exhibit 13-2
Fourteen observations were selected from each of four populations, and analysis of variance was performed on the data. Part of the ANOVA table is shown below.

Source of Variation	Sum of Squares	Degrees of Freedom	Mean Square	F
Between Treatments	60			
Error (Within Treatments)	260			

16. Refer to Exhibit 13-2. The number of degrees of freedom corresponding to between treatments is
a)   1
b)   2
c)   3
d)   4

17.   Refer to Exhibit 13-2. The number of degrees of freedom corresponding to within treatments is
a)   51
b)   52
c)   53
d)   54

18.   Refer to Exhibit 13-2. The mean square between treatments (MSTR) is
a)   15
b)   20
c)   30
d)   40

19.   Refer to Exhibit 13-2. The mean square within treatments or mean square error (MSE) is
a)   2
b)   3
c)   4
d)   5

20.   The computed F statistic is
a)   4
b)   3
c)   2
d)   1

ANSWERS TO THE SELF-TESTING QUESTIONS

1. d
2. c
3. c
4. a
5. d
6. b
7. c
8. b
9. c
10. a
11. d
12. b
13. b
14. c
15. b
16. c
17. b
18. b
19. d
20. a

ANSWERS TO CHAPTER THIRTEEN EXERCISES

2. (a) test statistic $F = 1.8$; p-value > 0.1 ($df_n = 2$, $df_d = 15$); do not reject H_0; there is no significant difference in the average lives of the three brands of tires
    (b) $F = 1.8 < 3.68$; thus, do not reject H_0
    (c) ANOVA: Single Factor

SUMMARY

Groups	Count	Sum	Average	Variance
Manufacturer A	6	240	40	8.4
Manufacturer B	6	252	42	18.8
Manufacturer C	6	264	44	12.8

ANOVA

Source of Variation	SS	df	MS	F	P-value	F crit
Between Groups	48	2	24	1.8	0.19922	3.68
Within Groups	200	15	13.33			
Total	248	17				

4. (a) test statistic $F = 0.6557$; p-value > 0.1 ($df_n = 2$, $df_d = 12$); do not reject H_0; we cannot conclude that there is a significant difference among the average heating bills (Excel results in a p-value of 0.5367)
    (b) $F = 0.66 < 3.89$; thus, do not reject H_0

5.
Source of Variation	Sum of Squares	Degrees of Freedom	Mean Square	F
Between Treatments	173.33	2	86.67	
				0.6557
Within Treatments (Error)	1586.00	12	132.17	
Total	1759.33	14		

7. (a) test statistic $F = 4.27$; p-value is between .05 and .025 (Excel p-value = .049); reject H_0; we conclude that there is a significant difference among the average speeds of the cars
    (b) $F = 4.27 > 4.26$; thus, reject H_0

9.

Source of Variation	Sum of Squares	Degrees of Freedom	Mean Square	F
Between Treatments	801	2	400.5	
				4.27
Within Treatments (Error)	804	9	93.78	

Since F = 4.27 > 4.26 reject H_0.   We conclude that there is a significant difference among the average speeds of the cars.

11.   (a)

Source of Variation	Sum of Squares	Degrees of Freedom	Mean Square	F
Between Treatments	69.33	2	34.665	
				6.07
Within Treatments (Error)	120.00	21	5.714	
Total	189.33	23		

Since F = 6.07 > 3.47, reject H_0. At least one mean is different from the others.

(b)   LSD = 2.47

$$\left|\bar{x}_1 - \bar{x}_2\right| = 1; \left|\bar{x}_1 - \bar{x}_3\right| = 3; \left|\bar{x}_2 - \bar{x}_3\right| = 4$$

Therefore, the mean of population 3 is different from the others.

12.   LSD = 22.75

$$\left|\bar{x}_1 - \bar{x}_2\right| = 32.9; \left|\bar{x}_1 - \bar{x}_3\right| = 49.7; \left|\bar{x}_2 - \bar{x}_3\right| = 16.8$$

Therefore, the mean of population 1 is different from the others.

14.   F = 1.428 < 7.71 (*p*-value > 0.1), thus, do not reject H_0

16.   Factor A treatment; F = 1.33 < 7.71 (*p*-value > 0.1), do not reject H_0, not significant
Factor B treatment; F = 1.33 < 7.71 (*p*-value > 0.1), do not reject H_0, not significant
Interaction (AB); F = 1.33 < 7.71 (*p*-value > 0.1), do not reject H_0, not significant

CHAPTER FOURTEEN

SIMPLE LINEAR REGRESSION

CHAPTER OUTLINE AND REVIEW

This chapter introduces two statistical techniques: regression and correlation. Regression and correlation are used for analyzing the relationship between variables by determining the best mathematical expression that describes their relationship and by measuring the strength of this relationship. The terms and concepts that you will learn are listed below.

ANOVA Table is the analysis of variance table used to summarize the computations associated with the F test for significance.

Coefficient of Determination (r^2) is a measure of the proportion of the variation in the dependent variable that is explained by the estimated regression equation. It is a measure of how well the estimated regression equation fits the data.

Confidence Interval Estimate is the interval estimate of the mean value of y for a given value of x.

Correlation Coefficient (r) is a statistical measure of the strength of the linear relationship between two variables.

Dependent Variable is the variable that is being predicted or explained. It is denoted by y in the regression equation.

Estimated Regression Equation is the estimate of the regression equation developed from sample data using the least squares method; that is, $\hat{y} = b_o + b_1 x$.

Independent Variable is the variable that is doing the predicting or explaining. It is denoted by x in the regression equation.

Influential Observation is an observation that has a strong influence or effect on the regression results.

ith Residual is the difference between the observed value of the dependent variable and the value predicted using the estimated regression equation; i.e., $y_i - \hat{y}_i$.

Least Squares Method is the approach used to develop the estimated regression equation that minimizes the sum of squares of the vertical distances from the points to the least squares fitted line. That is, it minimizes $\sum(y_i - \hat{y}_i)^2$.

Leverage is a measure of the influence an observation has on the regression results. Influential observations have high leverage.

Mean Square Error is the unbiased estimate of the variance, σ^2, of the error term ε. It is denoted by MSE or s^2.

Normal Probability Plot is a graph of normal scores plotted against values of the standardized residuals. This plot helps to determine if the assumption that the error term has a normal probability distribution appears to be valid.

Outlier is a data point or observation that is unusual compared to the remaining data.

Prediction Interval Estimate is the interval estimate of an individual value of y for a given value of x.

Regression Equation is the mathematical equation relating the independent variable to the expected value of the dependent variable; that is, $E(y) = \beta_0 + \beta_1 x$.

Regression Model is the probability model describing how the dependent variable (y) is related to the independent variable (x) in simple linear regression. The regression model has the form $y = \beta_0 + \beta_1 x + \varepsilon$.

Residual Analysis is the analysis of the residuals used to determine if the assumptions made about the regression model appear to be valid. Residual analysis is also used to identify unusual and influential observations.

Residual Plots are graphical representations of the residuals that can be used to determine if the assumptions made about the regression model appear to be valid.

Scatter Diagram is a graph of the data in which the independent variable appears on the horizontal axis and the dependent variable appears on the vertical axis.

Simple Linear Regression is the simplest kind of regression, involving only two variables (one independent and one dependent variable). The relationship between variables is approximated by a straight line.

Standard Error of the Estimate is the square root of the mean square error, denoted by s. It is the estimate of σ, the standard deviation of the error term ε.

Standardized Residual is the value obtained by dividing the residual by its standard deviation.

CHAPTER FORMULAS

Simple Linear Regression Model

$$y = \beta_0 + \beta_1 x + \varepsilon \tag{14.1}$$

Simple Linear Regression Equation

$$E(y) = \beta_0 + \beta_1 x \tag{14.2}$$

Least Squares Criterion

$$\text{Min} \sum (y_i - \hat{y}_i)^2 \tag{14.5}$$

Estimated Simple Linear Regression Equation

$$\hat{y} = b_o + b_1 x \tag{14.3}$$

where $\hat{y}$ = the estimated value of the dependent variable

b_0 = the y-intercept

b_1 = the slope of the line

and b_0 and b_1 are computed as

$$b_1 = \frac{\sum (x_i - \bar{x})(y_i - \bar{y})}{\sum (x_i - \bar{x})^2} \tag{14.6}$$

$$b_o = \bar{y} - b_1 \bar{x} \tag{14.7}$$

Sum of Squares due to Error

$$SSE = \sum (y_i - \hat{y}_i)^2 \tag{14.8}$$

Sum of Squares due to Regression

$$SSR = \sum (\hat{y} - \bar{y})^2 \qquad \text{Also,} \quad SSR = \frac{\left[\sum (x_i - \bar{x})(y_i - \bar{y}) \right]^2}{\sum (x_i - \bar{x})^2} \tag{14.10}$$

Total Sum of Squares

$$SST = \sum (y_i - \bar{y})^2 \tag{14.9}$$

Relationship among SST, SSR, and SSE

$$SST = SSR + SSE \tag{14.11}$$

CHAPTER FORMULAS
(Continued)

Coefficient of Determination

$$r^2 = \frac{SSR}{SST} \tag{14.12}$$

Sample Correlation Coefficient

$$r_{xy} = (\text{the sign of } b_1) \ \sqrt{\text{Coefficient of Determination}}$$
$$= (\text{the sign of } b_1) \ \sqrt{r^2} \tag{14.13}$$

where b_1 = the slope of the regression equation

Testing for Significance of the Correlation Coefficient

$$H_o: \rho_{xy} = 0$$
$$H_a: \rho_{xy} \neq 0$$

t statistic: $t = r_{xy}\sqrt{\dfrac{n-2}{1-r_{xy}^2}}$ $\tag{14.43}$

Decision Rules:

When using the *p*-value approach, reject H_0 if *p*-value $\leq \alpha$

When using the critical value approach, reject H_0 if $t \leq -t_{\alpha/2}$ or: $t \geq t_{\alpha/2}$
(degrees of freedom = n - 2)

Mean Square Error (Estimate of σ^2)

$$s^2 = MSE = \frac{SSE}{n-2} \tag{14.15}$$

Standard Error of the Estimate

$$s = \sqrt{MSE} = \sqrt{\frac{SSE}{n-2}} \tag{14.16}$$

CHAPTER FORMULAS
(Continued)

---

t Test for significance in Simple Linear Regression
(Testing for the Significance of the Slope)

$H_o: \beta_1 = 0$

$H_a: \beta_1 \neq 0$

t statistic: $t = \dfrac{b_1}{s_{b_1}}$ (14.19)

where s_{b_1} (Estimated Standard Deviation of b_1) is

$s_{b_1} = \dfrac{s}{\sqrt{\Sigma(x_i - \bar{x})^2}}$ (14.18)

Decision Rules:

When using the *p*-value approach, reject H_O if *p*-value $\leq \alpha$

When using the critical value approach, reject H_O if $t \leq -t_{\alpha/2}$ or: $t \geq t_{\alpha/2}$
(degrees of freedom = n - 2)

F Test for Significance in Simple Linear Regression

$H_o: \beta = 0$

$H_a: \beta \neq 0$

$F = \dfrac{MSR}{MSE}$ (14.21)

where MSR (Mean Square Due to Regression) is

$MSR = \dfrac{SSR}{\text{Number of Independent Variables}}$ (14.20)

Decision Rules:

When using the *p*-value approach, reject H_O if *p*-value $\leq \alpha$

When using the critical value approach, reject H_O if $F \geq F_{\alpha}$
(degrees of freedom = n - 2)

CHAPTER FORMULAS
(Continued)

> ## Confidence Interval Estimate of $E(y_p)$
> ## (for the Mean Value of y)

$$\hat{y}_p \pm t_{\alpha/2} s_{\hat{y}_p} \tag{14.24}$$

where Estimated Standard Deviation of $\hat{y}_p$ is

$$s_{\hat{y}_p} = s\sqrt{\frac{1}{n} + \frac{(x_p - \overline{x})^2}{\Sigma(x_i - \overline{x})^2}} \tag{14.23}$$

> ## Confidence Interval Estimate of y_p
> ## (for an Individual Value of y)

$$\hat{y}_p \pm t_{\alpha/2} s_{ind} \tag{14.27}$$

where

$$s_{ind} = s\sqrt{1 + \frac{1}{n} + \frac{(x_p - \overline{x})^2}{\Sigma(x_i - \overline{x})^2}} \tag{14.26}$$

Residual for Observation i

$$y_i - \hat{y}_i \tag{14.28}$$

Standard Deviation of the ith Residual

$$S_{y_i - \hat{y}_i} = S\sqrt{1 - h_i} \tag{14.30}$$

where h_i is the leverage for observation i.

$$h_i = \frac{1}{n} + \frac{\left(x_i - \overline{x}\right)^2}{\Sigma\left(x_i - \overline{x}\right)^2} \tag{14.31}$$

Standardized Residual for Observation i

$$\frac{y_i - \hat{y}_i}{s_{y_i - \hat{y}_i}} \tag{14.32}$$

EXERCISES

Solved Problem

1.   Note: Since the topics in this chapter are interrelated, the remaining exercises in this chapter that are marked with an "" are based on this exercise and have been worked for you.

Freeman, Inc. is a large carpet manufacturing firm. The following data represent Freeman's yearly sales volume and its advertising expenditures over a period of 10 years.

Year	Advertising Expenditure (x_i) ($ Millions)	Sales Volume (y_i) ($ Millions)
2001	1.8	26
2002	2.3	31
2003	2.6	28
2004	2.4	30
2005	2.8	34
2006	3.0	38
2007	3.4	41
2008	3.2	44
2009	3.6	40
2010	3.8	43

(a)   Develop a scatter diagram for the above data.

Answer: Plotting the advertising expenditures on the horizontal axis, the scatter diagram is shown in Figure 14.1.

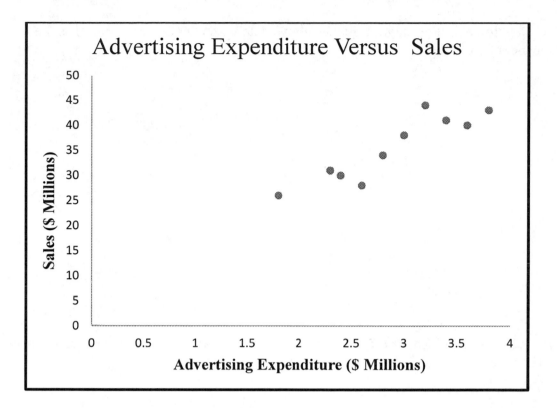

Figure 14.1

(b)   What does the scatter diagram developed in part (a) indicate about the relationship between the two variables?

Answer: The scatter diagram shows that there is a positive relationship between the variables. The overview of the data shows that as advertising expenditures increase so does the sales volume.

2.   Note: Exercises 5, 8, 11, 14, 16, and 18 are a continuation of this exercise and use the same data set.
Assume you have noted the following prices for paperback books and the number of pages that each book contains.

Book	Pages (x)	Price (y)
A	500	$7.00
B	700	7.50
C	750	9.00
D	590	6.50
E	540	7.50
F	650	7.00
G	480	4.50

(a)   Develop a scatter diagram for the above data with the number of pages as the independent variable.

(b)   What does the scatter diagram developed in part (a) indicate about the relationship between the two variables?

3.   Note: Exercises 6, 9, 12, and 19 are a continuation of this exercise and use the same data set.
The following data represent the number of weed-eaters sold per month at a local garden shop and their prices.

Price (x)	Units Sold (y)
$34	3
36	4
32	6
35	5
30	9
38	2
40	1

(a)   Develop a scatter diagram for the above data with the price as the independent variable.

(b)   What does the scatter diagram developed in part (a) indicate about the relationship between the two variables?

Solved Problem

*4.   Refer to exercise *1.

(a)   What kind of model would be appropriate for representing the relationship between the two variables?

Answer: Since one cannot guarantee a single value of y for each value of x, the relationship between the variables is explained by a probabilistic model. Noting the relationship between sales volume (y) and advertising expenditure (x), one can assume that this relationship can be approximated by a straight line in the form of

$$y = \beta_0 + \beta_1 x + \varepsilon$$

where β_0 = y-intercept.

β_1 = the slope of the line.

ε = the error, or deviation, of the actual y value from the line given by $\beta_0 + \beta_1 x$.

The above probabilistic model is known as a regression model, which provides a good approximation of the y value at each x. β_0 and β_1 are known as the parameters of the model.

(b)   In the regression model shown in part (a), what assumptions are made about the error term ε in the regression model $y = \beta_0 + \beta_1 x + \varepsilon$?

Answer: The 4 major assumptions about the regression model are

1.   The error term ε is a random variable with a mean or expected value of zero. That is, $E(\varepsilon) = 0$. Since $E(\varepsilon) = 0$, then $E(y) = \beta_0 + \beta_1 x$.

2.   The variance of ε is the same for all values of x.

3.   The values of the error are independent. That is, the size of error for a particular value of x is not related to the size of error for any other value of x.

4.   The error term ε is a normally distributed random variable that can take on negative or positive values. Thus, the error term represents the deviation between the y

value and the value given by $\beta_0 + \beta_1 x$. Since y is a linear function of ε, the above implies that y is also a normally distributed random variable.

(c)   Develop a least-squares estimated regression line.

Answer: In part (a), it was assumed that the regression model $y = \beta_0 + \beta_1 x + \varepsilon$ related x and y. Furthermore, it was assumed $E(\varepsilon) = 0$. Thus, the regression model became $E(y) = \beta_0 + \beta_1 x$. Now we can use the least squares method to estimate β_0 and β_1, thereby determining the following estimated regression equation.

$$\hat{y} = b_0 + b_1 x$$

where $\hat{y}$ = estimate of $E(y)$
b_0 = estimate of β_0
b_1 = estimate of β_1

The least squares method determines the estimated regression equation, which minimizes the sum of squares of the differences between the observed values of the dependent variable (y_i) and the estimated values of the dependent variable ($\hat{y}_i$). That is, the values of b_0 and b_1 are determined in such a way that

$$\sum_{i=1}^{n} (y_i - \hat{y}_i)^2 \text{ is minimized.}$$

Using differential calculus, it is determined that the following b_0 and b_1 minimizes the above sum of squares of the differences.

$$b_1 = \frac{\sum(x_i - \bar{x})(y_i - \bar{y})}{\sum(x_i - \bar{x})^2}$$

$$b_0 = \bar{y} - b_1 \bar{x}$$

where x_i = the value of the independent variable for the ith observation

y_i = the value of the dependent variable for the ith observation

$\bar{x}$ = the mean value for the independent variable

$\bar{y}$ = the mean value for the dependent variable

n = the total number of observations

Thus, we need the following calculations for estimating the regression line.

x_i	y_i	$(x_i - \bar{x})$	$(y_i - \bar{y})$	$(x_i - \bar{x})(y_i - \bar{y})$	$(x_i - \bar{x})^2$
1.8	26	-1.09	-9.5	10.355	1.1881
2.3	31	-0.59	-4.5	2.655	0.3481
2.6	28	-0.29	-7.5	2.175	0.0841
2.4	30	-0.49	-5.5	2.695	0.2401
2.8	34	-0.09	-1.5	0.135	0.0081
3	38	0.11	2.5	0.275	0.0121
3.4	41	0.51	5.5	2.805	0.2601
3.2	44	0.31	8.5	2.635	0.0961
3.6	40	0.71	4.5	3.195	0.5041
3.8	43	0.91	7.5	6.825	0.8281
Totals **28.9**	**355**			**33.75**	**3.569**
Σx_i	Σy_i			$\Sigma(x_i - \bar{x})(y_i - \bar{y})$	$\Sigma(x_i - \bar{x})^2$

The values of $\bar{x}$ and $\bar{y}$ are determined to be

$$\bar{x} = \frac{\Sigma x}{n} = \frac{28.9}{10} = 2.89$$

$$\bar{y} = \frac{\Sigma y}{n} = \frac{355}{10} = 35.5$$

Now using the above totals and the means we can compute the slope (b_1) as

$$b_1 = \frac{\Sigma(x_i - \bar{x})(y_i - \bar{y})}{\Sigma(x_i - \bar{x})^2} = \frac{33.75}{3.569} = 9.4564$$

Hence, the value of b_0 is computed as

$$b_0 = \bar{y} - b_1 \bar{x} = 35.5 - (9.4564)(2.89) = 8.171 \quad \text{(rounded)}$$

Therefore, the estimated regression function is

$$\hat{y} = 8.171 + 9.4564\, x_1$$

The slope of the estimated regression line is 9.4564. Since the slope is positive, it implies that as advertising expenditure increases, sales volume is expected to increase. Since both advertising expenditure and sales volume were measured in millions of dollars, it can be concluded that as advertising expenditure increases by 1 million dollars, sales volume is expected to increase by 9.4565 million dollars.

5.   Refer to exercise 2. Develop a least-squares estimated regression line.

6.   Refer to exercise 3. Develop a least-squares regression line and explain what the slope of the line indicates.

Solved Problem

*7. Refer to exercise *4.

(a) Compute the coefficient of determination, and comment on the strength of the relationship between advertising and sales.

Answer: The coefficient of determination (r^2) is a measure indicating how well the regression equation fits the observed data. The coefficient of determination is computed as

$$r^2 = \frac{SSR}{SST}$$

where   SSR = the sum of squares explained by regression
        SSE = the sum of squared due to error
        SST = the total sum of squares

We begin by computing the Sum of Squares Due to Error (SSE) as

$$SSE = \sum(y_i - \hat{y}_i)^2$$

The above equation shows the sum of the differences between individual observations (y_i) and their corresponding values as estimated by the line of regression ($\hat{y}_i$). For example, in 2001, the value of $x_{2001} = 1.8$ and the observed value of $y_{2001} = 26$. Since our regression equation is

$$\hat{y}_i = 8.171 + 9.4564x_i$$

we can estimate the value of $\hat{y}_{2001}$ as

$$\hat{y}_{2001} = 8.171 + 9.4564(1.8) = 25.1925$$

The difference between y_{2001} and $\hat{y}_{2001}$ is the error (residual) resulting from using the regression equation to estimate the observed value. Similarly, we can determine the errors for all years. The following table shows the steps needed for computing SSE.

Year	x_i	y_i	$\hat{y}_i = 8.1709 + 9.4564 x_i$	$(y_i - \hat{y}_i)$	$(y_i - \hat{y}_i)^2$
2001	1.8	26	25.1925	0.8075	0.6521
2002	2.3	31	29.9207	1.0793	1.1649
2003	2.6	28	32.7576	-4.7576	22.6351
2004	2.4	30	30.8663	-0.8663	0.7506
2005	2.8	34	34.6489	-0.6489	0.4211
2006	3	38	36.5402	1.4598	2.1310
2007	3.4	41	40.3228	0.6772	0.4586
2008	3.2	44	38.4315	5.5685	31.0083
2009	3.6	40	42.2141	-2.2141	4.9021
2010	3.8	43	44.1054	-1.1054	1.2218
				SSE =	**65.3455**

Next we compute the total sum of squares (SST) as SST = $\sum(y_i - \bar{y})^2$. Hence, the following computations are needed for calculating SST. **Remember:** $\bar{y} = 35.5$

Year	y_i	$(y_i - \bar{y})$	$(y_i - \bar{y})^2$
2001	26	-9.5	90.25
2001	31	-4.5	20.25
2003	28	-7.5	56.25
2004	30	-5.5	30.25
2005	34	-1.5	2.25
2006	38	2.5	6.25
2007	41	5.5	30.25
2008	44	8.5	72.25
2009	40	4.5	20.25
2010	43	7.5	56.25
		SST=	**384.5**

Now that we have determined SST = 384.5 and SSE = 65.3455, we can compute SSR. Since SST = SSR + SSE, we can compute SSR as

SSR = SST - SSE = 384.5 - 65.3455 = 319.1545

Finally, the coefficient of determination is computed as

$$r^2 = \frac{SSR}{SST} = \frac{319.1545}{384.5} = 0.83 \text{ (rounded)}$$

Therefore, it can be concluded that the estimated regression function has accounted for 83% of the total sum of the squares, which indicates that it provides a good fit for the data.

(b)   Compute the sample correlation coefficient between sales volumes and advertising expenditures.

Answer: The sample correlation coefficient is simply the square root of the coefficient of determination. In part (a) of this exercise the coefficient of determination was computed to be 0.83. Therefore the coefficient of correlation is

$$r_{xy} = \text{(the sign of } b_1) \ \sqrt{\text{Coefficient of Determination}} = + \ \sqrt{0.83} = 0.91 \text{ (rounded)}$$

(c)   At 95% confidence test the following hypotheses.

$$H_o: \rho_{xy} = 0$$
$$H_a: \rho_{xy} \neq 0$$

Answer: The test statistic is

$$t = r_{xy} \sqrt{\frac{n-2}{1-r^2}} - (0.91) \ \sqrt{\frac{10 - 2}{1 - (0.91)^2}} = 6.25$$

From the t distribution of the Appendix with 8 degrees of freedom, we have the following information.

Area in the upper tail	0.025	0.01	0.005
t value (8 df)	2.306	2.896	3.355

t = 6.25

The test statistic t = 6.2 is greater than 3.355. Therefore, the *p*-value must be less than .005. This being a two-tailed test, the *p*-value must be less than (2)(.005) = .01. Since the *p*-value < .01, the null hypothesis is rejected at 95% confidence; and we conclude that x and y are related. We could have used the critical value approach for this test. From Table 2 in the Appendix, we read the t value with n - 2 = 10 - 2 = 8 degrees of freedom as $t_{.025} = \pm 2.306$. Since 6.2 > 2.306, the null hypothesis is rejected, and we conclude that x and y are related.

8.   Refer to exercise 5.

(a)   Compute the coefficient of determination and explain its meaning.

(b)   Compute the correlation coefficient between the price and the number of pages. Test to see if x and y are related. Use $\alpha = 0.10$.
Hint: The solution procedure is shown to you in parts (b) and (c) of exercise *7.

9. Refer to exercise 6.

(a) Compute the coefficient of determination and comment on the strength of relationship between x and y.

(b) Compute the sample correlation coefficient between the price and the number of weed-eaters sold. Use $\alpha = 0.01$ to test the relationship between x and y. **Hint: The solution procedure is shown to you in parts (b) and (c) of exercise *7.**

Solved Problem

*10. Refer to exercise *7.

(a)   Using an F test, determine if the advertising expenditures and the sales volumes are related.   Let $\alpha = 0.05$.

Answer: If a relationship between x and y of the form $E(y) = \beta_0 + \beta_1 x$ really exists, then β_1 must be different from zero. Thus, the hypotheses to be tested are

> H_0: $\beta_1 = 0$ (variables are not related)

> H_a: $\beta_1 \neq 0$ (variables are related)

First we need to compute an F value as

$$F = \frac{MSR}{MSE}$$

Then, if this F value is less than or equal to the critical F value (F_α), the null hypothesis will not be rejected. In exercise *7 we computed the following.

> SSR = 319.1545

> SST = 384.5

> SSE = 65.3455

Then, the mean squares are computed as

$$MSR = \frac{SSR}{\text{Number of Independent Variables}}$$

Since there is one independent variable, MSR will be

$$MSR = \frac{319.1545}{1} = 319.1545$$

and

$$MSE = \frac{SSE}{n - 2} = \frac{65.3455}{10 - 2} = 8.1682$$

Now the F statistic is computed as

$$F = \frac{319.1545}{8.1682} = 39.07 \text{ (rounded)}$$

The F distribution of the Appendix shows that with 1 numerator degree of freedom (the number of independent variables) and n - 2 = 10 - 2 = 8 denominator degrees of freedom F = 11.26, providing an area of .01 in the upper tail. Therefore, the area in the upper tail (*p*-value) for F = 39.07 must be less than 0.01. Thus, the null hypothesis is rejected, and we conclude that there is a significant statistical relationship between sales volume and advertising expenditure.

We could have used the critical value approach for this test. From Table 4 of the Appendix, the critical value of F_α with 1 numerator degree of freedom (the number of independent variables) and n - 2 = 10 - 2 = 8 denominator degrees of freedom is determined to be $F_{.05} = 5.32$. Since 39.07 > 5.32, the null hypothesis is rejected.

(b)   Use a t test to answer the question asked in part (a).

Answer: The hypotheses to be tested are the same as shown in part (a), which are

$$H_0: \beta_1 = 0 \text{ (variables are not related)}$$

$$H_a: \beta_1 \neq 0 \text{ (variables are related)}$$

The test statistic is

$$t = \frac{b_1}{s_{b_1}}$$

where s_{b_1} (estimated standard deviation of b_1) is

$$s_{b_1} = \frac{s}{\sqrt{\Sigma(x_i - \bar{x})^2}}$$

In part (a) of this exercise, MSE was computed to be 8.1687. Using MSE, first we can compute the numerator of the above (s) as

$$s = \sqrt{MSE} = \sqrt{8.1682} = 2.858$$

In part (c) of exercise *4, we computed $\Sigma(x_i - \bar{x})^2 = 3.649$. Now we can compute s_{b_1} as

$$s_{b_1} = \frac{s}{\sqrt{\Sigma(x_i - \bar{x})^2}} = \frac{2.858}{\sqrt{3.569}} = 1.5129 \text{ (rounded)}$$

Now we can compute the t statistic. (Recall that b_1 was calculated in part (c) of exercise *4 as 9.4564.)

$$t = \frac{b_1}{s_{b_1}} = \frac{9.4564}{1.5129} = 6.25$$

From the t distribution table of the Appendix corresponding to n - 2 = 10 - 2 = 8 degrees of freedom, we have the following.

Area in the upper tail	**0.025**	**0.01**	**0.005**
t value (8 df)	2.306	2.896	3.355

$$t = 6.25$$

Since our test statistic t = 6.25 is larger than 3.355, it indicates that the area in the upper tail is less than .005; hence, the *p*-value is less than 2(.005) = .01 (two-tailed). Therefore, we reject the null hypothesis and conclude that there is a significant statistical relationship between sales volume and advertising expenditure. Note that this is the same conclusion we had in part (a).

If we use the critical value approach, the decision rule for the t test is

Reject H_0 if $t < -t_{\alpha/2}$ or $t \geq t_{\alpha/2}$

From Table 2 of the Appendix, we find that $t_{\alpha/2}$ with 8 degrees of freedom (n - 2) is $t_{.025} = 2.306$. Since 6.25 > 2.306, the null hypothesis is rejected.

11.   Refer to exercise 8.

(a)   Perform an F test and determine if the price and the number of pages of the books are related. Let $\alpha = 0.01$.

(b)   Perform a t test and determine if the price and the number of pages of the books are related. Let $\alpha = 0.01$.

12.   Refer to exercise 9.

(a)   Perform an F test and determine if the price and the number of weed-eaters sold are related. Let $\alpha = 0.01$

(b)   Perform a t test and determine if the price and the number of weed-eaters sold are related. Let $\alpha = 0.01$

Solved Problem

*13. Refer to exercises *4 and *10.

(a)   Determine the expected sales volume when the advertising expenditures are 3.5 million dollars.

Answer: With advertising expenditures of 3.5 million dollars, the expected sales volume is $\hat{y}_p$.

$$\hat{y}_p = 8.1709 + 9.4564 \,(3.5) = 41.2683$$

Thus, we conclude that the expected sales volume is \$41,268,300.

(b)   Develop a 95% confidence interval for estimating the mean sales volume with advertising expenditures of 3.5 million dollars.

Answer: The estimated standard deviation of $\hat{y}_p$ is

$$s_{\hat{y}_p} = s\sqrt{\frac{1}{n} + \frac{(x_p - \overline{x})^2}{\sum(x_i - \overline{x})^2}}$$

Recall that in part (c) of exercise *4 we calculated $\sum(x_i - \overline{x})^2 = 3.56$ and in part (b) of exercise *10, we determined $s = 2.8580$. Thus, we can calculate the standard deviation of $\hat{y}_p$ as

$$s_{\hat{y}_p} = s\sqrt{\frac{1}{n} + \frac{(x_p - \overline{x})^2}{\sum(x_i - \overline{x})^2}} = 2.8580\sqrt{\frac{1}{10} + \frac{(3.5 - 2.89)^2}{3.569}} = 1.29 \text{ (rounded)}$$

Therefore, we can find an interval estimate for $E(y_p)$ as

$$\hat{y}_p \pm t_{a/2}\, s_{\hat{y}_p}$$

From Table 2 of the Appendix, we can read the t value with $n - 2 = 10 - 2 = 8$ degrees of freedom as $t_{.025} = 2.306$. Hence, the confidence interval is shown below. (Note: $\hat{y}_p$ was determined in part (a) of this exercise.)

$$\hat{y}_p \pm t_{\alpha/2}\, s_{\hat{y}_p}$$

$$41.2683 \pm (2.306)\,(1.29) = 41.2683 \pm 2.9747$$

which yields 38.2936 to 44.2430. Thus, the 95% confidence interval estimate in terms of dollars is from $38,293,600 to $44,243,100.

14.   Refer to exercises 5 and 11. Develop a 90% confidence interval for estimating the average price of books that contain 800 pages.

Solved Problem

*15. Refer to exercise *13. Develop a 95% confidence interval to estimate the sales volume for a specific advertising expenditure of 3.5 million dollars.

Answer: In exercise *13, we determined an interval for the average sales volume. In this exercise, we are interested in determining an interval for the sales volume corresponding to a specific advertising expenditure of 3.5 million dollars. The procedure is basically the same as that which was shown in exercise 13. However, the standard deviation is

$$s_{ind} = s\sqrt{1 + \frac{1}{n} + \frac{(x_p - \bar{x})^2}{\sum(x_i - \bar{x})^2}} = 2.8580\sqrt{1 + \frac{1}{10} + \frac{(3.5 - 2.89)^2}{3.569}} = 3.14 \text{ (rounded)}$$

Thus, the interval estimate is

$$\hat{y}_p \pm t_{a/2}\, s_{ind}$$

$$41.2683 \pm (2.306)(3.14) = 41.2683 \pm 7.2408$$

which yields 34.0275 to 48.5091. Therefore, the 95% confidence interval estimate in terms of dollars is from \$34,027,500 to \$48,509,100.

16. As an extension of exercise 14, develop a 90% confidence interval to estimate the price of a specific book that has 800 pages.

Solved Problem

*17. Refer to exercise *4.

(a) Prepare a plot of the residuals against the independent variable x. Comment on it.

Answer: The residuals are computed as shown in Table 14.1.
(Note: $\hat{y} = 8.171 + 9.4564\,x$, and $\hat{y}$ values are computed by substituting x values in this equation.)

x_i	y_i	$\hat{y}_i$	$(y_i - \hat{y}_i)$
1.8	26	25.1925	0.8075
2.3	31	29.9207	1.0793
2.6	28	32.7576	-4.7576
2.4	30	30.8664	-0.8664
2.8	34	34.6489	-0.6489
3.0	38	36.5402	1.4598
3.4	41	40.3228	0.6772
3.2	44	38.4315	5.5685
3.6	40	42.2140	-2.2140
3.8	43	44.1053	-1.1053

Table 14.1

Now we plot the x_i on the horizontal and $(y_i - \hat{y}_i)$ on the vertical axis, thus producing the residual plot as shown in Figure 14.2

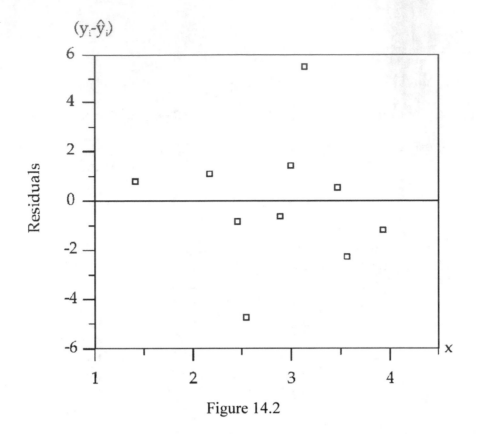

Figure 14.2

Note that the largest residual is 5.5685 and the smallest is - 4.7576. Also, residuals appear to be randomly distributed with no particular pattern. Therefore, it can be concluded that the assumptions made in part (b) of exercise *4 are satisfied and the proposed linear relationship between x and y is an appropriate model.

(b)   Prepare a residual plot of $\hat{y}_i$ versus ($y_i - \hat{y}_i$) and comment on it.

Answer: The residuals are computed as shown previously in Table 14.1. Now we plot the $\hat{y}_i$ on the horizontal and $(y_i - \hat{y}_i)$ on the vertical axis. This residual plot is shown in Figure 14.3.

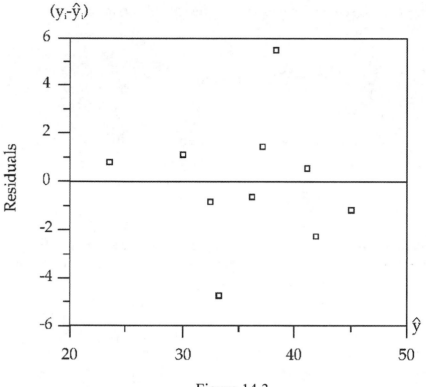

$(y_i - \hat{y}_i)$

Residuals

Figure 14.3

As you note, the pattern of this residual plot is the same as the residual plot shown in Figure 14.2. In fact, either residual plot can be constructed, and the same conclusions can be drawn.

(c) Construct a residual plot of the standardized residuals against the independent variable.

Answer: Any random variable is standardized by subtracting its mean from it and dividing the results by its standard deviation. Since the mean of the residuals is zero, we can simply divide each residual by its standard deviation and arrive at the standardized values. The standard deviation of the ith residual is given by

$$S_{y_i - \hat{y}_i} = S\sqrt{1 - h_i}$$

where $h_i = \dfrac{1}{n} + \dfrac{(x_i - \overline{x})^2}{\sum(x_i - \overline{x})^2}$

The above formula indicates that residuals corresponding to different values of x have different standard deviations. The standard deviation of each residual is computed using the above formula. Note that the denominator of h_i is simply $\sum(x_i - \overline{x})^2 = 3.569$.

As an example, let us compute the standard deviation for the first observation (i.e., x = 1.8). First, we can compute h_1 as

$$h_i = \frac{1}{n} + \frac{(x_i - \bar{x})^2}{\sum(x_i - \bar{x})^2} = \frac{1}{10} + \frac{(1.8 - 2.89)^2}{3.569} = 0.4329$$

All other values of h_i are computed in the same manner and are shown in Table 14.2. Next, we compute the standard deviation for the first observation as

$$S_{y_i - \hat{y}_i} = S\sqrt{1 - h_i} = 2.858\sqrt{(1 - 0.4329)} = 2.1523$$

For the above computations, the value of s = 2.8580, which was computed in part (b) of exercise *10. All other variances and ultimately the standard deviations are computed in the same manner and their values are shown in Table 14.2.

x_i	y_i	$\hat{y}$	$y_i - \hat{y}$	h_i	Standard Deviation	Standardized Residual
1.8	26	25.1925	0.8075	0.4329	2.1523	0.3752
2.3	31	29.9207	1.0793	0.1975	2.5603	0.4215
2.6	28	32.7576	-4.7576	0.1236	2.6757	-1.7781
2.4	30	30.8664	-0.8664	0.1673	2.6081	-0.3322
2.8	34	34.6489	-0.6489	0.1023	2.7080	-0.2396
3.0	38	36.5402	1.4598	0.1034	2.7063	0.5394
3.4	41	40.3228	0.6772	0.1729	2.5993	0.2605
3.2	44	38.4315	5.5685	0.1269	2.6706	2.0852
3.6	40	42.2140	-2.2140	0.2412	2.4896	-0.8893
3.8	43	44.1053	-1.1053	0.3320	2.3359	-0.4732

Table 14.2

Finally, the standardized residuals are computed by dividing each residual by its corresponding standard deviation. These values are also shown in Table 14.2. Now we can construct the plot of the standardized residuals against x values as shown in Figure 14.4.

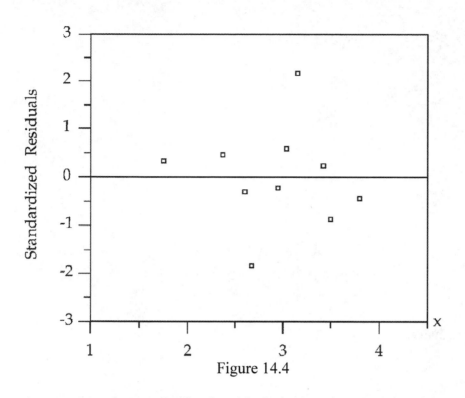

Figure 14.4

As you note, the standardized residual plot has the same general pattern as the original residual plot shown in Figure 14.2.

18. Refer to Exercise 5.

(a) Determine the residuals.

(b)   Prepare a residual plot of x_i versus $(y_i - \hat{y}_i)$.

19.   Refer to Exercise 6.

(a)   Determine the residuals.

(b)   Prepare a residual plot of x_i versus $(y_i - \hat{y}_i)$.

Solved Problem

*20. Use Excel (or any statistical software available to you) and perform a regression analysis on data provided in exercise *1.

Answer: I have used Microsoft Excel, and the results are given below.

SUMMARY
OUTPUT

Regression Statistics	
Multiple R	0.9111
R Square	0.8301
Adjusted R Square	0.8088
Standard Error	2.8580
Observations	10

ANOVA

	df	SS	MS	F	Significance F
Regression	1	319.1545	319.1545	39.0729	0.0002
Residual	8	65.3455	8.1682		
Total	9	384.5000			

	Coefficients	Standard Error	t Stat	P-value
Intercept	8.1709	4.4645	1.8302	0.1046
Advertising	9.4564	1.5128	6.2508	0.0002

As you notice, the results of Excel are precisely those shown to you in exercises *4, *7, and *10, which are extensions of exercise *1.

21.   Use Excel (or any statistical software available to you) and perform a regression analysis on data provided in exercise 2.

22.   Use Excel (or any statistical software available to you) and perform a regression analysis on data provided in exercise 3.

SELF-TESTING QUESTIONS

In the following multiple choice questions, circle the correct answer. An answer key is provided following the questions.

1.   In regression analysis, the variable that is being predicted is
a)   the independent variable
b)   the dependent variable
c)   usually denoted by x
d)   either the dependent or the independent variable

2.   In the regression equation $\hat{y} = b_0 + b_1x$, b_0 is the
a)   slope of the line
b)   independent variable
c)   y-intercept
d)   dependent variable

3.   In the regression equation $\hat{y} = b_0 + b_1x$, b_1 is
a)   the slope of the line
b)   an independent variable
c)   the y-intercept
d)   a dependent variable

4.   In regression analysis, the variable that is doing the predicting or explaining is
a)   the independent variable
b)   usually denoted by y
c)   the dependent variable
d)   either the dependent or the independent variable

5.   The coefficient of determination is
a)   the square root of the correlation coefficient
b)   usually less than zero
c)   the correlation coefficient squared
d)   usually larger than one

6.   The value of the coefficient of determination ranges between
a)   -1 to +1
b)   -1 to 0
c)   1 to infinity
d)   0 to +1

7.   The coefficient of correlation
a)   is the coefficient of determination squared
b)   is the square root of the coefficient of determination
c)   can never be negative
d)   is usually greater than one

8. The range of the correlation coefficient is
a) 0 to +1
b) -1 to 0
c) -1 to infinity
d) -1 to +1

9. If the slope of the regression equation $\hat{y} = b_0 + b_1 x$ is positive, then
a) as x increases y decreases
b) as x increases so does y
c) all y values must be positive
d) all x values must be positive

10. The residual refers to
a) $\overline{y}_i - \hat{y}_i$
b) $y_i - \hat{y}_i$
c) $\hat{y}_i - \overline{y}_i$
d) $\overline{y} - \overline{x}$

11. In a regression analysis, the error term ε is a random variable with a mean or expected value of
a) zero
b) one
c) any positive value
d) any value

12. The model developed from sample data that has the form of $\hat{y} = b_0 + b_1 x$ is known as
a) regression equation
b) correlation equation
c) estimated regression equation
d) regression model

13. In a regression analysis, if only MSE is known, you can compute the
a) r square
b) coefficient of determination
c) standard error
d) all of these alternatives are correct

14. In a regression analysis, the standard error is determined to be 9. In this situation, the MSE
a) is 3
b) is 81
c) depends on the sample size
d) depends on the degrees of freedom

15.   A regression analysis between sales (Y in $1000) and advertising (X in dollars) resulted in the following equation

$$\hat{Y} = 30,000 + 5X$$

The above equation implies that an
a)   increase of $4 in advertising is associated with an increase of $5,000 in sales
b)   increase of $1 in advertising is associated with an increase of $5 in sales
c)   increase of $1 in advertising is associated with an increase of $35,000 in sales
d)   increase of $1 in advertising is associated with an increase of $5,000 in sales

16.   In a regression analysis, the coefficient of determination is 0.16. the coefficient of correlation in this situation is
a)   0.4
b)   0.0256
c)   any positive value
d)   any value

17.   In a regression and correlation analysis if $r^2 = 1$, then
a)   SSE = SST
b)   SSE = 1
c)   SSR = SSE
d)   SSR = SST

18.   In a regression analysis if SSE = 400 and SSR = 600, then the coefficient of determination is
a)   0.6667
b)   0.6000
c)   0.4000
d)   1.5000

19.   Regression analysis was applied between demand for a product (Y) and the price of the product (X), and the following estimated regression equation was obtained.

$$\hat{Y} = 140 - 20X$$

Based on the above estimated regression equation, if price is increased by 2 units, then demand is expected to
a)   increase by 140 units
b)   decrease by 140 units
c)   increase by 40 units
d)   decrease by 40 units

20.   If the coefficient of correlation is 0.8, the percentage of variation in the dependent variable explained by the variation in the independent variable is
a)   0.80%
b)   80%
c)   0.64%
d)   64%

ANSWERS TO THE SELF-TESTING QUESTIONS

1. b
2. c
3. a
4. a
5. c
6. d
7. b
8. d
9. b
10. b
11. a
12. c
13. c
14. b
15. d
16. a
17. d
18. b
19. d
20. d

ANSWERS TO CHAPTER FOURTEEN EXERCISES

2. (a)

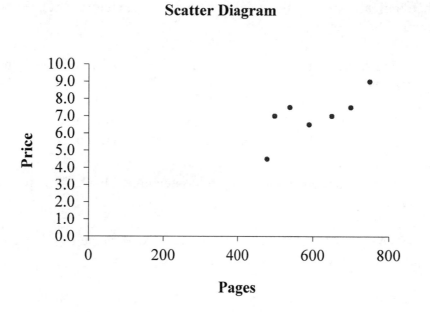

Scatter Diagram

(b) There appears to be a positive relationship between x and y.

3. (a)

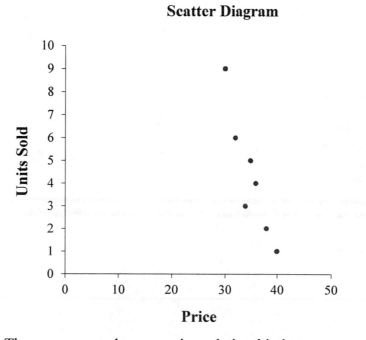

Scatter Diagram

(b) There appears to be a negative relationship between x and y.

5. $\hat{y} = 1.0416 + 0.0099x$

6. $\hat{y} = 29.7857 - 0.7286x$

    The slope indicates that as the price goes up by $1, the number of units sold goes down by 0.7286 units.

8. (a) $r^2 = .5629$; the regression equation has accounted for 56.29% of the total sum of squares
    (b) $r_{xy} = 0.75$
         $t = 2.54 > 2.015$ (df = 5); p-value is between .05 and 0.1; (Excel's result: p-value = .052); reject H_0, and conclude x and y are related

9. (a) $r^2 = .8556$; the regression equation has accounted for 85.56% of the total sum of squares
    (b) $r_{xy} = -0.92$
         $t = -5.44 < -4.032$ (df = 5); p-value < .01; (Excel's result: p-value = .0028); reject H_0, and conclude x and y are related

11. (a) $F = 6.439 < 16.26$; p-value is between .1 and .2; (Excel's result: p-value = .052); do not reject H_0; x and y are not related
    (b) $t = 2.5376 < 4.032$; p-value is between .1 and .2; (Excel's result: p-value = .052); do not reject H_0; x and y are not related

12. (a) $F = 29.624 > 16.26$; p-value < .01; (Excel's result: p-value = .0028); reject H_0, x and y are related
    (b) $t = -5.4428 < -4.032$; p-value < .01; (Excel's result: p-value = .0028); reject H_0, x and y are related

14. $7.29 to $10.63 (rounded)

16. $5.62 to $12.31 (rounded)

18. (a)   Residuals
               1.00487
              -0.476563
               0.528078
              -0.386777
               1.10858
              -0.481206
              -1.29699

(b)

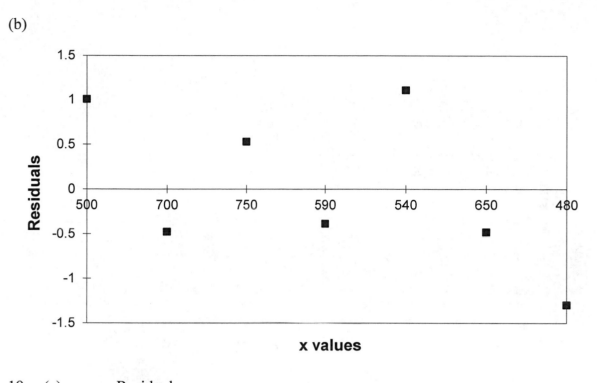

19. (a)
Residuals
-2.01429
0.44285
-0.47144
0.71428
1.07142
-0.10000
0.35714

(b)

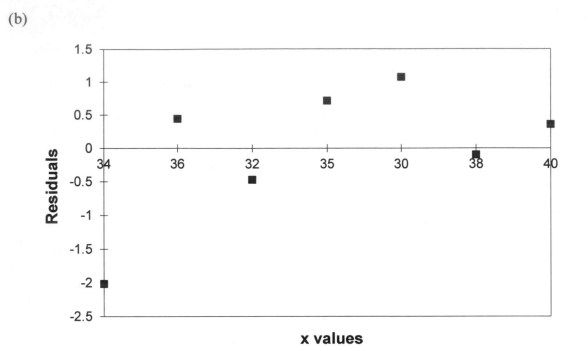

21.   Excel's output:

SUMMARY
OUTPUT

Regression Statistics	
Multiple R	0.7503
R Square	0.5629
Adjusted R Square	0.4755
Standard Error	0.9806
Observations	7

ANOVA

	df	SS	MS	F	Significance F
Regression	1	6.1920	6.1920	6.4392	0.0520
Residual	5	4.8080	0.9616		
Total	6	11			

	Coefficients	Standard Error	t Stat	P-value	Lower 95%	Upper 95%
Intercept	1.0416	2.3772	0.4381	0.6796	-5.0692	7.1523
Pages (x)	0.0099	0.0039	2.5376	0.0520	-0.0001	0.0199

22.   Excel's output:

SUMMARY
OUTPUT

Regression Statistics	
Multiple R	0.9250
R Square	0.8556
Adjusted R Square	0.8267
Standard Error	1.1199
Observations	7

ANOVA

	df	SS	MS	F	Significance F
Regression	1	37.1571	37.1571	29.62425	0.0028
Residual	5	6.2714	1.2543		
Total	6	43.4286			

	Coefficients	Standard Error	t Stat	P-value	Lower 95%	Upper 95%
Intercept	29.7857	4.7042	6.3318	0.0014	17.6933	41.8781
Price (x)	-0.7286	0.1339	-5.4428	0.0028	-1.0727	-0.3845

CHAPTER FIFTEEN

MULTIPLE REGRESSION

CHAPTER OUTLINE AND REVIEW

Chapter 14 introduced the concepts of regression and correlation. You learned how to determine a linear functional relationship between two variables, one dependent and one independent. However, there are many situations in which merely one independent variable (x) cannot explain or predict the dependent variable (y). Thus, we must rely on multiple regression analysis, where the dependent variable is explained or predicted by more than one independent variable. For instance, the estimated regression function, in which there are two independent variables (x_1 and x_2) that predict the dependent variable (y), has the form of

$$\hat{y} = b_0 + b_1 x_1 + b_2 x_2$$

The coefficients b_0, b_1, and b_2 are calculated from the available data. The procedure for their calculation is based on the least-squares method (as explained in Chapter 14). The mathematics involved in the estimation of b_0, b_1, and b_2 are very tedious. Thus, I recommend that you use a computer package available on your school's computer system for solving problems dealing with multiple regression. In the section of exercises, I will give you the output from a computer package that I used and interpret the results. Keep in mind that no matter what statistical software you use, the results are the same, even though the format of the output may differ among various software packages. In this chapter, you are also shown how categorical variables can be incorporated into a regression model. Some of the main terms that you will learn in this chapter include:

Adjusted Multiple Coefficient of Determination (R_a^2) is a measure of the goodness of fit for the estimated regression equation that accounts for the number of independent variables in the model.

Categorical Variable is a variable with categorical data. A categorical variable is not measured in terms of how much or how many.

Cook's D is a measure of the influence of an observation based on the residual and leverage.

Dummy Variable is a variable used to incorporate the effect of the categorical variable in a regression model. The dummy variable takes on the values of 0 or 1.

Estimated Logit is an estimate of the logit based on sample data; that is,
$$\hat{g}(x_1, x_2, \ldots, x_p) = b_0 + b_1 x_1 + b_2 x_2 + \cdots + b_p x_p.$$

Estimated Multiple Regression Equation: is the estimate of the multiple regression equation based on sample data and the least squares method; it is
$$\hat{y} = b_0 + b_1 x_1 + b_2 x_2 + \cdots + b_p x_p.$$

Influential Observation is an observation which has a great influence in determining the estimated regression equation.

Least Squares Method is the method used to develop the estimated regression equation. It minimizes the sum of squared residuals (the deviations between the observed values of the dependent variable, y_i, and the estimated values of the dependent variable, $\hat{y}_i$.

Leverage is a measure of the effect of an unusual x value on the regression results.

Logistic Regression Equation is the mathematical equation relating E(y), the probability that y = 1, to the values of the independent variables.

Logit is the natural logarithm of the odds in favor of y = 1; that is,
$$g(x_1, x_2, \ldots, x_p) = \beta_0 + \beta_1 x_1 + \beta_2 x_2 + \cdots + \beta_p x_p.$$

Multicollinearity is a term used to describe the case when the independent variables in a multiple regression model are correlated.

Multiple Coefficient of Determination (R^2) is a measure of the goodness of fit for the estimated regression equation. It provides the proportion of variability in the dependent variable that is explained by the estimated regression equation.

Multiple Regression Analysis is a regression analysis involving two or more independent variables.

Multiple Regression Equation is the mathematical equation relating the expected value or mean value of the dependent variable to the value of the independent variables; that is,

$$E(y) = \beta_0 + \beta_1 x_1 + \beta_2 x_2 + \cdots + \beta_p x_p.$$

Multiple Regression Model is the mathematical equation that explains how the dependent variable y is related to several independent variables x_1, x_2, ..., x_p and the error term ε.

Odd Ratio is the odds that y = 1 given that one of the independent variables has increased by one unit ($odds_1$) divided by the odds that y = 1 given no change in the values for the independent variables ($odds_0$); that is,

$$\text{Odds Ratio} = \frac{odds_1}{odds_0}$$

Odds in Favor of an Event is the probability the event will occur divided by the probability the event will not occur.

Outlier is an observation that does not fit the pattern of the rest of the data.

Studentized Deleted Residuals are standardized residuals that are based on deleting observation **i** from the data set and then performing the regression analysis and computing the standardized residual for observation **i** using the remaining **(n − 1)** observations.

CHAPTER FORMULAS

Multiple Regression Model

$$y = \beta_0 + \beta_1 x_1 + \beta_2 x_2 + \ldots \beta_p x_p + \varepsilon \tag{15.1}$$

Multiple Regression Equation

$$E(y) = \beta_0 + \beta_1 x_1 + \beta_2 x_2 + \ldots \beta_p x_p \tag{15.2}$$

Estimated Multiple Regression Equation

$$\hat{y} = b_0 + b_1 x_1 + b_2 x_2 + \ldots + b_p x_p \tag{15.3}$$

Least Squares Criterion

$$\text{Min } \Sigma\left(y_i - \hat{y}_i\right)^2 \tag{15.4}$$

where

y_i = observed value of the dependent variable for the ith observation.
$\hat{y}_i$ = estimated value of the dependent variable for the ith observation.

Relationship among SST, SSR, and SSE

$$SST = SSR + SSE \tag{15.7}$$

Multiple Coefficient of Determination

$$R^2 = \frac{SSR}{SST} \tag{15.8}$$

Adjusted Multiple Coefficient of Determination

$$R_a^2 = 1 - \left(1 - R^2\right)\left(\frac{n-1}{n-p-1}\right) \tag{15.9}$$

Mean Square Due to Regression

$$MSR = \frac{SSR}{p} \tag{15.12}$$

where p is the number of independent variables

CHAPTER FORMULAS
(Continued)

Mean Square Due to Error

$$MSE = \frac{SSE}{n-p-1} \tag{15.13}$$

F Test for Overall Significance in Multiple Regression

H_O: $\beta_1 = \beta_2 = ... = \beta_p = 0$

H_a: One or more of the coefficients is not equal to zero

Test Statistic

$$F = \frac{MSR}{MSE} \tag{15.14}$$

When using the *p*-value approach, reject H_O if the *p*-value $\leq \alpha$

When using the critical value approach, reject H_O if the test statistic $F \geq F_\alpha$ where F_α is based on an F distribution with p numerator degrees of freedom and $n - p - 1$ denominator degrees of freedom

---

t Test for Individual Significance in Multiple Regression

H_O: $\beta_i = 0$

H_a: $\beta_i \neq 0$ for any parameter β_i

Test Statistic

$$t = \frac{b_i}{s_{b_i}} \tag{15.15}$$

When using the *p*-value approach, reject H_O if the *p*-value $\leq \alpha$

When using the critical value approach, reject H_O if the test statistic $t \geq t_{\alpha/2}$ or if $t \leq -t_{\alpha/2}$, where $t_{\alpha/2}$ is based on a t distribution with n - p - 1 degrees of freedom

CHAPTER FORMULAS
(Continued)

Standardized Residual for Observation i

$$\frac{y_i - \hat{y}_i}{s_{y_i - \hat{y}_i}} \tag{15.23}$$

Standard Deviation of Residual i

$$s_{\overline{y_i - \hat{y}_i}} = s\sqrt{1 - h_i} \tag{15.24}$$

Cook's Distance Measure

$$D_i = \frac{(y_i - \hat{y}_i)^2}{(p-1)\,s^2}\left[\frac{h_i}{(1-h_i)^2}\right] \tag{15.25}$$

Logistic Regression Equation

$$E(y) = \frac{e^{\beta_0 + \beta_1 x_1 + \beta_2 x_2 + \cdots + \beta_p x_p}}{1 + e^{\beta_0 + \beta_1 x_1 + \beta_2 x_2 + \cdots + \beta_p x_p}} \tag{15.27}$$

Estimated Logistic Equation

$$\hat{y} = \text{estimate of } P(y = 1 \mid x_1, x_2, \ldots, x_p) = \frac{e^{b_0 + b_1 x_1 + b_2 x_2 + \cdots + b_p x_p}}{1 + e^{b_0 + b_1 x_1 + b_2 x_2 + \cdots + b_p x_p}} \tag{15.30}$$

Odds Ratio

$$\text{Odds Ratio} = \frac{\text{odds}_1}{\text{odds}_0} \tag{15.34}$$

Logit

$$g(x_1, x_2, \ldots, x_p) = \beta_0 + \beta_1 x_1 + \beta_2 x_2 + \cdots + \beta_p x_p \tag{15.35}$$

Estimated Logit

$$\hat{g}(x_1, x_2, \ldots, x_p) = b_0 + b_1 x_1 + b_2 x_2 + \cdots + b_p x_p \tag{15.37}$$

EXERCISES

Solved Problem

*1. In exercise *1 of Chapter 14, we looked at the sales volume of Freeman, Inc., and then determined a regression function relating sales volume to advertising expenditure. Obviously, advertising expenditure is not the only variable that affects sales volume. Assume we believe that besides the advertising expenditure, the number of salespeople also plays an important role in the sales volume. The following data show the sales volumes, the advertising expenditures (in millions of dollars), and the number of salespeople for the years 2001-2010.

Year	Sales Volume (y_i)	Advertising Expense (x_1)	Number of Salespeople (x_2)
2001	26	1.8	35
2002	31	2.3	38
2003	28	2.6	33
2004	30	2.4	40
2005	34	2.8	38
2006	38	3.0	32
2007	41	3.4	42
2008	44	3.2	49
2009	40	3.6	53
2010	43	3.8	55

(a) What is the regression model for the above?

Answer: If it is believed that the sales volume is related to the advertising expenditure (x_1) and the number of salespeople (x_2), then the regression model involving two independent variables will be

$$y = \beta_0 + \beta_1 x_1 + \beta_2 x_2 + \varepsilon$$

where ε is the error term. The same assumptions that were made in Chapter 14 will also apply here. In multiple regression analysis (similar to simple linear regression analysis), the least squares method is used to estimate the parameters β_0, β_1 and β_2. These estimates are denoted by b_0, b_1 and b_2. Thus, the estimated regression equation has the form of

$$\hat{y} = b_0 + b_1 x_1 + b_2 x_2$$

(b)   Use a computer package available at your computer center and determine a regression function.

Answer: I have used **Microsoft Excel** and have named my variables Advertising as (ADV) and the Number of Salespeople as (PEOPLE). Part of the output is presented below.

SUMMARY OUTPUT

Regression Statistics	
Multiple R	0.9139
R Square	0.8351
Adjusted R Square	0.7880
Standard Error	3.0092
Observations	10

ANOVA

	df	SS	MS	F	Significance F
Regression	2	321.1140	160.5570	17.7310	0.001819
Residual	7	63.3860	9.0551		
Total	9	384.5			

	Coefficients	Standard Error	t Stat	P-value
Intercept	7.0174	5.3146	1.3204	0.2282
ADV	8.6233	2.3968	3. 5978	0.0088
PEOPLE	0.0858	0.1845	0.4652	0.6559

From the above results, we note the following.

$$b_0 = 7.0174$$
$$b_1 = 8.6233$$
$$b_2 = 0.0858$$

Thus, the least-squares estimated regression function is

$$\hat{y} = 7.0174 + 8.6233\, x_1 + 0.0858\, x_2$$

which can be written with the variables' names:

$$\hat{y} = 7.0174 + 8.6233\ \text{ADV} + 0.0858\ \text{PEOPLE}$$

With the above equation, we can estimate the sales volume for a given value of advertising expenditure and the number of salespeople.

(c)   Interpret the coefficients of the estimated regression equation that were found in part (a).

Answer: In this equation $b_1 = 8.6233$, which indicates that for each 1 million dollar increase in advertising expenditure, the sales volume is expected to increase by 8.6233 million dollars when the number of salespeople is held constant. Similarly, $b_2 = 0.0858$, which indicates that as the number of salespeople is increased by 1, the sales volume is expected to increase by 0.0858 million dollars (that is $85,800), when advertising expenditure is held constant.

(d)   Estimate the sales volume for an advertising expenditure of 3.5 million dollars and 45 salespeople.

Answer: Using the given data and the regression equation as determined in part (a), we can estimate the sales volume:

$$\hat{y} = 7.0174 + 8.6233(3.5) + 0.0858(45) = 41.05995$$

Hence, the expected sales volume in terms of dollars is $41,059,950.

(e)   At 95% confidence, determine which variables are significant and which are not.

Answer: From the Excel output, we note that the p-value for ADV is 0.0088, which is less than 0.05; therefore, it is a significant variable. Whereas, the p-value for PEOPLE is 0.6559, which is greater than 0.05; therefore, it is not a significant variable.

2.   The following data represent the number of automobiles sold per month by Autos, Inc., their prices, and the number of advertising spots they used on a local television station.

Units Sold (y)	Price (In $1,000s) (PRICE)	Advertising Spots (ADV)
10	8.2	10
8	8.7	6
12	7.9	14
13	7.8	18
9	8.1	10
14	8.8	19
15	8.9	20

(a)   Using the above data, determine the least-squares regression function relating units sold (y) to PRICE and ADV. Use a computer software package available to you.

(b)   Excel was used to determine the least-squares regression equation. Part of the output is shown below.

ANOVA

	df	SS	MS	F	Significance F
Regression	2	40.699	20.350	80.196	0.0006
Residual	4	1.015	0.254		
Total	6	41.714			

	Coefficients	Standard Error	t Stat	P-value
Intercept	0.8051	3.8142	0.2111	0.8431
PRICE	0.4977	0.4617	1.0781	0.3417
ADV	0.4773	0.0387	12.3209	0.0002

Use the output shown above and write an equation that can be used to predict the monthly sales of automobiles.

(c)   Interpret the coefficients of the estimated regression equation that were determined in part (b).

(d)   If the company charges $8,000 for each car and uses 15 advertising spots, how many cars would you expect them to sell?

(e)   At 95% confidence, determine which variables are significant and which are not.

3. The prices of Rawlston, Inc. stock (y) over a period of 12 days, the number of shares (in 100s) of company stock sold (x_1), and the volume of exchange (in millions) on the New York Stock Exchange (x_2) are shown below.

Day	(y)	(x_1)	(x_2)
1	87.50	950	11.00
2	86.00	945	11.25
3	84.00	940	11.75
4	83.00	930	11.75
5	84.50	935	12.00
6	84.00	935	13.00
7	82.00	932	13.25
8	80.00	938	14.50
9	78.50	925	15.00
10	79.00	900	16.50
11	77.00	875	17.00
12	77.50	870	17.50

Excel was used to determine the least-squares regression equation. Part of the computer output is shown below.

ANOVA

	df	SS	MS	F	Significance F
Regression	2	118.8474	59.4237	40.9216	0.0000
Residual	9	13.0692	1.4521		
Total	11	131.9167			

	Coefficients	Standard Error	t Stat	P-value
Intercept	118.5059	33.5753	3.5296	0.0064
($x1$)	-0.0163	0.0315	-0.5171	0.6176
($x2$)	-1.5726	0.3590	-4.3807	0.0018

(a) Use the output shown above and write an equation that can be used to predict the price of the stock.

(b) Interpret the coefficients of the estimated regression equation that you found in part (a).

(c)   At 95% confidence, determine which variables are significant and which are not.

(d)   If in a given day, the number of shares of the company that were sold was 94,500 and the volume of exchange on the New York Stock Exchange was 16 million, what would you expect the price of the stock to be?

Solved Problem

*4.   At $\alpha = 0.01$ level of significance, test to determine if the fitted equation developed in exercise *1 represents a significant relationship between the independent variables and the dependent variable.

Answer: To determine whether or not the regression function is significant, we want to test the following hypotheses.

H_0: $\beta_1 = \beta_2 = 0$
H_a: At least one of the two coefficients is not equal to zero.

To test the above, we must determine an F value from the data and compare its value with F_α. The null hypothesis will be rejected if the test statistic $F > F_\alpha$. The F value is given in part (b) of exercise *1, and its value is computed as follows.

$$F = \frac{MSR}{MSE}$$

where

$$MSR = \frac{SSR}{p} \quad \text{(p represents the number of independent variables)}$$

$$MSE = \frac{SSE}{(n - p - 1)}$$

In this exercise, there are 2 independent variables (p = 2). Therefore, SSR has 2 degrees of freedom, and SSE has n - p - 1 = 10 - 2 - 1 = 7 degrees of freedom. Now we can compute MSR and MSE:

$$MSR = \frac{321.114}{2} = 160.557$$

$$MSE = \frac{63.386}{7} = 9.0551$$

Thus, the F value is calculated as

$$F = \frac{160.555}{9.0551} = 17.731$$

Now, from Table 4 of the Appendix in your textbook, we read the F value with 2 degrees of freedom for the numerator and 7 degrees of freedom for the denominator as $F_{.01} = 9.55$. Since the computed F = 17.731 is greater than $F_{.01}$, the null hypothesis is rejected; and we conclude that there is a significant linear relationship between the sales volume and the two independent variables.

We could have used the *p*-value approach to answer the above question. Using the F table (2 numerator and 7 denominator degrees of freedom) for F = 17.731, the *p*-value is less than 0.01. Using Excel and the function FDIST(17.731, 2, 7) the actual *p*-value = 0.001819. Since the *p*-value is $< \alpha = 0.01$, the null hypothesis H_o is rejected.

Now, refer to the computer output given in the solution to exercise *1. You can identify the following values.

SSR = 321.114	p = 2	MSR = 160.557	F = 17.731
SSE = 63.386	n - p - 1 = 7	MSE = 9.0551	

5. At $\alpha = 0.05$ level of significance, test to determine if the fitted equation that you developed in exercise 2 represents a significant relationship between the independent variables and the dependent variable.

6.   At $\alpha = 0.01$ level of significance, test to determine if the fitted equation that you developed in exercise 3 represents a significant relationship between the independent variables and the dependent variable.

Solved Problem

*7.   Refer to exercise *1. Use a level of significance of 0.05 to test the significance of β_1.

Answer: After using the F test, it was concluded that the multiple regression was significant, indicating that at least one of the two coefficients (β_1 or β_2) was not zero (see exercise *4). Now a t test can be applied for testing the significance of the individual parameters, in this case β_1. The hypotheses to be tested are

H_o: $\beta_1 = 0$

H_a: $\beta_1 \neq 0$

The null hypothesis will not be rejected if $- t_{\alpha/2} \leq t \leq t_{\alpha/2}$. Now referring to the Excel printout (exercise *1, part (b)), the t statistic can be computed as $8.6233/2.3968 = 3.5978$. From Table 2 of the Appendix, the critical t values with 7 degrees of freedom are

$t_{.025} = \pm 2.365$

Since $3.5978 > 2.365$, the null hypothesis is rejected, thus, concluding that β_1 is significantly different from zero. The *p*-value for this test is .0088.

8.   Refer to exercise *1. Use a level of significance of 0.05 to test the significance of β_2.

*9. Refer to exercise *1. Compute the multiple coefficient of determination.

Answer: The multiple coefficient of determination (R^2) is provided on the output of the computer, but we could compute its value as follows.

$$R^2 = \frac{SSR}{SST}$$

Thus, the R^2 for this situation is

$$R^2 = \frac{321.11}{384.5} = 0.8351$$

Therefore, 83.51% of the variability in sales volume is explained by the variability in both advertising expenditure and the number of salespeople.

10. Refer to exercise 2. Compute the multiple coefficient of determination.

Solved Problem

*11. Refer to exercise *1. Compute the adjusted R^2 (i.e., R_a^2).

Answer: To avoid overestimating the impact of adding an independent variable on the amount of explained variability, it is recommended to adjust the coefficient of determination:

$$R_a^2 = 1 - (1 - R^2)\left(\frac{n-1}{n-p-1}\right)$$

For this example, the adjusted R^2 is provided for you on the computer output. But we can compute its value as

$$R_a^2 = 1 - (1 - 0.835)\left(\frac{10 - 1}{10 - 2 - 1}\right) = 0.7879$$

12.   Refer to exercise 2. Determine the adjusted R_a^2.

Solved Problem

*13. Refer to exercise *1 of this chapter. Assume we also have data available on whether only TV advertising was used or whether multimedia advertising was used. To incorporate the effect of the type of advertising on the sales volume, let us define a new variable x_3, where

$$x_3 = \begin{cases} 0 & \text{if multimedia advertising was used} \\ \\ 1 & \text{if only TV advertising was used} \end{cases}$$

Thus, our available data appear as follows.

Year	Sales Volume (y)	Advertising Expenditure (ADV)	Number of Salespeople (PEOPLE)	Type of Advertising (ADTYPE)
2001	26	1.8	35	0
2002	31	2.3	38	0
2003	28	2.6	33	1
2004	30	2.4	40	0
2005	34	2.8	38	1
2006	38	3.0	32	0
2007	41	3.4	42	0
2008	44	3.2	49	0
2009	40	3.6	53	1
2010	43	3.8	55	1

(a)   Use the above data to determine a regression function relating y to ADV, PEOPLE, and ADTYPE.

Answer: The estimated regression function using the least-squares method and incorporating the type of advertising will have the form of

$$\hat{y} = b_0 + b_1x_1 + b_2x_2 + b_3x_3$$

Using the variables' names, it will be in the form of

$$\hat{y} = b_0 + b_1 ADV + b_2 PEOPLE + b_3 ADTYPE$$

Remember that ADTYPE represents the type of advertising used, and it can only take values of 0 or 1. Part of the Excel output is displayed below.

SUMMARY
OUTPUT

Regression Statistics	
Multiple R	0.9684
R Square	0.9378
Adjusted R Square	0.9067
Standard Error	1.9964
Observations	10

ANOVA

	df	SS	MS	F	Significance F
Regression	3	360.5854	120.1951	30.1561	0.0005
Residual	6	23.9146	3.9858		
Total	9	384.5000			

	Coefficients	Standard Error	t Stat	P-value
Intercept	4.0928	3.6464	1.1224	0.3046
ADV	10.0230	1.6512	6.0702	0.0009
PEOPLE	0.1020	0.1225	0.8327	0.4369
ADTYPE	-4.4811	1.4240	-3.1469	0.0199

Thus, the regression function will be as follows:

$$\hat{y} = 4.0928 + 10.0230 \, ADV + 0.1020 \, PEOPLE - 4.4811 \, ADTYPE$$

(b)   Interpret the meaning of the coefficient of ADTYPE (i.e., -4.4811).

Answer: Recall that ADTYPE is a dummy variable indicating the type of advertising used. ADTYPE = 0 if multimedia advertising was used, and ADTYPE = 1 if only TV advertising was used. Thus, -4.4811 indicates that in those years where only TV advertising was used (ADTYPE = 1), sales were lower by 4.4811 (in thousands) than those years in which multimedia advertising was used.

14. In exercise 2 of this chapter , data on units sold, price, and the number of television spots the company used per month were given. During some months the company also used a radio promotion campaign. This categorical variable is shown in the last column where 0 indicates that a radio promotion campaign was not used and 1 indicates that one was.

Units Sold (y)	Price (In $1000) ($x_1$)	Television Advertising Spots (x_2)	Radio Campaign (x_3)
10	8.2	10	1
8	8.7	6	0
12	7.9	14	0
13	7.8	18	1
9	8.1	10	0
14	8.8	19	1
15	8.9	20	1

(a) Use the above data to determine a regression function relating y to x_1, x_2, and x_3. Use a computer software available to you.

(b) Interpret the meaning of the coefficient of x_3.

15.   In exercise 3 of this chapter , the prices of Rawlston, Inc. stock (y) over a period of 12 days, the number of shares (in 100s) of the company's stocks sold (x_1), and the volume of exchange (in millions) on the New York Stock Exchange (x_2) were given. As an extension of that exercise, a dummy variable was also used for predicting the price of the stock. This dummy variable represents the volume of exchange on the NYSE on the previous day. If the volume of exchange on the previous day was high, $x_3 = 1$, otherwise $x_3 = 0$. These data are presented below.

Day	(y_i)	(x_1)	(x_2)	(x_3)
1	87.50	950	11.00	1
2	86.00	945	11.25	1
3	84.00	940	11.75	0
4	83.00	930	11.75	0
5	84.50	935	12.00	1
6	84.00	935	13.00	0
7	82.00	932	13.25	1
8	80.00	938	14.50	1
9	78.50	925	15.00	0
10	79.00	900	16.50	1
11	77.00	875	17.00	1
12	77.50	870	17.50	0

(a)   Use a computer software available to you to determine a regression function relating y to x_1, x_2, and x_3.

(b)   Interpret the meaning of the coefficient of x_3.

Solved Problem

*16. Refer to exercise *1 of this chapter.

(a)   Compute the estimated values of sales volume ($\hat{y}_i$) and the residuals.

Answer: In part (b) of exercise *1, Excel was used and the Least-Squares estimated regression function was determined:

$$\hat{y} = 7.0174 + 8.6233\ x_1 + 0.0858\ x_2$$

Thus, the $\hat{y}_i$ values can be computed by substituting x_1 and x_2 values in the above equation. Then the residuals are computed by subtracting the estimated values from the observed values. The results are shown below.

Year	Observed Sales Volume (y_i)	Predicted Values ($\hat{y}_i$)	Residuals ($y_i - \hat{y}_i$)
2001	26	25.54281	0.45719
2002	31	30.11190	0.88810
2003	28	32.26983	-4.26983
2004	30	31.14586	-1.14586
2005	34	34.42356	-0.42356
2006	38	35.63334	2.36666
2007	41	39.94079	1.05921
2008	44	38.81682	5.18318
2009	40	42.60940	-2.60940
2010	43	44.50569	-1.50569

(b)   Determine the standardized residuals and plot them versus $\hat{y}_i$. Does the standardized residual plot support the assumptions involving ε?

Answer: The computation of standardized residuals is too complex to be done manually. Excel was used and the values of $\hat{y}_i$ and the standardized residuals were determined to be as follows.

Year	Predicted Values ($\hat{y}_i$)	Standardized Residuals
2001	25.54281	0.15193
2002	30.11190	0.29513
2003	32.26983	-1.41894
2004	31.14586	-0.38079
2005	34.42356	-0.14075
2006	35.63334	0.78648
2007	39.94079	0.35199
2008	38.81682	1.72246
2009	42.60940	-0.86715
2010	44.50569	-0.50037

Now we can plot the predicted values ($\hat{y}_i$) versus the standardized residuals as shown below.

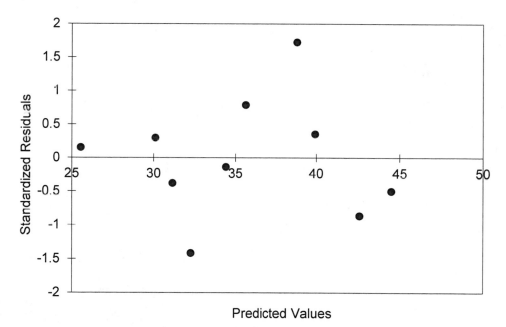

This standardized residuals plot does not show any abnormalities. The standardized residuals appear to be randomly distributed with no particular pattern and their values range between -2 and +2. Thus we conclude that the standardized residual plot supports the assumptions involving ε.

17.   Refer to exercise 2. Use a computer package available to you and determine the predicted values ($\hat{y}_i$) and the standardized residuals. Plot the standardized residuals against the predicted values. Does the standardized residual plot support the assumptions involving ε?

SELF-TESTING QUESTIONS

In the following multiple choice questions, circle the correct answer. Answers are provided following the questions.

1.   A regression model in which more than one independent variable is used to predict the dependent variable is called
a)   a simple linear regression model
b)   a multiple regression model
c)   an independent model
d)   a dependent model

2.   A term used to describe the case when the independent variables in a multiple regression model are correlated is
a)   regression
b)   correlation
c)   multicollinearity
d)   deterministic

3.   A multiple regression model has the form: $y = 2 + 3x_1 + 4x_2$.
As x_1 increases by 1 unit (holding x_2 constant), y will
a)   increase by 3 units
b)   decrease by 3 units
c)   increase by 4 units
d)   decrease by 4 units

4.   A multiple regression model has
a)   only one independent variable
b)   more than one dependent variable
c)   more than one independent variable
d)   several dependent, but only one independent variable

5.   A measure of goodness of fit for the estimated regression equation is the
a)   multiple coefficient of determination
b)   mean square due to error
c)   mean square due to regression
d)   sum of squares due to error

6.   The adjusted multiple coefficient of determination accounts for
a)   the number of dependent variables in the model
b)   the number of independent variables in the model
c)   unusually large predictors
d)   usually small predictions

7.   The multiple coefficient of determination is computed by
a)   dividing SSR by SST
b)   dividing SST by SSR
c)   dividing SST by SSE
d)   SST + SSE

8.   For a multiple regression model, SST = 200 and SSE = 50. The multiple coefficient of determination is
a)   0.25
b)   4.00
c)   0.75
d)   100

9.   The correct relationship between SST, SSR, and SSE is given by
a)   SSR = SST + SSE
b)   SST = SSR + SSE
c)   SSE = SSR - SST
d)   all of the above

10.   The ratio of MSR/MSE yields
a)   the t statistic
b)   SST
c)   the F statistic
d)   the chi-square statistic

11.   A variable that cannot be measured in terms of how much or how many is called
a)   an interaction.
b)   a constant variable.
c)   a dependent variable.
d)   a categorical variable.

12.   A variable that takes on the values of 0 or 1 and is used to incorporate the effect of categorical variables in a regression model is called
a)   an interaction
b)   a constant variable
c)   a dummy variable
d)   a qualifier variable

13.   For a multiple regression model, SSR = 600 and SSE = 200. The multiple coefficient of determination is
a)   0.333
b)   0.275
c)   0.300
d)   0.75

14.   A regression model involved 5 independent variables and 136 observations. The critical value of t for testing the significance of each of the independent variable's coefficients will have
a)   121 degrees of freedom
b)   135 degrees of freedom
c)   130 degrees of freedom
d)   4 degrees of freedom

15.   In order to test for the significance of a regression model involving 3 independent variables and 47 observations, the numerator and denominator degrees of freedom (respectively) for the critical value of F are
a)   47 and 3
b)   3 and 47
c)   2 and 43
d)   3 and 43

16.   In regression analysis, an outlier is an observation whose
a)   mean is larger than the standard deviation
b)   residual is zero
c)   mean is zero
d)   residual is much larger than the rest of the residual values

17   In a multiple regression model, the error term ε is assumed to be a random variable with a mean of
a)   zero
b)   -1
c)   1
d)   any value

18.   In regression analysis, the response variable is the
a)   independent variable
b)   dependent variable
c)   slope of the regression function
d)   intercept

19.   A multiple regression model has the form

$$\hat{y} = 65 + 5\,x_1 + 8\,x_2$$

As x_1 increases by 1 unit (holding x_2 constant), y is expected to
a)   increase by 70 units
b)   decrease by 70 units
c)   increase by 5 units
d)   decrease by 5 units

20.   The numerical value of the coefficient of determination
a)   is always larger than the coefficient of correlation
b)   is always smaller than the coefficient of correlation
c)   is negative if the coefficient of determination is negative
d)   can be larger or smaller than the coefficient of correlation

ANSWERS TO THE SELF-TESTING QUESTIONS

1. b
2. c
3. a
4. c
5. a
6. b
7. a
8. c
9. b
10. c
11. d
12. c
13. d
14. c
15. d
16. d
17. a
18. b
19. c
20. d

ANSWERS TO CHAPTER FIFTEEN EXERCISES

2. (a) $b_0 = 0.8051$
        $b_1 = 0.4977$
        $b_2 = 0.4773$
    (b) $\hat{y} = 0.8051 + 0.4977x_1 + 0.4773x_2$
    (c) As price increases by 1 unit ($1,000s), units sold will increase by 0.4977 (holding advertising spots constant). As advertising spots increase by 1 unit, units sold will increase by 0.4773 (holding the price constant).
    (d) 12 (rounded)
    (e) PRICE is not significant; the p-value $= 0.3417 > \alpha = 0.05$.
        ADV is significant; the p-value $= 0.0002 < \alpha = 0.05$.

3. (a) $\hat{y} = 118.5055 - 0.0163x_1 - 1.5726x_2$
    (b) As the number of shares of the stock increases by 1 unit, the stock price decreases by $0.0163 (holding the volume of exchange on the NYSE constant). As the volume of exchange on the NYSE increases by 1 unit, the stock price decreases by $1.5726 (holding the number of shares of the stock sold constant).
    (c) x_1 is not significant; the p-value $= 0.6176 > \alpha = 0.05$.
        x_2 is significant; the p-value $= 0.0018 < \alpha = 0.05$.
    (d) $77.94

5. test statistic $F = 80.2 > 6.94$; p-value $< .005$ (almost zero); reject H_0, there is a significant relationship

6. test statistic $F = 40.92 > 8.02$; p-value $< .005$ (almost zero); reject H_0, there is a significant relationship

8. test statistic $t = 0.4652 < 2.365$; p-value $> .4$ (df $= 7$); do not reject H_0, there is no significant relationship

10. $R^2 = 0.9756$

12. $R_a^2 = 0.9635$

14. (a)

	Coefficients	Standard Error	t Stat	P-value
Intercept	0.8545	4.5126	0.1894	0.8619
(x1)	0.4930	0.5412	0.9109	0.4295
(x2)	0.4753	0.0597	7.9575	0.0041
(x3)	0.0304	0.6092	0.0499	0.9633

$\hat{y} = 0.8545 + 0.4930 x_1 + 0.4753 x_2 + 0.0304 x_3$

   (b) When radio promotions were used, sales were higher by 0.0304.

15. (a)

	Coefficients	Standard Error	t Stat	P-value
Intercept	123.294	33.752	3.653	0.006
(x1)	-0.021	0.032	-0.670	0.522
(x2)	-1.618	0.360	-4.493	0.002
(x3)	0.738	0.711	1.037	0.330

$$\hat{y} = 123.294 - 0.021\, x_1 - 1.618\, x_2 + 0.738\, x_3$$

(b) When the volume of exchange was high on the previous day, the stock price was higher by 0.738.

17. (a)

Predicted Values ($\hat{y}$)	Standardized Residuals
9.65931	0.67633
7.99896	0.00207
11.4192	1.15299
13.27863	-0.55314
9.60954	-1.21004
14.25364	-0.50353
14.78072	0.43532

(b)

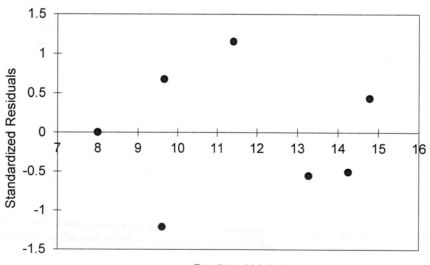

This standardized residuals plot does not show any abnormalities. The standardized residuals appear to be randomly distributed with no particular pattern and their values range between -1.5 and +1.5. Thus we conclude that the standardized residual plot supports the assumptions involving ε.

CHAPTER SIXTEEN

REGRESSION ANALYSIS: MODEL BUILDING

CHAPTER OUTLINE AND REVIEW

This chapter is an extension of Chapters 14 and 15. Chapter 16 introduces the concept of *general linear models* and shows how the general linear model can be used for situations where a curvilinear relationship exists between the independent variables and the dependent variable. The final topic is how to perform an F test in order to determine when to add or delete variables to or from the model. Some of the main terms that you will learn in this chapter are listed below.

Autocorrelation (Serial Correlation) is the correlation in the error terms at successive points in time. First order autocorrelation is when e_t and e_{t-1} are related. Second order is when e_t and e_{t-2} are related, and so on.

Durbin-Watson Test is a test used to determine whether or not first order autocorrelation is present.

General Linear Model is a model in the form of $y = \beta_0 + \beta_1 z_1 + \beta_2 z_2 + \ldots + \beta_p z_p + \varepsilon$ where each independent variable z_j (for $j = 1, 2, \ldots, p$) is a function of x_j. x_j is the variable for which data has been collected.

Interaction is the joint effect of two variables acting together.

Leverage is a measure that indicates how far an observation is from the others in terms of the values of the independent variables.

Variable Selection Procedures are computer based methods for selecting subsets of the potential independent variables for a regression model.

CHAPTER FORMULAS

General Linear Statistical Model

$$y = \beta_0 + \beta_1 z_1 + \beta_2 z_2 + \ldots + \beta_p z_p + \varepsilon \tag{16.1}$$

where z_j (for $j = 1, 2, \ldots, p$) is a function of x_j

First Order Model with One Predictor Variable

$$y = \beta_0 + \beta_1 x_1 + \varepsilon \tag{16.2}$$

Second Order Model with One Predictor Variable

$$y = \beta_0 + \beta_1 x_1 + \beta_1 x_1^2 + \varepsilon \tag{16.3}$$

Second Order Model with Interaction

$$y = \beta_0 + \beta_1 x_1 + \beta_2 x_2 + \beta_3 x_1^2 + \beta_4 x_2^2 + \beta_5 x_1 x_2 + \varepsilon \tag{16.4}$$

Exponential Model

$$E(y) = \beta_0 \beta_1^x \tag{16.7}$$

Exponential model can be transformed to linear logarithm model as

$$\text{Log } E(y) = \text{Log } \beta_0 + x \text{ Log } \beta_1 \tag{16.8}$$

F Statistic for Determining When to Add or Delete x_2

$$F = \frac{\dfrac{SSE(x_1) - SSE(x_1, x_2)}{1}}{\dfrac{SSE(x_1, x_2)}{n - p - 1}} \tag{16.10}$$

CHAPTER FORMULAS
(Continued)

General F Test for Adding or Deleting Variables

$$F = \frac{\dfrac{SSE(x_1, x_2, \ldots, x_q) - SSE(x_1, x_2 + \ldots + x_q, x_{q+1} + \ldots + x_p)}{p - q}}{\dfrac{SSE(x_1, x_2, \ldots, x_q, x_{q+1}, \ldots, x_p)}{n - p - 1}}$$

$$(16.13)$$

which can be written in the form

$$F = \frac{\dfrac{SSE(\text{reduced}) - SSE(\text{full})}{\text{number of extra items}}}{MSE(\text{full})}$$

$$(16.15)$$

or

$$F = \frac{\dfrac{SSR(\text{full}) - SSR(\text{reduced})}{\text{number of extra items}}}{MSE(\text{full})}$$

Autocorrelated Error Terms

$$e_t = \rho e_{t-1} + z_t \qquad (16.16)$$

Durbin-Watson Statistic

$$d = \frac{\sum\limits_{t=2}^{n}(e_t - e_{t-1})^2}{\sum\limits_{t=1}^{n} e_t^2} \qquad (16.17)$$

EXERCISES

Solved Problem

*1. Monthly total production costs and the number of units produced at a local company over a period of 10 months are shown below.

Month	Production Costs (y_i) (in \$ millions)	Units Produced (x_i) (in millions)
1	1	2
2	1	3
3	1	4
4	2	5
5	2	6
6	4	7
7	5	8
8	7	9
9	9	10
10	12	10

(a)   Using Excel, perform a regression analysis between Production Costs (y_i) and Units Produced (x_i).

Answer: The results of the regression analysis are shown below.

SUMMARY OUTPUT (y versus x)

Regression Statistics	
Multiple R	0.9108
R Square	0.8296
Adjusted R Square	0.8083
Standard Error	1.6793
Observations	10

ANOVA

	df	SS	MS	F	Significance F
Regression	1	109.8409	109.8409	38.9521	0.0002
Residual	8	22.5591	2.8199		
Total	9	132.4000			

	Coefficients	Standard Error	t Stat	P-value
Intercept	-3.3763	1.3544	-2.4928	0.0374
x	1.2151	0.1947	6.2412	0.0002

From the above output, the estimated regression model is

$$\hat{y} = -3.3763 + 1.2151x$$

R-square is 0.8296, indicating 82.96% of variability in production costs is explained by variability in units produced.

(b)   Draw a scatter diagram for the above data. Does the relationship between production costs and units produced appear to be linear?

Answer: The scatter diagram is shown in Figure 16.1.

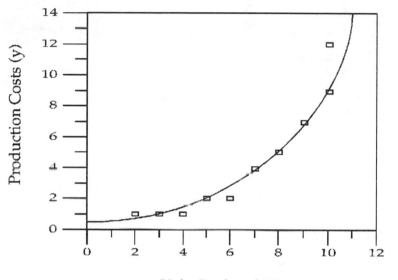

Figure 16.1

As you can see, the relationship between production costs and units produced appears to be curvilinear.

(c)   From the scatter diagram (Figure 16.1), it appears that a model in the following form best describes the relationship between x and y.

$$y = \beta_0 + \beta_1 x^2 + \varepsilon$$

Estimate the parameters of this curvilinear regression equation.

Answer: Let a new variable $z_i = x_i^2$. Then we have a simple linear regression model in the form of

$$y = \beta_0 + \beta_1 z + \varepsilon$$

Then the estimated regression model will be in the form of

$$\hat{y} = b_0 + b_1 z_i$$

The parameters of this new model can simply be computed by substituting z_i for x_i^2 and performing another regression analysis using Excel. The values of z_i that are substituted for x_i^2 are given below.

Month	y_i	x_i	$z_i = x_i^2$
1	1	2	4
2	1	3	9
3	1	4	16
4	2	5	25
5	2	6	36
6	4	7	49
7	5	8	64
8	7	9	81
9	9	10	100
10	12	10	100

The results of the new regression analysis are shown below.

SUMMARY OUTPUT (y versus z=x²)

Regression Statistics	
Multiple R	0.9593
R Square	0.9202
Adjusted R Square	0.9102
Standard Error	1.1494
Observations	10

ANOVA

	df	SS	MS	F	Significance F
Regression	1	121.8319	121.8319	92.2262	0.0000
Residual	8	10.5681	1.3210		
Total	9	132.4000			

	Coefficients	Standard Error	t Stat	P-value
Intercept	-0.4959	0.6261	-0.7921	0.4512
$z = x^2$	0.1012	0.0105	9.6034	0.0000

Thus, the regression function in terms of z is

$$\hat{y} = -0.4959 + 0.1012z$$

Since we had originally substituted z for x^2, now we can substitute x^2 back for z and arrive at the following curvilinear regression function.

$$\hat{y} = -0.4959 + 0.1012x^2$$

R-square for this new function is 0.9202, as compared to 0.8296, which was determined in part (a). This indicates that x^2 is a better predictor of y.

2.   For the following data,

y_i	x_i
2	1
3	4
5	6
8	7
10	8

(a)   Using Excel, develop an estimated linear regression function.

(b)   Draw a scatter diagram. Does the relationship between x and y appear to be linear?

(c)   Develop an estimated regression model. Assume the relationship between x and y can best be given by $\hat{y} = b_0 + b_1x^2$.

(d)   Which model (part (a) or (c)) is a better fit for the data?

3.   Consider the following data for two variables x and y. Use a computer software package available to you to solve this problem.

y	x
1	1
3	2
5	3
6	4
8	5
7	6
5	7
4	8

(a)   Develop an estimated regression equation for the above data of the form $\hat{y} = b_0 + b_1 x$. Comment on the adequacy of this equation for predicting y. Let $\alpha = .05$.

(b)   Develop an estimated regression equation for the above data of the form $\hat{y} = b_0 + b_1 x + b_2 x^2$. Comment on the adequacy of this equation for predicting y. Let $\alpha = .05$.

(c)   Use the results of part (b) and predict y when x = 4.

4.   Consider the following data for two variables x and y. Use a computer software package available to you to solve this problem.

x	y
1	1
4	6
7	9
8	7
9	4
10	3

(a)   Develop an estimated regression equation for the above data of the form $\hat{y} = b_0 + b_1 x$. Comment on the adequacy of this equation for predicting y. Let $\alpha = .05$.

(b)   Develop an estimated regression equation for the above data of the form $\hat{y} = b_0 + b_1 x + b_2 x^2$. Comment on the adequacy of this equation for predicting y. Let $\alpha = .05$.

(c)   Predict the value of y when x = 5.

5.   The following estimated regression equation has been developed for the relationship between y, the dependent variable, and x, the independent variable.

$$\hat{y} = 60 + 200x - 6x^2$$

The sample size for this regression model was 23, and SSR = 600 and SSE = 400.

(a)   Compute the coefficient of determination.

(b)   Using $\alpha = .05$, test for a significant relationship.

Solved Problem

*6. The following information was given in exercise *1 of Chapter 15.

Year	Sales Volume (y)	Advertising Expense (x_1)	Number of Salespeople (x_2)
2001	26	1.8	35
2002	31	2.3	38
2003	28	2.6	33
2004	30	2.4	40
2005	34	2.8	38
2006	38	3.0	32
2007	41	3.4	42
2008	44	3.2	49
2009	40	3.6	53
2010	43	3.8	55

Excel was first used to determine a regression function relating sales volume (y) and advertising expenditure (x_1). Part of the results of regression analysis is shown below.

ANOVA

	df	SS	MS	F	Significance F
Regression	1	319.1545	319.1545	39.0729	0.0002
Residual	8	65.3455	8.1682		
Total	9	384.5000			

	Coefficients	Standard Error	t Stat	P-value
Intercept	8.1709	4.4645	1.8302	0.1046
x1	9.4564	1.5128	6.2508	0.0002

From the above, the regression function is $\hat{y} = 8.1709 + 9.4564\,x_1$

Then regression analysis was performed relating sales volume (y) to both advertising expenditure (x_1) and number of salespeople (x_2). Part of the Excel output is shown below.

ANOVA

	df	SS	MS	F	Significance F
Regression	2	321.1140	160.5570	17.7310	0.0018
Residual	7	63.3860	9.0551		
Total	9	384.5000			

	Coefficients	Standard Error	t Stat	P-value
Intercept	7.0174	5.3146	1.3204	0.2282
x1	8.6233	2.3968	3.5978	0.0088
x2	0.0858	0.1845	0.4652	0.6559

From the above, the regression function is

$$\hat{y} = 7.0174 + 8.6233\,x_1 + 0.0858\,x_2$$

Use the above information and determine if x_2 contributes significantly to the model. Let $\alpha = 0.05$.

Answer: The second variable (x_2) should be added to the model if the reduction in SSE is significant. To test whether or not the reduction is significant, the following F statistic is used.

$$F = \frac{\dfrac{SSE(x_1) - SSE(x_1, x_2)}{1}}{\dfrac{SSE(x_1, x_2)}{n - p - 1}}$$

In this equation, SSE (x_1) represents the error sum of squares when x_1 is the only independent variable, and SSE (x_1, x_2) represents the error sum of squares when both x_1 and x_2 are independent variables. Note p is the number of independent variables.

Our hypotheses to be tested are

H_0: Adding x_2 to the model does not reduce the error sum of squares significantly.

H_a: Adding x_2 to the model does reduce the error sum of squares significantly.

If the null hypothesis is rejected, then we can conclude that x_2 contributes significantly to the model.

From the computer solutions (provided earlier in this problem), we note
SSE (x_1) = 65.35 and SSE (x_1, x_2) = 63.39. Now we can compute the F statistic:

$$F = \frac{\dfrac{SSE(x_1) - SSE(x_1,x_2)}{1}}{\dfrac{SSE(x_1,x_2)}{n-p-1}} = \frac{\dfrac{65.35 - 63.39}{1}}{\dfrac{63.39}{10-2-1}} = 0.216$$

From Table 4 of the Appendix, the F value is 5.59. Note that the numerator degrees of freedom is 1 and the denominator degrees of freedom is 7. Since the computed F statistic of 0.216 is less than 5.59, the null hypothesis is not rejected, and we conclude that the addition of x_2 to the model does not reduce the error sum of squares significantly. Thus, x_2 does not contribute to the model significantly.

7.   In exercise 3 of Chapter 15, you were given the following information.

Day	Stock Price (y)	No. of Shares Sold (x_1)	Volume of Exchange on NYSE (x_2)
1	87.50	950	11.00
2	86.00	945	11.25
3	84.00	940	11.75
4	83.00	930	11.75
5	84.50	935	12.00
6	84.00	935	13.00
7	82.00	932	13.25
8	80.00	938	14.50
9	78.50	925	15.00
10	79.00	900	16.50
11	77.00	875	17.00
12	77.50	870	17.50

If the number of shares sold (x_1) is used as the sole independent variable, the following function is provided.

$\hat{y} = 0.1081 - 17.8173x_1$

The SSE for the above model is 40.9359.

On the other hand, when both the number of shares sold (x_1) and the volume of exchange on the NYSE (x_2) are used, the following function is provided.

$\hat{y} = 118.5059 - 0.0163x_1 - 1.5726x_2$

This latter model's SSE is 13.0692.

(a)   Use a computer software package available to you and verify that the above functions and error sums of squares are correct.

(b)   Use an F test and determine if x_2 contributes significantly to the model. Let $\alpha = 0.05$.

8.   In exercise 2 of Chapter 15, the following information was provided.

Units Sold (y)	Price (In $1,000s) (x₁)	Advertising Spots (x₂)
10	8.2	10
8	8.7	6
12	7.9	14
13	7.8	18
9	8.1	10
14	8.8	19
15	8.9	20

Using price (x_1) as the only independent variable, the following function is provided.

$$\hat{y} = 0.408 + 1.338x_1$$

The SSE for the above model is 39.535.

Using both x_1 and x_2 as independent variables yields the following function.

$$\hat{y} = 0.805 + 0.498x_1 - 0.477x_2$$

The SSE for this latter function is 1.015.

Use an F test and determine if x_2 contributes significantly to the model. Let $\alpha = 0.05$.

9. A regression analysis was applied in order to determine the relationship between a dependent variable and 6 independent variables. The following information was obtained from the regression analysis.

$r^2 = 0.6$
SSR = 1,200
Total number of observations n = 32

(a) Fill in the blanks in the following ANOVA table.

Source of Variation	DF	SS	MS	F
Regression	_____?	_____?	_____?	_____?
Error (Residual)	_____?	_____?	_____?	
Total	_____?	_____?		

(b) Is the model significant? Let $\alpha = 0.05$.

10. In a regression analysis involving 21 observations and 4 independent variables, the following information was obtained.

$r^2 = 0.80$
S = 5.0

Based on the above information, fill in all the blanks in the following ANOVA.

Hint: $r^2 = \dfrac{SSR}{SST}$, but also $r^2 = 1 - \dfrac{SSE}{SST}$.

Source	DF	SS	MS	F
Regression	_____?	_____?	_____?	_____?
Error (Residual)	_____?	_____?	_____?	
Total	_____?	_____?		

Solved Problem

*11. We are interested in determining an estimated regression equation relating the yearly incomes of a sample of 20 professors and the following variables.

1. AGE = Age of the professor
2. EXP = Years of teaching experience
3. CONSULT = Years of consulting experience
4. GENDER = Gender of the professor (male = 1, female = 0)

The Minitab program was used for the analysis of the data, and the results are shown below.

The regression equation is

INCOME = 19,855.8 + 642.3 AGE + 273.4 EXP + 3.4 CONSULT - 14,906.9 SEX

Predictor	coef	Stdv	t-ratio	p-value
Constant	19,855.8	6,581.2	3.02	0.009
AGE	642.3	158.4	4.05	0.001
EXP	273.4	528.5	0.52	0.618
CONSULT	3.4	583.2	0.01	0.991
GENDER	-14,906.9	3,190.9	-4.67	0.001

$s = 6,498.821$ R-sq = 82.3%   R-sq (adj) = 77.5%

Analysis of Variance

Source	DF	SS	MS	F	p-value
Regression	4	2,937,268,224	734,317,056	17.387	0.000
Error	15	633,520,128	42,234,676		
Total	19	3,570,788,352			

(a)   Is the relationship between y and the independent variables significant? Let $\alpha = .05$.

Answer: In this case, we need to perform an F test in order to test the following hypotheses.

$H_0: \beta_1 = \beta_2 = \beta_3 = \beta_4 = 0$
$H_a:$ One or more of the coefficients is not equal to zero

If H_O is rejected, we can conclude that there is a significant relationship, which means the estimated regression equation is useful for predicting the yearly salaries. From the computer output provided above, we note the F statistic is 17.387. Then we read F_α with 4 numerator and 15 denominator degrees of freedom as $F_{.05} = 3.06$. Since $17.387 > 3.06$, H_O is rejected, and we conclude that the relationship is significant.

Note that we could have used the p-value for our test. The p-value for the analysis of variance is almost zero (0.000), which is less than $\alpha = .05$. Thus, H_O is rejected.

(b) Is AGE a significant variable? Let $\alpha = .05$.

Answer: Now we are interested in testing for the significance of an individual variable where the hypotheses are

$$H_O: \beta_1 = 0$$

$$H_a: \beta_1 \neq 0$$

First, let us read $t_{\alpha/2}$ with 15 degrees of freedom from Table 2 of the Appendix as $t_{0.025} = 2.131$. Then from the computer printout, we note that the t-ratio has a value of 4.05. Since $4.05 > 2.131$, H_O is rejected; and we conclude that AGE is a significant variable. Note, we could have considered the p-value for the variable AGE whose value is 0.001, which is less than .05, and rejected H_O.

12. Refer to exercise *11.

(a) At 95% confidence, test to see which other coefficient is significant.

(b) Interpret the meaning of the coefficient of GENDER (i.e., -14,906.90).

SELF-TESTING QUESTIONS

In the following multiple choice questions, circle the correct answer. Answers are provided following the questions.

1.   A regression model in the form of $y = \beta_0 + \beta_1 x_1 + \varepsilon$ is referred to as a
a)   simple first-order model with two predictor variables
b)   simple second-order model with one predictor variable
c)   simple second-order model with two predictor variables
d)   simple first-order model with one predictor variables

2.   A regression model in the form of $y = \beta_0 + \beta_1 x_1 + \beta_2 x_1^2 + \varepsilon$ is referred to as a
a)   second-order model with three predictor variables
b)   second-order model with two predictor variables
c)   second-order model with one predictor variable
d)   first-order model with one predictor variables

3.   Serial correlation is the
a)   correlation between serial numbers of products
b)   same as autocorrelation
c)   same as leverage
d)   multiple coefficient of correlation

4.   The joint effect of two variables acting together is called
a)   autocorrelation
b)   interaction
c)   serial correlation
d)   joint coefficient of determination

5.   A test to determine whether or not first order autocorrelation is present is
a)   a t test
b)   an F test
c)   a test of interaction
d)   a test of correlation

6.   Which of the following tests is used to determine whether an additional variable makes a significant contribution to a multiple regression model?
a)   a t test
b)   a Z test
c)   an F test
d)   a chi-square test

7. In multiple regression analysis, the general linear model
a) cannot be used to accommodate curvilinear relationships between dependent variables and independent variables
b) can be used to accommodate curvilinear relationships between independent variables and dependent variables
c) must contain more than two independent variables
d) always crosses at the origin

8. The range of the Durbin-Watson statistic is between
a) -1 and 1
b) 0 and 1
c) - infinity and + infinity
d) 0 and 4

9. If SSR = 200 and SSE = 50, then r^2 will be
a) 0.25
b) 4.00
c) 0.80
d) 0.20

10. If r^2 = 0.25 and SST = 2,000, then SSE will have a value of
a) 2,666.6
b) 500.0
c) 8,000.0
d) 1,500.0

11. The following model is referred to as a

$$Y = \beta_0 + \beta_1 X_1 + \varepsilon$$

a) curvilinear model
b) curvilinear model with one predictor variable
c) simple second-order model with one predictor variable
d) simple first-order model with one predictor variable

12. A variable such as Z, whose value is $Z = X_1 X_2$ is added to a general linear model in order to account for potential effects of two variables X_1 and X_2 acting together. This type of effect is
a) impossible to occur
b) called interaction
c) called multicollinearity effect
d) called transformation effect

13.   The parameters of nonlinear models have exponents
a)   larger than zero
b)   larger than 1
c)   larger than 2
d)   larger than 3

14.   All the variables in a multiple regression analysis
a)   must be quantitative
b)   must be either quantitative or categorical but not a mix of both
c)   must be positive
d)   None of these alternatives is correct.

Exhibit 16-1
In a regression analysis involving 25 observations, the following estimated regression equation was developed.

$$\hat{Y} = 10 - 18X_1 + 3X_2 + 14X_3$$

Also, the following standard errors and the sum of squares were obtained.

$$S_{b1} = 3 \quad S_{b2} = 6 \; S_{b3} = 7$$

$$SST = 4{,}800 \qquad SSE = 1{,}296$$

15.   Refer to Exhibit 16-1. If you want to determine whether or not the coefficients of the independent variables are significant, the critical value of t statistic at $\alpha = 0.05$ is
a)   2.080
b)   2.060
c)   2.064
d)   1.96

16.   Refer to Exhibit 16-1. The coefficient of X_1
a)   is significant
b)   is not significant
c)   can not be tested, because not enough information is provided
d)   None of these alternatives is correct.

17. Refer to Exhibit 16-1. The coefficient of X_2
a) is significant
b) is not significant
c) cannot be tested, because not enough information is provided
d) None of these alternatives is correct.

18. Refer to Exhibit 16-1. The coefficient of X_3
a) is significant
b) is not significant
c) cannot be tested, because not enough information is provided
d) None of these alternatives is correct.

19. Refer to Exhibit 16-1. The multiple coefficient of determination is
a) 0.27
b) 0.73
c) 0.50
d) 0.33

20. Refer to Exhibit 16-1. If we are interested in testing for the significance of the relationship among the variables (i.e., significance of the model) the critical value of F at $\alpha = 0.05$ is
a) 2.76
b) 2.78
c) 3.10
d) 3.07

ANSWERS TO SELF-TESTING QUESTIONS

1. d
2. c
3. b
4. b
5. d
6. c
7. b
8. d
9. c
10. d
11. d
12. b
13. b
14. d
15. a
16. a
17. b
18. b
19. b
20. d

ANSWERS TO CHAPTER SIXTEEN EXERCISES

2.   (a)

Regression Statistics	
Multiple R	0.9220
R Square	0.8500
Adjusted R Square	0.8000
Standard Error	1.5032
Observations	5

ANOVA

	df	SS	MS	F	Significance F
Regression	1	38.4208	38.4208	17.0023	0.0259
Residual	3	6.7792	2.2597		
Total	4	45.2			

	Coefficients	*Standard Error*	*t Stat*	*P-value*
Intercept	-0.2078	1.5607	-0.1331	0.9025
Xi	1.11688	0.2709	4.1234	0.0259

$$\hat{y} = -0.2078 + 1.1169x$$

(b)   As can be seen below, the relationship appears to be curvilinear.

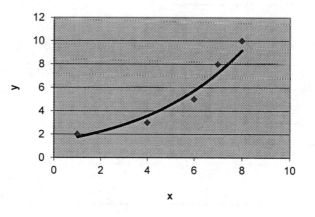

(c)

Regression Statistics	
Multiple R	0.9812
R Square	0.9628
Adjusted R Square	0.9505
Standard Error	0.7482
Observations	5

ANOVA

	df	SS	MS	F	Significance F
Regression	1	43.5205	43.5205	77.7367	0.0031
Residual	3	1.6795	0.5598		
Total	4	45.2			

	Coefficients	Standard Error	t Stat
Intercept	1.2532	0.5958	2.1032
x-squared	0.1309	0.0148	8.8168

(d)   The model developed in part (c) is a better fit. R-square is 0.9628 as compared to 0.85 of part (a).

3.   (a)   Linear function

SUMMARY OUTPUT

Regression Statistics	
Multiple R	0.5095
R Square	0.2596
Adjusted R Square	0.1362
Standard Error	2.0745
Observations	8

ANOVA

	df	SS	MS	F	Significance F
Regression	1	9.0536	9.0536	2.1037	0.1971
Residual	6	25.8214	4.3036		
Total	7	34.875			

	Coefficients	Standard Error	t Stat	P-value
Intercept	2.7857	1.6164	1.7234	0.1356
x	0.4643	0.3201	1.4504	0.1971

$\hat{y} = 2.7857 + 0.4643\ x,\ r^2 = 0.2596$ Only 25.96% of variation is explained. P-value = 0.1971; no significant relationship exists. The model is not adequate for predicting y.

(b) Curvilinear

SUMMARY OUTPUT

Regression Statistics	
Multiple R	0.9680
R Square	0.9370
Adjusted R Square	0.9118
Standard Error	0.6628
Observations	8

ANOVA

	df	SS	MS	F	Significance F
Regression	2	32.6786	16.3392	37.1951	0.0010
Residual	5	2.1964	0.4393		
Total	7	34.875			

	Coefficients	Standard Error	t Stat	P-value
Intercept	-2.8393	0.9247	-3.0706	0.0278
x	3.8393	0.4714	8.1437	0.0005
x-squared	-0.375	0.0511	-7.3335	0.0007

$\hat{y} = -2.8392 + 3.8392 x - 0.375 x^2$

$r^2 = 93.7\%$, which means 93.7% of variation in y is explained by both x and x^2. Both x and x^2 are significant. (Both p-values < 0.05.) The p-value for the analysis of variance is 0.002, which is less than 0.05. Therefore, the model is adequate for predicting y.

(c) 6.517

4. (a) Linear
SUMMARY OUTPUT

Regression Statistics	
Multiple R	0.3052
R Square	0.0932
Adjusted R Square	-0.1335
Standard Error	3.0857
Observations	6

ANOVA

	df	SS	MS	F	Significance F
Regression	1	3.9130	3.9130	0.4110	0.5564
Residual	4	38.0870	9.5217		
Total	5	42			

	Coefficients	Standard Error	t Stat	P-value
Intercept	3.3043	2.9297	1.1279	0.3224
x	0.2609	0.4069	0.6411	0.5564

$\hat{y} = 3.3043 + 0.2618 x$

$r^2 = 0.09317$ Only 9.317% of variation is explained.

P-value = 0.5563, no significant relationship exists.

The model is not adequate for predicting y.

(b) Curvilinear

SUMMARY OUTPUT

Regression Statistics	
Multiple R	0.9508
R Square	0.9041
Adjusted R Square	0.8401
Standard Error	1.1588
Observations	6

ANOVA

	df	SS	MS	F	Significance F
Regression	2	37.9713	18.9856	14.1376	0.0297
Residual	3	4.0287	1.343		
Total	5	42			

	Coefficients	Standard Error	t Stat	P-value
Intercept	-2.6808	1.6196	-1.655	0.1964
x	3.6803	0.6960	5.2879	0.0132
x-squared	-0.3133	0.0622	-5.036	0.0151

$\hat{y} = -2.6808 + 3.6803 x - 0.3133 x^2$

$r^2 = 0.9040$, which indicates 90.4% of variation in y is explained by both x and x^2. The p-value for x is 0.013 and for x^2 is 0.015. Both are significant. The p-value for the analysis of variance is 0.0297, which is less than 0.05. Therefore, the model is adequate for predicting y.

(c) 7.894

5. (a) $r^2 = 0.60$
   (b) $F = 15 > 3.49$; reject H_o, the relationship is significant.

7. (a)

SUMMARY OUTPUT (x1 only)

ANOVA

	df	SS	MS	F	Significance F
Regression	1	90.9808	90.9808	22.2252	0.0008
Residual	10	40.9359	4.0936		
Total	11	131.9167			

	Coefficients	Standard Error	t Stat	P-value
Intercept	-17.8173	21.1634	-0.8419	0.4195
x1	0.1081	0.0229	4.7144	0.0008

SUMMARY OUTPUT (x1 and x2)

Regression Statistics	
Multiple R	0.9492
R Square	0.9009
Adjusted R Square	0.8789
Standard Error	1.2050
Observations	12

ANOVA

	df	SS	MS	F	Significance F
Regression	2	118.8474	59.4237	40.9216	0.0000
Residual	9	13.0692	1.4521		
Total	11	131.9167			

	Coefficients	Standard Error	t Stat	P-value
Intercept	118.5059	33.5753	3.5296	0.0064
x1	-0.0163	0.0315	-0.5171	0.6176
x2	-1.5726	0.3590	-4.3807	0.0018

(b) $F = 19.19$ and $F_{.05} = 5.12$
   Since $19.19 > 5.12$, reject H_0 and conclude x_2 contributes significantly to the model.

8. $F = 151.8$ and $F_{.05} = 7.71$

Since $151.8 > 7.71$, reject H_0 and conclude x_2 contributes significantly to the model.

9.   (a)

Source of Variation	DF	SS	MS	F
Regression	6	1,200	200	6.25
Error (Residual)	25	800	32	
Total	31	2,000		

(b)   Since $F = 6.25 > 2.49$, reject H_0. The model is significant.

10.

Source of Variation	DF	SS	MS	F
Regression	4	1,600	400	16
Error (Residual)	16	400	25	
Total	20	2,000		

12.   (a)

Variable	P-value	
EXP	$0.618 > .05$	not significant
CONSULT	$0.991 > .05$	not significant
GENDER	$0.001 < .05$	significant

(b)   A value of 1 was used for male and 0 for female. Therefore, this coefficient indicates that in this data set, females' incomes were higher than males by $14,906.90.

APPENDIX

• •

Tables

1. Standard Normal Distribution

2. t Distribution

3. Chi-Square Distribution

4. F Distribution

5. Binomial Probabilities

6. Values of $e^{-\mu}$

7. Poisson Probabilities

TABLE 1 Cumulative probabilities for the Standard Normal Distribution

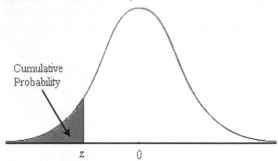

Cumulative
Probability

Entries in this table give the area
under the curve to the left of the
z value. For example, for z = -2.0,
the cumulative probability is 0.0228.

z	0.00	0.01	0.02	0.03	0.04	0.05	0.06	0.07	0.08	0.09
-3.00	0.0013	0.0013	0.0013	0.0012	0.0012	0.0011	0.0011	0.0011	0.0010	0.0010
-2.90	0.0019	0.0018	0.0018	0.0017	0.0016	0.0016	0.0015	0.0015	0.0014	0.0014
-2.80	0.0026	0.0025	0.0024	0.0023	0.0023	0.0022	0.0021	0.0021	0.0020	0.0019
-2.70	0.0035	0.0034	0.0033	0.0032	0.0031	0.0030	0.0029	0.0028	0.0027	0.0026
-2.60	0.0047	0.0045	0.0044	0.0043	0.0041	0.0040	0.0039	0.0038	0.0037	0.0036
-2.50	0.0062	0.0060	0.0059	0.0057	0.0055	0.0054	0.0052	0.0051	0.0049	0.0048
-2.40	0.0082	0.0080	0.0078	0.0075	0.0073	0.0071	0.0069	0.0068	0.0066	0.0064
-2.30	0.0107	0.0104	0.0102	0.0099	0.0096	0.0094	0.0091	0.0089	0.0087	0.0084
-2.20	0.0139	0.0136	0.0132	0.0129	0.0125	0.0122	0.0119	0.0116	0.0113	0.0110
-2.10	0.0179	0.0174	0.0170	0.0166	0.0162	0.0158	0.0154	0.0150	0.0146	0.0143
-2.00	0.0228	0.0222	0.0217	0.0212	0.0207	0.0202	0.0197	0.0192	0.0188	0.0183
-1.90	0.0287	0.0281	0.0274	0.0268	0.0262	0.0256	0.0250	0.0244	0.0239	0.0233
-1.80	0.0359	0.0351	0.0344	0.0336	0.0329	0.0322	0.0314	0.0307	0.0301	0.0294
-1.70	0.0446	0.0436	0.0427	0.0418	0.0409	0.0401	0.0392	0.0384	0.0375	0.0367
-1.60	0.0548	0.0537	0.0526	0.0516	0.0505	0.0495	0.0485	0.0475	0.0465	0.0455
-1.50	0.0668	0.0655	0.0643	0.0630	0.0618	0.0606	0.0594	0.0582	0.0571	0.0559
-1.40	0.0808	0.0793	0.0778	0.0764	0.0749	0.0735	0.0721	0.0708	0.0694	0.0681
-1.30	0.0968	0.0951	0.0934	0.0918	0.0901	0.0885	0.0869	0.0853	0.0838	0.0823
-1.20	0.1151	0.1131	0.1112	0.1093	0.1075	0.1056	0.1038	0.1020	0.1003	0.0985
-1.10	0.1357	0.1335	0.1314	0.1292	0.1271	0.1251	0.1230	0.1210	0.1190	0.1170
-1.00	0.1587	0.1562	0.1539	0.1515	0.1492	0.1469	0.1446	0.1423	0.1401	0.1379
-0.90	0.1841	0.1814	0.1788	0.1762	0.1736	0.1711	0.1685	0.1660	0.1635	0.1611
-0.80	0.2119	0.2090	0.2061	0.2033	0.2005	0.1977	0.1949	0.1922	0.1894	0.1867
-0.70	0.2420	0.2389	0.2358	0.2327	0.2296	0.2266	0.2236	0.2206	0.2177	0.2148
-0.60	0.2743	0.2709	0.2676	0.2643	0.2611	0.2578	0.2546	0.2514	0.2483	0.2451
-0.50	0.3085	0.3050	0.3015	0.2981	0.2946	0.2912	0.2877	0.2843	0.2810	0.2776
-0.40	0.3446	0.3409	0.3372	0.3336	0.3300	0.3264	0.3228	0.3192	0.3156	0.3121
-0.30	0.3821	0.3783	0.3745	0.3707	0.3669	0.3632	0.3594	0.3557	0.3520	0.3483
-0.20	0.4207	0.4168	0.4129	0.4090	0.4052	0.4013	0.3974	0.3936	0.3897	0.3859
-0.10	0.4602	0.4562	0.4522	0.4483	0.4443	0.4404	0.4364	0.4325	0.4286	0.4247
-0.00	0.5000	0.4960	0.4920	0.4880	0.4840	0.4801	0.4761	0.4721	0.4681	0.4641

TABLE 1 Cumulative probabilities for the Standard Normal Distribution

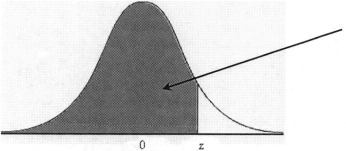

Cumulative probability

Entries in this table give the area under the curve to the left of the z value. For example, for z = 1.96, the cumulative probability is 0.9750.

z	0.00	0.01	0.02	0.03	0.04	0.05	0.06	0.07	0.08	0.09
0.00	0.5000	0.5040	0.5080	0.5120	0.5160	0.5199	0.5239	0.5279	0.5319	0.5359
0.10	0.5398	0.5438	0.5478	0.5517	0.5557	0.5596	0.5636	0.5675	0.5714	0.5753
0.20	0.5793	0.5832	0.5871	0.5910	0.5948	0.5987	0.6026	0.6064	0.6103	0.6141
0.30	0.6179	0.6217	0.6255	0.6293	0.6331	0.6368	0.6406	0.6443	0.6480	0.6517
0.40	0.6554	0.6591	0.6628	0.6664	0.6700	0.6736	0.6772	0.6808	0.6844	0.6879
0.50	0.6915	0.6950	0.6985	0.7019	0.7054	0.7088	0.7123	0.7157	0.7190	0.7224
0.60	0.7257	0.7291	0.7324	0.7357	0.7389	0.7422	0.7454	0.7486	0.7517	0.7549
0.70	0.7580	0.7611	0.7642	0.7673	0.7704	0.7734	0.7764	0.7794	0.7823	0.7852
0.80	0.7881	0.7910	0.7939	0.7967	0.7995	0.8023	0.8051	0.8078	0.8106	0.8133
0.90	0.8159	0.8186	0.8212	0.8238	0.8264	0.8289	0.8315	0.8340	0.8365	0.8389
1.00	0.8413	0.8438	0.8461	0.8485	0.8508	0.8531	0.8554	0.8577	0.8599	0.8621
1.10	0.8643	0.8665	0.8686	0.8708	0.8729	0.8749	0.8770	0.8790	0.8810	0.8830
1.20	0.8849	0.8869	0.8888	0.8907	0.8925	0.8944	0.8962	0.8980	0.8997	0.9015
1.30	0.9032	0.9049	0.9066	0.9082	0.9099	0.9115	0.9131	0.9147	0.9162	0.9177
1.40	0.9192	0.9207	0.9222	0.9236	0.9251	0.9265	0.9279	0.9292	0.9306	0.9319
1.50	0.9332	0.9345	0.9357	0.9370	0.9382	0.9394	0.9406	0.9418	0.9429	0.9441
1.60	0.9452	0.9463	0.9474	0.9484	0.9495	0.9505	0.9515	0.9525	0.9535	0.9545
1.70	0.9554	0.9564	0.9573	0.9582	0.9591	0.9599	0.9608	0.9616	0.9625	0.9633
1.80	0.9641	0.9649	0.9656	0.9664	0.9671	0.9678	0.9686	0.9693	0.9699	0.9706
1.90	0.9713	0.9719	0.9726	0.9732	0.9738	0.9744	0.9750	0.9756	0.9761	0.9767
2.00	0.9772	0.9778	0.9783	0.9788	0.9793	0.9798	0.9803	0.9808	0.9812	0.9817
2.10	0.9821	0.9826	0.9830	0.9834	0.9838	0.9842	0.9846	0.9850	0.9854	0.9857
2.20	0.9861	0.9864	0.9868	0.9871	0.9875	0.9878	0.9881	0.9884	0.9887	0.9890
2.30	0.9893	0.9896	0.9898	0.9901	0.9904	0.9906	0.9909	0.9911	0.9913	0.9916
2.40	0.9918	0.9920	0.9922	0.9925	0.9927	0.9929	0.9931	0.9932	0.9934	0.9936
2.50	0.9938	0.9940	0.9941	0.9943	0.9945	0.9946	0.9948	0.9949	0.9951	0.9952
2.60	0.9953	0.9955	0.9956	0.9957	0.9959	0.9960	0.9961	0.9962	0.9963	0.9964
2.70	0.9965	0.9966	0.9967	0.9968	0.9969	0.9970	0.9971	0.9972	0.9973	0.9974
2.80	0.9974	0.9975	0.9976	0.9977	0.9977	0.9978	0.9979	0.9979	0.9980	0.9981
2.90	0.9981	0.9982	0.9982	0.9983	0.9984	0.9984	0.9985	0.9985	0.9986	0.9986
3.00	0.9987	0.9987	0.9987	0.9988	0.9988	0.9989	0.9989	0.9989	0.9990	0.9990

TABLE 2   t Distribution

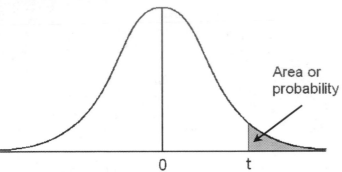

Area or probability

Entries in this table give the t values for an area or probability in the upper tail of the t distribution. For example, with 2 degrees of freedom and 0.10 area in the upper tail, $t_{0.10} = 1.886$

			Area in the upper tail			
Degrees of Freedom	0.20	0.10	0.05	0.025	0.01	0.005
1	1.376	3.078	6.314	12.706	31.821	63.656
2	1.061	1.886	2.920	4.303	6.965	9.925
3	0.978	1.638	2.353	3.182	4.541	5.841
4	0.941	1.533	2.132	2.776	3.747	4.604
5	0.920	1.476	2.015	2.571	3.365	4.032
6	0.906	1.440	1.943	2.447	3.143	3.707
7	0.896	1.415	1.895	2.365	2.998	3.499
8	0.889	1.397	1.860	2.306	2.896	3.355
9	0.883	1.383	1.833	2.262	2.821	3.250
10	0.879	1.372	1.812	2.228	2.764	3.169
11	0.876	1.363	1.796	2.201	2.718	3.106
12	0.873	1.356	1.782	2.179	2.681	3.055
13	0.870	1.350	1.771	2.160	2.650	3.012
14	0.868	1.345	1.761	2.145	2.624	2.977
15	0.866	1.341	1.753	2.131	2.602	2.947
16	0.865	1.337	1.746	2.120	2.583	2.921
17	0.863	1.333	1.740	2.110	2.567	2.898
18	0.862	1.330	1.734	2.101	2.552	2.878
19	0.861	1.328	1.729	2.093	2.539	2.861
20	0.860	1.325	1.725	2.086	2.528	2.845
21	0.859	1.323	1.721	2.080	2.518	2.831
22	0.858	1.321	1.717	2.074	2.508	2.819
23	0.858	1.319	1.714	2.069	2.500	2.807
24	0.857	1.318	1.711	2.064	2.492	2.797
25	0.856	1.316	1.708	2.060	2.485	2.787
26	0.856	1.315	1.706	2.056	2.479	2.779
27	0.855	1.314	1.703	2.052	2.473	2.771
28	0.855	1.313	1.701	2.048	2.467	2.763
29	0.854	1.311	1.699	2.045	2.462	2.756
30	0.854	1.310	1.697	2.042	2.457	2.750
31	0.853	1.309	1.696	2.040	2.453	2.744
32	0.853	1.309	1.694	2.037	2.449	2.738
33	0.853	1.308	1.692	2.035	2.445	2.733
34	0.852	1.307	1.691	2.032	2.441	2.728

TABLE 2   t Distribution (*Continued*)

Degrees of Freedom	Area in the upper tail					
	0.20	0.10	0.05	0.025	0.01	0.005
35	0.852	1.306	1.690	2.030	2.438	2.724
36	0.852	1.306	1.688	2.028	2.434	2.719
37	0.851	1.305	1.687	2.026	2.431	2.715
38	0.851	1.304	1.686	2.024	2.429	2.712
39	0.851	1.304	1.685	2.023	2.426	2.708
40	0.851	1.303	1.684	2.021	2.423	2.704
41	0.850	1.303	1.683	2.020	2.421	2.701
42	0.850	1.302	1.682	2.018	2.418	2.698
43	0.850	1.302	1.681	2.017	2.416	2.695
44	0.850	1.301	1.680	2.015	2.414	2.692
45	0.850	1.301	1.679	2.014	2.412	2.690
46	0.850	1.300	1.679	2.013	2.410	2.687
47	0.849	1.300	1.678	2.012	2.408	2.685
48	0.849	1.299	1.677	2.011	2.407	2.682
49	0.849	1.299	1.677	2.010	2.405	2.680
50	0.849	1.299	1.676	2.009	2.403	2.678
51	0.849	1.298	1.675	2.008	2.402	2.676
52	0.849	1.298	1.675	2.007	2.400	2.674
53	0.848	1.298	1.674	2.006	2.399	2.672
54	0.848	1.297	1.674	2.005	2.397	2.670
55	0.848	1.297	1.673	2.004	2.396	2.668
56	0.848	1.297	1.673	2.003	2.395	2.667
57	0.848	1.297	1.672	2.002	2.394	2.665
58	0.848	1.296	1.672	2.002	2.392	2.663
59	0.848	1.296	1.671	2.001	2.391	2.662
60	0.848	1.296	1.671	2.000	2.390	2.660
61	0.848	1.296	1.670	2.000	2.389	2.659
62	0.847	1.295	1.670	1.999	2.388	2.657
63	0.847	1.295	1.669	1.998	2.387	2.656
64	0.847	1.295	1.669	1.998	2.386	2.655
65	0.847	1.295	1.669	1.997	2.385	2.654
66	0.847	1.295	1.668	1.997	2.384	2.652
67	0.847	1.294	1.668	1.996	2.383	2.651
68	0.847	1.294	1.668	1.995	2.382	2.650
69	0.847	1.294	1.667	1.995	2.382	2.649
70	0.847	1.294	1.667	1.994	2.381	2.648
71	0.847	1.294	1.667	1.994	2.380	2.647
72	0.847	1.293	1.666	1.993	2.379	2.646
73	0.847	1.293	1.666	1.993	2.379	2.645
74	0.847	1.293	1.666	1.993	2.378	2.644
75	0.846	1.293	1.665	1.992	2.377	2.643
76	0.846	1.293	1.665	1.992	2.376	2.642
77	0.846	1.293	1.665	1.991	2.376	2.641
78	0.846	1.292	1.665	1.991	2.375	2.640

TABLE 2   t Distribution *(Continued)*

Degrees of Freedom	Area in the upper tail					
	0.20	0.10	0.05	0.025	0.01	0.005
79	0.846	1.292	1.664	1.990	2.374	2.639
80	0.846	1.292	1.664	1.990	2.374	2.639
81	0.846	1.292	1.664	1.990	2.373	2.638
82	0.846	1.292	1.664	1.989	2.373	2.637
83	0.846	1.292	1.663	1.989	2.372	2.636
84	0.846	1.292	1.663	1.989	2.372	2.636
85	0.846	1.292	1.663	1.988	2.371	2.635
86	0.846	1.291	1.663	1.988	2.370	2.634
87	0.846	1.291	1.663	1.988	2.370	2.634
88	0.846	1.291	1.662	1.987	2.369	2.633
89	0.846	1.291	1.662	1.987	2.369	2.632
90	0.846	1.291	1.662	1.987	2.368	2.632
91	0.846	1.291	1.662	1.986	2.368	2.631
92	0.846	1.291	1.662	1.986	2.368	2.630
93	0.846	1.291	1.661	1.986	2.367	2.630
94	0.845	1.291	1.661	1.986	2.367	2.629
95	0.845	1.291	1.661	1.985	2.366	2.629
96	0.845	1.290	1.661	1.985	2.366	2.628
97	0.845	1.290	1.661	1.985	2.365	2.627
98	0.845	1.290	1.661	1.984	2.365	2.627
99	0.845	1.290	1.660	1.984	2.365	2.626
100	0.845	1.290	1.660	1.984	2.364	2.626
∞	0.842	1.282	1.645	1.960	2.326	2.576

TABLE 3 Chi-Square Distribution

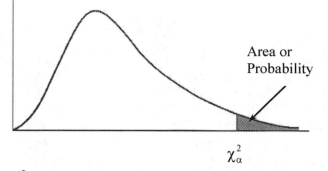

$$\chi_{\alpha}^{2}$$

Entries in table give χ_{α}^{2} values, where α is the area or probability in the upper tail of the chi-square distribution. For example with 5 degrees of freedom *(labeled as df)* and 0.05 area in the upper tail $\chi_{.05}^{2} = 11.070$.

Area in the Upper Tail

df	0.995	0.990	0.975	0.950	0.900	0.100	0.050	0.025	0.010	0.005
1	0.000	0.000	0.001	0.004	0.016	2.706	3.841	5.024	6.635	7.879
2	0.010	0.020	0.051	0.103	0.211	4.605	5.991	7.378	9.210	10.597
3	0.072	0.115	0.216	0.352	0.584	6.251	7.815	9.348	11.345	12.838
4	0.207	0.297	0.484	0.711	1.064	7.779	9.488	11.143	13.277	14.860
5	0.412	0.554	0.831	1.145	1.610	9.236	11.070	12.832	15.086	16.750
6	0.676	0.872	1.237	1.635	2.204	10.645	12.592	14.449	16.812	18.548
7	0.989	1.239	1.690	2.167	2.833	12.017	14.067	16.013	18.475	20.278
8	1.344	1.647	2.180	2.733	3.490	13.362	15.507	17.535	20.090	21.955
9	1.735	2.088	2.700	3.325	4.168	14.684	16.919	19.023	21.666	23.589
10	2.156	2.558	3.247	3.940	4.865	15.987	18.307	20.483	23.209	25.188
11	2.603	3.053	3.816	4.575	5.578	17.275	19.675	21.920	24.725	26.757
12	3.074	3.571	4.404	5.226	6.304	18.549	21.026	23.337	26.217	28.300
13	3.565	4.107	5.009	5.892	7.041	19.812	22.362	24.736	27.688	29.819
14	4.075	4.660	5.629	6.571	7.790	21.064	23.685	26.119	29.141	31.319
15	4.601	5.229	6.262	7.261	8.547	22.307	24.996	27.488	30.578	32.801
16	5.142	5.812	6.908	7.962	9.312	23.542	26.296	28.845	32.000	34.267
17	5.697	6.408	7.564	8.672	10.085	24.769	27.587	30.191	33.409	35.718
18	6.265	7.015	8.231	9.390	10.865	25.989	28.869	31.526	34.805	37.156
19	6.844	7.633	8.907	10.117	11.651	27.204	30.144	32.852	36.191	38.582
20	7.434	8.260	9.591	10.851	12.443	28.412	31.410	34.170	37.566	39.997
21	8.034	8.897	10.283	11.591	13.240	29.615	32.671	35.479	38.932	41.401
22	8.643	9.542	10.982	12.338	14.041	30.813	33.924	36.781	40.289	42.796
23	9.260	10.196	11.689	13.091	14.848	32.007	35.172	38.076	41.638	44.181
24	9.886	10.856	12.401	13.848	15.659	33.196	36.415	39.364	42.980	45.558
25	10.520	11.524	13.120	14.611	16.473	34.382	37.652	40.646	44.314	46.928
26	11.160	12.198	13.844	15.379	17.292	35.563	38.885	41.923	45.642	48.290
27	11.808	12.878	14.573	16.151	18.114	36.741	40.113	43.195	46.963	49.645
28	12.461	13.565	15.308	16.928	18.939	37.916	41.337	44.461	48.278	50.994
29	13.121	14.256	16.047	17.708	19.768	39.087	42.557	45.722	49.588	52.335
30	13.787	14.953	16.791	18.493	20.599	40.256	43.773	46.979	50.892	53.672

TABLE 3   Chi-Square Distribution *(Continued)*

Area in the Upper Tail

df	0.995	0.990	0.975	0.950	0.900	0.100	0.050	0.025	0.010	0.005
31	14.458	15.655	17.539	19.281	21.434	41.422	44.985	48.232	52.191	55.002
32	15.134	16.362	18.291	20.072	22.271	42.585	46.194	49.480	53.486	56.328
33	15.815	17.073	19.047	20.867	23.110	43.745	47.400	50.725	54.775	57.648
34	16.501	17.789	19.806	21.664	23.952	44.903	48.602	51.966	56.061	58.964
35	17.192	18.509	20.569	22.465	24.797	46.059	49.802	53.203	57.342	60.275
36	17.887	19.233	21.336	23.269	25.643	47.212	50.998	54.437	58.619	61.581
37	18.586	19.960	22.106	24.075	26.492	48.363	52.192	55.668	59.893	62.883
38	19.289	20.691	22.878	24.884	27.343	49.513	53.384	56.895	61.162	64.181
39	19.996	21.426	23.654	25.695	28.196	50.660	54.572	58.120	62.428	65.475
40	20.707	22.164	24.433	26.509	29.051	51.805	55.758	59.342	63.691	66.766
41	21.421	22.906	25.215	27.326	29.907	52.949	56.942	60.561	64.950	68.053
42	22.138	23.650	25.999	28.144	30.765	54.090	58.124	61.777	66.206	69.336
43	22.860	24.398	26.785	28.965	31.625	55.230	59.304	62.990	67.459	70.616
44	23.584	25.148	27.575	29.787	32.487	56.369	60.481	64.201	68.710	71.892
45	24.311	25.901	28.366	30.612	33.350	57.505	61.656	65.410	69.957	73.166
46	25.041	26.657	29.160	31.439	34.215	58.641	62.830	66.616	71.201	74.437
47	25.775	27.416	29.956	32.268	35.081	59.774	64.001	67.821	72.443	75.704
48	26.511	28.177	30.754	33.098	35.949	60.907	65.171	69.023	73.683	76.969
49	27.249	28.941	31.555	33.930	36.818	62.038	66.339	70.222	74.919	78.231
50	27.991	29.707	32.357	34.764	37.689	63.167	67.505	71.420	76.154	79.490
51	28.735	30.475	33.162	35.600	38.560	64.295	68.669	72.616	77.386	80.746
52	29.481	31.246	33.968	36.437	39.433	65.422	69.832	73.810	78.616	82.001
53	30.230	32.019	34.776	37.276	40.308	66.548	70.993	75.002	79.843	83.253
54	30.981	32.793	35.586	38.116	41.183	67.673	72.153	76.192	81.069	84.502
55	31.735	33.571	36.398	38.958	42.060	68.796	73.311	77.380	82.292	85.749
56	32.491	34.350	37.212	39.801	42.937	69.919	74.468	78.567	83.514	86.994
57	33.248	35.131	38.027	40.646	43.816	71.040	75.624	79.752	84.733	88.237
58	34.008	35.914	38.844	41.492	44.696	72.160	76.778	80.936	85.950	89.477
59	34.770	36.698	39.662	42.339	45.577	73.279	77.930	82.117	87.166	90.715
60	35.534	37.485	40.482	43.188	46.459	74.397	79.082	83.298	88.379	91.952
61	36.300	38.273	41.303	44.038	47.342	75.514	80.232	84.476	89.591	93.186
62	37.068	39.063	42.126	44.889	48.226	76.630	81.381	85.654	90.802	94.419
63	37.838	39.855	42.950	45.741	49.111	77.745	82.529	86.830	92.010	95.649
64	38.610	40.649	43.776	46.595	49.996	78.860	83.675	88.004	93.217	96.878
65	39.383	41.444	44.603	47.450	50.883	79.973	84.821	89.177	94.422	98.105
66	40.158	42.240	45.431	48.305	51.770	81.085	85.965	90.349	95.626	99.330
67	40.935	43.038	46.261	49.162	52.659	82.197	87.108	91.519	96.828	100.554
68	41.714	43.838	47.092	50.020	53.548	83.308	88.250	92.688	98.028	101.776
69	42.493	44.639	47.924	50.879	54.438	84.418	89.391	93.856	99.227	102.996
70	43.275	45.442	48.758	51.739	55.329	85.527	90.531	95.023	100.425	104.215
71	44.058	46.246	49.592	52.600	56.221	86.635	91.670	96.189	101.621	105.432
72	44.843	47.051	50.428	53.462	57.113	87.743	92.808	97.353	102.816	106.647
73	45.629	47.858	51.265	54.325	58.006	88.850	93.945	98.516	104.010	107.862
74	46.417	48.666	52.103	55.189	58.900	89.956	95.081	99.678	105.202	109.074
75	47.206	49.475	52.942	56.054	59.795	91.061	96.217	100.839	106.393	110.285

TABLE 3 Chi-Square Distribution *(Continued)*

Area in the Upper Tail

df	0.995	0.990	0.975	0.950	0.900	0.100	0.050	0.025	0.010	0.005
76	47.996	50.286	53.782	56.920	60.690	92.166	97.351	101.999	107.582	111.495
77	48.788	51.097	54.623	57.786	61.586	93.270	98.484	103.158	108.771	112.704
78	49.581	51.910	55.466	58.654	62.483	94.374	99.617	104.316	109.958	113.911
79	50.376	52.725	56.309	59.522	63.380	95.476	100.749	105.473	111.144	115.116
80	51.172	53.540	57.153	60.391	64.278	96.578	101.879	106.629	112.329	116.321
81	51.969	54.357	57.998	61.262	65.176	97.680	103.010	107.783	113.512	117.524
82	52.767	55.174	58.845	62.132	66.076	98.780	104.139	108.937	114.695	118.726
83	53.567	55.993	59.692	63.004	66.976	99.880	105.267	110.090	115.876	119.927
84	54.368	56.813	60.540	63.876	67.876	100.980	106.395	111.242	117.057	121.126
85	55.170	57.634	61.389	64.749	68.777	102.079	107.522	112.393	118.236	122.324
86	55.973	58.456	62.239	65.623	69.679	103.177	108.648	113.544	119.414	123.522
87	56.777	59.279	63.089	66.498	70.581	104.275	109.773	114.693	120.591	124.718
88	57.582	60.103	63.941	67.373	71.484	105.372	110.898	115.841	121.767	125.912
89	58.389	60.928	64.793	68.249	72.387	106.469	112.022	116.989	122.942	127.106
90	59.196	61.754	65.647	69.126	73.291	107.565	113.145	118.136	124.116	128.299
91	60.005	62.581	66.501	70.003	74.196	108.661	114.268	119.282	125.289	129.490
92	60.815	63.409	67.356	70.882	75.100	109.756	115.390	120.427	126.462	130.681
93	61.625	64.238	68.211	71.760	76.006	110.850	116.511	121.571	127.633	131.871
94	62.437	65.068	69.068	72.640	76.912	111.944	117.632	122.715	128.803	133.059
95	63.250	65.898	69.925	73.520	77.818	113.038	118.752	123.858	129.973	134.247
96	64.063	66.730	70.783	74.401	78.725	114.131	119.871	125.000	131.141	135.433
97	64.878	67.562	71.642	75.282	79.633	115.223	120.990	126.141	132.309	136.619
98	65.693	68.396	72.501	76.164	80.541	116.315	122.108	127.282	133.476	137.803
99	66.510	69.230	73.361	77.046	81.449	117.407	123.225	128.422	134.641	138.987
100	67.328	70.065	74.222	77.929	82.358	118.498	124.342	129.561	135.807	140.170

TABLE 4 F Distribution

Entries in the table give F_α values, where α is the area or probability in the upper tail of the F distribution.
For example, with 2 numerator degrees of freedom, and 3 denominator degrees of freedom *(Labeled as DF_d)*, and a 0.05 area in the upper tail $F_{.05} = 9.55$.

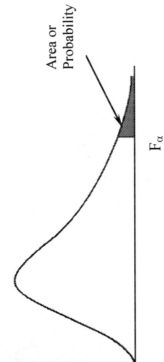

Area or Probability

F_α

Numerator Degrees of Freedom

DF_d	α	1	2	3	4	5	6	7	8	9	10	15	20	25	30	40	60	100	1000
1	.10	39.86	49.50	53.59	55.83	57.24	58.20	58.91	59.44	59.86	60.19	61.22	61.74	62.05	62.26	62.53	62.79	63.01	63.30
	.05	161.45	199.50	215.71	224.58	230.16	233.99	236.77	238.88	240.54	241.88	245.95	248.02	249.26	250.10	251.14	252.20	253.04	254.19
	.025	647.79	799.48	864.15	899.60	921.83	937.11	948.20	956.64	963.28	968.63	984.87	993.08	998.09	1001.40	1005.60	1009.79	1013.16	1017.76
	.01	4052.18	4999.34	5403.53	5624.26	5763.96	5858.95	5928.33	5980.95	6022.40	6055.93	6156.97	6208.66	6239.86	6260.35	6286.43	6312.97	6333.92	6362.80
2	.10	8.53	9.00	9.16	9.24	9.29	9.33	9.35	9.37	9.38	9.39	9.42	9.44	9.45	9.46	9.47	9.47	9.48	9.49
	.05	18.51	19.00	19.16	19.25	19.30	19.33	19.35	19.37	19.38	19.40	19.43	19.45	19.46	19.46	19.47	19.48	19.49	19.49
	.025	38.51	39.00	39.17	39.25	39.30	39.33	39.36	39.37	39.39	39.40	39.43	39.45	39.46	39.46	39.47	39.48	39.49	39.50
	.01	98.50	99.00	99.16	99.25	99.30	99.33	99.36	99.38	99.39	99.40	99.43	99.45	99.46	99.47	99.48	99.48	99.49	99.50
3	.10	5.54	5.46	5.39	5.34	5.31	5.28	5.27	5.25	5.24	5.23	5.20	5.18	5.17	5.17	5.16	5.15	5.14	5.13
	.05	10.13	9.55	9.28	9.12	9.01	8.94	8.89	8.85	8.81	8.79	8.70	8.66	8.63	8.62	8.59	8.57	8.55	8.53
	.025	17.44	16.04	15.44	15.10	14.88	14.73	14.62	14.54	14.47	14.42	14.25	14.17	14.12	14.08	14.04	13.99	13.96	13.91
	.01	34.12	30.82	29.46	28.71	28.24	27.91	27.67	27.49	27.34	27.23	26.87	26.69	26.58	26.50	26.41	26.32	26.24	26.14

TABLE 4 F Distribution *(Continued)*

Numerator Degrees of Freedom

DF_d	α	1	2	3	4	5	6	7	8	9	10	15	20	25	30	40	60	100	1000
4	.10	4.54	4.32	4.19	4.11	4.05	4.01	3.98	3.95	3.94	3.92	3.87	3.84	3.83	3.82	3.80	3.79	3.78	3.76
	.05	7.71	6.94	6.59	6.39	6.26	6.16	6.09	6.04	6.00	5.96	5.86	5.80	5.77	5.75	5.72	5.69	5.66	5.63
	.025	12.22	10.65	9.98	9.60	9.36	9.20	9.07	8.98	8.90	8.84	8.66	8.56	8.50	8.46	8.41	8.36	8.32	8.26
	.01	21.20	18.00	16.69	15.98	15.52	15.21	14.98	14.80	14.66	14.55	14.20	14.02	13.91	13.84	13.75	13.65	13.58	13.47
5	.10	4.06	3.78	3.62	3.52	3.45	3.40	3.37	3.34	3.32	3.30	3.24	3.21	3.19	3.17	3.16	3.14	3.13	3.11
	.05	6.61	5.79	5.41	5.19	5.05	4.95	4.88	4.82	4.77	4.74	4.62	4.56	4.52	4.50	4.46	4.43	4.41	4.37
	.025	10.01	8.43	7.76	7.39	7.15	6.98	6.85	6.76	6.68	6.62	6.43	6.33	6.27	6.23	6.18	6.12	6.08	6.02
	.01	16.26	13.27	12.06	11.39	10.97	10.67	10.46	10.29	10.16	10.05	9.72	9.55	9.45	9.38	9.29	9.20	9.13	9.03
6	.10	3.78	3.46	3.29	3.18	3.11	3.05	3.01	2.98	2.96	2.94	2.87	2.84	2.81	2.80	2.78	2.76	2.75	2.72
	.05	5.99	5.14	4.76	4.53	4.39	4.28	4.21	4.15	4.10	4.06	3.94	3.87	3.83	3.81	3.77	3.74	3.71	3.67
	.025	8.81	7.26	6.60	6.23	5.99	5.82	5.70	5.60	5.52	5.46	5.27	5.17	5.11	5.07	5.01	4.96	4.92	4.86
	.01	13.75	10.92	9.78	9.15	8.75	8.47	8.26	8.10	7.98	7.87	7.56	7.40	7.30	7.23	7.14	7.06	6.99	6.89
7	.10	3.59	3.26	3.07	2.96	2.88	2.83	2.78	2.75	2.72	2.70	2.63	2.59	2.57	2.56	2.54	2.51	2.50	2.47
	.05	5.59	4.74	4.35	4.12	3.97	3.87	3.79	3.73	3.68	3.64	3.51	3.44	3.40	3.38	3.34	3.30	3.27	3.23
	.025	8.07	6.54	5.89	5.52	5.29	5.12	4.99	4.90	4.82	4.76	4.57	4.47	4.40	4.36	4.31	4.25	4.21	4.15
	.01	12.25	9.55	8.45	7.85	7.46	7.19	6.99	6.84	6.72	6.62	6.31	6.16	6.06	5.99	5.91	5.82	5.75	5.66
8	.10	3.46	3.11	2.92	2.81	2.73	2.67	2.62	2.59	2.56	2.54	2.46	2.42	2.40	2.38	2.36	2.34	2.32	2.30
	.05	5.32	4.46	4.07	3.84	3.69	3.58	3.50	3.44	3.39	3.35	3.22	3.15	3.11	3.08	3.04	3.01	2.97	2.93
	.025	7.57	6.06	5.42	5.05	4.82	4.65	4.53	4.43	4.36	4.30	4.10	4.00	3.94	3.89	3.84	3.78	3.74	3.68
	.01	11.26	8.65	7.59	7.01	6.63	6.37	6.18	6.03	5.91	5.81	5.52	5.36	5.26	5.20	5.12	5.03	4.96	4.87
9	.10	3.36	3.01	2.81	2.69	2.61	2.55	2.51	2.47	2.44	2.42	2.34	2.30	2.27	2.25	2.23	2.21	2.19	2.16
	.05	5.12	4.26	3.86	3.63	3.48	3.37	3.29	3.23	3.18	3.14	3.01	2.94	2.89	2.86	2.83	2.79	2.76	2.71
	.025	7.21	5.71	5.08	4.72	4.48	4.32	4.20	4.10	4.03	3.96	3.77	3.67	3.60	3.56	3.51	3.45	3.40	3.34
	.01	10.56	8.02	6.99	6.42	6.06	5.80	5.61	5.47	5.35	5.26	4.96	4.81	4.71	4.65	4.57	4.48	4.41	4.32
10	.10	3.29	2.92	2.73	2.61	2.52	2.46	2.41	2.38	2.35	2.32	2.24	2.20	2.17	2.16	2.13	2.11	2.09	2.06
	.05	4.96	4.10	3.71	3.48	3.33	3.22	3.14	3.07	3.02	2.98	2.85	2.77	2.73	2.70	2.66	2.62	2.59	2.54
	.025	6.94	5.46	4.83	4.47	4.24	4.07	3.95	3.85	3.78	3.72	3.52	3.42	3.35	3.31	3.26	3.20	3.15	3.09
	.01	10.04	7.56	6.55	5.99	5.64	5.39	5.20	5.06	4.94	4.85	4.56	4.41	4.31	4.25	4.17	4.08	4.01	3.92
11	.10	3.23	2.86	2.66	2.54	2.45	2.39	2.34	2.30	2.27	2.25	2.17	2.12	2.10	2.08	2.05	2.03	2.01	1.98
	.05	4.84	3.98	3.59	3.36	3.20	3.09	3.01	2.95	2.90	2.85	2.72	2.65	2.60	2.57	2.53	2.49	2.46	2.41
	.025	6.72	5.26	4.63	4.28	4.04	3.88	3.76	3.66	3.59	3.53	3.33	3.23	3.16	3.12	3.06	3.00	2.96	2.89
	.01	9.65	7.21	6.22	5.67	5.32	5.07	4.89	4.74	4.63	4.54	4.25	4.10	4.01	3.94	3.86	3.78	3.71	3.61
12	.10	3.18	2.81	2.61	2.48	2.39	2.33	2.28	2.24	2.21	2.19	2.10	2.06	2.03	2.01	1.99	1.96	1.94	1.91
	.05	4.75	3.89	3.49	3.26	3.11	3.00	2.91	2.85	2.80	2.75	2.62	2.54	2.50	2.47	2.43	2.38	2.35	2.30
	.025	6.55	5.10	4.47	4.12	3.89	3.73	3.61	3.51	3.44	3.37	3.18	3.07	3.01	2.96	2.91	2.85	2.80	2.73
	.01	9.33	6.93	5.95	5.41	5.06	4.82	4.64	4.50	4.39	4.30	4.01	3.86	3.76	3.70	3.62	3.54	3.47	3.37

TABLE 4 F Distribution *(Continued)*

DF_d	α	1	2	3	4	5	6	7	8	9	10	15	20	25	30	40	60	100	1000
								Numerator Degrees of Freedom											
13	.10	3.14	2.76	2.56	2.43	2.35	2.28	2.23	2.20	2.16	2.14	2.05	2.01	1.98	1.96	1.93	1.90	1.88	1.85
	.05	4.67	3.81	3.41	3.18	3.03	2.92	2.83	2.77	2.71	2.67	2.53	2.46	2.41	2.38	2.34	2.30	2.26	2.21
	.025	6.41	4.97	4.35	4.00	3.77	3.60	3.48	3.39	3.31	3.25	3.05	2.95	2.88	2.84	2.78	2.72	2.67	2.60
	.01	9.07	6.70	5.74	5.21	4.86	4.62	4.44	4.30	4.19	4.10	3.82	3.66	3.57	3.51	3.43	3.34	3.27	3.18
14	.10	3.10	2.73	2.52	2.39	2.31	2.24	2.19	2.15	2.12	2.10	2.01	1.96	1.93	1.91	1.89	1.86	1.83	1.80
	.05	4.60	3.74	3.34	3.11	2.96	2.85	2.76	2.70	2.65	2.60	2.46	2.39	2.34	2.31	2.27	2.22	2.19	2.14
	.025	6.30	4.86	4.24	3.89	3.66	3.50	3.38	3.29	3.21	3.15	2.95	2.84	2.78	2.73	2.67	2.61	2.56	2.50
	.01	8.86	6.51	5.56	5.04	4.69	4.46	4.28	4.14	4.03	3.94	3.66	3.51	3.41	3.35	3.27	3.18	3.11	3.02
15	.10	3.07	2.70	2.49	2.36	2.27	2.21	2.16	2.12	2.09	2.06	1.97	1.92	1.89	1.87	1.85	1.82	1.79	1.76
	.05	4.54	3.68	3.29	3.06	2.90	2.79	2.71	2.64	2.59	2.54	2.40	2.33	2.28	2.25	2.20	2.16	2.12	2.07
	.025	6.20	4.77	4.15	3.80	3.58	3.41	3.29	3.20	3.12	3.06	2.86	2.76	2.69	2.64	2.59	2.52	2.47	2.40
	.01	8.68	6.36	5.42	4.89	4.56	4.32	4.14	4.00	3.89	3.80	3.52	3.37	3.28	3.21	3.13	3.05	2.98	2.88
16	.10	3.05	2.67	2.46	2.33	2.24	2.18	2.13	2.09	2.06	2.03	1.94	1.89	1.86	1.84	1.81	1.78	1.76	1.72
	.05	4.49	3.63	3.24	3.01	2.85	2.74	2.66	2.59	2.54	2.49	2.35	2.28	2.23	2.19	2.15	2.11	2.07	2.02
	.025	6.12	4.69	4.08	3.73	3.50	3.34	3.22	3.12	3.05	2.99	2.79	2.68	2.61	2.57	2.51	2.45	2.40	2.32
	.01	8.53	6.23	5.29	4.77	4.44	4.20	4.03	3.89	3.78	3.69	3.41	3.26	3.16	3.10	3.02	2.93	2.86	2.76
17	.10	3.03	2.64	2.44	2.31	2.22	2.15	2.10	2.06	2.03	2.00	1.91	1.86	1.83	1.81	1.78	1.75	1.73	1.69
	.05	4.45	3.59	3.20	2.96	2.81	2.70	2.61	2.55	2.49	2.45	2.31	2.23	2.18	2.15	2.10	2.06	2.02	1.97
	.025	6.04	4.62	4.01	3.66	3.44	3.28	3.16	3.06	2.98	2.92	2.72	2.62	2.55	2.50	2.44	2.38	2.33	2.26
	.01	8.40	6.11	5.19	4.67	4.34	4.10	3.93	3.79	3.68	3.59	3.31	3.16	3.07	3.00	2.92	2.83	2.76	2.66
18	.10	3.01	2.62	2.42	2.29	2.20	2.13	2.08	2.04	2.00	1.98	1.89	1.84	1.80	1.78	1.75	1.72	1.70	1.66
	.05	4.41	3.55	3.16	2.93	2.77	2.66	2.58	2.51	2.46	2.41	2.27	2.19	2.14	2.11	2.06	2.02	1.98	1.92
	.025	5.98	4.56	3.95	3.61	3.38	3.22	3.10	3.01	2.93	2.87	2.67	2.56	2.49	2.44	2.38	2.32	2.27	2.20
	.01	8.29	6.01	5.09	4.58	4.25	4.01	3.84	3.71	3.60	3.51	3.23	3.08	2.98	2.92	2.84	2.75	2.68	2.58
19	.10	2.99	2.61	2.40	2.27	2.18	2.11	2.06	2.02	1.98	1.96	1.86	1.81	1.78	1.76	1.73	1.70	1.67	1.64
	.05	4.38	3.52	3.13	2.90	2.74	2.63	2.54	2.48	2.42	2.38	2.23	2.16	2.11	2.07	2.03	1.98	1.94	1.88
	.025	5.92	4.51	3.90	3.56	3.33	3.17	3.05	2.96	2.88	2.82	2.62	2.51	2.44	2.39	2.33	2.27	2.22	2.14
	.01	8.18	5.93	5.01	4.50	4.17	3.94	3.77	3.63	3.52	3.43	3.15	3.00	2.91	2.84	2.76	2.67	2.60	2.50
20	.10	2.97	2.59	2.38	2.25	2.16	2.09	2.04	2.00	1.96	1.94	1.84	1.79	1.76	1.74	1.71	1.68	1.65	1.61
	.05	4.35	3.49	3.10	2.87	2.71	2.60	2.51	2.45	2.39	2.35	2.20	2.12	2.07	2.04	1.99	1.95	1.91	1.85
	.025	5.87	4.46	3.86	3.51	3.29	3.13	3.01	2.91	2.84	2.77	2.57	2.46	2.40	2.35	2.29	2.22	2.17	2.09
	.01	8.10	5.85	4.94	4.43	4.10	3.87	3.70	3.56	3.46	3.37	3.09	2.94	2.84	2.78	2.69	2.61	2.54	2.43
21	.10	2.96	2.57	2.36	2.23	2.14	2.08	2.02	1.98	1.95	1.92	1.83	1.78	1.74	1.72	1.69	1.66	1.63	1.59
	.05	4.32	3.47	3.07	2.84	2.68	2.57	2.49	2.42	2.37	2.32	2.18	2.10	2.05	2.01	1.96	1.92	1.88	1.82
	.025	5.83	4.42	3.82	3.48	3.25	3.09	2.97	2.87	2.80	2.73	2.53	2.42	2.36	2.31	2.25	2.18	2.13	2.05
	.01	8.02	5.78	4.87	4.37	4.04	3.81	3.64	3.51	3.40	3.31	3.03	2.88	2.79	2.72	2.64	2.55	2.48	2.37

TABLE 4 F Distribution *(Continued)*

DF$_d$	α	1	2	3	4	5	6	7	8	9	10	15	20	25	30	40	60	100	1000
								Numerator Degrees of Freedom											
22	.10	2.95	2.56	2.35	2.22	2.13	2.06	2.01	1.97	1.93	1.90	1.81	1.76	1.73	1.70	1.67	1.64	1.61	1.57
	.05	4.30	3.44	3.05	2.82	2.66	2.55	2.46	2.40	2.34	2.30	2.15	2.07	2.02	1.98	1.94	1.89	1.85	1.79
	.025	5.79	4.38	3.78	3.44	3.22	3.05	2.93	2.84	2.76	2.70	2.50	2.39	2.32	2.27	2.21	2.14	2.09	2.01
	.01	7.95	5.72	4.82	4.31	3.99	3.76	3.59	3.45	3.35	3.26	2.98	2.83	2.73	2.67	2.58	2.50	2.42	2.32
23	.10	2.94	2.55	2.34	2.21	2.11	2.05	1.99	1.95	1.92	1.89	1.80	1.74	1.71	1.69	1.66	1.62	1.59	1.55
	.05	4.28	3.42	3.03	2.80	2.64	2.53	2.44	2.37	2.32	2.27	2.13	2.05	2.00	1.96	1.91	1.86	1.82	1.76
	.025	5.75	4.35	3.75	3.41	3.18	3.02	2.90	2.81	2.73	2.67	2.47	2.36	2.29	2.24	2.18	2.11	2.06	1.98
	.01	7.88	5.66	4.76	4.26	3.94	3.71	3.54	3.41	3.30	3.21	2.93	2.78	2.69	2.62	2.54	2.45	2.37	2.27
24	.10	2.93	2.54	2.33	2.19	2.10	2.04	1.98	1.94	1.91	1.88	1.78	1.73	1.70	1.67	1.64	1.61	1.58	1.54
	.05	4.26	3.40	3.01	2.78	2.62	2.51	2.42	2.36	2.30	2.25	2.11	2.03	1.97	1.94	1.89	1.84	1.80	1.74
	.025	5.72	4.32	3.72	3.38	3.15	2.99	2.87	2.78	2.70	2.64	2.44	2.33	2.26	2.21	2.15	2.08	2.02	1.94
	.01	7.82	5.61	4.72	4.22	3.90	3.67	3.50	3.36	3.26	3.17	2.89	2.74	2.64	2.58	2.49	2.40	2.33	2.22
25	.10	2.92	2.53	2.32	2.18	2.09	2.02	1.97	1.93	1.89	1.87	1.77	1.72	1.68	1.66	1.63	1.59	1.56	1.52
	.05	4.24	3.39	2.99	2.76	2.60	2.49	2.40	2.34	2.28	2.24	2.09	2.01	1.96	1.92	1.87	1.82	1.78	1.72
	.025	5.69	4.29	3.69	3.35	3.13	2.97	2.85	2.75	2.68	2.61	2.41	2.30	2.23	2.18	2.12	2.05	2.00	1.91
	.01	7.77	5.57	4.68	4.18	3.85	3.63	3.46	3.32	3.22	3.13	2.85	2.70	2.60	2.54	2.45	2.36	2.29	2.18
26	.10	2.91	2.52	2.31	2.17	2.08	2.01	1.96	1.92	1.88	1.86	1.76	1.71	1.67	1.65	1.61	1.58	1.55	1.51
	.05	4.23	3.37	2.98	2.74	2.59	2.47	2.39	2.32	2.27	2.22	2.07	1.99	1.94	1.90	1.85	1.80	1.76	1.70
	.025	5.66	4.27	3.67	3.33	3.10	2.94	2.82	2.73	2.65	2.59	2.39	2.28	2.21	2.16	2.09	2.03	1.97	1.89
	.01	7.72	5.53	4.64	4.14	3.82	3.59	3.42	3.29	3.18	3.09	2.81	2.66	2.57	2.50	2.42	2.33	2.25	2.14
27	.10	2.90	2.51	2.30	2.17	2.07	2.00	1.95	1.91	1.87	1.85	1.75	1.70	1.66	1.64	1.60	1.57	1.54	1.50
	.05	4.21	3.35	2.96	2.73	2.57	2.46	2.37	2.31	2.25	2.20	2.06	1.97	1.92	1.88	1.84	1.79	1.74	1.68
	.025	5.63	4.24	3.65	3.31	3.08	2.92	2.80	2.71	2.63	2.57	2.36	2.25	2.18	2.13	2.07	2.00	1.94	1.86
	.01	7.68	5.49	4.60	4.11	3.78	3.56	3.39	3.26	3.15	3.06	2.78	2.63	2.54	2.47	2.38	2.29	2.22	2.11
28	.10	2.89	2.50	2.29	2.16	2.06	2.00	1.94	1.90	1.87	1.84	1.74	1.69	1.65	1.63	1.59	1.56	1.53	1.48
	.05	4.20	3.34	2.95	2.71	2.56	2.45	2.36	2.29	2.24	2.19	2.04	1.96	1.91	1.87	1.82	1.77	1.73	1.66
	.025	5.61	4.22	3.63	3.29	3.06	2.90	2.78	2.69	2.61	2.55	2.34	2.23	2.16	2.11	2.05	1.98	1.92	1.84
	.01	7.64	5.45	4.57	4.07	3.75	3.53	3.36	3.23	3.12	3.03	2.75	2.60	2.51	2.44	2.35	2.26	2.19	2.08
29	.10	2.89	2.50	2.28	2.15	2.06	1.99	1.93	1.89	1.86	1.83	1.73	1.68	1.64	1.62	1.58	1.55	1.52	1.47
	.05	4.18	3.33	2.93	2.70	2.55	2.43	2.35	2.28	2.22	2.18	2.03	1.94	1.89	1.85	1.81	1.75	1.71	1.65
	.025	5.59	4.20	3.61	3.27	3.04	2.88	2.76	2.67	2.59	2.53	2.32	2.21	2.14	2.09	2.03	1.96	1.90	1.82
	.01	7.60	5.42	4.54	4.04	3.73	3.50	3.33	3.20	3.09	3.00	2.73	2.57	2.48	2.41	2.33	2.23	2.16	2.05
30	.10	2.88	2.49	2.28	2.14	2.05	1.98	1.93	1.88	1.85	1.82	1.72	1.67	1.63	1.61	1.57	1.54	1.51	1.46
	.05	4.17	3.32	2.92	2.69	2.53	2.42	2.33	2.27	2.21	2.16	2.01	1.93	1.88	1.84	1.79	1.74	1.70	1.63
	.025	5.57	4.18	3.59	3.25	3.03	2.87	2.75	2.65	2.57	2.51	2.31	2.20	2.12	2.07	2.01	1.94	1.88	1.80
	.01	7.56	5.39	4.51	4.02	3.70	3.47	3.30	3.17	3.07	2.98	2.70	2.55	2.45	2.39	2.30	2.21	2.13	2.02

TABLE 4 F Distribution *(Continued)*

DF$_d$	α	\<center>Numerator Degrees of Freedom\</center>																	
		1	2	3	4	5	6	7	8	9	10	15	20	25	30	40	60	100	1000
40	.10	2.84	2.44	2.23	2.09	2.00	1.93	1.87	1.83	1.79	1.76	1.66	1.61	1.57	1.54	1.51	1.47	1.43	1.38
	.05	4.08	3.23	2.84	2.61	2.45	2.34	2.25	2.18	2.12	2.08	1.92	1.84	1.78	1.74	1.69	1.64	1.59	1.52
	.025	5.42	4.05	3.46	3.13	2.90	2.74	2.62	2.53	2.45	2.39	2.18	2.07	1.99	1.94	1.88	1.80	1.74	1.65
	.01	7.31	5.18	4.31	3.83	3.51	3.29	3.12	2.99	2.89	2.80	2.52	2.37	2.27	2.20	2.11	2.02	1.94	1.82
60	.10	2.79	2.39	2.18	2.04	1.95	1.87	1.82	1.77	1.74	1.71	1.60	1.54	1.50	1.48	1.44	1.40	1.36	1.30
	.05	4.00	3.15	2.76	2.53	2.37	2.25	2.17	2.10	2.04	1.99	1.84	1.75	1.69	1.65	1.59	1.53	1.48	1.40
	.025	5.29	3.93	3.34	3.01	2.79	2.63	2.51	2.41	2.33	2.27	2.06	1.94	1.87	1.82	1.74	1.67	1.60	1.49
	.01	7.08	4.98	4.13	3.65	3.34	3.12	2.95	2.82	2.72	2.63	2.35	2.20	2.10	2.03	1.94	1.84	1.75	1.62
100	.10	2.76	2.36	2.14	2.00	1.91	1.83	1.78	1.73	1.69	1.66	1.56	1.49	1.45	1.42	1.38	1.34	1.29	1.22
	.05	3.94	3.09	2.70	2.46	2.31	2.19	2.10	2.03	1.97	1.93	1.77	1.68	1.62	1.57	1.52	1.45	1.39	1.30
	.025	5.18	3.83	3.25	2.92	2.70	2.54	2.42	2.32	2.24	2.18	1.97	1.85	1.77	1.71	1.64	1.56	1.48	1.36
	.01	6.90	4.82	3.98	3.51	3.21	2.99	2.82	2.69	2.59	2.50	2.22	2.07	1.97	1.89	1.80	1.69	1.60	1.45
1000	.10	2.71	2.31	2.09	1.95	1.85	1.78	1.72	1.68	1.64	1.61	1.49	1.43	1.38	1.35	1.30	1.25	1.20	1.08
	.05	3.85	3.00	2.61	2.38	2.22	2.11	2.02	1.95	1.89	1.84	1.68	1.58	1.52	1.47	1.41	1.33	1.26	1.11
	.025	5.04	3.70	3.13	2.80	2.58	2.42	2.30	2.20	2.13	2.06	1.85	1.72	1.64	1.58	1.50	1.41	1.32	1.13
	.01	6.66	4.63	3.80	3.34	3.04	2.82	2.66	2.53	2.43	2.34	2.06	1.90	1.79	1.72	1.61	1.50	1.38	1.16

TABLE 5 Binomial probabilities

Entries in the table give the probability of x successes in n trials of a binomial experiment, where p is the probability of a success on one trial. For example, with 2 trials ($n=2$) and $p=.02$, the probability of $x = 1$ success is 0.0392.

						p				
n	x	.01	.02	.03	.04	.05	.06	.07	.08	.09
2	0	0.9801	0.9604	0.9409	0.9216	0.9025	0.8836	0.8649	0.8464	0.8281
	1	0.0198	0.0392	0.0582	0.0768	0.095	0.1128	0.1302	0.1472	0.1638
	2	0.0001	0.0004	0.0009	0.0016	0.0025	0.0036	0.0049	0.0064	0.0081
3	0	0.9703	0.9412	0.9127	0.8847	0.8574	0.8306	0.8044	0.7787	0.7536
	1	0.0294	0.0576	0.0847	0.1106	0.1354	0.1590	0.1816	0.2031	0.2236
	2	0.0003	0.0012	0.0026	0.0046	0.0071	0.0102	0.0137	0.0177	0.0221
	3	0.0000	0.0000	0.0000	0.0001	0.0001	0.0002	0.0003	0.0005	0.0007
4	0	0.9606	0.9224	0.8853	0.8493	0.8145	0.7807	0.7481	0.7164	0.6857
	1	0.0388	0.0753	0.1095	0.1416	0.1715	0.1993	0.2252	0.2492	0.2713
	2	0.0006	0.0023	0.0051	0.0088	0.0135	0.0191	0.0254	0.0325	0.0402
	3	0.0000	0.0000	0.0001	0.0002	0.0005	0.0008	0.0013	0.0019	0.0027
	4	0.0000	0.0000	0.0000	0.0000	0.0000	0.0000	0.0000	0.0000	0.0001
5	0	0.9510	0.9039	0.8587	0.8154	0.7738	0.7339	0.6957	0.6591	0.6240
	1	0.0480	0.0922	0.1328	0.1699	0.2036	0.2342	0.2618	0.2866	0.3086
	2	0.0010	0.0038	0.0082	0.0142	0.0214	0.0299	0.0394	0.0498	0.0610
	3	0.0000	0.0001	0.0003	0.0006	0.0011	0.0019	0.0030	0.0043	0.0060
	4	0.0000	0.0000	0.0000	0.0000	0.0000	0.0001	0.0001	0.0002	0.0003
	5	0.0000	0.0000	0.0000	0.0000	0.0000	0.0000	0.0000	0.0000	0.0000
6	0	0.9415	0.8858	0.8330	0.7828	0.7351	0.6899	0.6470	0.6064	0.5679
	1	0.0571	0.1085	0.1546	0.1957	0.2321	0.2642	0.2922	0.3164	0.3370
	2	0.0014	0.0055	0.0120	0.0204	0.0305	0.0422	0.0550	0.0688	0.0833
	3	0.0000	0.0002	0.0005	0.0011	0.0021	0.0036	0.0055	0.0080	0.0110
	4	0.0000	0.0000	0.0000	0.0000	0.0001	0.0002	0.0003	0.0005	0.0008
	5	0.0000	0.0000	0.0000	0.0000	0.0000	0.0000	0.0000	0.0000	0.0000
	6	0.0000	0.0000	0.0000	0.0000	0.0000	0.0000	0.0000	0.0000	0.0000
7	0	0.9321	0.8681	0.8080	0.7514	0.6983	0.6485	0.6017	0.5578	0.5168
	1	0.0659	0.1240	0.1749	0.2192	0.2573	0.2897	0.3170	0.3396	0.3578
	2	0.0020	0.0076	0.0162	0.0274	0.0406	0.0555	0.0716	0.0886	0.1061
	3	0.0000	0.0003	0.0008	0.0019	0.0036	0.0059	0.0090	0.0128	0.0175
	4	0.0000	0.0000	0.0000	0.0001	0.0002	0.0004	0.0007	0.0011	0.0017
	5	0.0000	0.0000	0.0000	0.0000	0.0000	0.0000	0.0000	0.0001	0.0001
	6	0.0000	0.0000	0.0000	0.0000	0.0000	0.0000	0.0000	0.0000	0.0000
	7	0.0000	0.0000	0.0000	0.0000	0.0000	0.0000	0.0000	0.0000	0.0000

TABLE 5 Binomial probabilities (*Continued*)

						P				
n	*x*	.01	.02	.03	.04	.05	.06	.07	.08	.09
8	0	0.9227	0.8508	0.7837	0.7214	0.6634	0.6096	0.5596	0.5132	0.4703
	1	0.0746	0.1389	0.1939	0.2405	0.2793	0.3113	0.3370	0.3570	0.3721
	2	0.0026	0.0099	0.0210	0.0351	0.0515	0.0695	0.0888	0.1087	0.1288
	3	0.0001	0.0004	0.0013	0.0029	0.0054	0.0089	0.0134	0.0189	0.0255
	4	0.0000	0.0000	0.0001	0.0002	0.0004	0.0007	0.0013	0.0021	0.0031
	5	0.0000	0.0000	0.0000	0.0000	0.0000	0.0000	0.0001	0.0001	0.0002
	6	0.0000	0.0000	0.0000	0.0000	0.0000	0.0000	0.0000	0.0000	0.0000
	7	0.0000	0.0000	0.0000	0.0000	0.0000	0.0000	0.0000	0.0000	0.0000
	8	0.0000	0.0000	0.0000	0.0000	0.0000	0.0000	0.0000	0.0000	0.0000
9	0	0.9135	0.8337	0.7602	0.6925	0.6302	0.5730	0.5204	0.4722	0.4279
	1	0.0830	0.1531	0.2116	0.2597	0.2985	0.3292	0.3525	0.3695	0.3809
	2	0.0034	0.0125	0.0262	0.0433	0.0629	0.0840	0.1061	0.1285	0.1507
	3	0.0001	0.0006	0.0019	0.0042	0.0077	0.0125	0.0186	0.0261	0.0348
	4	0.0000	0.0000	0.0001	0.0003	0.0006	0.0012	0.0021	0.0034	0.0052
	5	0.0000	0.0000	0.0000	0.0000	0.0000	0.0001	0.0002	0.0003	0.0005
	6	0.0000	0.0000	0.0000	0.0000	0.0000	0.0000	0.0000	0.0000	0.0000
	7	0.0000	0.0000	0.0000	0.0000	0.0000	0.0000	0.0000	0.0000	0.0000
	8	0.0000	0.0000	0.0000	0.0000	0.0000	0.0000	0.0000	0.0000	0.0000
	9	0.0000	0.0000	0.0000	0.0000	0.0000	0.0000	0.0000	0.0000	0.0000
10	0	0.9044	0.8171	0.7374	0.6648	0.5987	0.5386	0.4840	0.4344	0.3894
	1	0.0914	0.1667	0.2281	0.2770	0.3151	0.3438	0.3643	0.3777	0.3851
	2	0.0042	0.0153	0.0317	0.0519	0.0746	0.0988	0.1234	0.1478	0.1714
	3	0.0001	0.0008	0.0026	0.0058	0.0105	0.0168	0.0248	0.0343	0.0452
	4	0.0000	0.0000	0.0001	0.0004	0.0010	0.0019	0.0033	0.0052	0.0078
	5	0.0000	0.0000	0.0000	0.0000	0.0001	0.0001	0.0003	0.0005	0.0009
	6	0.0000	0.0000	0.0000	0.0000	0.0000	0.0000	0.0000	0.0000	0.0001
	7	0.0000	0.0000	0.0000	0.0000	0.0000	0.0000	0.0000	0.0000	0.0000
	8	0.0000	0.0000	0.0000	0.0000	0.0000	0.0000	0.0000	0.0000	0.0000
	9	0.0000	0.0000	0.0000	0.0000	0.0000	0.0000	0.0000	0.0000	0.0000
	10	0.0000	0.0000	0.0000	0.0000	0.0000	0.0000	0.0000	0.0000	0.0000

TABLE 5 Binomial probabilities (*Continued*)

						p				
n	*x*	.01	.02	.03	.04	.05	.06	.07	.08	.09
12	0	0.8864	0.7847	0.6938	0.6127	0.5404	0.4759	0.4186	0.3677	0.3225
	1	0.1074	0.1922	0.2575	0.3064	0.3413	0.3645	0.3781	0.3837	0.3827
	2	0.0060	0.0216	0.0438	0.0702	0.0988	0.1280	0.1565	0.1835	0.2082
	3	0.0002	0.0015	0.0045	0.0098	0.0173	0.0272	0.0393	0.0532	0.0686
	4	0.0000	0.0001	0.0003	0.0009	0.0021	0.0039	0.0067	0.0104	0.0153
	5	0.0000	0.0000	0.0000	0.0001	0.0002	0.0004	0.0008	0.0014	0.0024
	6	0.0000	0.0000	0.0000	0.0000	0.0000	0.0000	0.0001	0.0001	0.0003
	7	0.0000	0.0000	0.0000	0.0000	0.0000	0.0000	0.0000	0.0000	0.0000
	8	0.0000	0.0000	0.0000	0.0000	0.0000	0.0000	0.0000	0.0000	0.0000
	9	0.0000	0.0000	0.0000	0.0000	0.0000	0.0000	0.0000	0.0000	0.0000
	10	0.0000	0.0000	0.0000	0.0000	0.0000	0.0000	0.0000	0.0000	0.0000
	11	0.0000	0.0000	0.0000	0.0000	0.0000	0.0000	0.0000	0.0000	0.0000
	12	0.0000	0.0000	0.0000	0.0000	0.0000	0.0000	0.0000	0.0000	0.0000
15	0	0.8601	0.7386	0.6333	0.5421	0.4633	0.3953	0.3367	0.2863	0.2430
	1	0.1303	0.2261	0.2938	0.3388	0.3658	0.3785	0.3801	0.3734	0.3605
	2	0.0092	0.0323	0.0636	0.0988	0.1348	0.1691	0.2003	0.2273	0.2496
	3	0.0004	0.0029	0.0085	0.0178	0.0307	0.0468	0.0653	0.0857	0.1070
	4	0.0000	0.0002	0.0008	0.0022	0.0049	0.0090	0.0148	0.0223	0.0317
	5	0.0000	0.0000	0.0001	0.0002	0.0006	0.0013	0.0024	0.0043	0.0069
	6	0.0000	0.0000	0.0000	0.0000	0.0000	0.0001	0.0003	0.0006	0.0011
	7	0.0000	0.0000	0.0000	0.0000	0.0000	0.0000	0.0000	0.0001	0.0001
	8	0.0000	0.0000	0.0000	0.0000	0.0000	0.0000	0.0000	0.0000	0.0000
	9	0.0000	0.0000	0.0000	0.0000	0.0000	0.0000	0.0000	0.0000	0.0000
	10	0.0000	0.0000	0.0000	0.0000	0.0000	0.0000	0.0000	0.0000	0.0000
	11	0.0000	0.0000	0.0000	0.0000	0.0000	0.0000	0.0000	0.0000	0.0000
	12	0.0000	0.0000	0.0000	0.0000	0.0000	0.0000	0.0000	0.0000	0.0000
	13	0.0000	0.0000	0.0000	0.0000	0.0000	0.0000	0.0000	0.0000	0.0000
	14	0.0000	0.0000	0.0000	0.0000	0.0000	0.0000	0.0000	0.0000	0.0000
	15	0.0000	0.0000	0.0000	0.0000	0.0000	0.0000	0.0000	0.0000	0.0000
18	0	0.8345	0.6951	0.5780	0.4796	0.3972	0.3283	0.2708	0.2229	0.1831
	1	0.1517	0.2554	0.3217	0.3597	0.3763	0.3772	0.3669	0.3489	0.3260
	2	0.0130	0.0443	0.0846	0.1274	0.1683	0.2047	0.2348	0.2579	0.2741
	3	0.0007	0.0048	0.0140	0.0283	0.0473	0.0697	0.0942	0.1196	0.1446
	4	0.0000	0.0004	0.0016	0.0044	0.0093	0.0167	0.0266	0.0390	0.0536
	5	0.0000	0.0000	0.0001	0.0005	0.0014	0.0030	0.0056	0.0095	0.0148
	6	0.0000	0.0000	0.0000	0.0000	0.0002	0.0004	0.0009	0.0018	0.0032

TABLE 5   Binomial probabilities (*Continued*)

| | | | | | | | *p* | | | |
n	*x*	.01	.02	.03	.04	.05	.06	.07	.08	.09
18	7	0.0000	0.0000	0.0000	0.0000	0.0000	0.0000	0.0001	0.0003	0.0005
	8	0.0000	0.0000	0.0000	0.0000	0.0000	0.0000	0.0000	0.0000	0.0001
	9	0.0000	0.0000	0.0000	0.0000	0.0000	0.0000	0.0000	0.0000	0.0000
	10	0.0000	0.0000	0.0000	0.0000	0.0000	0.0000	0.0000	0.0000	0.0000
	11	0.0000	0.0000	0.0000	0.0000	0.0000	0.0000	0.0000	0.0000	0.0000
	12	0.0000	0.0000	0.0000	0.0000	0.0000	0.0000	0.0000	0.0000	0.0000
	13	0.0000	0.0000	0.0000	0.0000	0.0000	0.0000	0.0000	0.0000	0.0000
	14	0.0000	0.0000	0.0000	0.0000	0.0000	0.0000	0.0000	0.0000	0.0000
	15	0.0000	0.0000	0.0000	0.0000	0.0000	0.0000	0.0000	0.0000	0.0000
	16	0.0000	0.0000	0.0000	0.0000	0.0000	0.0000	0.0000	0.0000	0.0000
	17	0.0000	0.0000	0.0000	0.0000	0.0000	0.0000	0.0000	0.0000	0.0000
	18	0.0000	0.0000	0.0000	0.0000	0.0000	0.0000	0.0000	0.0000	0.0000
20	0	0.8179	0.6676	0.5438	0.4420	0.3585	0.2901	0.2342	0.1887	0.1516
	1	0.1652	0.2725	0.3364	0.3683	0.3774	0.3703	0.3526	0.3282	0.3000
	2	0.0159	0.0528	0.0988	0.1458	0.1887	0.2246	0.2521	0.2711	0.2818
	3	0.0010	0.0065	0.0183	0.0364	0.0596	0.0860	0.1139	0.1414	0.1672
	4	0.0000	0.0006	0.0024	0.0065	0.0133	0.0233	0.0364	0.0523	0.0703
	5	0.0000	0.0000	0.0002	0.0009	0.0022	0.0048	0.0088	0.0145	0.0222
	6	0.0000	0.0000	0.0000	0.0001	0.0003	0.0008	0.0017	0.0032	0.0055
	7	0.0000	0.0000	0.0000	0.0000	0.0000	0.0001	0.0002	0.0005	0.0011
	8	0.0000	0.0000	0.0000	0.0000	0.0000	0.0000	0.0000	0.0001	0.0002
	9	0.0000	0.0000	0.0000	0.0000	0.0000	0.0000	0.0000	0.0000	0.0000
	10	0.0000	0.0000	0.0000	0.0000	0.0000	0.0000	0.0000	0.0000	0.0000
	11	0.0000	0.0000	0.0000	0.0000	0.0000	0.0000	0.0000	0.0000	0.0000
	12	0.0000	0.0000	0.0000	0.0000	0.0000	0.0000	0.0000	0.0000	0.0000
	13	0.0000	0.0000	0.0000	0.0000	0.0000	0.0000	0.0000	0.0000	0.0000
	14	0.0000	0.0000	0.0000	0.0000	0.0000	0.0000	0.0000	0.0000	0.0000
	15	0.0000	0.0000	0.0000	0.0000	0.0000	0.0000	0.0000	0.0000	0.0000
	16	0.0000	0.0000	0.0000	0.0000	0.0000	0.0000	0.0000	0.0000	0.0000
	17	0.0000	0.0000	0.0000	0.0000	0.0000	0.0000	0.0000	0.0000	0.0000
	18	0.0000	0.0000	0.0000	0.0000	0.0000	0.0000	0.0000	0.0000	0.0000
	19	0.0000	0.0000	0.0000	0.0000	0.0000	0.0000	0.0000	0.0000	0.0000
	20	0.0000	0.0000	0.0000	0.0000	0.0000	0.0000	0.0000	0.0000	0.0000

TABLE 5 Binomial probabilities (*Continued*)

						p				
n	*x*	0.1	0.15	0.2	0.25	0.3	0.35	0.4	0.45	0.5
2	0	0.8100	0.7225	0.6400	0.5625	0.4900	0.4225	0.3600	0.3025	0.2500
	1	0.1800	0.2550	0.3200	0.3750	0.4200	0.4550	0.4800	0.4950	0.5000
	2	0.0100	0.0225	0.0400	0.0625	0.0900	0.1225	0.1600	0.2025	0.2500
3	0	0.7290	0.6141	0.5120	0.4219	0.3430	0.2746	0.2160	0.1664	0.1250
	1	0.2430	0.3251	0.3840	0.4219	0.4410	0.4436	0.4320	0.4084	0.3750
	2	0.0270	0.0574	0.0960	0.1406	0.1890	0.2389	0.2880	0.3341	0.3750
	3	0.0010	0.0034	0.0080	0.0156	0.0270	0.0429	0.0640	0.0911	0.1250
4	0	0.6561	0.5220	0.4096	0.3164	0.2401	0.1785	0.1296	0.0915	0.0625
	1	0.2916	0.3685	0.4096	0.4219	0.4116	0.3845	0.3456	0.2995	0.2500
	2	0.0486	0.0975	0.1536	0.2109	0.2646	0.3105	0.3456	0.3675	0.3750
	3	0.0036	0.0115	0.0256	0.0469	0.0756	0.1115	0.1536	0.2005	0.2500
	4	0.0001	0.0005	0.0016	0.0039	0.0081	0.0150	0.0256	0.0410	0.0625
5	0	0.5905	0.4437	0.3277	0.2373	0.1681	0.1160	0.0778	0.0503	0.0313
	1	0.3281	0.3915	0.4096	0.3955	0.3602	0.3124	0.2592	0.2059	0.1563
	2	0.0729	0.1382	0.2048	0.2637	0.3087	0.3364	0.3456	0.3369	0.3125
	3	0.0081	0.0244	0.0512	0.0879	0.1323	0.1811	0.2304	0.2757	0.3125
	4	0.0005	0.0022	0.0064	0.0146	0.0284	0.0488	0.0768	0.1128	0.1563
	5	0.0000	0.0001	0.0003	0.0010	0.0024	0.0053	0.0102	0.0185	0.0313
6	0	0.5314	0.3771	0.2621	0.1780	0.1176	0.0754	0.0467	0.0277	0.0156
	1	0.3543	0.3993	0.3932	0.3560	0.3025	0.2437	0.1866	0.1359	0.0938
	2	0.0984	0.1762	0.2458	0.2966	0.3241	0.3280	0.3110	0.2780	0.2344
	3	0.0146	0.0415	0.0819	0.1318	0.1852	0.2355	0.2765	0.3032	0.3125
	4	0.0012	0.0055	0.0154	0.0330	0.0595	0.0951	0.1382	0.1861	0.2344
	5	0.0001	0.0004	0.0015	0.0044	0.0102	0.0205	0.0369	0.0609	0.0938
	6	0.0000	0.0000	0.0001	0.0002	0.0007	0.0018	0.0041	0.0083	0.0156
7	0	0.4783	0.3206	0.2097	0.1335	0.0824	0.0490	0.0280	0.0152	0.0078
	1	0.3720	0.3960	0.3670	0.3115	0.2471	0.1848	0.1306	0.0872	0.0547
	2	0.1240	0.2097	0.2753	0.3115	0.3177	0.2985	0.2613	0.2140	0.1641
	3	0.0230	0.0617	0.1147	0.1730	0.2269	0.2679	0.2903	0.2918	0.2734
	4	0.0026	0.0109	0.0287	0.0577	0.0972	0.1442	0.1935	0.2388	0.2734
	5	0.0002	0.0012	0.0043	0.0115	0.0250	0.0466	0.0774	0.1172	0.1641
	6	0.0000	0.0001	0.0004	0.0013	0.0036	0.0084	0.0172	0.0320	0.0547
	7	0.0000	0.0000	0.0000	0.0001	0.0002	0.0006	0.0016	0.0037	0.0078

TABLE 5 Binomial probabilities (*Continued*)

						p				
n	*x*	0.1	0.15	0.2	0.25	0.3	0.35	0.4	0.45	0.5
8	0	0.4305	0.2725	0.1678	0.1001	0.0576	0.0319	0.0168	0.0084	0.0039
	1	0.3826	0.3847	0.3355	0.2670	0.1977	0.1373	0.0896	0.0548	0.0313
	2	0.1488	0.2376	0.2936	0.3115	0.2965	0.2587	0.2090	0.1569	0.1094
	3	0.0331	0.0839	0.1468	0.2076	0.2541	0.2786	0.2787	0.2568	0.2188
	4	0.0046	0.0185	0.0459	0.0865	0.1361	0.1875	0.2322	0.2627	0.2734
	5	0.0004	0.0026	0.0092	0.0231	0.0467	0.0808	0.1239	0.1719	0.2188
	6	0.0000	0.0002	0.0011	0.0038	0.0100	0.0217	0.0413	0.0703	0.1094
	7	0.0000	0.0000	0.0001	0.0004	0.0012	0.0033	0.0079	0.0164	0.0313
	8	0.0000	0.0000	0.0000	0.0000	0.0001	0.0002	0.0007	0.0017	0.0039
9	0	0.3874	0.2316	0.1342	0.0751	0.0404	0.0207	0.0101	0.0046	0.0020
	1	0.3874	0.3679	0.3020	0.2253	0.1556	0.1004	0.0605	0.0339	0.0176
	2	0.1722	0.2597	0.3020	0.3003	0.2668	0.2162	0.1612	0.1110	0.0703
	3	0.0446	0.1069	0.1762	0.2336	0.2668	0.2716	0.2508	0.2119	0.1641
	4	0.0074	0.0283	0.0661	0.1168	0.1715	0.2194	0.2508	0.2600	0.2461
	5	0.0008	0.0050	0.0165	0.0389	0.0735	0.1181	0.1672	0.2128	0.2461
	6	0.0001	0.0006	0.0028	0.0087	0.0210	0.0424	0.0743	0.1160	0.1641
	7	0.0000	0.0000	0.0003	0.0012	0.0039	0.0098	0.0212	0.0407	0.0703
	8	0.0000	0.0000	0.0000	0.0001	0.0004	0.0013	0.0035	0.0083	0.0176
	9	0.0000	0.0000	0.0000	0.0000	0.0000	0.0001	0.0003	0.0008	0.0020
10	0	0.3487	0.1969	0.1074	0.0563	0.0282	0.0135	0.0060	0.0025	0.0010
	1	0.3874	0.3474	0.2684	0.1877	0.1211	0.0725	0.0403	0.0207	0.0098
	2	0.1937	0.2759	0.3020	0.2816	0.2335	0.1757	0.1209	0.0763	0.0439
	3	0.0574	0.1298	0.2013	0.2503	0.2668	0.2522	0.2150	0.1665	0.1172
	4	0.0112	0.0401	0.0881	0.1460	0.2001	0.2377	0.2508	0.2384	0.2051
	5	0.0015	0.0085	0.0264	0.0584	0.1029	0.1536	0.2007	0.2340	0.2461
	6	0.0001	0.0012	0.0055	0.0162	0.0368	0.0689	0.1115	0.1596	0.2051
	7	0.0000	0.0001	0.0008	0.0031	0.0090	0.0212	0.0425	0.0746	0.1172
	8	0.0000	0.0000	0.0001	0.0004	0.0014	0.0043	0.0106	0.0229	0.0439
	9	0.0000	0.0000	0.0000	0.0000	0.0001	0.0005	0.0016	0.0042	0.0098
	10	0.0000	0.0000	0.0000	0.0000	0.0000	0.0000	0.0001	0.0003	0.0010
12	0	0.2824	0.1422	0.0687	0.0317	0.0138	0.0057	0.0022	0.0008	0.0002
	1	0.3766	0.3012	0.2062	0.1267	0.0712	0.0368	0.0174	0.0075	0.0029
	2	0.2301	0.2924	0.2835	0.2323	0.1678	0.1088	0.0639	0.0339	0.0161
	3	0.0852	0.1720	0.2362	0.2581	0.2397	0.1954	0.1419	0.0923	0.0537
	4	0.0213	0.0683	0.1329	0.1936	0.2311	0.2367	0.2128	0.1700	0.1208
	5	0.0038	0.0193	0.0532	0.1032	0.1585	0.2039	0.2270	0.2225	0.1934
	6	0.0005	0.0040	0.0155	0.0401	0.0792	0.1281	0.1766	0.2124	0.2256
	7	0.0000	0.0006	0.0033	0.0115	0.0291	0.0591	0.1009	0.1489	0.1934
	8	0.0000	0.0001	0.0005	0.0024	0.0078	0.0199	0.0420	0.0762	0.1208

TABLE 5 Binomial probabilities (*Continued*)

						p				
n	*x*	0.1	0.15	0.2	0.25	0.3	0.35	0.4	0.45	0.5
	9	0.0000	0.0000	0.0001	0.0004	0.0015	0.0048	0.0125	0.0277	0.0537
	10	0.0000	0.0000	0.0000	0.0000	0.0002	0.0008	0.0025	0.0068	0.0161
	11	0.0000	0.0000	0.0000	0.0000	0.0000	0.0001	0.0003	0.0010	0.0029
	12	0.0000	0.0000	0.0000	0.0000	0.0000	0.0000	0.0000	0.0001	0.0002
15	0	0.2059	0.0874	0.0352	0.0134	0.0047	0.0016	0.0005	0.0001	0.0000
	1	0.3432	0.2312	0.1319	0.0668	0.0305	0.0126	0.0047	0.0016	0.0005
	2	0.2669	0.2856	0.2309	0.1559	0.0916	0.0476	0.0219	0.0090	0.0032
	3	0.1285	0.2184	0.2501	0.2252	0.1700	0.1110	0.0634	0.0318	0.0139
	4	0.0428	0.1156	0.1876	0.2252	0.2186	0.1792	0.1268	0.0780	0.0417
	5	0.0105	0.0449	0.1032	0.1651	0.2061	0.2123	0.1859	0.1404	0.0916
	6	0.0019	0.0132	0.0430	0.0917	0.1472	0.1906	0.2066	0.1914	0.1527
	7	0.0003	0.0030	0.0138	0.0393	0.0811	0.1319	0.1771	0.2013	0.1964
	8	0.0000	0.0005	0.0035	0.0131	0.0348	0.0710	0.1181	0.1647	0.1964
	9	0.0000	0.0001	0.0007	0.0034	0.0116	0.0298	0.0612	0.1048	0.1527
	10	0.0000	0.0000	0.0001	0.0007	0.0030	0.0096	0.0245	0.0515	0.0916
	11	0.0000	0.0000	0.0000	0.0001	0.0006	0.0024	0.0074	0.0191	0.0417
	12	0.0000	0.0000	0.0000	0.0000	0.0001	0.0004	0.0016	0.0052	0.0139
	13	0.0000	0.0000	0.0000	0.0000	0.0000	0.0001	0.0003	0.0010	0.0032
	14	0.0000	0.0000	0.0000	0.0000	0.0000	0.0000	0.0000	0.0001	0.0005
	15	0.0000	0.0000	0.0000	0.0000	0.0000	0.0000	0.0000	0.0000	0.0000
18	0	0.1501	0.0536	0.0180	0.0056	0.0016	0.0004	0.0001	0.0000	0.0000
	1	0.3002	0.1704	0.0811	0.0338	0.0126	0.0042	0.0012	0.0003	0.0001
	2	0.2835	0.2556	0.1723	0.0958	0.0458	0.0190	0.0069	0.0022	0.0006
	3	0.1680	0.2406	0.2297	0.1704	0.1046	0.0547	0.0246	0.0095	0.0031
	4	0.0700	0.1592	0.2153	0.2130	0.1681	0.1104	0.0614	0.0291	0.0117
	5	0.0218	0.0787	0.1507	0.1988	0.2017	0.1664	0.1146	0.0666	0.0327
	6	0.0052	0.0301	0.0816	0.1436	0.1873	0.1941	0.1655	0.1181	0.0708
	7	0.0010	0.0091	0.0350	0.0820	0.1376	0.1792	0.1892	0.1657	0.1214
	8	0.0002	0.0022	0.0120	0.0376	0.0811	0.1327	0.1734	0.1864	0.1669
	9	0.0000	0.0004	0.0033	0.0139	0.0386	0.0794	0.1284	0.1694	0.1855
	10	0.0000	0.0001	0.0008	0.0042	0.0149	0.0385	0.0771	0.1248	0.1669
	11	0.0000	0.0000	0.0001	0.0010	0.0046	0.0151	0.0374	0.0742	0.1214
	12	0.0000	0.0000	0.0000	0.0002	0.0012	0.0047	0.0145	0.0354	0.0708
	13	0.0000	0.0000	0.0000	0.0000	0.0002	0.0012	0.0045	0.0134	0.0327
	14	0.0000	0.0000	0.0000	0.0000	0.0000	0.0002	0.0011	0.0039	0.0117
	15	0.0000	0.0000	0.0000	0.0000	0.0000	0.0000	0.0002	0.0009	0.0031
	16	0.0000	0.0000	0.0000	0.0000	0.0000	0.0000	0.0000	0.0001	0.0006
	17	0.0000	0.0000	0.0000	0.0000	0.0000	0.0000	0.0000	0.0000	0.0001
	18	0.0000	0.0000	0.0000	0.0000	0.0000	0.0000	0.0000	0.0000	0.0000

TABLE 5   Binomial probabilities (*Continued*)

						p				
n	x	0.1	0.15	0.2	0.25	0.3	0.35	0.4	0.45	0.5
20	0	0.1216	0.0388	0.0115	0.0032	0.0008	0.0002	0.0000	0.0000	0.0000
	1	0.2702	0.1368	0.0576	0.0211	0.0068	0.0020	0.0005	0.0001	0.0000
	2	0.2852	0.2293	0.1369	0.0669	0.0278	0.0100	0.0031	0.0008	0.0002
	3	0.1901	0.2428	0.2054	0.1339	0.0716	0.0323	0.0123	0.0040	0.0011
	4	0.0898	0.1821	0.2182	0.1897	0.1304	0.0738	0.0350	0.0139	0.0046
	5	0.0319	0.1028	0.1746	0.2023	0.1789	0.1272	0.0746	0.0365	0.0148
	6	0.0089	0.0454	0.1091	0.1686	0.1916	0.1712	0.1244	0.0746	0.0370
	7	0.0020	0.0160	0.0545	0.1124	0.1643	0.1844	0.1659	0.1221	0.0739
	8	0.0004	0.0046	0.0222	0.0609	0.1144	0.1614	0.1797	0.1623	0.1201
	9	0.0001	0.0011	0.0074	0.0271	0.0654	0.1158	0.1597	0.1771	0.1602
	10	0.0000	0.0002	0.0020	0.0099	0.0308	0.0686	0.1171	0.1593	0.1762
	11	0.0000	0.0000	0.0005	0.0030	0.0120	0.0336	0.0710	0.1185	0.1602
	12	0.0000	0.0000	0.0001	0.0008	0.0039	0.0136	0.0355	0.0727	0.1201
	13	0.0000	0.0000	0.0000	0.0002	0.0010	0.0045	0.0146	0.0366	0.0739
	14	0.0000	0.0000	0.0000	0.0000	0.0002	0.0012	0.0049	0.0150	0.0370
	15	0.0000	0.0000	0.0000	0.0000	0.0000	0.0003	0.0013	0.0049	0.0148
	16	0.0000	0.0000	0.0000	0.0000	0.0000	0.0000	0.0003	0.0013	0.0046
	17	0.0000	0.0000	0.0000	0.0000	0.0000	0.0000	0.0000	0.0002	0.0011
	18	0.0000	0.0000	0.0000	0.0000	0.0000	0.0000	0.0000	0.0000	0.0002
	19	0.0000	0.0000	0.0000	0.0000	0.0000	0.0000	0.0000	0.0000	0.0000
	20	0.0000	0.0000	0.0000	0.0000	0.0000	0.0000	0.0000	0.0000	0.0000

TABLE 5 Binomial probabilities (*Continued*)

						P				
n	x	0.55	0.60	0.65	0.70	0.75	0.80	0.85	0.90	0.95
2	0	0.2025	0.1600	0.1225	0.0900	0.0625	0.0400	0.0225	0.0100	0.0025
	1	0.4950	0.4800	0.4550	0.4200	0.3750	0.3200	0.2550	0.1800	0.0950
	2	0.3025	0.3600	0.4225	0.4900	0.5625	0.6400	0.7225	0.8100	0.9025
3	0	0.0911	0.0640	0.0429	0.0270	0.0156	0.0080	0.0034	0.0010	0.0001
	1	0.3341	0.2880	0.2389	0.1890	0.1406	0.0960	0.0574	0.0270	0.0071
	2	0.4084	0.4320	0.4436	0.4410	0.4219	0.3840	0.3251	0.2430	0.1354
	3	0.1664	0.2160	0.2746	0.3430	0.4219	0.5120	0.6141	0.7290	0.8574
4	0	0.0410	0.0256	0.0150	0.0081	0.0039	0.0016	0.0005	0.0001	0.0000
	1	0.2005	0.1536	0.1115	0.0756	0.0469	0.0256	0.0115	0.0036	0.0005
	2	0.3675	0.3456	0.3105	0.2646	0.2109	0.1536	0.0975	0.0486	0.0135
	3	0.2995	0.3456	0.3845	0.4116	0.4219	0.4096	0.3685	0.2916	0.1715
	4	0.0915	0.1296	0.1785	0.2401	0.3164	0.4096	0.5220	0.6561	0.8145
5	0	0.0185	0.0102	0.0053	0.0024	0.0010	0.0003	0.0001	0.0000	0.0000
	1	0.1128	0.0768	0.0488	0.0284	0.0146	0.0064	0.0022	0.0005	0.0000
	2	0.2757	0.2304	0.1811	0.1323	0.0879	0.0512	0.0244	0.0081	0.0011
	3	0.3369	0.3456	0.3364	0.3087	0.2637	0.2048	0.1382	0.0729	0.0214
	4	0.2059	0.2592	0.3124	0.3602	0.3955	0.4096	0.3915	0.3281	0.2036
	5	0.0503	0.0778	0.1160	0.1681	0.2373	0.3277	0.4437	0.5905	0.7738
6	0	0.0083	0.0041	0.0018	0.0007	0.0002	0.0001	0.0000	0.0000	0.0000
	1	0.0609	0.0369	0.0205	0.0102	0.0044	0.0015	0.0004	0.0001	0.0000
	2	0.1861	0.1382	0.0951	0.0595	0.0330	0.0154	0.0055	0.0012	0.0001
	3	0.3032	0.2765	0.2355	0.1852	0.1318	0.0819	0.0415	0.0146	0.0021
	4	0.2780	0.3110	0.3280	0.3241	0.2966	0.2458	0.1762	0.0984	0.0305
	5	0.1359	0.1866	0.2437	0.3025	0.3560	0.3932	0.3993	0.3543	0.2321
	6	0.0277	0.0467	0.0754	0.1176	0.1780	0.2621	0.3771	0.5314	0.7351
7	0	0.0037	0.0016	0.0006	0.0002	0.0001	0.0000	0.0000	0.0000	0.0000
	1	0.0320	0.0172	0.0084	0.0036	0.0013	0.0004	0.0001	0.0000	0.0000
	2	0.1172	0.0774	0.0466	0.0250	0.0115	0.0043	0.0012	0.0002	0.0000
	3	0.2388	0.1935	0.1442	0.0972	0.0577	0.0287	0.0109	0.0026	0.0002
	4	0.2918	0.2903	0.2679	0.2269	0.1730	0.1147	0.0617	0.0230	0.0036
	5	0.2140	0.2613	0.2985	0.3177	0.3115	0.2753	0.2097	0.1240	0.0406
	6	0.0872	0.1306	0.1848	0.2471	0.3115	0.3670	0.3960	0.3720	0.2573
	7	0.0152	0.0280	0.0490	0.0824	0.1335	0.2097	0.3206	0.4783	0.6983

TABLE 5 Binomial probabilities (*Continued*)

						P				
n	x	0.55	0.60	0.65	0.70	0.75	0.80	0.85	0.90	0.95
8	0	0.0017	0.0007	0.0002	0.0001	0.0000	0.0000	0.0000	0.0000	0.0000
	1	0.0164	0.0079	0.0033	0.0012	0.0004	0.0001	0.0000	0.0000	0.0000
	2	0.0703	0.0413	0.0217	0.0100	0.0038	0.0011	0.0002	0.0000	0.0000
	3	0.1719	0.1239	0.0808	0.0467	0.0231	0.0092	0.0026	0.0004	0.0000
	4	0.2627	0.2322	0.1875	0.1361	0.0865	0.0459	0.0185	0.0046	0.0004
	5	0.2568	0.2787	0.2786	0.2541	0.2076	0.1468	0.0839	0.0331	0.0054
	6	0.1569	0.2090	0.2587	0.2965	0.3115	0.2936	0.2376	0.1488	0.0515
	7	0.0548	0.0896	0.1373	0.1977	0.2670	0.3355	0.3847	0.3826	0.2793
	8	0.0084	0.0168	0.0319	0.0576	0.1001	0.1678	0.2725	0.4305	0.6634
9	0	0.0008	0.0003	0.0001	0.0000	0.0000	0.0000	0.0000	0.0000	0.0000
	1	0.0083	0.0035	0.0013	0.0004	0.0001	0.0000	0.0000	0.0000	0.0000
	2	0.0407	0.0212	0.0098	0.0039	0.0012	0.0003	0.0000	0.0000	0.0000
	3	0.1160	0.0743	0.0424	0.0210	0.0087	0.0028	0.0006	0.0001	0.0000
	4	0.2128	0.1672	0.1181	0.0735	0.0389	0.0165	0.0050	0.0008	0.0000
	5	0.2600	0.2508	0.2194	0.1715	0.1168	0.0661	0.0283	0.0074	0.0006
	6	0.2119	0.2508	0.2716	0.2668	0.2336	0.1762	0.1069	0.0446	0.0077
	7	0.1110	0.1612	0.2162	0.2668	0.3003	0.3020	0.2597	0.1722	0.0629
	8	0.0339	0.0605	0.1004	0.1556	0.2253	0.3020	0.3679	0.3874	0.2985
	9	0.0046	0.0101	0.0207	0.0404	0.0751	0.1342	0.2316	0.3874	0.6302
10	0	0.0003	0.0001	0.0000	0.0000	0.0000	0.0000	0.0000	0.0000	0.0000
	1	0.0042	0.0016	0.0005	0.0001	0.0000	0.0000	0.0000	0.0000	0.0000
	2	0.0229	0.0106	0.0043	0.0014	0.0004	0.0001	0.0000	0.0000	0.0000
	3	0.0746	0.0425	0.0212	0.0090	0.0031	0.0008	0.0001	0.0000	0.0000
	4	0.1596	0.1115	0.0689	0.0368	0.0162	0.0055	0.0012	0.0001	0.0000
	5	0.2340	0.2007	0.1536	0.1029	0.0584	0.0264	0.0085	0.0015	0.0001
	6	0.2384	0.2508	0.2377	0.2001	0.1460	0.0881	0.0401	0.0112	0.0010
	7	0.1665	0.2150	0.2522	0.2668	0.2503	0.2013	0.1298	0.0574	0.0105
	8	0.0763	0.1209	0.1757	0.2335	0.2816	0.3020	0.2759	0.1937	0.0746
	9	0.0207	0.0403	0.0725	0.1211	0.1877	0.2684	0.3474	0.3874	0.3151
	10	0.0025	0.0060	0.0135	0.0282	0.0563	0.1074	0.1969	0.3487	0.5987
12	0	0.0001	0.0000	0.0000	0.0000	0.0000	0.0000	0.0000	0.0000	0.0000
	1	0.0010	0.0003	0.0001	0.0000	0.0000	0.0000	0.0000	0.0000	0.0000
	2	0.0068	0.0025	0.0008	0.0002	0.0000	0.0000	0.0000	0.0000	0.0000
	3	0.0277	0.0125	0.0048	0.0015	0.0004	0.0001	0.0000	0.0000	0.0000
	4	0.0762	0.0420	0.0199	0.0078	0.0024	0.0005	0.0001	0.0000	0.0000
	5	0.1489	0.1009	0.0591	0.0291	0.0115	0.0033	0.0006	0.0000	0.0000
	6	0.2124	0.1766	0.1281	0.0792	0.0401	0.0155	0.0040	0.0005	0.0000

TABLE 5 Binomial probabilities (*Continued*)

						P				
n	*x*	0.55	0.60	0.65	0.70	0.75	0.80	0.85	0.90	0.95
12	7	0.2225	0.2270	0.2039	0.1585	0.1032	0.0532	0.0193	0.0038	0.0002
	8	0.1700	0.2128	0.2367	0.2311	0.1936	0.1329	0.0683	0.0213	0.0021
	9	0.0923	0.1419	0.1954	0.2397	0.2581	0.2362	0.1720	0.0852	0.0173
	10	0.0339	0.0639	0.1088	0.1678	0.2323	0.2835	0.2924	0.2301	0.0988
	11	0.0075	0.0174	0.0368	0.0712	0.1267	0.2062	0.3012	0.3766	0.3413
	12	0.0008	0.0022	0.0057	0.0138	0.0317	0.0687	0.1422	0.2824	0.5404
15	0	0.0000	0.0000	0.0000	0.0000	0.0000	0.0000	0.0000	0.0000	0.0000
	1	0.0001	0.0000	0.0000	0.0000	0.0000	0.0000	0.0000	0.0000	0.0000
	2	0.0010	0.0003	0.0001	0.0000	0.0000	0.0000	0.0000	0.0000	0.0000
	3	0.0052	0.0016	0.0004	0.0001	0.0000	0.0000	0.0000	0.0000	0.0000
	4	0.0191	0.0074	0.0024	0.0006	0.0001	0.0000	0.0000	0.0000	0.0000
	5	0.0515	0.0245	0.0096	0.0030	0.0007	0.0001	0.0000	0.0000	0.0000
	6	0.1048	0.0612	0.0298	0.0116	0.0034	0.0007	0.0001	0.0000	0.0000
	7	0.1647	0.1181	0.0710	0.0348	0.0131	0.0035	0.0005	0.0000	0.0000
	8	0.2013	0.1771	0.1319	0.0811	0.0393	0.0138	0.0030	0.0003	0.0000
	9	0.1914	0.2066	0.1906	0.1472	0.0917	0.0430	0.0132	0.0019	0.0000
	10	0.1404	0.1859	0.2123	0.2061	0.1651	0.1032	0.0449	0.0105	0.0006
	11	0.0780	0.1268	0.1792	0.2186	0.2252	0.1876	0.1156	0.0428	0.0049
	12	0.0318	0.0634	0.1110	0.1700	0.2252	0.2501	0.2184	0.1285	0.0307
	13	0.0090	0.0219	0.0476	0.0916	0.1559	0.2309	0.2856	0.2669	0.1348
	14	0.0016	0.0047	0.0126	0.0305	0.0668	0.1319	0.2312	0.3432	0.3658
	15	0.0001	0.0005	0.0016	0.0047	0.0134	0.0352	0.0874	0.2059	0.4633
18	0	0.0000	0.0000	0.0000	0.0000	0.0000	0.0000	0.0000	0.0000	0.0000
	1	0.0000	0.0000	0.0000	0.0000	0.0000	0.0000	0.0000	0.0000	0.0000
	2	0.0001	0.0000	0.0000	0.0000	0.0000	0.0000	0.0000	0.0000	0.0000
	3	0.0009	0.0002	0.0000	0.0000	0.0000	0.0000	0.0000	0.0000	0.0000
	4	0.0039	0.0011	0.0002	0.0000	0.0000	0.0000	0.0000	0.0000	0.0000
	5	0.0134	0.0045	0.0012	0.0002	0.0000	0.0000	0.0000	0.0000	0.0000
	6	0.0354	0.0145	0.0047	0.0012	0.0002	0.0000	0.0000	0.0000	0.0000
	7	0.0742	0.0374	0.0151	0.0046	0.0010	0.0001	0.0000	0.0000	0.0000
	8	0.1248	0.0771	0.0385	0.0149	0.0042	0.0008	0.0001	0.0000	0.0000
	9	0.1694	0.1284	0.0794	0.0386	0.0139	0.0033	0.0004	0.0000	0.0000
	10	0.1864	0.1734	0.1327	0.0811	0.0376	0.0120	0.0022	0.0002	0.0000
	11	0.1657	0.1892	0.1792	0.1376	0.0820	0.0350	0.0091	0.0010	0.0000
	12	0.1181	0.1655	0.1941	0.1873	0.1436	0.0816	0.0301	0.0052	0.0002
	13	0.0666	0.1146	0.1664	0.2017	0.1988	0.1507	0.0787	0.0218	0.0014
	14	0.0291	0.0614	0.1104	0.1681	0.2130	0.2153	0.1592	0.0700	0.0093
	15	0.0095	0.0246	0.0547	0.1046	0.1704	0.2297	0.2406	0.1680	0.0473
	16	0.0022	0.0069	0.0190	0.0458	0.0958	0.1723	0.2556	0.2835	0.1683
	17	0.0003	0.0012	0.0042	0.0126	0.0338	0.0811	0.1704	0.3002	0.3763
	18	0.0000	0.0001	0.0004	0.0016	0.0056	0.0180	0.0536	0.1501	0.3972

TABLE 5 Binomial probabilities (*Continued*)

P

n	x	0.55	0.60	0.65	0.70	0.75	0.80	0.85	0.90	0.95
20	0	0.0000	0.0000	0.0000	0.0000	0.0000	0.0000	0.0000	0.0000	0.0000
	1	0.0000	0.0000	0.0000	0.0000	0.0000	0.0000	0.0000	0.0000	0.0000
	2	0.0000	0.0000	0.0000	0.0000	0.0000	0.0000	0.0000	0.0000	0.0000
	3	0.0002	0.0000	0.0000	0.0000	0.0000	0.0000	0.0000	0.0000	0.0000
	4	0.0013	0.0003	0.0000	0.0000	0.0000	0.0000	0.0000	0.0000	0.0000
	5	0.0049	0.0013	0.0003	0.0000	0.0000	0.0000	0.0000	0.0000	0.0000
	6	0.0150	0.0049	0.0012	0.0002	0.0000	0.0000	0.0000	0.0000	0.0000
	7	0.0366	0.0146	0.0045	0.0010	0.0002	0.0000	0.0000	0.0000	0.0000
	8	0.0727	0.0355	0.0136	0.0039	0.0008	0.0001	0.0000	0.0000	0.0000
	9	0.1185	0.0710	0.0336	0.0120	0.0030	0.0005	0.0000	0.0000	0.0000
	10	0.1593	0.1171	0.0686	0.0308	0.0099	0.0020	0.0002	0.0000	0.0000
	11	0.1771	0.1597	0.1158	0.0654	0.0271	0.0074	0.0011	0.0001	0.0000
	12	0.1623	0.1797	0.1614	0.1144	0.0609	0.0222	0.0046	0.0004	0.0000
	13	0.1221	0.1659	0.1844	0.1643	0.1124	0.0545	0.0160	0.0020	0.0000
	14	0.0746	0.1244	0.1712	0.1916	0.1686	0.1091	0.0454	0.0089	0.0003
	15	0.0365	0.0746	0.1272	0.1789	0.2023	0.1746	0.1028	0.0319	0.0022
	16	0.0139	0.0350	0.0738	0.1304	0.1897	0.2182	0.1821	0.0898	0.0133
	17	0.0040	0.0123	0.0323	0.0716	0.1339	0.2054	0.2428	0.1901	0.0596
	18	0.0008	0.0031	0.0100	0.0278	0.0669	0.1369	0.2293	0.2852	0.1887
	19	0.0001	0.0005	0.0020	0.0068	0.0211	0.0576	0.1368	0.2702	0.3774
	20	0.0000	0.0000	0.0002	0.0008	0.0032	0.0115	0.0388	0.1216	0.3585

Table 6   Values of $e^{-\mu}$

μ	$e^{-\mu}$	μ	$e^{-\mu}$	μ	$e^{-\mu}$
0.00	1.0000	2.00	0.135	4.00	0.0183
0.05	0.9512	2.05	0.129	4.05	0.0174
0.10	0.9048	2.10	0.122	4.10	0.0166
0.15	0.8607	2.15	0.116	4.15	0.0158
0.20	0.8187	2.20	0.111	4.20	0.0150
0.25	0.7788	2.25	0.105	4.25	0.0143
0.30	0.7408	2.30	0.100	4.30	0.0136
0.35	0.7047	2.35	0.095	4.35	0.0129
0.40	0.6703	2.40	0.091	4.40	0.0123
0.45	0.6376	2.45	0.086	4.45	0.0117
0.50	0.6065	2.50	0.082	4.50	0.0111
0.55	0.5769	2.55	0.078	4.55	0.0106
0.60	0.5488	2.60	0.074	4.60	0.0101
0.65	0.5220	2.65	0.071	4.65	0.0096
0.70	0.4966	2.70	0.067	4.70	0.0091
0.75	0.4724	2.75	0.064	4.75	0.0087
0.80	0.4493	2.80	0.061	4.80	0.0082
0.85	0.4274	2.85	0.058	4.85	0.0078
0.90	0.4066	2.90	0.055	4.90	0.0074
0.95	0.3867	2.95	0.052	4.95	0.0071
1.00	0.3679	3.00	0.050	5.00	0.0067
1.05	0.3499	3.05	0.047	6.00	0.0025
1.10	0.3329	3.10	0.045	7.00	0.0009
1.15	0.3166	3.15	0.043	8.00	0.000335
1.20	0.3012	3.20	0.041	9.00	0.000123
1.25	0.2865	3.25	0.039	10.00	0.000045
1.30	0.2725	3.30	0.037		
1.35	0.2592	3.35	0.035		
1.40	0.2466	3.40	0.033		
1.45	0.2346	3.45	0.032		
1.50	0.2231	3.50	0.030		
1.55	0.2122	3.55	0.029		
1.60	0.2019	3.60	0.027		
1.65	0.1920	3.65	0.026		
1.70	0.1827	3.70	0.025		
1.75	0.1738	3.75	0.024		
1.80	0.1653	3.80	0.022		
1.85	0.1572	3.85	0.021		
1.90	0.1496	3.90	0.020		
1.95	0.1423	3.95	0.019		

TABLE 7   Poisson Probabilities
Entries in this table give the probability of x occurrences for a Poisson process with a mean μ.
For example, when $\mu = 0.2$, the probability of $x = 1$ occurrence is 0.1637.

	μ									
x	0.1	0.2	0.3	0.4	0.5	0.6	0.7	0.8	0.9	1.0
0	0.9048	0.8187	0.7408	0.6703	0.6065	0.5488	0.4966	0.4493	0.4066	0.3679
1	0.0905	0.1637	0.2222	0.2681	0.3033	0.3293	0.3476	0.3595	0.3659	0.3679
2	0.0045	0.0164	0.0333	0.0536	0.0758	0.0988	0.1217	0.1438	0.1647	0.1839
3	0.0002	0.0011	0.0033	0.0072	0.0126	0.0198	0.0284	0.0383	0.0494	0.0613
4	0.0000	0.0001	0.0003	0.0007	0.0016	0.0030	0.0050	0.0077	0.0111	0.0153
5	0.0000	0.0000	0.0000	0.0001	0.0002	0.0004	0.0007	0.0012	0.0020	0.0031
6	0.0000	0.0000	0.0000	0.0000	0.0000	0.0000	0.0001	0.0002	0.0003	0.0005
7	0.0000	0.0000	0.0000	0.0000	0.0000	0.0000	0.0000	0.0000	0.0000	0.0001

	μ									
x	1.1	1.2	1.3	1.4	1.5	1.6	1.7	1.8	1.9	2.0
0	0.3329	0.3012	0.2725	0.2466	0.2231	0.2019	0.1827	0.1653	0.1496	0.1353
1	0.3662	0.3614	0.3543	0.3452	0.3347	0.3230	0.3106	0.2975	0.2842	0.2707
2	0.2014	0.2169	0.2303	0.2417	0.2510	0.2584	0.2640	0.2678	0.2700	0.2707
3	0.0738	0.0867	0.0998	0.1128	0.1255	0.1378	0.1496	0.1607	0.1710	0.1804
4	0.0203	0.0260	0.0324	0.0395	0.0471	0.0551	0.0636	0.0723	0.0812	0.0902
5	0.0045	0.0062	0.0084	0.0111	0.0141	0.0176	0.0216	0.0260	0.0309	0.0361
6	0.0008	0.0012	0.0018	0.0026	0.0035	0.0047	0.0061	0.0078	0.0098	0.0120
7	0.0001	0.0002	0.0003	0.0005	0.0008	0.0011	0.0015	0.0020	0.0027	0.0034
8	0.0000	0.0000	0.0001	0.0001	0.0001	0.0002	0.0003	0.0005	0.0006	0.0009
9	0.0000	0.0000	0.0000	0.0000	0.0000	0.0000	0.0001	0.0001	0.0001	0.0002

	μ									
x	2.1	2.2	2.3	2.4	2.5	2.6	2.7	2.8	2.9	3.0
0	0.1225	0.1108	0.1003	0.0907	0.0821	0.0743	0.0672	0.0608	0.0550	0.0498
1	0.2572	0.2438	0.2306	0.2177	0.2052	0.1931	0.1815	0.1703	0.1596	0.1494
2	0.2700	0.2681	0.2652	0.2613	0.2565	0.2510	0.2450	0.2384	0.2314	0.2240
3	0.1890	0.1966	0.2033	0.2090	0.2138	0.2176	0.2205	0.2225	0.2237	0.2240
4	0.0992	0.1082	0.1169	0.1254	0.1336	0.1414	0.1488	0.1557	0.1622	0.1680
5	0.0417	0.0476	0.0538	0.0602	0.0668	0.0735	0.0804	0.0872	0.0940	0.1008
6	0.0146	0.0174	0.0206	0.0241	0.0278	0.0319	0.0362	0.0407	0.0455	0.0504
7	0.0044	0.0055	0.0068	0.0083	0.0099	0.0118	0.0139	0.0163	0.0188	0.0216

TABLE 7 Poisson Probabilities *(Continued)*

8	0.0011	0.0015	0.0019	0.0025	0.0031	0.0038	0.0047	0.0057	0.0068	0.0081
9	0.0003	0.0004	0.0005	0.0007	0.0009	0.0011	0.0014	0.0018	0.0022	0.0027
10	0.0001	0.0001	0.0001	0.0002	0.0002	0.0003	0.0004	0.0005	0.0006	0.0008
11	0.0000	0.0000	0.0000	0.0000	0.0000	0.0001	0.0001	0.0001	0.0002	0.0002
12	0.0000	0.0000	0.0000	0.0000	0.0000	0.0000	0.0000	0.0000	0.0000	0.0001

$$\mu$$

x	3.1	3.2	3.3	3.4	3.5	3.6	3.7	3.8	3.9	4.0
0	0.0450	0.0408	0.0369	0.0334	0.0302	0.0273	0.0247	0.0224	0.0202	0.0183
1	0.1397	0.1304	0.1217	0.1135	0.1057	0.0984	0.0915	0.0850	0.0789	0.0733
2	0.2165	0.2087	0.2008	0.1929	0.1850	0.1771	0.1692	0.1615	0.1539	0.1465
3	0.2237	0.2226	0.2209	0.2186	0.2158	0.2125	0.2087	0.2046	0.2001	0.1954
4	0.1733	0.1781	0.1823	0.1858	0.1888	0.1912	0.1931	0.1944	0.1951	0.1954
5	0.1075	0.1140	0.1203	0.1264	0.1322	0.1377	0.1429	0.1477	0.1522	0.1563
6	0.0555	0.0608	0.0662	0.0716	0.0771	0.0826	0.0881	0.0936	0.0989	0.1042
7	0.0246	0.0278	0.0312	0.0348	0.0385	0.0425	0.0466	0.0508	0.0551	0.0595
8	0.0095	0.0111	0.0129	0.0148	0.0169	0.0191	0.0215	0.0241	0.0269	0.0298
9	0.0033	0.0040	0.0047	0.0056	0.0066	0.0076	0.0089	0.0102	0.0116	0.0132
10	0.0010	0.0013	0.0016	0.0019	0.0023	0.0028	0.0033	0.0039	0.0045	0.0053
11	0.0003	0.0004	0.0005	0.0006	0.0007	0.0009	0.0011	0.0013	0.0016	0.0019
12	0.0001	0.0001	0.0001	0.0002	0.0002	0.0003	0.0003	0.0004	0.0005	0.0006
13	0.0000	0.0000	0.0000	0.0000	0.0001	0.0001	0.0001	0.0001	0.0002	0.0002
14	0.0000	0.0000	0.0000	0.0000	0.0000	0.0000	0.0000	0.0000	0.0000	0.0001

$$\mu$$

x	4.1	4.2	4.3	4.4	4.5	4.6	4.7	4.8	4.9	5.0
0	0.0166	0.0150	0.0136	0.0123	0.0111	0.0101	0.0091	0.0082	0.0074	0.0067
1	0.0679	0.0630	0.0583	0.0540	0.0500	0.0462	0.0427	0.0395	0.0365	0.0337
2	0.1393	0.1323	0.1254	0.1188	0.1125	0.1063	0.1005	0.0948	0.0894	0.0842
3	0.1904	0.1852	0.1798	0.1743	0.1687	0.1631	0.1574	0.1517	0.1460	0.1404
4	0.1951	0.1944	0.1933	0.1917	0.1898	0.1875	0.1849	0.1820	0.1789	0.1755
5	0.1600	0.1633	0.1662	0.1687	0.1708	0.1725	0.1738	0.1747	0.1753	0.1755
6	0.1093	0.1143	0.1191	0.1237	0.1281	0.1323	0.1362	0.1398	0.1432	0.1462
7	0.0640	0.0686	0.0732	0.0778	0.0824	0.0869	0.0914	0.0959	0.1002	0.1044
8	0.0328	0.0360	0.0393	0.0428	0.0463	0.0500	0.0537	0.0575	0.0614	0.0653
9	0.0150	0.0168	0.0188	0.0209	0.0232	0.0255	0.0281	0.0307	0.0334	0.0363

TABLE 7 Poisson Probabilities *(Continued)*

10	0.0061	0.0071	0.0081	0.0092	0.0104	0.0118	0.0132	0.0147	0.0164	0.0181
11	0.0023	0.0027	0.0032	0.0037	0.0043	0.0049	0.0056	0.0064	0.0073	0.0082
12	0.0008	0.0009	0.0011	0.0013	0.0016	0.0019	0.0022	0.0026	0.0030	0.0034
13	0.0002	0.0003	0.0004	0.0005	0.0006	0.0007	0.0008	0.0009	0.0011	0.0013
14	0.0001	0.0001	0.0001	0.0001	0.0002	0.0002	0.0003	0.0003	0.0004	0.0005
15	0.0000	0.0000	0.0000	0.0000	0.0001	0.0001	0.0001	0.0001	0.0001	0.0002

μ

x	5.1	5.2	5.3	5.4	5.5	5.6	5.7	5.8	5.9	6.0
0	0.0061	0.0055	0.0050	0.0045	0.0041	0.0037	0.0033	0.0030	0.0027	0.0025
1	0.0311	0.0287	0.0265	0.0244	0.0225	0.0207	0.0191	0.0176	0.0162	0.0149
2	0.0793	0.0746	0.0701	0.0659	0.0618	0.0580	0.0544	0.0509	0.0477	0.0446
3	0.1348	0.1293	0.1239	0.1185	0.1133	0.1082	0.1033	0.0985	0.0938	0.0892
4	0.1719	0.1681	0.1641	0.1600	0.1558	0.1515	0.1472	0.1428	0.1383	0.1339
5	0.1753	0.1748	0.1740	0.1728	0.1714	0.1697	0.1678	0.1656	0.1632	0.1606
6	0.1490	0.1515	0.1537	0.1555	0.1571	0.1584	0.1594	0.1601	0.1605	0.1606
7	0.1086	0.1125	0.1163	0.1200	0.1234	0.1267	0.1298	0.1326	0.1353	0.1377
8	0.0692	0.0731	0.0771	0.0810	0.0849	0.0887	0.0925	0.0962	0.0998	0.1033
9	0.0392	0.0423	0.0454	0.0486	0.0519	0.0552	0.0586	0.0620	0.0654	0.0688
10	0.0200	0.0220	0.0241	0.0262	0.0285	0.0309	0.0334	0.0359	0.0386	0.0413
11	0.0093	0.0104	0.0116	0.0129	0.0143	0.0157	0.0173	0.0190	0.0207	0.0225
12	0.0039	0.0045	0.0051	0.0058	0.0065	0.0073	0.0082	0.0092	0.0102	0.0113
13	0.0015	0.0018	0.0021	0.0024	0.0028	0.0032	0.0036	0.0041	0.0046	0.0052
14	0.0006	0.0007	0.0008	0.0009	0.0011	0.0013	0.0015	0.0017	0.0019	0.0022
15	0.0002	0.0002	0.0003	0.0003	0.0004	0.0005	0.0006	0.0007	0.0008	0.0009
16	0.0001	0.0001	0.0001	0.0001	0.0001	0.0002	0.0002	0.0002	0.0003	0.0003
17	0.0000	0.0000	0.0000	0.0000	0.0000	0.0001	0.0001	0.0001	0.0001	0.0001

μ

x	6.1	6.2	6.3	6.4	6.5	6.6	6.7	6.8	6.9	7.0
0	0.0022	0.0020	0.0018	0.0017	0.0015	0.0014	0.0012	0.0011	0.0010	0.0009
1	0.0137	0.0126	0.0116	0.0106	0.0098	0.0090	0.0082	0.0076	0.0070	0.0064
2	0.0417	0.0390	0.0364	0.0340	0.0318	0.0296	0.0276	0.0258	0.0240	0.0223
3	0.0848	0.0806	0.0765	0.0726	0.0688	0.0652	0.0617	0.0584	0.0552	0.0521
4	0.1294	0.1249	0.1205	0.1162	0.1118	0.1076	0.1034	0.0992	0.0952	0.0912

TABLE 7 Poisson Probabilities *(Continued)*

x										
5	0.1579	0.1549	0.1519	0.1487	0.1454	0.1420	0.1385	0.1349	0.1314	0.1277
6	0.1605	0.1601	0.1595	0.1586	0.1575	0.1562	0.1546	0.1529	0.1511	0.1490
7	0.1399	0.1418	0.1435	0.1450	0.1462	0.1472	0.1480	0.1486	0.1489	0.1490
8	0.1066	0.1099	0.1130	0.1160	0.1188	0.1215	0.1240	0.1263	0.1284	0.1304
9	0.0723	0.0757	0.0791	0.0825	0.0858	0.0891	0.0923	0.0954	0.0985	0.1014
10	0.0441	0.0469	0.0498	0.0528	0.0558	0.0588	0.0618	0.0649	0.0679	0.0710
11	0.0244	0.0265	0.0285	0.0307	0.0330	0.0353	0.0377	0.0401	0.0426	0.0452
12	0.0124	0.0137	0.0150	0.0164	0.0179	0.0194	0.0210	0.0227	0.0245	0.0263
13	0.0058	0.0065	0.0073	0.0081	0.0089	0.0099	0.0108	0.0119	0.0130	0.0142
14	0.0025	0.0029	0.0033	0.0037	0.0041	0.0046	0.0052	0.0058	0.0064	0.0071
15	0.0010	0.0012	0.0014	0.0016	0.0018	0.0020	0.0023	0.0026	0.0029	0.0033
16	0.0004	0.0005	0.0005	0.0006	0.0007	0.0008	0.0010	0.0011	0.0013	0.0014
17	0.0001	0.0002	0.0002	0.0002	0.0003	0.0003	0.0004	0.0004	0.0005	0.0006
18	0.0000	0.0001	0.0001	0.0001	0.0001	0.0001	0.0001	0.0002	0.0002	0.0002
19	0.0000	0.0000	0.0000	0.0000	0.0000	0.0000	0.0001	0.0001	0.0001	0.0001

μ

x	7.1	7.2	7.3	7.4	7.5	7.6	7.7	7.8	7.9	8.0
0	0.0008	0.0007	0.0007	0.0006	0.0006	0.0005	0.0005	0.0004	0.0004	0.0003
1	0.0059	0.0054	0.0049	0.0045	0.0041	0.0038	0.0035	0.0032	0.0029	0.0027
2	0.0208	0.0194	0.0180	0.0167	0.0156	0.0145	0.0134	0.0125	0.0116	0.0107
3	0.0492	0.0464	0.0438	0.0413	0.0389	0.0366	0.0345	0.0324	0.0305	0.0286
4	0.0874	0.0836	0.0799	0.0764	0.0729	0.0696	0.0663	0.0632	0.0602	0.0573
5	0.1241	0.1204	0.1167	0.1130	0.1094	0.1057	0.1021	0.0986	0.0951	0.0916
6	0.1468	0.1445	0.1420	0.1394	0.1367	0.1339	0.1311	0.1282	0.1252	0.1221
7	0.1489	0.1486	0.1481	0.1474	0.1465	0.1454	0.1442	0.1428	0.1413	0.1396
8	0.1321	0.1337	0.1351	0.1363	0.1373	0.1381	0.1388	0.1392	0.1395	0.1396
9	0.1042	0.1070	0.1096	0.1121	0.1144	0.1167	0.1187	0.1207	0.1224	0.1241
10	0.0740	0.0770	0.0800	0.0829	0.0858	0.0887	0.0914	0.0941	0.0967	0.0993
11	0.0478	0.0504	0.0531	0.0558	0.0585	0.0613	0.0640	0.0667	0.0695	0.0722
12	0.0283	0.0303	0.0323	0.0344	0.0366	0.0388	0.0411	0.0434	0.0457	0.0481
13	0.0154	0.0168	0.0181	0.0196	0.0211	0.0227	0.0243	0.0260	0.0278	0.0296
14	0.0078	0.0086	0.0095	0.0104	0.0113	0.0123	0.0134	0.0145	0.0157	0.0169
15	0.0037	0.0041	0.0046	0.0051	0.0057	0.0062	0.0069	0.0075	0.0083	0.0090
16	0.0016	0.0019	0.0021	0.0024	0.0026	0.0030	0.0033	0.0037	0.0041	0.0045
17	0.0007	0.0008	0.0009	0.0010	0.0012	0.0013	0.0015	0.0017	0.0019	0.0021

TABLE 7 Poisson Probabilities *(Continued)*

18	0.0003	0.0003	0.0004	0.0004	0.0005	0.0006	0.0006	0.0007	0.0008	0.0009
19	0.0001	0.0001	0.0001	0.0002	0.0002	0.0002	0.0003	0.0003	0.0003	0.0004
20	0.0000	0.0000	0.0001	0.0001	0.0001	0.0001	0.0001	0.0001	0.0001	0.0002
21	0.0000	0.0000	0.0000	0.0000	0.0000	0.0000	0.0000	0.0000	0.0001	0.0001

μ

x	8.1	8.2	8.3	8.4	8.5	8.6	8.7	8.8	8.9	9.0
0	0.0003	0.0003	0.0002	0.0002	0.0002	0.0002	0.0002	0.0002	0.0001	0.0001
1	0.0025	0.0023	0.0021	0.0019	0.0017	0.0016	0.0014	0.0013	0.0012	0.0011
2	0.0100	0.0092	0.0086	0.0079	0.0074	0.0068	0.0063	0.0058	0.0054	0.0050
3	0.0269	0.0252	0.0237	0.0222	0.0208	0.0195	0.0183	0.0171	0.0160	0.0150
4	0.0544	0.0517	0.0491	0.0466	0.0443	0.0420	0.0398	0.0377	0.0357	0.0337
5	0.0882	0.0849	0.0816	0.0784	0.0752	0.0722	0.0692	0.0663	0.0635	0.0607
6	0.1191	0.1160	0.1128	0.1097	0.1066	0.1034	0.1003	0.0972	0.0941	0.0911
7	0.1378	0.1358	0.1338	0.1317	0.1294	0.1271	0.1247	0.1222	0.1197	0.1171
8	0.1395	0.1392	0.1388	0.1382	0.1375	0.1366	0.1356	0.1344	0.1332	0.1318
9	0.1256	0.1269	0.1280	0.1290	0.1299	0.1306	0.1311	0.1315	0.1317	0.1318
10	0.1017	0.1040	0.1063	0.1084	0.1104	0.1123	0.1140	0.1157	0.1172	0.1186
11	0.0749	0.0776	0.0802	0.0828	0.0853	0.0878	0.0902	0.0925	0.0948	0.0970
12	0.0505	0.0530	0.0555	0.0579	0.0604	0.0629	0.0654	0.0679	0.0703	0.0728
13	0.0315	0.0334	0.0354	0.0374	0.0395	0.0416	0.0438	0.0459	0.0481	0.0504
14	0.0182	0.0196	0.0210	0.0225	0.0240	0.0256	0.0272	0.0289	0.0306	0.0324
15	0.0098	0.0107	0.0116	0.0126	0.0136	0.0147	0.0158	0.0169	0.0182	0.0194
16	0.0050	0.0055	0.0060	0.0066	0.0072	0.0079	0.0086	0.0093	0.0101	0.0109
17	0.0024	0.0026	0.0029	0.0033	0.0036	0.0040	0.0044	0.0048	0.0053	0.0058
18	0.0011	0.0012	0.0014	0.0015	0.0017	0.0019	0.0021	0.0024	0.0026	0.0029
19	0.0005	0.0005	0.0006	0.0007	0.0008	0.0009	0.0010	0.0011	0.0012	0.0014
20	0.0002	0.0002	0.0002	0.0003	0.0003	0.0004	0.0004	0.0005	0.0005	0.0006
21	0.0001	0.0001	0.0001	0.0001	0.0001	0.0002	0.0002	0.0002	0.0002	0.0003
22	0.0000	0.0000	0.0000	0.0000	0.0001	0.0001	0.0001	0.0001	0.0001	0.0001

TABLE 7 Poisson Probabilities *(Continued)*

| | | | | | | μ | | | | |
x	9.1	9.2	9.3	9.4	9.5	9.6	9.7	9.8	9.9	10.0
0	0.0001	0.0001	0.0001	0.0001	0.0001	0.0001	0.0001	0.0001	0.0001	0.0000
1	0.0010	0.0009	0.0009	0.0008	0.0007	0.0007	0.0006	0.0005	0.0005	0.0005
2	0.0046	0.0043	0.0040	0.0037	0.0034	0.0031	0.0029	0.0027	0.0025	0.0023
3	0.0140	0.0131	0.0123	0.0115	0.0107	0.0100	0.0093	0.0087	0.0081	0.0076
4	0.0319	0.0302	0.0285	0.0269	0.0254	0.0240	0.0226	0.0213	0.0201	0.0189
5	0.0581	0.0555	0.0530	0.0506	0.0483	0.0460	0.0439	0.0418	0.0398	0.0378
6	0.0881	0.0851	0.0822	0.0793	0.0764	0.0736	0.0709	0.0682	0.0656	0.0631
7	0.1145	0.1118	0.1091	0.1064	0.1037	0.1010	0.0982	0.0955	0.0928	0.0901
8	0.1302	0.1286	0.1269	0.1251	0.1232	0.1212	0.1191	0.1170	0.1148	0.1126
9	0.1317	0.1315	0.1311	0.1306	0.1300	0.1293	0.1284	0.1274	0.1263	0.1251
10	0.1198	0.1210	0.1219	0.1228	0.1235	0.1241	0.1245	0.1249	0.1250	0.1251
11	0.0991	0.1012	0.1031	0.1049	0.1067	0.1083	0.1098	0.1112	0.1125	0.1137
12	0.0752	0.0776	0.0799	0.0822	0.0844	0.0866	0.0888	0.0908	0.0928	0.0948
13	0.0526	0.0549	0.0572	0.0594	0.0617	0.0640	0.0662	0.0685	0.0707	0.0729
14	0.0342	0.0361	0.0380	0.0399	0.0419	0.0439	0.0459	0.0479	0.0500	0.0521
15	0.0208	0.0221	0.0235	0.0250	0.0265	0.0281	0.0297	0.0313	0.0330	0.0347
16	0.0118	0.0127	0.0137	0.0147	0.0157	0.0168	0.0180	0.0192	0.0204	0.0217
17	0.0063	0.0069	0.0075	0.0081	0.0088	0.0095	0.0103	0.0111	0.0119	0.0128
18	0.0032	0.0035	0.0039	0.0042	0.0046	0.0051	0.0055	0.0060	0.0065	0.0071
19	0.0015	0.0017	0.0019	0.0021	0.0023	0.0026	0.0028	0.0031	0.0034	0.0037
20	0.0007	0.0008	0.0009	0.0010	0.0011	0.0012	0.0014	0.0015	0.0017	0.0019
21	0.0003	0.0003	0.0004	0.0004	0.0005	0.0006	0.0006	0.0007	0.0008	0.0009
22	0.0001	0.0001	0.0002	0.0002	0.0002	0.0002	0.0003	0.0003	0.0004	0.0004
23	0.0000	0.0001	0.0001	0.0001	0.0001	0.0001	0.0001	0.0001	0.0002	0.0002
24	0.0000	0.0000	0.0000	0.0000	0.0000	0.0000	0.0000	0.0001	0.0001	0.0001

| | | | | | | μ | | | | |
x	11	12	13	14	15	16	17	18	19	20
0	0.0000	0.0000	0.0000	0.0000	0.0000	0.0000	0.0000	0.0000	0.0000	0.0000
1	0.0002	0.0001	0.0000	0.0000	0.0000	0.0000	0.0000	0.0000	0.0000	0.0000
2	0.0010	0.0004	0.0002	0.0001	0.0000	0.0000	0.0000	0.0000	0.0000	0.0000
3	0.0037	0.0018	0.0008	0.0004	0.0002	0.0001	0.0000	0.0000	0.0000	0.0000
4	0.0102	0.0053	0.0027	0.0013	0.0006	0.0003	0.0001	0.0001	0.0000	0.0000

TABLE 7 Poisson Probabilities *(Continued)*

5	0.0224	0.0127	0.0070	0.0037	0.0019	0.0010	0.0005	0.0002	0.0001	0.0001
6	0.0411	0.0255	0.0152	0.0087	0.0048	0.0026	0.0014	0.0007	0.0004	0.0002
7	0.0646	0.0437	0.0281	0.0174	0.0104	0.0060	0.0034	0.0019	0.0010	0.0005
8	0.0888	0.0655	0.0457	0.0304	0.0194	0.0120	0.0072	0.0042	0.0024	0.0013
9	0.1085	0.0874	0.0661	0.0473	0.0324	0.0213	0.0135	0.0083	0.0050	0.0029
10	0.1194	0.1048	0.0859	0.0663	0.0486	0.0341	0.0230	0.0150	0.0095	0.0058
11	0.1194	0.1144	0.1015	0.0844	0.0663	0.0496	0.0355	0.0245	0.0164	0.0106
12	0.1094	0.1144	0.1099	0.0984	0.0829	0.0661	0.0504	0.0368	0.0259	0.0176
13	0.0926	0.1056	0.1099	0.1060	0.0956	0.0814	0.0658	0.0509	0.0378	0.0271
14	0.0728	0.0905	0.1021	0.1060	0.1024	0.0930	0.0800	0.0655	0.0514	0.0387
15	0.0534	0.0724	0.0885	0.0989	0.1024	0.0992	0.0906	0.0786	0.0650	0.0516
16	0.0367	0.0543	0.0719	0.0866	0.0960	0.0992	0.0963	0.0884	0.0772	0.0646
17	0.0237	0.0383	0.0550	0.0713	0.0847	0.0934	0.0963	0.0936	0.0863	0.0760
18	0.0145	0.0255	0.0397	0.0554	0.0706	0.0830	0.0909	0.0936	0.0911	0.0844
19	0.0084	0.0161	0.0272	0.0409	0.0557	0.0699	0.0814	0.0887	0.0911	0.0888
20	0.0046	0.0097	0.0177	0.0286	0.0418	0.0559	0.0692	0.0798	0.0866	0.0888
21	0.0024	0.0055	0.0109	0.0191	0.0299	0.0426	0.0560	0.0684	0.0783	0.0846
22	0.0012	0.0030	0.0065	0.0121	0.0204	0.0310	0.0433	0.0560	0.0676	0.0769
23	0.0006	0.0016	0.0037	0.0074	0.0133	0.0216	0.0320	0.0438	0.0559	0.0669
24	0.0003	0.0008	0.0020	0.0043	0.0083	0.0144	0.0226	0.0328	0.0442	0.0557
25	0.0001	0.0004	0.0010	0.0024	0.0050	0.0092	0.0154	0.0237	0.0336	0.0446
26	0.0000	0.0002	0.0005	0.0013	0.0029	0.0057	0.0101	0.0164	0.0246	0.0343
27	0.0000	0.0001	0.0002	0.0007	0.0016	0.0034	0.0063	0.0109	0.0173	0.0254
28	0.0000	0.0000	0.0001	0.0003	0.0009	0.0019	0.0038	0.0070	0.0117	0.0181
29	0.0000	0.0000	0.0001	0.0002	0.0004	0.0011	0.0023	0.0044	0.0077	0.0125
30	0.0000	0.0000	0.0000	0.0001	0.0002	0.0006	0.0013	0.0026	0.0049	0.0083
31	0.0000	0.0000	0.0000	0.0000	0.0001	0.0003	0.0007	0.0015	0.0030	0.0054
32	0.0000	0.0000	0.0000	0.0000	0.0001	0.0001	0.0004	0.0009	0.0018	0.0034
33	0.0000	0.0000	0.0000	0.0000	0.0000	0.0001	0.0002	0.0005	0.0010	0.0020
34	0.0000	0.0000	0.0000	0.0000	0.0000	0.0000	0.0001	0.0002	0.0006	0.0012
35	0.0000	0.0000	0.0000	0.0000	0.0000	0.0000	0.0000	0.0001	0.0003	0.0007
36	0.0000	0.0000	0.0000	0.0000	0.0000	0.0000	0.0000	0.0001	0.0002	0.0004
37	0.0000	0.0000	0.0000	0.0000	0.0000	0.0000	0.0000	0.0000	0.0001	0.0002
38	0.0000	0.0000	0.0000	0.0000	0.0000	0.0000	0.0000	0.0000	0.0000	0.0001
39	0.0000	0.0000	0.0000	0.0000	0.0000	0.0000	0.0000	0.0000	0.0000	0.0001